THE LANDLORD'S LAW BOOK

RIGHTS AND RESPONSIBILITIES

By Attorneys David Brown
and Ralph Warner

Illustrations: Linda Allison

NOLO PRESS • 950 Parker St., Berkeley, CA 94710

Printing History

Nolo Press is committed to keeping its books up-to-date. Each new printing, whether or not it is called a new edition, has been revised to reflect the latest law changes. This book was printed and updated on the last date indicated below. Before you rely on information in it, you might wish to call Nolo Press (415) 549-1976 to check whether a later printing or edition has been issued.

First Edition	May 1985
Second Printing	February 1986
Third Printing	August 1986
Second Edition	April 1987
Second Printing	September 1987
Third Printing	July 1988

Difference between new "Editions" and "Printings"

New "Printing" means there have been some minor changes, but usually not enough so that people will need to trade in or discard an earlier printing of the same edition. Obviously, this is a judgment call and any change, no matter how minor, might affect you.

New "Edition" means one or more major, or a number of minor, law changes since the previous edition.

PLEASE READ THIS: Please be aware that laws and procedures are constantly changing and are subject to differing interpretations. You have the responsibility to check all material you read here before relying on it. Of necessity, neither Nolo Press nor the authors make any guarantees concerning the information in this book or the use to which it is put.

Linda Allison	Illustrations
Nelg Nihsolov	
Stephanie Harolde	Production
Keija Kimura	Book Design and Layout
Toni Ihara	
Glenn Voloshin	
Marianne Morgan	Index
Delta Lithograph	Printing
Van Nuys, CA	

ISBN 0-87337-046-5
Library of Congress Card Catalog No.: 85-61224
Copyright © 1985 & 1987 David Brown & Ralph Warner

Update Service
• Introductory Offer •

Our books are as current as we can make them, but sometimes the laws do change between editions. You can read about law changes which may affect this book in the NOLO NEWS, a 24-page newspaper which we publish quarterly.

In addition to the Update Service, each issue contains comprehensive articles about the growing self-help law movement as well as areas of law that are sure to affect you (regular subscription rate is $7.00).

To receive the next 4 issues of the NOLO NEWS, please send us $2.00:

Name _____

Address_____

_____

Send to: NOLO PRESS, 950 Parker St., Berkeley CA 94710

LLBE9/87

Recycle Your Out-of-Date Books & Get 25%off your next purchase!

Using an old edition can be dangerous if information in it is wrong. Unfortunately, laws and legal procedures change often. To help you keep up to date we extend this offer. If you cut out and deliver to us the title portion of the cover of any old Nolo book we'll give you a 25% discount off the retail price of any new Nolo book. For example, if you have a copy of TENANT'S RIGHTS, 4th edition and want to trade it for the latest CALIFORNIA MARRIAGE AND DIVORCE LAW, send us the TENANT'S RIGHTS cover and a check for the current price of MARRIAGE & DIVORCE, less a 25% discount. Information on current prices and editions is listed in the NOLO NEWS (see above box). Generally speaking, any book more than two years old is of questionable value. Books more than four or five years old are a menace.

OUT OF DATE = DANGEROUS

This offer is to individuals only.

Acknowledgements

This book could not have been published without the generous assistance of many people. A special thank-you to Stephanie Harolde, who, in addition to keyboarding virtually the entire manuscript, made numerous helpful suggestions, nearly all of which were incorporated. Steve Elias, Carol Pladsen and Carol Marciel also made extremely helpful comments and suggestions. We would also like to acknowledge the generous help of Mike Mansel, a commercial insurance specialist in Walnut Creek, Joe Kelly, President of K & S Company, specialists in property management, and D.J. Soviero, an attorney specializing in landlord/tenant law based in San Francisco. Thanks, too, to Darlene Hopper and Coral Swain for their assistance in typing the earlier and later manuscripts, respectively.

Thanks also to Toni Ihara, Amy Ihara, John O'Donnell, Barbara Hodovan, Kate Miller, and especially Keija Kimura, who was responsible for the paste-up and layout of this book, as well as the wonderful front cover design.

Finally, Dave Brown expresses his special thanks to his wife, Nancy Brown, and his mother, Jane Fajardo, for their support and encouragement in putting together this book.

Table of Contents

Introduction

Here is a concise legal guide for California landlords. It is designed to cover the statutes and court decisions relevant to the average California landlord, as well as a number of proven techniques to keep you out of legal trouble. We do not cover mobile home, condominium or hotel rentals. Our emphasis is twofold. First we concentrate on explaining California landlord-tenant law in as straightforward a manner as possible. Second, we focus on how you can use this legal knowledge to anticipate and, where possible, avoid legal problems.

This book, **The Landlord's Law Book: Rights and Responsibilities** is the first of a two-volume set. Here we concentrate on the legal rules associated with most aspects of renting and

managing residential real property. For example, we include information on leases, rental agreements, managers, credit checks, discrimination, invasion of privacy, the landlord's duty to maintain the premises, and much more. **Volume II, The Landlord's Law Book: Evictions**, contains all the forms and instructions necessary to end a tenancy, including a step-by-step guide to doing your own evictions.

We recommend that you purchase several other books which we feel are essential additions to every landlord's (tax-deductible) library. The first of these is **Landlording**, by Leigh Robinson, which we feel is the best practical guide to the landlord business. In addition, we feel every California landlord should own copies of the basic laws which regulate his or her business. These are the California Civil Code and the California Code of Civil Procedure (C.C.P.). Although we review all the important statutes that set out your rights and responsibilities, we do not have space to print them in their entirety, and there are many times when you will surely want to refer to the complete statute.

Right here at the beginning let us confess an important bias. We believe that in the long run a landlord is best served if he establishes a positive relationship with his tenants. Why? First, because it's our personal view that adherence to the law and principles of fairness is a good way to live. Second, your tenants are your most important economic asset and should be treated as such. Think of it this way. From a long-term perspective, the business of renting residential properties is often less profitable than is cashing in on the appreciation of that property. Your tenants are crucial to this process, as it is their rent payments that allow you to carry the cost of the real property while you wait for it to go up in value. And just as other businesses place great importance on conserving natural resources, it makes sense for you to adopt legal and practical strategies designed to establish and maintain a good relationship with your tenants.

But while we advocate adhering to the letter of the law and treating tenants fairly, we are equally mindful of these facts:

● There are many tenants who will unfairly take advantage of you, if you let them. Or, in other words, just because you follow the law doesn't mean your tenants will;

● California courts and legislatures have created a plethora of tenant protection laws in the last generation (sometimes with little thought to how they negatively affect landlords). Failure to understand and follow these laws is a recipe for economic suicide;

● Many tenant lawyers make a good living out of exploiting the fine print of tenant protection laws;

● It's up to you to know the law well enough to protect your interests. No one will do it for you.

Now, here are a few tips about using this book. Landlord-tenant law is a complicated and intertwined subject. Necessarily, when laying it out in a linear fashion on the pages of this book we have had to make dozens of organizational decisions. Thus, while we deal with your legal liability for a tenant's physical injuries in Chapter 11, we discuss your potential financial liability for the illegal acts of your employees in Chapters 6 and 10. To take another example, the penalties for illegal discrimination are discussed in Chapter 8, potential financial liability for invading a tenant's privacy is discussed in Chapter 12, and your legal liability for retaliatory evictions is discussed in Chapter 13. The point is that unless you are very knowledgeable about California landlord-tenant law to begin with, your best bet is to read this entire book at least once. You will then have the perspective and background necessary to be able to focus on those specific areas which concern you.

And there is another reason to read this entire book carefully. We believe that with sensible advanced planning the majority of serious legal problems encountered by landlords can be either minimized or avoided. For example, in Chapter 10 we show you how to plan ahead to deal with those few tenants who will inevitably try to invent bogus reasons why they were legally entitled to withhold rent. Similarly, in Chapter 8 we discuss ways to be sure that you, your managers and other employees, know and follow anti-discrimination laws and, at least as important, make it clear that you are doing so.

A special word is appropriate for those of you who live in areas covered by rent control ordinances. These laws not only establish how much you can charge for most residential living spaces, they also override state law in a number of other ways. For example, in many areas rent control ordinances restrict a landlord's ability to terminate month-to-month tenancies and require "just cause for eviction." We handle rent control in two ways. First, as we explain your rights and responsibilities under state law in the bulk of this book, we indicate those areas in which rent control laws are likely to modify or change these rules. Second, we provide a detailed discussion of rent control in Chapter 4. This chapter is designed to be used along with a careful reading of your local rent-control ordinance.

We obviously believe that the average educated American landlord must familiarize herself with the laws and legal procedures which so closely regulate the landlord business and that leaving all legal decisions to lawyers is not wise (we discuss this in Chapter 7). In this regard, we confess our own hostility to what passes for justice in this country and our bias against lawyers as a group, even though it is a group in which we are counted as members. This isn't the place for an extended diatribe about the high cost and low efficiency and other problems of our legal system, except to caution you that there are doubtless many people who would advise you to rely on lawyers more often than we do.

We come now to the pesky personal pronoun. Our solution to the problem of how to handle gender is by using "he" and "she" more or less alternatively throughout the book. While this isn't perfect, it makes more sense than "she/he" or other cumbersome devices, such as writing "he and she" every time an abstract person must be identified.

Finally, may we wish you nothing but good managers, good tenants, and above all else, good luck.

Dave Brown
Ralph Warner

Berkeley, California

1

Renting Your Property: How to Avoid Legal Pitfalls

In this chapter, we examine the typical process of renting a home or apartment with an eye to avoiding several potential legal problems. We recognize that a landlord with 40 (or even 400) units is in a far different situation than a person with a mother-in-law cottage in the back yard and a duplex around the corner. Still, the basic legal rules apply to all.

Because this book is a legal guide, we concentrate on legal rules. Obviously, all sorts of practical considerations, including how to find and keep good tenants, are at least as important. In this regard, we recommend **Landlording** by Leigh Robinson (see back of this book for order information). It's quite simply the best book available on the business of being a landlord.

A. Adopt a Rental Plan and Stick to It

Before you advertise your property for rent, you'll want to make some basic decisions so that you can intelligently respond to inquiries. Obviously, these include how much rent to charge, when it is payable, whether to offer a fixed-term lease or a month-to-month or other periodic tenancy, and how much of a security deposit or "last month's rent" to require.

From a legal point of view, each of these decisions has major implications. We discuss the details of all these as we proceed. However, it's important to also understand one general point: in renting residential property, it's wise to decide the major details of your rental plan in advance and be consistent when dealing with prospective tenants. The reason for this is simple. If you don't treat all tenants more or less equally, you can fairly easily be accused of discriminatory conduct (see Chapter 8). Of course, there will be times when you will want to bargain a little with a prospective tenant (i.e., change several terms of the tenancy in exchange for concessions by the tenant in other areas), but again, as a general rule, you're better off to figure out your rental plan in advance and stick to it.

B. A Few Words About Rent

As we discuss in some detail, in Chapter 3, the rent you can legally charge in most of California is limited only by the market, or, in other words, the amount tenants will pay. However, in cities with rent control, the legal rules as to the maximum you can charge are very different. If the city in which your property is located has rent control, get a copy of your rent control ordinance to see if your property is covered by the law,* unless the property is being rented for the first time, in which case you can charge whatever you want. We discuss rent control in some detail in Chapter 4.

---

* It might not, if it's a single family home or if the property was vacated voluntarily in a city that has what's called "vacancy decontrol," or for several other reasons.

C. Advertising

Once you've decided how much rent to charge and when it will be due, whether to rent from month to month or for a fixed term, and how large a deposit to require, you will probably want to get on with the job of finding a tenant. In some areas, small landlords are lucky enough to fill all vacancies by word of mouth. If you fit this category, skip to the next section. For many of us, however, life is a little harder. At least occasionally, if not routinely, we have to advertise vacancies and deal with strangers.

Since this is primarily a law book, we will not go into advertising theory in detail. Still, there is one crucial point you should think about if you haven't already done so: Where you advertise is more important than how you advertise. If you are a quiet person who loves gardening and insists on neat surroundings, it obviously makes more sense to post a vacancy notice on the bulletin board at your favorite environmental organization or back pack store than at "Hot Rock Records." The same sort of thinking will serve you well when it comes to advertising in newspapers or other mass media. Many publications, rental services, etc. serve fairly defined market segments. Be sure the publication you choose to advertise in reaches the sort of people you want to rent to.

As far as legal problems are concerned, you should have no trouble if you follow these simple rules:

• If you put a price in your ad, make it an honest one. If a tenant shows up promptly and agrees to all the terms you set out in your ad, you may run afoul of the law if you arbitrarily raise the price. This doesn't mean you are always legally required to rent at this price, however. If a tenant asks for more services, different lease terms or some other change that you feel requires more rent, it's fine to bargain and raise your price;

• Don't engage in "bait-and-switch" tactics or advertising something you don't have. In the past, large landlords, management companies, and rental services have advertised units that weren't really available in order to produce a large number of prospective tenants who could then be "switched" to higher priced or inferior units. There have been a number of prosecutions involving this practice. Given the scarcity of rental housing in most California cities, this practice is not only illegal, it's just plain silly. You should be able to tell the absolute truth about your property and still be barraged with inquiries from prospective tenants;

• Be sure your ad can't be construed as discriminatory. We discuss this in detail in Chapter 8. Particular no-no's involve mentioning age, sex, race, religion, or adults-only (no children), but you should realize that any discrimination against any group that is unrelated to a legitimate landlord concern is illegal. It is an excellent idea to include the sentence: "[Your name or name of building] is an equal opportunity renter," or something similar, in all your ads, just as most businesses routinely include this statement in employment ads.

EXAMPLE: An ad for an apartment that says "Young, female, non-smoker preferred" is illegal on at least two counts, and perhaps three, since sex discrimination is forbidden by both state and federal law and age discrimination is illegal under California law. Even an ad for a non-smoker could be illegal, since the apparent assumption that all smokers are inconsiderate and are likely to damage or destroy your property has not yet been ruled on by the California courts.

• If you have any particular (non-illegally discriminatory) rules, such as "no pets," it's a good idea to put them in your ad. However, the wording of your ad does not legally obligate you to rent on any particular terms. In other words, just because your ad doesn't specify "no pets," you are not obligated to rent to Brenda Breeder and her two Dobermans.

D. Dealing with Prospective Tenants

Landlords with a unit or two may wish to deal with each prospective tenant personally and handle their own credit checks, reference checking, etc. Obviously, if you only rent a unit every year or two, it's not worth the effort to develop a detailed property rental system. Larger landlords, on the other hand, should understand that it's good business, as well as sound legal protection strategy, to adopt a detailed system and stick to it. Of course, no matter what approach you take, your goal is the same--to select tenants with an eye to avoiding legal and practical hassles later. Probably, the most common tenant problem you are trying to avoid is non-payment for rent, but there are a number of others.

Your first step in dealing with a prospective tenant should be to get them to fill out a written application. Here is a sample. (You will find a tear-out version at the back of this book.)

RENTAL APPLICATION

Property Address _____

                                          Home   Work

Name _____ Phone_____ Phone_____

Driver's License No. _____ Social Security No. _____

Current Address _____
   Years at   Reason for Wanting
   Address _____ to Move _____

   Owner/Manager _____ Phone _____

Previous Address_____
   Years at   Reason for
   Address _____ Leaving _____

   Person to Contact _____ Phone _____

                                  Please indicate any
Do you have   Type of   water-filled furni-
any pets? ____ Pet(s) _____ ture you own _____

                         Name of
Current Occupation _____ Employer _____ Phone _____
   Years with this   Name of
   employer? _____ Supervisor _____ Phone _____

Previous   Name of
Employment _____ of Employer _____ Phone _____
   Years on   Name of
   the job? _____ Supervisor _____ Phone _____

Monthly Employment Income
(before deductions) $ _____

Sources and Amounts of
Other Income (if any)   _____

                         _____

Name and relationship of every adult
person to live with you (each person
to attach separate application)

_____   _____

_____   _____

_____   _____

Name and age of every minor
child to live with you   _____   _____

                          _____   _____

                          _____   _____

Total Monthly Household Income
(Include gross and other income
of yourself and other adults to
live with you) $ _____

Savings
Account   Bank _____ Branch _____ Acct. No. _____

Checking
Account   Bank _____ Branch _____ Acct. No. _____

Money Market
Accounts _____

          _____

Major Credit Card _____ Acct. No. _____

Credit   Acct.   Amount   Av. Monthly
Reference _____ No. _____   Owed _____   Payment _____

Credit   Acct.   Amount   Av. Monthly
Reference _____ No. _____   Owed _____   Payment _____

Have you ever   Have you ever   Have you ever
filed bankruptcy? _____ been sued? _____   been evicted? _____

Explain any "yes" to the above _____

_____

Vehicle
Make _____ Model _____ Year _____ License No. _____

Personal
Reference _____ Address _____ Phone _____

Contact in
Emergency _____ Address _____ Phone _____

    I certify that all the information given above is true and correct, and I
hereby authorize the Owner and/or Manager of the property listed above to verify
any and all of the information and/or references provided to obtain all relevant
credit information pertaining to me.

Date _____   Signed _____

Assuming the application looks good, you should take the following additional steps (or at least most of them):

• Check with previous landlords given as references. Make sure you speak to a legitimate landlord, not a "friend" of the prospective tenant, posing as one. In this regard, you should realize that bad tenants almost always provide phony references. One suggestion is to call any number given and ask for the tenant by name, rather than starting off by saying that you are checking references. If you have really been given a friend's name, they will probably say something inappropriate. Also, if you have doubts, drive to the former address if possible and check things out in person. Finally, ask the previous landlord to pull out the tenant's rental application so you can verify certain facts, such as the tenant's birthdate. If the so-called landlord can't do this, you may be being conned;

• Obtain a credit report from a private credit reporting agency. These are listed in the phone book. Obviously, you want a tenant who pays bills in a timely and consistent manner;

• Check with the tenant's bank. You may need an authorization form such as the one included at the bottom of the rental application;

• Call the prospective tenant's employer to verify her income and length of employment. Some employers will require a written authorization from your prospective tenant. Again, this is included at the bottom of the sample rental application form above;

• If your prospective tenant has lived in the area, you may want to check local court records to see if she has been named as a defendant in any collection or eviction suits. This information is available to the public. Simply go to your local "municipal" or "justice" court (check your phone book under county listings) and ask the civil clerk to let you see the "defendant's index," usually kept in microfiche form. If the prospective tenant's name is listed, jot down the case number so you can check the actual case file to see what the lawsuit was about and how it was resolved. You can often determine if the prospective tenant asserted a reasonable defense and if any judgment against her was paid off. Checking court records may seem like overkill in many situations, but now and then it's an invaluable tool if you suspect a prospective tenant may be a potential troublemaker.

WARNING! Landlords are often faced with anxious, often desperate people who need a place to live immediately. Some of these people tell terrific hard luck stories as to why an exception to normal credit and reference checking rules should be made in their case and why they should be allowed to move right in. Don't believe any of it. People who have planned so poorly that they will literally have to sleep in the street if they don't get the place that day are all too likely to come up with a similar emergency when it comes time to pay the rent. And never, never let anyone stay in your property on a temporary basis. Even if nothing is signed and you have accepted no rent, you give anyone the legally-protected status of a tenant by allowing them to move in as much as a toothbrush. If they don't leave voluntarily, you will have to file a lawsuit to get them out.

Once you have several (or maybe even fifty) applications, make your selection. Assuming you are choosing the candidate who has the best qualifications to be a tenant (job, credit history, references, etc.), you have no legal problem no matter what their race, religion, sex, age, etc. This is true even if a less qualified prospective tenant, who happens to be a member of one or another minority group, also applies (see discussion on how to avoid discrimination lawsuits in detail in Chapter 8). Be warned that if you choose a clearly less-qualified tenant from a group you like (e.g., a white student with a low income), at the same time that you turn down a member of a minority group who is better qualified (e.g., an Asian professor with $10,000 in T-bills), you are very likely to be in legal hot water (see Chapter 8) if a discrimination complaint is filed.

But what if you have a number of more or less equally qualified applicants? Can you safely choose one who happens to be Caucasian over a member of a minority group? The answer is "Yes," so long as you don't make a habit of always eliminating minority group applicants. In other words, once you use an objective criteria to qualify people, and they rate equally, the choice is up to you without legal risk in any particular situation, but not if you make it a consistent policy to avoid equally-qualified minority applicants.

RECORD KEEPING NOTE: Obviously, a crucial part of any system to rent property is to be sure you can document how and why you chose a particular tenant. Assuming you did choose a highly qualified tenant, you want your records to back you up. So, keep all applications, credit reports, etc. in an organized way for at least one year after you rent a particular unit. And, if you make a decision not to rent to a tenant based on verbal in-

formation provided by someone such as a former landlord or employer, make a brief note of your conversation and include it in your file. Oh, and one more piece of advice about records: Make sure you keep them current after a tenant moves in. You always want to know where a tenant works and banks (you can get this latter information from their monthly rent check). If a tenant leaves owing you money above the amount of the security deposit, you can enforce your judgment by garnisheeing their wages or bank account.

EXAMPLE: 3/15/86 at 11:35 a.m.-- Called Anna Applicant's former landlord (for property at 123 State St., Apt. #4, San Francisco), Larry G. Landlord, at 555-1313. He said that Applicant was occasionally 1-2 weeks late with her rent and kept a cat in her apartment, contrary to the rental agreement.

E. Credit-Check Fees

Most landlords will not rent to anyone until they have checked their credit history with one or more credit reporting agencies. We believe this approach is essential. It is legal to charge the tenant for the cost of the report itself, and perhaps a small additional charge to cover the administrative cost of getting the report. It is customary to collect this charge at the time the credit application is taken. Be warned, though, it is not legal to assess this charge if you do not use it for the stated purpose, and pocket it instead.* It is wise to put the amount of the credit-check charge and the purpose for which it will be used in writing, either as a part of the rental application or separately. Here is an example:

CREDIT-CHECKING FEE

[NAME OF APPLICANT]
hereby pays to   [YOUR NAME]
the non-refundable fee of $20.00, receipt of which is acknowledged. This fee will be used by Lessor for the purpose of checking Applicant's credit history, including paying for a report on Applicant's credit for a credit reporting agency. It will be refunded to Applicant only if Lessor chooses to rent to another applicant prior to ordering such a report.

---

* There have been a few situations where landlords took hundreds of applications, charged a credit check fee and pocketed the money. What can we say but that everyone who does that deserves to be caught.

F. Holding Deposits

Charging a holding deposit is also legal, but we don't advise it. This type of deposit is usually offered by a tenant to try and hold the unit pending the result of a credit check, or until the tenant can come up with enough money for the rent and a formal deposit. (We discuss deposits in Chapter 5). Why should you avoid taking a holding deposit? Simply because they do you little or no good from a business point of view, and all too often result in legal fights and misunderstandings. You are far better off taking applications at your own pace, checking people's credit and references, and taking no deposits until you are sure you want to enter into a landlord-tenant relationship with the person.

The problem with taking a holding deposit is that it commonly leads to confusion. If you take a deposit of several hundred dollars from someone, what exactly are you promising them in return? To rent them the premises? To rent them the premises only if their credit checks out to your satisfaction? To rent to them only if they come up with the rest of the money before you rent to someone who you like better? If you and the tenant disagree about the answer to any of these questions, it can lead to needless anger and bitterness. This can sometimes even spill over into a small claims court lawsuit alleging breach of contract.

Another prime reason to avoid these deposits is that the law is very unclear as to what portion of a holding deposit a landlord can keep if a would-be tenant changes her mind about renting the property or doesn't come up with the rest of the rent and deposit money. The basic rule is that the landlord can keep an amount that approximates a "reasonable" relation to the landlord's costs, i.e., for more advertising and for pro-rated rent during the time the property was held vacant. A landlord who keeps a larger amount is said to be imposing an unlawful "penalty."

If contrary to our advice you should decide to take a holding deposit, it is essential that both you and your prospective tenant are clear as to all the specifics of your agreement. The only way to accomplish this is to write it down, preferably on the holding-deposit receipt. Here are two samples which cover several possibilities:

RECEIPT AND HOLDING-DEPOSIT AGREEMENT

This will acknowledge receipt of the sum of $200.00 by Rufus Rentor, "Landlord," from Arnie Applicant, "Applicant," as a holding deposit to hold vacant the rental property at 123 State Street, City of Los Angeles, California, until February 5, 198_ at 5:00 p.m., to be rented to Applicant on a month-to-month basis at a rent of $600 per month. The property will be rented to Applicant if s/he signs Landlord's written rental agreement and pays Landlord the first month's rent and a $600 security deposit on or before that date, in which event the holding deposit will be applied to the first month's rent. Landlord and Applicant agree that if Applicant cancels or fails to sign the agreement and pay the funds, Landlord may retain of this holding deposit a sum equal to the pro-rated daily rent of $20 per day plus a $50.00 charge to compensate Landlord for the inconvenience.

Date: February 2, 198_

_____
Applicant

_____
Landlord

RECEIPT AND HOLDING-DEPOSIT AGREEMENT

This will acknowledge receipt of the sum of $200.00 by Rufus Rentor, "Landlord" from Arnie Applicant, "Applicant," as a holding deposit to hold vacant the rental property at 123 State Street, City of Los Angeles, California, until February 5, 198_ at 5:00 p.m., to be rented to Applicant on a month-to-month basis at a rent of $600 per month. The property will be rented to Applicant if s/he signs Landlord's written rental agreement and pays Landlord the first month's rent and a $600.00 security deposit on or before that date, in which event the holding deposit will be applied to the first month's rent. Landlord and Applicant agree that if Applicant cancels or fails to sign the agreement and pay the funds, Landlord may retain the deposit.

[NOTE: This provision is probably not legal if the holding deposit is fairly high, say $100 or more, and the landlord only holds the unit for a day or two.]

Date: February 2, 198_

_____
Applicant

_____
Landlord

G. Cashing Checks

In talking to landlords, one problem that has been mentioned repeatedly involves tenants who give landlords deposit and rent checks which bounce after the tenant moves in. Sometimes this means that you have to evict a tenant from whom you never collected anything. One way to get around this is to cash the tenant's check at his bank before allowing him to move in. Another, perhaps easier, approach is to demand a certified check for the first month's rent and security deposits.

H. The Landlord/Tenant Checklist

Before you and your prospective tenant sign the lease or rental agreement, it is absolutely necessary to check the place over for damage. Do this together if at all possible, using the "Landlord/Tenant Checklist" form, such as the ones shown here and contained in the Appendix of this book. After you agree on all of the particulars, you should both sign and date the form.

Landlord-Tenant Checklist
(Dwelling Only — See Reverse Side for Furnishings)

The following is a summary of the conditions of the premises at _____, California, on the date listed below.

	Condition on Arrival	Condition on Departure	Estimated Cost of Any Repair
LIVING ROOM			
Floors & Floor Covering			
Drapes			
Walls & Ceilings			
Light Fixtures			
Windows, Screens & Doors			
Other:			
Other:			
KITCHEN			
Floor Covering			
Cupboards			
Stove & Refrigerator			
Dishwasher			
Disposal			
Sink & Plumbing			
Light Fixtures			
Other:			
Other:			
DINING AREA			
Floor & Floor Covering			
Walls & Ceilings			
Light Fixtures			
Windows, Screens & Doors			
Other:			
Other:			
BATHROOM(S)			
Floor & Floor Coverings			
Walls & Ceiling			
Windows, Screens & Doors			
Light Fixtures			
Other:			
Other:			
BEDROOMS			
Floors & Floor Covering			
Windows, Screens & Doors			
Walls & Ceilings			
Light Fixtures			
Other:			
Other:			
OTHER AREAS			
Floors & Floor Covering			
Windows, Screens & Doors			
Walls & Ceilings			
Furnace/Heater			
Air Conditioning			
Lawn/Ground Covering			
Patio, Terrace, Deck, etc.			
Other:			
Other:			

Dwelling checklist filled out on moving in on_____, 19____, and approved by _____
Landlord
and_____.
Tenant

Dwelling checklist filled out on moving out on_____, 19____, and approved by_____
Landlord
and_____.
Tenant

IMPORTANT NOTICE: We are committed to keeping the premises at _____

in good repair. Please notify us at _____

immediately of any defects in and around your dwelling unit. We will make necessary repairs as soon as possible.

Sincerely,

_____

Landlord-Tenant Checklist

(Side 2 — Furnished Property)

The following is a summary of the condition of any furnishings or implements in the premises described on the reverse side, on the date indicated below.

	Condition on Arrival	Condition on Departure	Estimated Cost of Any Repair
LIVING ROOM			
Coffee Table			
End Tables			
Lamps			
Lounge Chairs			
Sofa			
Other:			
Other:			
KITCHEN			
Broiler Pan			
Ice Trays			
Other:			
Other:			
DINING ROOM			
Chairs			
Stools			
Table			
Other:			
Other:			
BATHROOM(S)			
Dresser Tables			
Mirrors			
Shower Curtain			
Hamper			
Other:			
Other:			
BEDROOMS			
Beds (Single)			
Beds (Double)			
Chairs			
Chests			
Dressing Tables			
Lamps			
Mirrors			
Night Tables			
Other:			
Other:			
OTHER AREAS			
Bookcases			
Desks			
Pictures			
Other:			
Other:			

Furnishings/Implements checklist filled out on moving in on _____, 19_____, and approved by _____
Landlord

and _____ .
Tenant

Furnishings/Implements checklist filled out on moving out on _____, 19_____, and approved by _____
Landlord

and _____ .
Tenant

IMPORTANT NOTICE:

We are committed to keeping the premises at _____

in good repair. Please notify us at _____,
immediately of any defects in and around your dwelling unit. We will make necessary repairs as soon as possible.

Sincerely,

_____

Why bother with this checklist, you may ask? Because it is an excellent device to protect both you and your tenant when the tenant moves out and wants his security deposit returned. Without some record as to the condition of the unit, you and the tenant are all too likely to get into arguments about things like whether there was a hole in the kitchen linoleum or cracked tile in the bathroom at the time the tenant moved in, or whether they occurred later. The Landlord/Tenant Checklist is an aid to the all too fallible memories of both you and your tenant.

As you will note, the combined lease and rental agreement form in the Appendix of this book presupposes that you will use the checklist and incorporates it into the agreement by reference. When you complete and sign the checklist, make a copy. As part of signing the lease/rental agreement form, staple a copy of the checklist to both your copy and the tenant's.

If for any reason you decide not to use the Landlord/Tenant Checklist, cross out the reference to it in your lease/rental agreement form. Of course, both you and the tenant should place your initials next to the crossed out material.

I. Taking Pictures

An even better way to protect yourself from uncertainties over whether a particular tenant should be responsible for cleaning and/or repair costs is to compare "before" and "after" photographs of the property--pictures taken before the tenant moved in and after he or she moved out. Nothing is more convincing in a tenant's lawsuit over amounts withheld by a landlord from a security deposit than pictures showing that the unit was immaculate when the tenant moved in and less than immaculate when she moved out. This is also true in a landlord's lawsuit against a tenant for cleaning and repairs costs above the deposit amount. In this situation, a picture is truly worth a thousand words (see Chapter 5 on deposits and Chapter 18 on moving out for what to do if the property is left damaged and messy).

Perhaps the best way to get pictures taken and verified is to use a Polaroid or other camera that develops the pictures automatically and have the tenant date and sign or initial the pictures on the spot. If possible, you should repeat this process with "after" pictures, to be signed or initialled by the tenant as part of your established check-out or move-out procedure.

2

Understanding Leases and Rental Agreements

It is essential that every landlord understand California law as it applies to rental agreements and leases. Let's begin with the basics. There are just three legal ways in which residential rentals can be made: the lease, the written rental agreement, and the oral rental agreement. An oral agreement is made without anything being written down--you and the tenant just verbally agree on the deal. The other two, the lease and the written rental agreement, require all terms to be written and signed by you and the tenant.

Now, let's look at each of these types of agreements in detail.

A. Oral Agreements

It is perfectly legal to make a deal orally--that is, without writing anything down, and no signatures, as long as it is for a year or less. Typically, you agree to let the tenant move in and she agrees to pay a certain amount of rent on a particular schedule, such as weekly, every other week, or once a month. The period between rent payments is what determines how much notice you must give to raise the rent (subject to any rent control restrictions that apply) or terminate the tenancy, unless you have specifically agreed to allow the tenant to stay for a longer period at an established rent.* If a tenant pays weekly or

---

* Civil Code Sections 827, 1944, and 1946.

monthly, then she's entitled to a week or 30 days' notice, respectively.

The oral agreement has the advantages of being easy and informal. Just the same, it is rarely, if ever, wise to use one. As a businessperson, you are better off with the clarity that results when everything is written down. This is particularly true if you want to impose conditions on the tenancy, such as no pets, no subletting, no water beds, or you want to have a clause requiring that the tenant pay your attorneys' fees if you ever have to file a lawsuit.

The main problem with oral agreements is obvious. As time passes and circumstances change, people's memories (including yours) have a funny habit of becoming unreliable. Then, if something goes wrong, both sides are all too likely to end up in front of a judge, arguing over who said what to whom, when and in what context. For this reason, this book is based on the assumption that you will exclusively use either a written rental agreement or a lease.

B. Written Agreements

The wording of the written lease* and the written rental agreement is basically the same, except for one crucial difference. The written lease

contains language which fixes the terms of the agreement for a longer period of time than does a written rental agreement--most often six months or a year, but sometimes longer. If you use a fixed-term lease, you can't raise the rent until the lease runs out (unless the lease says you can), nor can you tell the tenant to move before the lease term expires, unless she breaks one or more terms of the lease. Similarly, the tenant is, at least in theory, legally bound to abide by the terms of the lease for its entire term. Should the tenant move out early, she is still contractually liable for the rent until you find a suitable replacement tenant, or could have reasonably found one if you tried. We discuss moving out and breaking leases in detail in Chapter 17, Section C.

The written rental agreement also reduces all the terms of the landlord-tenant relationship to writing. The difference is that the time period covered by the agreement is short-- usually 30 days (a month-to-month rental agreement). This means that you can raise the rent or ask the tenant to leave on 30 days' notice** (sometimes less). However, it also means that the tenant need normally only give you 30 days' notice if she wants to leave.

---

* Oral leases for less than a year are legally possible, but should be avoided. They are even more dangerous than oral rental agreements in that they require that one important term (the length of the lease) be accurately remembered by both parties over a considerable time.

** Several communities which have adopted rent-control ordinances have modified this rule to require "just cause" for eviction in certain circumstances. We discuss this in detail in Chapter 4.

Except for these very important differences, leases and written rental agreements are so similar that they are sometimes hard to tell apart.* Both cover the basic terms of rental (names, addresses, amount of rent and date due, deposits, etc.), and both contain a number of other provisions governing the terms and conditions of the tenancy. When they are printed, they look almost identical, except for the title at the top of the document. Sometimes even this can be misleading. It is also possible to use a single form to create either a lease or a rental agreement, depending on which boxes are checked. This is the approach we use.

Legally, a written agreement can be typed or written out in long-hand on any kind of paper, so long as the terms are understandable. However, as a practical matter, you will almost surely wish to use a printed fill-in-the-blank form such as the one at the back of this book, or one of those obtainable from the California Association of Realtors or the California Apartment Association.** These forms have been designed to protect your broad legal interests, but it is important to realize that they may not fit your exact circumstances and, if so, will require modification. For example, many form agreements contain clauses prohibiting pets. Some landlords, who like animals, or who have concluded that they get a more responsible class of tenant if they rent to pet owners, may wish to eliminate this one.

Lease and written rental agreement forms need not look like death certificates, nor read like a United Nations resolution, but such is often the case. Some of the sillier ones include a

number of illegal and unenforceable clauses, such as those requiring the tenant to waive her statutory right of privacy (see Chapter 12), accept responsibility for fixing things for which the landlord is responsible by law (see Chapter 10), or allow the landlord to keep the tenant's deposit if she doesn't stay some minimum period. To repeat, all of these provisions are illegal and unenforceable, and for reasons discussed in Section E of this chapter, should not be included in the lease or rental agreement.

The combined lease and rental agreement at the back of this book is a good one, but again, you may well need to modify it to fit your circumstances. You can do this by retyping our form and making the necessary changes. If you make fundamental changes, however, you may wish to have your work reviewed by an experienced landlords' lawyer (see Chapter 7).

SPANISH LANGUAGE NOTE: If the lease or written month-to-month rental agreement is negotiated primarily in Spanish, you must give the tenant notice

---

* In the Appendix of this book you will find a combined lease/rental agreement form. Clause number 3 allows you to elect whether you want to rent under a month-to-month tenancy or lease for a longer period of time.
** We list the addresses of these associations in Section F of this chapter.

in Spanish of her right to request a Spanish translation of the lease or rental agreement. To avoid confusion in this area, we recommend that you routinely make Spanish language translations available to tenants who speak Spanish as their first language.*

C. Which is Better, a Lease or a Rental Agreement?

Landlords often ask whether there is a legal reason to prefer a lease to a rental agreement or vice-versa. The answer is that there is less legal difference between the two than there used to be because of legal developments in the last generation. And what legal difference remains can probably be seen, on balance, to favor the use of rental agreements. But don't jump to any conclusions. Read what follows, think about your own situation, and then decide.

When a landlord rents property under a month-to-month rental agreement, she can change the terms of the tenancy (which includes raising the rent) or even end an undesirable tenant's tenancy, on 30 days' written notice, in all those cities without rent-control ordinances.** With a fixed-term lease, the terms can't be changed without the tenant's consent until the lease expires, and the landlord can evict before this time only if the tenant fails to pay the rent, or breaches another significant term of the agreement.

---

* Civil Code Section 1632.

** Under "just-cause eviction" provisions of some cities' rent-control ordinances, a tenant in effect has a lifetime tenancy unless one of the conditions allowing for just-cause eviction prevails. We discuss rent control in detail in Chapter 4.

It used to be that the major advantage of leasing for fixed terms of six months or a year or more was that a landlord obtained a fair degree of security because the tenant was on the hook to pay for a given length of time. Put another way, if the tenant broke the lease and left before it expired, she was still legally responsible for the balance of the rent for the entire lease term. And, if she could be located and sued, the landlord could obtain a court judgment for this amount. This is no longer true in most circumstances. Nowadays, as part of any effort to sue the departing (lease-breaking) tenant for the rent due for the rest of the lease term, landlords are required to "mitigate" (or minimize) the damage they suffer as a result of a tenant breaking a lease.

How does this "mitigation of damages" rule work? You can probably guess. The landlord must try to rent the unit to another suitable tenant at the same or a greater rent. If this is done (or even if it isn't done, but a judge believes it could have been done with a reasonable amount of effort), the landlord is presumed to have suffered little or no damage and the lease-breaking tenant is off the hook. This all adds up to a simple truth. A lease no longer provides much income security to a landlord. Indeed, arguably, a lease is now something of a one-way street, running in the tenant's direction. This is because, as a practical matter, the mitigation of damages rule allows a tenant to easily break a lease with little or no financial responsibility. And, even if the tenant does end up owing the landlord some money for the time in which the unit was empty, collecting the money can be more trouble than it is worth. Not surprisingly, many landlords prefer to rent from month to month, particularly in urban areas where new tenants can be found in hours or, at most, a few days.

Despite these legal rules favoring the tenant, there can, of course, still be practical advantages to leasing for a fixed period. This is because many people view entering into a lease for a period of time as a serious personal commitment. In other words, if you get the right tenant willing to sign a lease, you may reduce your turnover rate, even though the tenant could probably get out of the lease if they wished. Some landlords who make reducing tenant turnover a priority insist on leases with good results.

Finally, there is one other situation in which a lease is often preferable. This is in a geographical area where there is a high vacancy factor and it is difficult to find another tenant. Remember, if you can't find another suitable tenant to move in, the former tenant with a lease which hasn't expired is still liable for the rent. What all this adds up to is this--if you are renting next to a college which is only in session for eight months a year, or in a vacation area which is deserted during some months, you are far better off with a year's lease.

Remember, though, that a seasonal tenant is almost sure to try and get someone to take over the tenancy, and you may very well not like the person they produce. This can put you in the awkward position of having a legal duty to mitigate damages, but not wanting to.

NOTE ON LONG-TERM LEASES: Most leases are for one year. This makes sense, as it allows you to raise the rent at reasonably-frequent intervals if market conditions allow. Occasionally, landlords do wish to lease a unit for a longer period--two, three or even five years. This can be appropriate, for example, if the tenant plans to make major repairs or remodel the property.* One danger with a long-term lease is that inflation can eat away at the real value of the rent amount. A good way to hedge against this danger is to provide in all leases of more than a year for annual rent increases which are tied to the Consumer Price Index increases during the previous year. Here is a sample clause:

"Landlord and Tenant agree that the rent charged under this lease shall increase on the ___ of each year by the same percentage as the Consumer Price Index has increased during the previous twelve months. This calculation shall be made by comparing the Consumer Price Index level on __(Date)__ with its level one year earlier."

NOTE ON OPTIONS TO RENEW A LEASE: In commercial situations, it is common to lease a property for a set period of time, with an option to renew when that period runs out, perhaps at a higher rent. An option to renew is essentially a standing offer by the

_____

* It's possible to create innovative long-term leases which give tenants some limited equity interest in improvements they make and greater than normal security as regards notice to move. One interesting model is the "Living Lease," by Michael Phillips, which you will find in The People's Law Review, Warner (ed.), Nolo Press.

landlord to the tenant, which the tenant can accept or not in a manner and time frame set forth in the option. The "option to renew" concept is not commonly used in residential rentals, but a tenant occasionally requests one.

We usually advise against using option clauses for several reasons. First, an option to renew a lease leaves it entirely up to the tenant as to whether to continue the tenancy, whereas, without such an option, both the tenant and the landlord must agree on a renewal. After all, by the time the lease is about to expire, you might feel different about continuing the tenancy than you felt when you originally signed the lease containing the option clause. Unless you've received something of particular value, such as a very high guaranteed rent for the initial term or an extra up-front payment in consideration for including the option clause, you have very little to gain and a lot to lose by giving an option to renew.

Second, options are often drafted to allow the tenancy to continue, assuming the tenant exerts the option, on the same terms as before.* Since you may be able to obtain a higher rent after the initial term of six or twelve months, an option which allows the tenant to choose to remain at the same rent obviously is not in your best interest. Finally, drafting option clauses can be very tricky, and even the slightest mistake may do you a great deal of harm, or at the very least, render the option clause of no effect and add uncertainty to the entire situations. If you insist on in-

---

* Option clauses must clearly set forth the terms of the renewed tenancy, including the new term, the rent (which can be different from the rent for the first term if the option clause clearly says so), and so forth. Most clauses do this by simply referring to the same terms of tenancy under the initial lease terms. An option clause which leaves any significant term, such as rent or length of term, to "further negotiation," or words to that effect, is of no effect and not legally binding.

cluding a renewal or other option in a lease, you should contact an attorney.

D. How to Change a Written Agreement

If you and your prospective tenant wish to change one or more provisions of any pre-printed written rental agreement or lease, it is simple to accomplish, particularly if changes are made before the agreement is signed. Simply cross out unwanted portions and/or write in desired changes. Then, have all parties who are going to sign the document initial the changes at the time they sign the document. If the changes are lengthy, use a separate sheet of paper. Type the same heading as you use on the original document, identify the parties, and make it clear that you are adding additional provisions to the lease or rental agreement. For example, if you agree that the unit will be repainted, with you supplying the paint and painting supplies, and the tenant contributing labor, this could be accomplished as follows:

ADDITION TO RENTAL AGREEMENT

The rental agreement for the premises at 2550 Sacramento St., San Diego, CA., entered into between Leo Lessor, Landlord, and Lon Lessee, Tenant, is hereby added to as follows:

Landlord will supply up to $150 dollars worth of paint and painting supplies to Tenant. Tenant will paint the living room, hall and two bedrooms, using off-white latex paint on the walls, and water-based enamel on all wood surfaces (doors and trim). Paint and supplies shall be picked up by Tenant from ABC Hardware and billed to Landlord.

DATE: _____

SIGNATURE _____
          Leo Lessor, Landlord

DATE: _____

SIGNATURE _____
          Lon Lessee, Tenant

AMENDMENT TO RENTAL AGREEMENT

The written agreement for rental of the premises at 1625 California Street, Mountain View, California, entered into by Logan D. Landlord ("Landlord") and Tania D. Tenant ("Tenant") on April 1, 1985 is hereby amended as follows:

Beginning on June 1, 198_ , Tenant shall rent a one-car garage, adjacent to the main premises, from landlord for the sum of $75 per month. Accordingly, the rent of $600 per month set out in Clause 1 of rented agreement shall be increased to $675, effective June 1, 198_ .

DATED: May 16, 198_

SIGNATURE: _____
           Logan D. Landlord

DATED: May 16, 198_

SIGNATURE: _____
           Tania D. Tenant

If you wish to make mutually agreed-upon changes to a written rental agreement or lease after it is signed, there are two good ways to accomplish it. The first is to agree to substitute a whole new agreement for the old one. The second is to add the new provision as an amendment to the original agreement. An amendment need not have any special form, so long as it clearly refers to the agreement it's changing, and is signed by the same people who signed the original agreement.

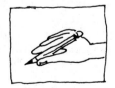

If you want to change one or more clauses in a written rental agreement, there is, of course, no legal requirement that you get the tenant's consent (it's always a good idea, of course). You can simply send a 30-day notice (see Chapter 14, Section A), unless you live in a city with a rent-control ordinance and the change is prohibited by the ordinance. However, if you have rented under a lease, you can't unilaterally change the term of the tenancy until the lease expires. We discuss the mechanics of changing terms of a written rental agreement by use of a 30-day notice in Chapter 14.

WARNING! When you have a written agreement, additional oral agreements may not be worth the air it takes to speak them. This is because whenever there is a written agreement, the law presumes that the parties have written out all of the provisions before signing. In other words, if a tenant with a written rental agreement or lease makes oral promises--such as paying extra rent if another person moves in--and doesn't do so, the law will usually assume such promises weren't made because they weren't written down. To repeat, get everything you want included in your rental agreement in writing before you sign. Any agreements made later should be done in writing in the form of an amendment.

E. Common Provisions in Lease and Rental Agreement Forms

Here we review the clauses normally contained in written rental agreements and leases. There are hundreds of different printed forms in use in California, which means that provisions designed to accomplish the same result are commonly worded differently. Unfortunately, some of these agreements are written so obtusely, it is hard to understand what they mean. Contrary to what many form writers seem to believe, it is not illegal to use plain English on lease and rental agreement forms. We have done our best to do so in the tear-out agreement at the back of this book.

As you will see, some provisions commonly included in lease and rental agreements are illegal, and therefore unenforceable. Some of these are meaningless relics from earlier days and reflect the fact that more than a few

landlords continue to use out-of-date lease forms. Since they are worthless, you should not include them in your agreements. Unfortunately, a few landlords disregard this advice and intentionally include illegal provisions to try and intimidate tenants. Doing this is counterproductive, because a lease containing too many illegal clauses may be disregarded in its entirety should you ever end up in court. In addition, you should know that several district attorneys have brought civil suits against landlords who routinely and flagrantly use leases with illegal clauses and, as a result, several landlords were fined.

1. Provisions Which Are Legal

Here are a number of common legal provisions found in printed lease and rental agreement forms. This list is not all-inclusive, but is representative of the most important provisions you will almost surely wish to include in your lease or rental agreement form. You will find most of these provisions contained in the tear-out agreement at the back of this book, although not always worded in exactly the same way. We do this intentionally to underline the fact that dozens, if not hundreds, of residential lease forms, all worded a little differently, all designed to accomplish pretty much the same thing, are in use in California.

a. Provision to Identify the Landlord and Tenant

This agreement is made and entered into on _____19__ , between _____ , hereinafter "Tenants," and _____ _____ , hereinafter "Owner."

Every lease or rental agreement must identify the landlord and the tenant (usually called the "parties" to the agreement). It must also include the street address at which the landlord and anyone authorized to manage the premises may be personally served with legal papers (Civil Code § 1962).

We suggest that you always list the name of all adults who will live in the premises, even if they are husband and wife. (We discuss co-tenants in Chapter 9.) If you are renting to a family with minor chioldren, you may want to simply list them as "minor children" (e.g., "Sally Phillips and Michael Phillips and their children"). However, if you are worried about the possibility of overcrowding if the family has more children, you should state the number of minor children (e.g., "Robin Ho and Cynthia Ho and their two children, Reginald and Amy").

b. Provision to Identify the Premises

Subject to the terms and conditions below, Owner rents to Tenants, and Tenants rent from Owner, for residential purposes only, the premises known as _____ _____ , located at _____ , California.

This provision normally involves no more than filling in the blanks with the address of your property, with perhaps a reference to whether you are renting a house, an apartment, etc. However, identifying exactly what the tenant is renting can be more difficult in shared housing situations. Suppose, for example, you are looking for a suitable tenant for a small cottage in your backyard that comes with kitchen and living room privileges in your house, or you are renting a portion, but not all, of a house in which you plan to continue living. The best way to handle these sorts of situations is to add an attachment sheet to the lease or rental agreement identifying exactly what property you are renting.

To accomplish this, simply fill in the address of the property and then add the words "as more fully described in Attachment 1 to this agreement." Then, take a piece of typing paper, label it "Attachment 1" and define the particulars of what you are renting. Finally, staple the attachment to the lease or rental agreement. When you and the tenant complete the paperwork, it's a good idea to ask the tenant to initial the attachment, as well as signing the agreement.

NOTE ON GARAGES AND OUT-BUILDINGS: If any part of a particular property is not being rented, such as a garage or shed you wish to use yourself or rent to someone else, make this clear by specifically excluding it from your description of the premises. For example, you might lease your "single-family house at 1212 Parker St., Visalia, California, except for the two-car garage located behind the house."

c. Provision Defining the Terms of the Tenancy

The term of the rental or lease shall begin on _____ , 19__ , and shall continue as follows (check/fill in one only):

( ) MONTH-TO-MONTH RENTAL AGREEMENT: On a month-to-month basis, the tenancy terminable by Owner or Tenants by the giving of 30 days' written notice to the other.

( ) FIXED-TERM LEASE: For a period of __ months thereafter, expiring on _____ _____ , 19 __ .

This provision is extremely important, as it establishes whether you are leasing your property for a fixed period of time, or renting it on a month-to-month basis. As we discuss in detail earlier in this chapter, a number of important legal rights and responsibilities for both you and your tenant depend on your choice. Of course, many lease and rental agreement forms are designed differently to offer only one type of tenancy on each form. We follow the combination lease/rental agreement form approach because we believe it's more efficient given the fact that all other clauses of both agreements are the same. However, if you exclusively use leases or rental agreements in your business, you may want to re-type our form to eliminate any reference to the type of tenancy you do not employ.

d. Provision For the Payment of Rent

On signing this agreement, Tenants shall pay to Owner the sum of $ _____ as rent, payable in advance, for the period of _____ _____ , 19__ through _____ , 19 __ . Thereafter, Tenants shall pay to owners a monthly rent of $ _____ , payable in advance on the first day of each month. Rent shall be paid at _____ , _____ , California.

We discuss the law as it applies to the payment of rent in detail in Chapter 3. Please read this discussion and consider whether you wish to modify this clause. For example, some landlords require that rent be paid in cash or by a money order; others want rent paid twice a month, etc.

e. Provisions for Late Fees and Bounced-Check Charges

If Tenant fails to pay the rent in full within three days after it is due, Tenant shall pay Landlord a late charge of $5.00, plus $2.00 for each additional day that the rent continues to be unpaid. The total late charge for any one month shall not exceed $35.00. By this provision, Landlord does not waive the right to insist on payment of the rent in full on the day it is due.

In the event any check offered by Tenant to Landlord in payment of rent or any other amount due under this agreement is returned for lack of sufficient funds, Tenant shall pay to Landlord a check-return charge in the amount of $10.00.

It's legal for a lease or rental agreement to require the tenant to pay an extra fee if the rent is late or if the tenant's rent check bounces (assuming you agree to accept checks), if such fees are reasonable. If a check-bounce fee or late charge is plainly excessive, chances are that a judge in an eviction lawsuit will rule that it is void. Normally, a charge shouldn't be assessed until after the rent is late more than a certain number of days, and should contain an upper limit if you adopt a provision that gets bigger the later the rent. A typical legal late charge provision on a low- or moderate-rent place is $5 on the third day after the rent is due, plus $2 for each additional day up to a maximum of $30 or $35. If you rent an expensive home or luxury apartment where the monthly rental amount is large, a bigger late fee will be legally enforceable. For more on late charges, see Chapter 3, Section C. As for fees charged when the tenant's rent check bounces, the amount should be no more than what your bank charges you for a returned item, plus a few dollars for your trouble. This is normally in the $10 to $15 range.

f. Provision for the Payment of Deposits

On signing this agreement, Tenants shall pay to Owner the sum of $ _____ as and for security as that term is defined by Section 1950.5 of the California Civil Code. Tenants, or either of them, may not, without owner's prior written consent, apply this security deposit to rent or to any other sum due under this agreement. Within two weeks after Tenants have vacated the premises, Owner shall furnish Tenants with an itemized written statement of the basis for, and the amount of, any of the security deposit retained by the Owner. Owner may withhold only that portion of Tenant's security deposit necessary (a) to remedy any default by Tenants in the payment of rent, (b) to repair damages to the premises exclusive of ordinary wear and tear, and/or, (c) to clean the premises if necessary.

We discuss deposits in detail in Chapter 5. Make sure you understand the maximum amount you may charge before completing this section.

g. Provision Reducing Notice Period

Landlord may terminate this agreement, and the tenancy under it, or may modify any of its terms, by giving seven days' written notice to Tenant.

You learned earlier in this chapter that a month-to-month tenancy can be terminated or the terms of tenancy changed on 30 days' written notice, unless you are in a city with a rent control ordinance which requires "just cause for eviction." These laws also allow a rental agreement provision to contain a clause reducing the 30-day period to as low as seven days. Though this may seem advantageous to landlords, very few written rental agreements contain this provision. This is because it is unclear under the law whether such a clause also allows the tenant to terminate his tenancy on short notice too, even if the provision is worded to only allow the landlord to do so.

Another legal uncertainty involves whether a landlord can use this sort of short-notice clause to terminate a tenancy in less than 30 days if she has already accepted rent to cover a period beyond the end of the short-notice period. In other words, if you accept rent on January 1st for the whole month, your seven-day notice may not be valid unless served on or after the 24th, to take effect on the first day not covered by any rent you've accepted. Because of these uncertainties, and because a 30-day notice provision is the one traditionally used, we adopt the 30-day standard in the agreement at the back of this book, and do not include a provision reducing the notice period as set out above.

h.   Provision Extending Notice Period

Landlord may terminate this agreement, and the tenancy under it, or may modify any of its terms, by giving ___ days' written notice to Tenant.

It is perfectly legal to adopt a clause in a rental agreement giving a tenant a longer notice period--say 60 or 90 days. This may very well be appropriate where a tenant has occupied your premises for a long time, and some landlords report that they have fewer evictions when they give tenants a generous amount of time in which to find another place. Again, the provision in the written rental agreement at the back of this book sticks to the (standard) 30-day notice period, but you may want to modify it.

i.   Provision Limiting Occupancy and Forbidding Subletting or "Assignment"

The premises shall be occupied only as a residence by Tenants. Occupancy is specifically limited to a total of __ occupants. Tenants shall not let anyone not specifically named in this agreement live in the premises, nor shall they sublet any part of the premises or assign the agreement with-

out the prior written consent of Landlord. Guests may stay up to 10 days in any six-month period. All guests that stay three or more consecutive days must register with the owner. Occupancy by guests staying more than 10 days is prohibited without owner's written consent and shall be considered to be a breach of this agreement.

It is a good idea to include this type of provision in order to be able to exercise some control over who lives in your property should it become necessary. You do not want the tenant to be able to turn your property over to someone else you wouldn't rent to if you had the choice. This provision is designed to prevent your tenant from leaving in the middle of a lease term and finding whomever she chooses to take her place, without your consent. It also prevents a tenant from subleasing during a vacation or other absence, or renting out a room to someone you don't know about unless you specifically agree.

It's important for you to understand, however, that even if you have this sort of provision in a lease, and your tenant with a lease wishes to leave early and provides you with another suitable tenant, you can't both hold the tenant financially liable for breaking the lease **and** unreasonably refuse to allow her to substitute another tenant who is in every way suitable. (We discuss this "mitigation of damages" concept in detail in Chapter 17.) You can, of course, refuse to rent to the new tenant the old tenant provides. If you are willing to waive the remainder of the former tenant's obligation to pay rent for the rest of the lease term, that's the end of the matter. However, if you plan to pursue the former tenant for any portion of the rent due under the remainder of the lease, you should document why you are refusing to rent to the new tenant. In this regard, a bad financial report or references would legally justify your action. In any event, you will be very glad to have the option not to accept a sublet or assignment if you don't like or trust the person your former tenant proposes to take over her lease.

We also think some control over guests makes sense. You may not enforce this provision strictly, but it will be very handy to have if a tenant tries to move in a friend or relative for a month or two, calling her a guest.

j. Provision Against Pets

No animal or other pet (except properly-trained dogs needed by blind, deaf or physically handicapped persons) shall be kept on the premises without Landlord's prior written consent.

This provision is designed to keep the tenant from keeping pets without your written permission. This is not to say that you will want to apply a flat "no-pets" rule and refuse to ever give such permission.* It does provide you with a legal mechanism designed to

---

* Some landlords allow pets but require the tenant to establish a separate deposit or "pet escrow" account to cover any damages caused by the pet. This is not legal if the deposit charged for the pet, when added to the amount charged for the security deposit and last month's rent, exceeds the maximum amount that can be charged for a deposit (see Chapter 5). Generally, we do not think pet escrow accounts are good ideas because it limits what you can use that part of the security deposit for. If you want to protect yourself from damage done by a pet, you are probably better off charging a slightly higher rent (and the maximum security deposit) to start with, assuming your rent is not covered by rent control.

keep your premises from being knee deep in Irish wolfhounds. Without this sort of provision, particularly in a fixed-term lease that can't be terminated on 30 days' notice, there's little, except for city ordinances prohibiting tigers and the like, to prevent your tenant from keeping dangerous or non-house-broken pets on the property.

WARNING! You may not use a no-pets clause to keep a blind person from keeping a trained "seeing-eye" dog, a deaf person from keeping a trained "signal dog," or a physically handicapped person from keeping a trained "service dog" on the premises.**

k. Provision Covering Condition of the Premises

Tenant(s) acknowledge that they have examined the premises, including carpets, drapes, and paint, and have found them to be in good, safe, and clean condition and repair, except as otherwise noted on the "Landlord/Tenant Checklist" which Tenant(s) has completed and given Owner, a copy of which Tenant(s) hereby acknowledges receipt of, and which is hereby deemed to be incorporated into this agreement by this reference. Tenant(s) agrees to (a) keep the premises in good order and repair, and, upon termination of tenancy, to return the premises to Owner in a condition identical to that which existed when Tenant(s) took occupancy, except for ordinary wear and tear, (b) immediately notify Owner of any defects or dangerous conditions in and about the premises of which

---

** Civil Code Section 54.1.

they become aware, and (c) reimburse to Owner, on demand by Owner or his or her agent, for the reasonable cost of any repairs to the premises damaged by Tenant(s) or their guests or invitees.

It is essential to include this type of clause for several obvious reasons, not the least of which is that it makes it clear that if a tenant damages the premises (e.g., breaks a window, plugs up the toilet with a toothbrush, etc.), it's up to him to pay for the cost of fixing the problem.

1. Provision Restricting Water-Filled Furniture.

    No waterbed or other item of water-filled furniture shall be kept on the premises unless the tenant obtains $100,000 of insurance to cover potential damage caused by the waterbed.

    It is no longer legal to ban waterbeds or other items of water-filled furniture outright. You may, however, require the tenant to have $100,000 in liability insurance to cover potential damage. Such insurance is available for $25 to $50 a year, according to the legislator who sponsored the bill that made this change in the law.

    Note that the agreement in the Appendix of this book does not contain a waterbed provision. You may or may not want to add it.

m. Provision Forbidding Repairs or Alterations

    Except as provided by law, Tenants shall not make any repairs or alterations to the premises without Landlord's prior written consent.

    Especially with fixed-term leases for a year or more, the law is unclear on the extent to which a tenant may, in the absence of a provision in the agreement, remodel or make substantial alterations to the building. This provision makes it clear that alterations and repairs without the landlord's consent aren't allowed. If you wish, you can make this clause more specific to prohibit the use of nails or tacks in the walls (very bad for lath-and-plaster walls, but okay on sheet-rock walls), adhesive hangers (which tear the outer layer off sheet-rock walls when removed), etc.

    You should know that the "except as provided by law" language in the above provision is a reference to the "repair-and-deduct" remedy the tenant may use to repair health- or safety-threatening defects. As we'll see shortly in Section 2(c) below, the tenant's right to use this statutory procedure can't be taken away with a lease or rental agreement provision.

Fixtures are things that are firmly attached to rental property. They belong to the landlord except where "the removal can be affected without injury to the premises, unless the thing has by the manner in which it is affixed become an integral part of the premises." They are completely defined in Civil Code Section 1019. Bookshelves nailed into the wall, kitchen cupboards screwed to studs, and heavy equipment bolted to the floor are all fixtures. If a tenant installs a fixture without your agreement to the contrary, it belongs to you, at least in theory (we discuss what to do if a tenant leaves and takes fixtures with him in Chapter 18.

We don't mention fixtures in our tear-out lease/rental agreement form for the obvious reason that it contains a provision by the tenant forbidding any kind of alteration or modification of the premises by the tenant, and the installation of anything which would constitute a fixture would be a violation by the tenant of her lease or rental agreement. Should your tenant ask permission to install anything that might constitute a fixture, and should you allow the tenant to do this, you should remind her that the fixture is to remain in place when she leaves, perhaps also having her sign a statement indicating that she understands things. (You might also insist on installing the shelves or other fixture yourself or having a worker install it, to assure that it's installed in a workman-like manner.)

AGREEMENT FOR INSTALLATION
OF FIXTURE

Otis Owner, the owner of the premises at 123 Flower Lane, San Diego, California, hereby grants to Teresa Tenant permission to install two bookshelves by use of four-inch screws attached to the long wall of the rear bedroom of the premises. Teresa acknowledges and understand that the bookshelves, once installed, are to be considered part of the premises, and are not to be removed when her tenancy ends.

Date: _____

Signature: _____
              Otis Owner

Date: _____

Signature: _____
              Teresa Tenant

---

n.   Provision Defining Who Will Pay for Utilities

Tenants shall be responsible for payments of all utility charges, except for the following, which shall be paid by Owner: _____
_____.

It's wise to include this provision to avoid the possibility of misunderstandings. Normally, landlords pay for garbage (and sometimes water, if there is a yard) to make sure that the premises don't turn into a dump. Tenants are normally required to pay for other services.

In a shared housing situation involving the landlord personally, or where there is only one meter for several units, you may want to define who is responsible for what portion of the utilities in more detail. If you do, simply cross out the provision in our form, type in their place, "As more fully explained in Attachment __ ." Use a separate sheet of paper to carefully delineate who is to pay what, and attach it to the lease or rental agreement. It's a good idea to have the tenant sign or initial the attachment when signing the agreement.

o. Provision Against Violating Laws, Causing Disturbances, Etc.

Tenants shall not violate any law or ordinance, commit waste or nuisance, or annoy, disturb, inconvenience, or interfere with any other tenant, in the use of the premises.

This type of provision is commonly found in most form leases and rental agreements. It is a good idea. If the tenant causes a nuisance* or seriously damages the property or violates the law in the use of the premises, you may be able to successfully evict them even without such a provision in the agreement, but it will be easier if you have an explicit lease provision to point to. You may never need to rely on this language, but then again, if your ten-

_____

* A nuisance consists of repeated or continuous conduct which prevents neighbors from fully enjoying the use of their own owned or rented real property. For example, frequently loud parties, blaring music, noxious odors, or even heavier-than-usual traffic in and out of an adjoining residence, may be considered a legal nuisance.

ant opens a marijuana store in the kitchen or a typography shop in the bedroom, you will be delighted it's there.

p. Provision for Payment of Attorneys' Fees in a Lawsuit

In any legal action or proceeding to enforce any part of this agreement, the prevailing party shall recover reasonable attorneys' fees and court costs.

Many people assume that if they sue someone and win, the court will order the losing person to pay their attorneys' fees. This is usually wrong. As a general rule, a court will order the loser to pay the winner's attorneys' fees only where a written agreement specifically provides for it. This is why it can be important to have an "attorneys' fees" clause in your lease. To repeat, if you hire a lawyer to bring an eviction suit against your tenant for nonpayment of rent, the judge won't order your tenant to pay your attorneys' fees even if you win-- unless the lease or rental agreement has an attorneys' fees clause. Of course, as you doubtless know, getting a court order for attorneys' fees and collecting them are two very different animals. Many landlords we know don't use this provision precisely because of their experience that, if they win a suit, these fees are very hard to collect, but if they are successfully sued by a tenant, and the tenant is awarded attorneys' fees (we discuss the reciprocal nature of Civil Code Section 1717, just below), they end up paying them.

This leads us to an important legal point. Under Civil Code Section 1717, an attorneys' fees clause in a lease, rental agreement, or other type of contract, works both ways. That is, if your tenant prevails in a lawsuit, where a lease or written rental agreement contains such a clause, you must pay her "reasonable attorneys' fees," in an amount determined by the judge. This is true even if the clause is worded in a "one-way" fashion to require payment of attorneys' fees only by the tenant if you win and not vice-versa.

Knowing this may also give you pause if you intend to do your own legal work in any potential eviction or other lawsuit, even if the tenant hires a lawyer. If so, you will probably conclude that it is wiser not to include this clause in your agreements. You don't want to be in a situation where you'd have to pay the tenant's attorneys' fees if she won, but she wouldn't have to pay yours if you won because you didn't hire a lawyer in the first place. So, again, if you are sure you will never hire an attorney, you will probably want to eliminate this clause.

q. Provision to Authorize Your Manager to Handle Legal Paperwork

Owner or the person signing this agreement on Owner's behalf is authorized to manage the said premises, and is authorized to act for and on behalf of Owner for the purpose of service of process and for the purpose of receiving all notices and demands, at the address indicated below Owner/Agent's signature herein.

We discuss your legal rights vis-a-vis managers in Chapter 6. If you plan to turn over to a manager authority to serve and receive legal papers, include this clause.

r. "Entire Agreement" Provision

This document constitutes the entire agreement between the parties, and no promises or representations, other than those contained here and those implied in law, have been made by either party.

The meaning of this provision is obvious. It protects you from liability for anything a tenant claims you promised verbally. It is a good idea to include it and to insist that any agreement made between you and your tenant be in writing.

s. Inspection of Premises

Tenant shall permit Landlord or his agents, upon reasonable notice of not less than 24 hours, to enter the premises, to make repairs, or to show them to prospective tenants or purchasers. If Landlord cannot locate tenant in order to give this notice after reasonable attempts to do so, he or his agents may enter the premises at a reasonable time for the above-stated purposes. In order to facilitate Owner's right of access, Tenant(s) shall not, without Owner's prior written consent, alter or rekey any locks to the premises. At all times, Owner or Owner's agent shall be provided with a key or keys capable of unlocking all such locks and gaining entry.

This clause makes it clear to the tenant that you as a landlord have a legal right of access to the property to make repairs or show the premises for sale or rental, provided you give the tenant reasonable notice in advance. As we'll see in Chapter 12, the law provides for this anyway, and makes illegal and unenforceable any provision which provides for less notice than the law allows, or for any other waiver by the tenant of his right to privacy. Still, we believe it's a good idea to spell this out in writing.

t. Provision Concerning Financial Responsibility for Damage to Premises

In the event the premises are damaged by fire or other casualty covered by insurance, Owner shall have the option either to (1) repair such damage and restore the premises, this Agreement continuing in full force and effect, or (2) give notice to Tenants at any time within thirty (30) days after such damage terminating this Agreement as of a date to be specified in such notice. In the event of the giving of such notice, this Agreement shall expire and all rights of Tenants pursuant to this Agreement shall terminate. Owner shall not be required to make any repair or replacement of any property brought into the premises by

Tenant. Tenants agree to accept financial responsibility for any damage to the premises and losses of use of the premises from fire or casualty caused by Tenants' negligence. Tenants shall carry a standard renter's insurance policy from a recognized insurance firm, or as an alternative, warrants that they will be financially responsible for losses not covered by Owner's fire and extended coverage insurance policy. Damages or plumbing stoppages caused by Tenant negligence or misuse will be paid by Tenant.

This provision speaks to what happens if the premises are seriously damaged by fire or other calamity. Basically, it seeks to reduce your risk to thirty (30) days rental value if the damage was your responsibility and to eliminate it entirely if it was caused by the tenant. The tenant is forced to assume complete responsibility for damage to her own belongings. One change you may wish to make in this clause involves requiring tenants' insurance. We discuss the pros and cons of this in Chapter 5. If you do require tenants to carry such insurance, you should also require proof not only that it has been purchased, but that it is kept in force.

u. Provision for Tenant Rules and Regulations

Tenants acknowledge receipt of, and have read a copy of the Tenant Rules and Regulations, which are hereby incorporated into this agreement by this reference. Owner may terminate this Agreement as provided by law if any of these Tenant Rules and Regulations are violated.

Many landlords don't worry about detailed rules and regulations, especially when they rent single-family homes or duplexes. However, in large buildings, rules are usually a must to control the use of such things as elevator, pools, parking garages, security systems, etc. to name just a few. They are also commonly employed to lay down rules about such things as excessive noise, use of grounds, maintenance of balconies (e.g., no drying clothes on the balcony). If you do plan to use tenant rules and want the power to enforce them if a tenant doesn't want to cooperate, it is necessary to include a clause such as this in your lease or rental agreement, especially if you use a lease. Doing this gives you the authority to evict a tenant who persists in seriously violating your code of Tenant Rules and Regulations.

2. Illegal Lease and Rental Agreement Provisions

Because some landlords have in the past drafted leases and rental agreements that contained provisions that attempted to take away various tenant protection provisions of California law, the Civil Code now expressly forbids the use of many types of "illegal" provisions.*

Let's look at several lease and rental agreement provisions that the law specifically says have no legal effect.

---

* Civil Code Section 1953.

a. Waiver of Rent Control Laws

As you will see in Chapter 4, California has no statewide rent control law. However, several cities do have such ordinances, and all these cities' rent control ordinances specifically forbid lease or rental agreement provisions by which a tenant waives or gives up any rights under the rent control ordinance.

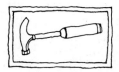

b. Waiver of "Repair-and-Deduct" Rights Under Civil Code Section 1942

As you will see in Chapter 10, Civil Code Section 1941 requires a landlord to maintain and repair the rental property in accordance with certain minimum standards. Section 1942 of the Civil Code allows a tenant whose landlord refuses to do so to arrange for certain repairs herself and deduct the cost from the next month's rent. Further, Section 1942.1 says that a lease or rental agreement provision by which the tenant agrees to waive or modify her rights under these laws is void and unenforceable. It's important to understand that there is one exception to this rule, however. If the tenant specifically agrees to repair and maintain all or part of the property "as part of the consideration for the rental," the repair-and-deduct rule can be waived. Although in principal this would seem to be a broad exception, it is far less broad in practice. Why? Because judges will look to see if the tenant's promise to keep the premises in repair was really part of a bargain by which he received lower rent and was not just a way for the landlord to avoid her legal responsibilities. Chances are the tenant's waiver will be upheld if a tenant handy with tools agrees to repair or maintain the property in exchange for rent that's considerably lower than fair market rent, but not otherwise.

Here is an example of a valid clause:

Helen Handy agrees to be responsible for all routine repairs and maintenance to the premises covered by this agreement, in consideration for a monthly rent of $250. This amount is approximately $150 less than the fair market rent for the premises, which is agreed to be $400.

NOTE: Even if a landlord enters into this sort of provision, it doesn't relieve her of her obligation to the city or county to comply with local housing codes. The landlord retains this obligation even if the tenant breaches a rental agreement or lease provision requiring her to maintain the premises in compliance with city and county regulations. In other words, the city and county has no interest in what the landlord and tenant agree to, but will hold the landlord responsible if there is a code violation problem.

c. Right of Inspection

As you will see in Chapter 12, a landlord can't just walk in any time to inspect or repair the property, or even to show it to prospective renters or buyers. Except in an emergency, the law requires a landlord to give a tenant reasonable advance notice. Nevertheless, some leases and rental agreements have provisions which purport to allow a landlord to enter with little or no notice. This type of provision

is of no effect (Civil Code Section 1953).

d. Provision That the Landlord Is Not Responsible for Tenant Injuries Or Injuries to a Tenant's Guests

Often called an "exculpatory clause," this provision says that if the landlord fails to maintain the property and the tenant or her guests suffer injury or property damage as a result, the landlord can't be held responsible for paying for the loss. This provision is void and of absolutely no use to a landlord, should a tenant or a guest suffer personal injury or damage to their property and sue the landlord.

e. Provision Giving Landlord "Right of Entry"

Some leases and rental agreements contain a clause that appears to allow the landlord to come in and throw the tenant out, or at least change the locks and remove her property if she doesn't pay the rent. This clause is void. If you do resort to extra-legal means to evict a tenant, this type of clause won't protect you in a tenant's lawsuit for unlawful eviction. In other words, no matter what the lease says, you have to sue and get a court order to legally remove an unwilling tenant (see Volume II of this book, on evictions).

f. Waiver of Right to Legal Notice, Trial, Jury or Appeal

A lease or rental agreement clause under which a tenant gives up, or modifies, her legal right to any procedural right in a lawsuit you might bring is also void. This includes the right to proper service of a three-day notice to pay rent or quit (three-day notice periods **cannot** be reduced by agreement) or other termination notice and the rights to present a defense in a lawsuit, trial by jury, appeal, etc.

g. Waiver of Right to Deposit Refund

Civil Code Section 1950.5 provides that a landlord must, within two weeks after the tenant vacates the property, mail the tenant a refund of his deposit or, if the deposit is not completely refunded, a written itemization as to how it was applied to back rent, costs of cleaning, repairs, etc. Any provision waiving or modifying the tenant's rights in this respect is void and of no effect (Civil Code 1953). As with right-of-inspection provisions, however some lease and rental agreement forms do state what the law provides. We believe this is a good idea and include such a provision in our agreements.

h. Other Illegal Provisions

Just because a particular type of lease clause isn't listed above doesn't mean it's legally enforceable. Courts can and do exercise the power to refuse to enforce what they consider to be illegal and outrageous clauses in leases, rental agreements and other contracts. This includes provisions for excessive late charges, short-cuts the landlord can use to recover possession if she believes the property to be abandoned, and anything else the court feels is manifestly unfair.

F. Lease and Rental Agreement Forms

There is no reason to draft your own lease or rental agreement from scratch for the same reason it makes no sense to invent an electric can opener--it has already been done. And it may even be counter-productive if you insert unenforceable clauses. As we noted earlier in this chapter, judges and district attorneys are beginning to get tough with landlords who knowingly insert illegal language in lease or rental agreement forms. You will find a tear-out form good to establish both a lease and rental agreement at the back of this book, or you can use the ones published by the California Apartment Association, 1107 9th St., Sacramento, (916) 447-7881, or the California Association of Realtors, 1129 10th St., Sacramento, (916) 444-2045. Forms are available for purchase from these organizations and usually from local landlord associations.

Does this mean that these pre-printed clauses will solve all your problems? Probably not. It is extremely common that you will want to cover one or more additional points not covered in standard leases. For example, if your building has a pool, you may want to incorporate pool rules in the lease, or you may want to add specific requirements regarding parking, noise, yard care, pets, etc. to the lease. If you do, simply re-type our form, adding your own provisions.

3

Basic Rent Rules

The right to receive rent is obviously a primary motive when a property owner authorizes someone else to live in his property. Given this truth, it's odd that so many landlords frequently confuse and misapply the legal rules which govern rent. While occasional misunderstandings between landlord and tenant over rent are probably inevitable, many landlords exacerbate these problems because of their own shaky knowledge of the law. In short, it's our belief that the business of renting residential property would often run more smoothly if landlords clearly understood the legal rules that control their right to receive money in exchange for the right of their tenants to occupy residential property.

Before we begin, keep the following in mind: although the rules given in this chapter are quite logical and straightforward, it is presumed that your tenant has no legal excuse for refusing to pay all or part of the rent. In fact, as we'll see in Chapter 10, the landlord's failure to repair and maintain the property may in some cases provide a tenant with a basis for withholding rent in an amount that can only be determined by a judge in an eviction lawsuit. So, although the rules in this chapter are pretty cut-and-dried, i.e., the tenant owes the precise rent stated in the lease or rental agreement on the date specified, a landlord's failure to keep up the premises can reduce this precision to somewhere between the nebulous and the uncertain.

We discuss the relationship of landlord's duty to keep property habitable and the tenant's duty to pay rent in detail in Chapter 10.

In the meantime, let's review California's basic rent laws.

A. How Much Can You Charge?

There is no state or federal law governing how much rent a landlord can charge. In other words, you can legally charge as much rent as you want (and a tenant will pay), unless your premises are subject to a local rent control ordinance. Rent control exists in a relatively few geographic areas of California, although several of these, such as San Francisco and the City of Los Angeles, have dense populations. Where it does exist, rent-control laws are established under the legal authority of the particular city.* Because rent control laws differ considerably from place to place, and because it's a fairly involved subject, we refer you to Chapter 4 for a full discussion.

Of course, common sense will tell you that even in areas without rent control, market conditions control the maximum rent you can charge, unless you enjoy making mortgage payments on vacant property. And, many wise landlords charge slightly less than the going rate as part of a policy designed to find and keep excellent tenants. Obviously, the amount of rent you do decide to charge and, in the case of a lease, the length of time for which it is established, should be set out in

writing in your written rental agreement or lease.**

As with any business arrangement, it usually pays in the long run to have your tenants feel they have a good deal. In exchange (often tacit), you hope the tenants will be responsive to your sensibilities as a landlord. This doesn't always work, of course, but it's our experience that tenants who feel they enjoy a fair rent are less likely to complain over trifling matters, often so as not to bring the landlord's attention to the low rent. Certainly, it's obvious that a tenant who thinks you are trying to squeeze every last nickel out of her is unlikely to think twice before calling you about a clogged toilet at 2 a.m.

B. When Rent Is Due

The rent clause in your lease and written rental agreement is the most important part of the agreement. It should state not only the amount of the rent, but the date it is due. If your agreement with the tenant is oral, the rent will be whatever you and the tenant agree on.

When it comes to written rental agreements and leases, rent is due on the date set out in the agreement.

---

* In addition, several important California Supreme Court decisions establish guidelines that rent control ordinances must meet in order to be found constitutional.

** This policy can backfire on landlords if the area in which they are located adopts a rent control ordinance at a time when they are charging a rent below market rates. If you are in one of the several California locations where rent control ordinances are regularly placed on the ballot and may be adopted, you may want to raise rents now on the theory that your flexibility will be restricted later.

This is true in all situations, including units governed by rent control ordinances. Most agreements, including the one in this book, call for rent to be paid monthly, in advance, on the first day of the month. It is perfectly proper to require rent to be paid on a different day of the month, and may make sense if the tenant is paid at odd times. Some landlords make rent payable each month on the date the tenant first moved in. We think it's easier to pro-rate rent for a short first month and then require that it be paid on the first of the next month; but if you only have a few tenants, and/or don't mind having different tenants paying you on different days of the month, it makes no legal difference.

You are not legally required to have your tenant pay rent on a monthly basis. If you wish, you and the tenant can agree that the rent be paid twice a month, each week, etc. The most common variation on the monthly payment arrangement is to require that rent be paid twice a month. This is a particularly good idea if you are dealing with tenants who receive government benefits or have relatively low-paying jobs and get paid twice a month. They may not always be able to save the needed portion of their mid-month check until the first of the month.

If you have a written or verbal rental agreement with your tenant for an unspecified term (as opposed to a lease), you should be aware that the length of the interval between rent payments affects other important rights. Specifically, the notice period you are required to give your tenant in order to terminate the tenancy (and the one she must give you), is normally the same number of days as the period between rent payments.* This is true unless your rental agreement specifically establishes a different notice period, or you rent in a rent con-

* Civil Code Section 1944.

trol area requiring just cause for eviction (see Chapter 4). This general rule also applies to the notice period you must give your tenants to raise the rent, subject, of course, to any rent-increase limitations of local rent control ordinances.

EXAMPLE 1: On March 10, Olivia Owner rents the other half of her duplex to Tassie Tenant for $350, payable on the tenth day of each month. Nothing more is said, and Tassie pays her rent every month. Because the interval between rent payments is a month, Olivia must give Tassie at least 30 days' written notice if she wants to raise the rent or ask Tassie to move out. If Tassie wants to leave, she too must give 30 days' notice to Olivia. This notice can be given at any time during the month, and is effective 30 days later, even if the 30th day doesn't fall on the 10th of the month, when rent is normally due.

EXAMPLE 2: Ramona Rooming-house rents rooms on a weekly basis with the rent payable every Friday. Because the interval between rent payments is one week, Ramona must give her tenants one full week's notice if she wishes to raise the rent or have them move out. This means that in order for a rent increase or termination of tenancy to take effect the following Friday, Ramona must give her tenant written notice to that effect no later than the Friday before.

Once you have established the rental amount and the day of payment, you should insist that your tenant's rent be paid in advance to cover the following month or other period. For example, rent should be due on the first day of the month for the month ahead, and it should be paid on or before that day. Perhaps requiring a tenant to pay rent in advance seems obvious. You would probably never consider allowing a tenant who moved in on the first day of the month to wait to pay rent until the 31st. We do have a reason to belabor this point, however. Under an ancient rule traceable to feudal times, California law states that in the absence of an agreement to the contrary, rent is due at the end of the rental term.* In other words, unless your lease or rental agreement, whether written or oral, provides that the rent is due in advance, you may have trouble enforcing your tenant's obligation to pay at the beginning of the rental period.

NOTE: The written rental agreement and lease in the Appendix of this book require rent to be paid in advance.

1. Sundays and Holidays

Even if a rental agreement says the rent is due on a certain day of the month, there are some exceptions. One instance is when the date rent is due in your lease or rental agreements falls on a Sunday or other legal holiday. (Saturdays count as ordinary business days for this purpose.) When rent would actually be due on a Sunday or holiday, it is legally due on the next business day.** For example, if your lease or rental agreement says a tenant's rent is due on the first day of each month, and April 1st falls on Sunday, rent isn't due until Monday, April 2nd. If Sunday is followed by a legal holiday, rent normally due on the

---
* Civil Code Section 1947.
** Civil Code Section 11.

first of the month isn't legally due until Tuesday. This isn't really all that important unless you have to file an eviction lawsuit based on the tenant's nonpayment of the rent, where counting days correctly can be crucial. This is covered in Chapter 15 on three-day notices, and then again in the second volume, the **The Landlord's Law Book: Evictions.**

2. Grace Periods

Now let's clear up a giant myth. Lots of tenants are absolutely convinced that if they pay by the 3rd (or sometimes the 5th, 7th, or even the 10th) of the month, they have legally paid their rent on time and should suffer no penalty because they are within a legal grace period. This is not true. Quite simply, there is no such law that gives tenants a mandatory three-day grace period, or any other grace period, when it comes to paying the rent. As we'll discuss more thoroughly in Chapter 15, a landlord can legally proceed with the first step necessary to evict a tenant--serving a three-day notice to pay rent or quit-- the day after the rent is legally due but unpaid. While it's true that some landlords customarily don't get upset about late rent until it's more than a few days late, and many rental agreements and leases do not begin assessing the tenant late charges until three or five days after the due date, let us repeat that no grace period is required by law. You are definitely within your legal rights to insist that the rent be paid on the day it is due, allowing for

Sundays and legal holidays. And in our opinion, if you allow more than a three- to five-day grace period, you are running your business unwisely, unless you have a good reason particular to the circumstances.

C. Late Charges

A fairly common and sensible practice is to assess tenants who are late with their rent an extra late fee or charge. Some large cities with rent control ordinances regulate the amount of these extra charges. Check any rent control ordinances applicable to your properties. In the great majority of California cities and unincorporated areas, however, there are no written regulations as to what you can charge.

Late charges provide an incentive for the tenant to pay on time, and, when used with discretion, make sense. Unfortunately, many landlords try to charge excessive late fees and, by so doing, get themselves into legal hot water, as well as incurring tenant hostility. Why can sizeable late charges cause legal problems? Because courts have been known to hold that provisions in rental agreements and lease clauses that provide for unreasonably high late charges are not enforceable.*

While there are no statutory guidelines as to how much you can reasonably charge as a late fee, you should be on safe ground if your provision adheres to these principles:

● The late charge should be either a flat charge of no more than $10-$35,

_____

* See **Fox v. Federated Department Stores** (1979) 94 Cal.App.3d 867, 156 Cal.Rptr. 893, where the court held invalid a late charge clause in a promissory note because the charge exceeded reasonable administrative costs.

depending on the amount of rent, unless you rent luxury units with very high rents. A late charge that is out of proportion to the rent (say, $50 for being one day late with rent on a $450-per-month apartment) would probably not be upheld in court;

● Or, if you adopt a late charge which increases with each additional day of lateness, it should be moderate and have an upper limit. For example, $5 for the first day rent is late, plus $2 for each additional day, with a maximum late charge of $25-35, would be acceptable to a judge, unless your property carries a high rent, in which case somewhat higher amounts might be allowed;

● If you do end up in court, it looks better if the late charge does not begin until after a reasonable grace period of three days or so has elapsed. In other words, imposing a stiff late charge if the rent is only one or two days late may not be upheld in court.

Some landlords try to disguise excessive late charges as a "discount" for early payment of rent. One landlord we know concluded he couldn't get away with charging a $50 late charge on a late $425 rent payment, so instead, he designed a rental agreement calling for a rent of $475 with a $50 "discount" if the rent was paid before the third day after it was due. Ingenious as this ploy sounds, it is unlikely to stand up in court, unless the discount for timely payment is very modest. This is because the effect of giving a relatively large discount is the same as charging an excessive late fee, and a judge is likely to see it as such and throw it out.

Anyway, we think all this fooling around with late charges is amateurish. If you want more rent for your unit, raise the rent (unless you live in a rent control area). If you are concerned about tenants paying on time-- and who isn't--put your energy into choosing responsible tenants. If you have a tenant with a month-to-month tenancy who drives you nuts with late rent payments, and a reasonable late charge doesn't resolve the situation, give her a 30-day notice. (Local rent control or just-cause eviction ordinances may regulate how this can be done in some areas covered by rent control.)

EVICTION WARNING! Do not demand late charges as part of giving a tenant a three-day notice to pay rent or quit. As we discuss in Chapter 15, and in more detail in the second volume on evictions, a three-day notice must precede an eviction lawsuit based on non-payment of rent. At present, the law is unclear as to whether sums other than rent can be demanded in such notices, and tenants' defense lawyers

have become adept at attacking landlord's eviction suits based on three-day notices which ask for more than the exact amount of unpaid rent. In other words, inclusion of late charges in a three-day notice may possibly delay the eviction of a nonpaying tenant and prolong her rent-free stay.

D. Partial Rent Payments

On occasion, a tenant suffering a temporary financial setback will offer something less than the full month's rent, with a promise to catch up in dribbles as the month proceeds, or at the first of the next month. Although, as a general rule, it isn't a good business practice to allow this, you may wish to go along with such a proposal in situations where the tenant's financial problems truly appear to be temporary, and you have a high regard for the person. In this connection, we recommend that you verify a tenant's hard-luck story by asking questions and then checking the story out by calling the hospital, employer, or anyone else the tenant says can back her up.

WARNING: If you do give a tenant a little more time to pay, monitor the situation carefully. You don't want to wake up one day to find that your reasonableness has contributed to a situation in which the tenant is three months in arrears, with no chance to bring her account current. If you do, you are likely to be so angry that you won't give the next tenant with a small problem the time of day.

One way to prevent this from happening is to put your agreement to accept partial rent payments in writing. This binds you to the agreement (you can't get mad at the tenant and demand the rent sooner), but, more important, it also gives both you and the tenant a benchmark against which to measure her efforts to catch up on the rent. Thus, if you give the tenant two weeks to catch up and she doesn't, the written agreement precludes any argument that you had really said "two to three weeks."

SAMPLE AGREEMENT

Nick Niceguy and Tania Tardy agree as follows:

1. That Tania Tardy has only paid one-half of her $500 rent for Apartment #2 at 111 Billy St., Fair Oaks, CA., on March 1, 19__ , which is the date the rent for the month of March is due.

2. That Nick Niceguy agrees to accept all the remainder of the rent on or before March 15, 19__ and to hold off on any legal proceeding to evict Tania until that date.

_____
Nick Niceguy

_____
Tania Tardy

_____

So much for advice. Now for the legal aspects of accepting partial rent payments. There is generally no legal problem if you accept partial rent payments. If you accept less than a full month's rent from a tenant, you

certainly do not give up the right to the balance. If the tenant does not pay the rest of the rent when promised, you can, and should, follow through with a three-day notice to pay rent or quit (see Chapter 15), and if need be, initiate an eviction lawsuit if payment is still not forthcoming. Indeed, you can normally accept a partial payment one day and demand full payment the next.

There are three major exceptions to this rule, however. If you specifically agree in writing that the tenant can have a longer time to pay, or if you agree orally and you get the tenant to promise something in exchange for your agreement to accept late payments (e.g., the tenant agreed to pay a late fee), you have created a binding contract to accept rent late and must abide by it. This is because in order for your agreement to accept rent late to be a contract, a tenant must offer you some legal consideration (advantage) over and above a promise to pay rent already due.

What does this have to do with whether an agreement is reduced to writing? Simply that there is a quirky legal rule that says if you put your agreement to accept partial payments in writing, it will be presumed that you received some advantage ("consideration," in legal jargon), and your agreement will probably be enforced by a court.

EXAMPLE 1: Teresa Tenant approaches Luke Landlord with a sad story about needing to send money to her ailing mother and asks if she can pay half the rent on the first of the month (the day it is due) and half two weeks late. Luke agrees, but nothing is written and Teresa does not promise to provide any extra payment or other advantage in exchange for Luke's forebearance. The next day, Luke finds out Teresa has lost her job and been arrested for possession of cocaine. He asks her to pay the full rent immediately. This is legal. Luke's original promise was not legally binding because Teresa provided no legal consideration in exchange for it.

NOTE: Had Luke agreed to the late payment in writing, the law would have "presumed" that there was legal consideration, and Luke would have had to wait the two weeks, despite the unlikelihood of payment.

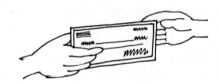

EXAMPLE 2: Now let's change this example slightly and assume that in exchange for the right to pay half of the rent late, Teresa promised to sweep the parking lot twice a week and turn on the pool filter every morning. Now, Teresa and Luke have entered into a valid contract (it can be oral or written), and Luke has a legal obligation to stick to his end of the bargain as long as Teresa honors her agreement.

The third exception is if you regularly allow a tenant to pay rent in installments despite its theoretically being due in one payment in advance. By regularly accepting rent in installment payments, you may have legally changed the terms of your rental agreement.

EXAMPLE: You routinely allow Lucy Late, whose $800 rent is due on the first of the month, to pay $400 on the first and the other $400 on the 15th. A year later, you get tired of this arrangement. After receiving $400 on the first, you give Lucy a three-day notice on the second of the month to pay the rest of the rent or quit. This may not work. You may be stuck with getting $400 on the first and $400 on the 15th for the balance of the term of the lease, or in the case of a written or oral rental agreement, until you give her a written notice of change in the terms of tenancy (see Chapter 14). Why? Because a judge in an eviction lawsuit may rule that, by giving Lucy this break every month for a year, coupled with her reliance on your doing this, you in effect changed the terms of the lease or rental agreement. Viewed this way, your three-day notice to pay the full rent or leave would be premature because the second $400 isn't due until the 15th. Of course, you don't have to worry about this happening if you accept partial payments only a few times on an irregular basis. And accepting partial payments more often than this really isn't good landlording anyway, unless you really are willing to change the terms of the lease or rental agreement. If you are, do it in writing.

Acceptance of partial rent payments after giving the tenant a three-day notice to pay the rent in full or quit is trickier. The basic legal rule is that if your tenant responds to a three-day notice with less than the amount stated in the notice, you can either refuse to accept it or accept the lesser amount and serve a new three-day notice demanding the balance. In this situation, you probably cannot accept the partial payment and base an eviction lawsuit on the original three-day notice. This is simply because the law requires that in any eviction lawsuit you file, the rent that's past due as of the date of filing be the same as the rent demanded in the three-day notice. For example, if you served a notice demanding the rent of $600, and the tenant paid $500, you would be filing an eviction suit based on a $600 three-day notice when only $100 was due. Also, any acceptance of rent by the landlord after serving the tenant a three-day notice is considered a "waiver" of the breach complained of in the notice, so that a new notice, demanding only the balance, would have to be given. This is more fully explained in the second volume of this book, which covers evictions for nonpayment of rent in detail and shows you how to do your own, step by step.

E. Where and How Rent Is Due

Once in a while, when relations between a landlord and a tenant are beginning to break down for other reasons, there will be misunderstandings about where and how the rent must be paid. Sometimes a landlord who's been burned by bounced checks from a particular tenant will suddenly decree that she'll accept nothing less than cash or a certified check or money order, and that rent may be paid only during certain hours at the manager's office. Be careful of doing this unless your rental agreement or lease spells out how and where the rent should be paid. If it states that you only accept cash or a money order, you are on solid ground when you tell a check-bouncing tenant that you'll no longer accept her

checks, and that your previous practice of doing so was merely an accommodation not required of you under the rental agreement. If, however, as is typical, your lease or rental agreement is silent on these subjects, the law states that past practice generally controls how rent is paid, until you notify the tenant of a change.

Suppose you wish to change your rent payment terms. If, as is usual, your tenant mails the rent to you, it's as if the lease or rental agreement allowed payment by mail. If you want to change this rule to require rent to be paid at your office, you must do it formally. If you operate under a month-to-month rental agreement, do so with a written 30-day notice (see Chapter 14). If you rent under a lease, you will have to wait until the lease runs out and insert this clause in the new one.

Now suppose you wish to make a change with regard to whether the rent must be paid by cash or check. The law presumes that a lease which is silent in this regard requires the rent to be paid in cash.* So, if you don't want to continue accepting a tenant's checks, simply notify her of this fact (it's best to do this in writing). This kind of notice is effective immediately. In addition, if you have to serve a three-day notice on a tenant accustomed to paying by (and bouncing) checks, be sure the three-day notice specifies that the payment be by cash, money order or certified check.

---

* Strom v. Union Oil Co., (1948) 88 Cal.App.2d 78, 84, 198 P.2d 347.

4

Rent Control

A. Local Laws

California has no statewide rent control law. It is not likely to adopt one, except possibly to limit the power of some extremely pro rent-control cities to pass what many see as being almost confiscatory ordinances. As of this writing, cities and counties may establish rent control on a local basis, either through the initiative process or by the act of a city council or a county board of supervisors.* Accordingly, some cities and counties have enacted local ordinances which limit the rents property owners can charge, and which also regulate the landlord-tenant relationship in other ways.

While landlords traditionally oppose all restrictions on their ability to rent their property for a fair market determined value, some of the milder rent control ordinances have proved to be reasonably livable. That is, landlords can follow the law and still make a decent profit, and afford to keep up their property. In a few cities, such as Berkeley and Santa Monica, however, rent control ordinances are so pro-tenant as to discourage the ownership

* The California Supreme Court upheld this right in the cases of **Fisher v. City of Berkeley** (1984) 37 Cal. 3d 644 and **Birkenfeld v. City of Berkeley** (1976) 17 Cal. 3d 129.

48

of rental property. In these cities, since rent control has been in force, the quantity and, arguably, the quality of rental housing has fallen, as many landlords have either reduced the level of maintenance on their property or have sold out and moved on.

Some form of rent regulation now exists in a number of California communities, including Los Angeles (city only), San Francisco, Oakland, San Jose, Berkeley, Santa Monica, Hayward, Palm Springs and several smaller cities, including Beverly Hills, Cotati, Los Gatos and West Hollywood (see the chart in Section E, below). Before we describe how such regulations work, here are a few words of caution:

● Rent control is a rapidly changing field. Many ordinances automatically expire after an established period of time. Hardly a month goes by without one or another city changing an ordinance. In addition, several rent control provisions are presently being challenged in court. In short, you should read the material here to get a broad idea of the field, not to establish the details of any particular ordinance. If the area in which you rent is covered by rent control, it is absolutely necessary that you also contact your city or county to get a copy of the ordinance, and any regulations interpreting it.

● No two rent control ordinances are exactly alike. Some cities have elected or appointed boards which have the power to adjust rents; others automatically allow a certain percentage increase each year as part of their ordinances. Some cities have ordinances with a "just-cause" eviction provision which requires landlords to give and prove, in court if necessary, valid reasons for terminating month-to-month tenancies, while the ordinances of other cities contain no such provisions. Also, some cities have some

form of "vacancy decontrol," whereby property from which a tenant voluntarily moves or is evicted for good cause is either no longer subject to rent control, or is subject to rent control again only after the new (and presumably higher) rent is agreed on between the landlord and the new tenant.

● For additional information, you might wish to contact either your local apartment owner's association or the California Apartment Association, 1107 9th St., Sacramento, CA 95814, (916) 447-7881 or the California Association of Realtors, 1129 10th St., Sacramento, CA 95814, (916) 444-2045 or 525 South Virgil Avenue in Los Angeles, (213) 739-8200.

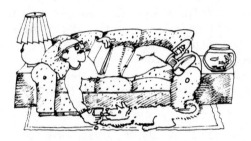

B. Common Terms and Phrases

Although no two cities' rent-control laws are identical, those of several cities are broadly similar. Indeed, it is possible to broadly categorize California rent control ordinances into three general groups--"mild," "moderate," and "strict." In Section C below, we summarize the important features of each group, and in Section E, you will find a "Rent Regulation Chart," which more specifically summarizes each city's ordinance. But before we do either of these things, let's define some critical "rent-control" terms.

EXEMPTIONS: No city's rent-control ordinance covers all rental housing within the particular city. Commonly, owner-occupied buildings with four (or sometimes three or two) units or less, as well as new construction, are exempted from rent control ordinances. Some cities also exempt luxury units that rent for more than a certain amount, and single-family dwellings, etc.

REGISTRATION: Several cities having rent control, including Berkeley, Los Angeles, and Santa Monica, require the owners of units subject to control to register their units with the agency which administers the rent control ordinance. This allows the "rent board" to keep track of the city's rental units, as well as to obtain operating funds from the registration fees. Berkeley, Los Angeles, and Santa Monica allow tenants to withhold rent payments if a landlord fails to register, and impose other penalties against non-registering landlords. Other cities require no registration at all.

ADMINISTRATION: Most rent control ordinances are administered by a rent control board whose members are appointed (elected in Santa Monica and Berkeley) by the mayor or city council. The formal name, address and phone number of each board is given in the Rent Regulation Chart.

RENT FORMULA AND INDIVIDUAL ADJUSTMENTS: Each city has a slightly different mechanism for allowing rent increases. All cities allow periodic (usually yearly) across-the-board increases, either by action of the board (as in Santa Monica and Berkeley) or by providing for a periodic increase of either a fixed flat percentage or one tied to a local or national consumer price index. In most cities, landlords who want to charge more than the allowed across-the-board increase may petition the board for a higher rent level based on certain criteria con-

tained in the ordinance, such as the right to recover the costs of major improvements amortized over their useful life, the right to recover increases in finance costs, etc. A few cities, such as Berkeley and Santa Monica, also allow a tenant to petition for lower rents based on criteria such as lack of maintenance or repairs. Some "mild" rent control cities, such as San Jose and Oakland, allow the landlord to increase rents by any amount, with the tenant having the burden of complaining and arguing that the increase be limited to the across-the-board amount. See Section C(1), below.

VACANCY DECONTROL: Most localities apply rent control to a particular rental unit only as long as a particular tenant lives there.* If that tenant voluntarily leaves, or in some cities is evicted for just cause (see below), the landlord can charge the new tenant any rent he wants. In some cities, including Los Angeles and San Francisco, once the rent for the new tenant is established, the unit again becomes subject to the rent control law at the higher rent. This is called "vacancy decontrol." However, several cities, including Berkeley, Santa Monica, and Cotati, keep units under rent control even when a tenant moves out. Under ordinances in these cities, the new tenant gets the unit at the same rent as the old, unless it is time for a percentage increase under the city-wide formula.

_____

* When more than one tenant shares an apartment or house, the rule in San Francisco and some other cities with vacancy-decontrol provisions in their ordinance is that the rent can't be raised more than the annual increase amounts allowed by the ordinance until all of the original tenants whose names were on the lease or rental agreement leave. At this point the landlord can raise the rent as much as he wants under the "vacancy-decontrol" provision. But please be aware that since this rule is subject to a number of different interpretations, depending both on the city and the precise fact situation, it's up to you to check locally.

EVICTION PROTECTION: If a city has a "vacancy decontrol" provision (in other words, the rent can be raised when a tenant moves), it is almost essential to the success of the ordinance that a tenant can only be evicted for "just cause." This is because if the rents can be raised as much as the landlord wants when a tenant leaves, landlords will have a motive to avoid rent control by giving a 30-day notice to a month-to-month tenant whose rents are controlled. What constitutes "just cause to evict"? Under most rent control ordinances, a landlord has "just cause" to evict a tenant in the following situations:

● Non-payment of rent following service on the tenant of a three-day notice to pay rent or quit;

● Violation of a lease or rental agreement provision after service of a three-day notice to correct the violation or leave.

However, you must first notify the tenant of the problem and give them a chance to correct it (see Strict Rent Control Note, below).

NOTE: In some cities, such as Los Angeles and San Francisco, where rent control is in force until a unit officially changes hands, at which point the rent is temporarily decontrolled, tenants will often try to keep

the rent low by unofficially subletting part or all of the premises to a new tenant, who may in turn sublet to someone else, and so forth. In these areas, a lease or rental agreement provision forbidding subleasing or assignment (see Section E of Chapter 2 and Section C of Chapter 9) is particularly important. As long as subletting is a breach of the lease or rental agreement,* it allows the landlord to evict a tenant and any so-called subtenants whom the tenant improperly allows to move in.

● The tenant has caused substantial damage to the premises and has been served an unconditional three-day notice specifying the damage done and telling her to vacate;

● The tenant is seriously disturbing other tenants or neighbors, and has been given a three-day notice specifically stating when and how this occurred;

● The tenant has committed illegal activity on the premises, and has been given a three-day notice setting forth the specifics. Minor illegal activity, such as smoking marijuana, is not sufficient cause, although dealing drugs, engaging in an illegal business (such as prostitution), or even an otherwise legal one that's in violation of local zoning laws, or overcrowding the unit in violation of local health codes, does constitute cause for eviction.

STRICT RENT CONTROL NOTE: In several "strict" rent control cities, such as Berkeley and Santa Monica and some of the "moderate" rent control cities with just-cause-for-eviction

---

* A landlord's consent to a sublease cannot be unreasonably withheld. See Section E of Chapter 2 and Section C of Chapter 9. However, if the tenant's subleasing of the property is designed to circumvent the rent-control ordinance's provision for higher rent when occupancy changes, the landlord's refusal to consent to the sublease isn't unreasonable.

provisions in their ordinances, the tenant who violates a lease or rental agreement (e.g., moves in too many people, damages the premises, makes too much noise, uses the premises for illegal activities, etc.) must first be notified of the problem in a written notice--often called a cease-and-desist notice--and given a reasonable time to correct it. Only if this is not done can the tenant be evicted for the lease or rental agreement violation. We discuss how to do this in Chapter 17.

In addition to the above reasons, the landlord can also terminate a month-to-month or other periodic tenancy for any of the following reasons, but must use a 30-day termination notice which specifically sets out the basis for the eviction:

• The tenant refuses to enter into a new lease or rental agreement containing the same terms as the previous expired one;

• The tenant refuses, following a written request, to allow the landlord to enter the premises when he had a right to do so (see Chapter 12 on privacy and access);

• The landlord wants to reside in the unit himself, or wants to provide it to an immediate family member **and** no similar unit is available for the landlord or family member to move into in the same building or in another one the landlord owns;

NOTE: There has been some abuse of this provision by landlords who evict a tenant claiming they, themself, or a family member, want to rent the premises, but then, after the tenant has moved out, simply re-rent to a non-family member.* In response, cities have amended their ordinances to impose serious civil penalties (fines) on landlords who do this;

• The landlord seeks to substantially remodel the property, after having obtained the necessary permits. However, the existing tenant in the unit must be allowed the right of first refusal to move back in after the remodeling is completed--at the original rent plus any extra "pass-through" increases allowed by the particular rent control ordinance. (This provision is designed to allow the landlord to recoup part of the cost of capital improvements);

• The landlord, after having complied with any local condominium-conversion ordinance and having applied for and received the necessary permits, seeks to convert an apartment complex to a condominium complex.

NOTE: Few cities that have no just-cause-for-eviction protection do forbid "retaliatory eviction," where the landlord gives the tenant a 30-day notice to quit in order to retaliate

---

* "Family member" is defined differently in different cities. In Berkeley and Santa Monica, family members include only parents and children. In cities with somewhat less restrictive laws, such as San Francisco and Los Angeles, family members also include brothers, sisters, grandparents, and grandchildren. In situations where property is owned by several people, either as co-tenants or through a joint venture, small corporation or a partnership, cities define who qualifies for the status of a landlord for purposes of claiming priority over an existing tenant if they, or a family member, wish to live in the property differently. In some cities you must own half or more of a property to be able to claim priority. In others, your percentage of ownership necessary to evict a tenant in favor of yourself or a close family member is much less.

against the tenant's exercise of her rights under the rent control law (i.e., by insisting on not paying any more than the legal rent, or by objecting to an illegal rent increase). Under this type of ordinance, the tenant has to prove in court that the landlord's reason for eviction was retaliatory in nature. However, it's important to realize that even without such a provision, this kind of retaliation is illegal under California law. See Chapter 13.

C. General Types of Rent Control Laws

As noted above, although no two cities' rent-control laws are identical, they can be broadly categorized into three types. Obviously, this sort of gross division isn't perfect, but it should help you place your city in the scheme of things.

1. Mild Rent Regulations

Let's start with the Bay Area cities of San Jose, Oakland, Hayward and Los Gatos, all of which have mild rent control ordinances. Although the rent-control ordinances of these areas set forth a certain formula (usually fairly generous) by which rents can be increased each year, it is possible for a landlord to raise the rent above this figure and still stay within the law. This is because each of these cities' ordinances require a tenant whose rent is increased above the formula level to petition the board within a certain period (usually 30 days) and protest the increase. If the increase isn't protested within the time allowed, it's effective, even though it is higher than the formula increase allowed. If the increase is protested, a hearing is held at which the board decides if the entire increase should be allowed.

In addition, the rent control ordinances in most of these cities do not require the landlord to show "just cause" for eviction. (It is required in Hayward, however.) In other words, a landlord can evict tenants following normal procedures under state law (see Chapter 17 and Volume II, on evictions). Perhaps because month-to-month tenants whose rents are increased above the formula level suspect they will receive a 30-day tenancy termination notice if they protest an increase, few tenants petition the board to object to larger-than-formula increases.* Needless-to-say, landlords in these cities should not encourage this type of fear by threatening retaliation against tenants who protest rent increases. This sort of conduct is illegal under both local and state law, and could lead to the assessment of penalties. Nevertheless, the possibility of a 30-day termination notice, even from a landlord who has made no threats in this area, is enough to deter most complaints to the board concerning moderate rent increases over the yearly recommended amount.

Finally, all these cities have "vacancy decontrol," none of their ordinances require landlords to register their units with the board, and only Oakland's applies to single-family homes.

---

* The ordinances in these cities do prohibit and penalize a landlord who retaliates against a tenant for contesting a rent increase, however, although the burden of proving the landlord's motive was retaliatory is on the tenant.

2. Strict Rent Control

California's most extreme rent-control laws are found in the cities of Berkeley, Cotati,* and Santa Monica. Not even single-family rentals are exempt from these cities' laws, unless a rental property has two or fewer units and the landlord lives on the property. Landlords must register their units with the board, which decides on the amount of the across-the-board rent increase allowed citywide each year. This tends to be very low. A landlord who increases rent by a greater percentage than that established by the board faces civil penalties unless the board has allowed an additional increase following the landlord's application. In these cities, the burden of justifying the need for a higher than routinely-allowable rent increase is entirely on the landlord. In addition, these ordinances provide for reducing rent increases on application of a tenant who contends that the landlord has poorly-maintained the property.

Finally, as you might have guessed, there is no vacancy decontrol in Berkeley, Santa Monica or Cotati. Again, this means that even if a tenant moves out, the maximum rent for a property remains fixed. In addition, a landlord must show just cause for eviction to evict a tenant in all "strict" rent control cities.

---

* Cotati's rent-control ordinance seems to be modeled on Berkeley's, although the across-the-board amount that rents can be raised is tied to the local consumer price index, rather than set by the board (the consumer price index is almost always more generous than are rent boards). However, no further individual adjustments are allowed. In this later respect, Cotati's ordinance is even more extreme than those of Berkeley and Santa Monica.

3. Moderate Rent Control

The rent-control laws of Los Angeles, San Francisco, Beverly Hills, and Palm Springs can all be described as "moderate." Although the laws in these moderate rent control cities do differ somewhat from city to city, they all require landlords who wish to increase the rent by more than a fixed formula amount to petition the board for a higher increase. In addition, all of them (except for Palm Springs) provide for some form of vacancy decontrol and require "just cause" for eviction. As you will remember, vacancy decontrol means that when a tenant moves out voluntarily (or is asked to leave for a "just cause"), the unit can be re-rented at the market rate. But what happens if a property is rented to several tenants and one moves out, but the others stay? The rule in most cities with vacancy decontrol is that the unit is covered by rent control as long as any of the original tenants who signed a lease or rental agreement remains, and the rent can't be raised above the amount allowed by the annual increase until all original tenants leave. There is a lot of confusion about this rule in several cities, however, and the law is in a state of rapid flux, so check locally.

Other than these regulations, there is little similarity in the rent-control laws of these four cities. For example, only Los Angeles requires landlords to register their units, and only San Francisco and Palm Springs regulate rents for single-family dwellings. For more detailed information, consult the Rent Regulation Chart in Section E, below.

MRS. PEEBLES...ABOUT THE RAISE IN RENT...

D. Hearings

As we've seen in Section B, almost all cities with rent control provide for a hearing procedure to deal with certain types of complaints and requests for rent adjustments. In cities with "mild" rent control, a tenant's protest of a rent increase higher than that allowed by the applicable rent-increase formula will result in a hearing at which the landlord has to justify the increase. In other rent-control cities, the landlord must request a hearing in order to increase rent above the formula amount. Finally, a few cities--such as Santa Monica and Berkeley--allow tenants to initiate hearings to decrease rents on the basis of the landlord's alleged neglect or lack of maintenance on the property.

In the first two types of hearings above, whether initiated by a tenant who protests a rent increase over the formula amount in a "mild" rent-control city, or by a landlord in a city that requires her to first obtain permission before exceeding the formula increase,

the landlord must demonstrate at the hearing that she needs a rent increase higher than that normally allowed, in order to obtain a fair return on her investment. This most often means establishing that taxes, or maintenance and upkeep costs, or applicable utility charges, or other business expenses, as well as the amortized cost of any capital improvements, make it difficult to obtain a fair return on one's investment given the existing level of rent.

1. Initiating the Hearing

A hearing is normally initiated by the filing of a "petition" or "application" with the rent board. In describing this process, let's assume that a landlord is filing a petition in a "strict" or "moderate" rent-control city that requires her to obtain permission before raising rents above the formula increase allowed. Remember, this process is approximately reversed in "mild" rent-control cities that require the tenant to protest such an increase.

In some cities, including Los Angeles and San Francisco, there are two types of petitions a landlord seeking an above-formula rent increase can file. If an increase is sought on account of recent capital improvements the landlord has made, a "petition for certification" of such improvements is filed. If a rent increase is sought on other grounds, a "petition for arbitration" is filed. Make sure you obtain the right form.

Usually, a nominal filing fee, often based on the number of units or properties for which an increase is being sought, must accompany the filing of the application. The application form will ask for your name and mailing address, the address of the property or properties for which you're seeking the extra increase, including the numbers of any apartments involved, the affected tenants' names and mailing addresses, the amounts of the proposed increases, and the reason for the requested increase, such as increased repair, maintenance, or utility charges, pass-through of recent capital improvements, etc. Make sure that the reason you state to justify your increase is one that is specifically allowed by your local ordinance. After your application is filed and your fees paid, you and the tenant (who in some cities may file a written reply to your application), are notified by mail of the date and place of the hearing. In Los Angeles, San Francisco, and other cities, the filing of a petition may result in your property being inspected by city employees. You are, of course, well-advised to cooperate as fully as possible in allowing such inspections.

2. Preparing for the Hearing

As a general rule, you will greatly increase your chances of winning your increase if you appear at the hearing fully prepared. The hearing officer will be much better disposed to listen to your concerns if you are thoroughly familiar with the issues and make your presentation in an organized way. Possibly, the tenant, if he or she appears, will not be well-prepared, which should make you look good.

As part of planning your preparation, first obtain a copy of the ordinance and any applicable regulations for the area in which your property is located. Then determine which factors the hearing officer must weigh in considering whether to give you an upward individual adjustment from the formula increase. Your job is to show that the increase you are asking for is allowed by the rent control ordinance. Assuming they are relevant to your case, be sure you obtain all tax statements, employee pay statements, bills for repairs, maintenance, and any other costs having to do with the property, including the costs of any extensive remodeling, repairs, or other capital improvements. For example, San Francisco's ordinance allows the consideration of the cost of capital improvements, energy conservation measures, utilities, taxes, janitorial, security, and maintenance services. Increased mortgage payments resulting from a recent purchase of the property by a new owner may be passed along in some, but not all, circumstances.*

You should also be prepared to produce a witness who is familiar with any items which you think might be contested. For example, if you know tenants are likely to argue that you didn't make major improvements to the building, when, in fact, you did, you will want to present cancelled checks for the work done. And, if possible, you should also arrange for the contractor who did the work to appear at the hearing. If for some reason your witness cannot appear in person, you may still present a written statement or "declaration" from that person. The declaration should be as specific as possible, including a description of the work done, dates, costs, and any other relevant information. At the end of the declaration, the contractor or other person should write the words "I

---

* Some cities have anti-speculation ordinances which do not allow increases in mortgage rates to be passed through to tenants if a building is sold and resold frequently. Check your rent-control ordinance on this point.

declare under penalty of perjury under the laws of the State of California that the foregoing is true and correct," putting the date and her signature afterward.

Before the date set for your hearing, go and watch someone else's hearing. (Most cities' hearings are open to the public, and even if they are sometimes closed, you can almost always arrange to attend as an observer if you call ahead.) Seeing another hearing may even make the difference between winning and losing at yours. This is because both your confidence and your capabilities will grow as you understand what the hearing officers are interested in and how they conduct the hearing. By watching a hearing, you will learn that while they are relatively informal, all follow some procedural rules. It is a great help to know what these are so you can swim with the current, not against it.

You are permitted to have an attorney or any other person represent you at a rent-adjustment hearing. (Many landlords are represented at such hearings by their apartment managers or management companies.) Hiring someone to speak for you is probably not necessary. If you do a careful job in preparing your case, you will probably do as well alone as with a lawyer or other representative. And remember, hearing officers (and rent boards) are local citizens who may well react negatively to a landlord who pleads poverty at the same time he is obviously able to pay a lawyer to argue his case. One good alternative is to consult with an attorney or someone else thoroughly familiar with rent-board hearings to discuss strategy, but handle the hearing yourself.

3. The Actual Hearing

Arrive at the hearing room at least a few minutes before it is set to begin. Go to the clerk or other official and establish who you are. Ask to see the file which contains the papers relevant to your application. Go through this material to see if there are any comments by office workers, rent-board investigators, or your tenant(s). Read the latter very closely and prepare to answer questions from the hearing officer on any of these points.

As you sit in the hearing room, you will probably see a long table, with the hearing officer seated at the head. (In a few cities, the hearing is held before several members of the rent board, and they may sit more formally on a dais or raised platform used by the city council, planning commission, etc.) In any event, you, any tenants who appear, your representative, and any witnesses, will be asked to sit at a table or come to the front of the room. A clerk or other employee may make summary notes of testimony given at the hearing. Or, in some cities, an electric recording device is used to make a record of the hearing. (If under the procedure followed in your city no record is kept, you have the right to have the proceedings transcribed or tape-recorded, though at your own expense.)

The hearing officer or chairperson of the rent board will introduce himself or herself and the other people in the room. If you have witnesses, tell the hearing officer. The hearing officer, or sometimes an employee of the rent board, will usually summarize your application, taking the information from your file. At some point, you will be sworn to tell the truth (it is perjury to lie at the hearing). When these preliminaries are complete, you or your tenant (depending on who initiated the proceeding) will have an opportunity to present your (his or her) case.

NOTE ON HEARING OFFICERS: Most hearing officers, rent board employees and members of rent boards tend to be pro-rent control and pro-tenant. This is not the same thing as saying they will treat you unfairly. In our experience, most make an honest effort to follow the law. In a sense, your job is to understand these people's position so you don't needlessly antagonize them, at the same time you work to make your legal position as unassailable as possible.

Before 1987, hearing officers and rent boards in strict and some moderate rent controlled cities that require registration of properties, unfairly penalized landlords who made innocent mistakes filing or serving legal notices. This is now illegal. Under CC§1947.7, a landlord's good-faith ("substantial compliance") in attempting to obey an ordinance prevents a rent board from imposing penalties.

A rent adjustment hearing is not like court. There are no formal rules of evidence. Hearing officers will usually allow you to bring in any information that may be important, though in a court of law it might not be admissible. Relax and just be yourself.

Present your points clearly, but do not do this in an argumentative way. Sometimes an outline on a 3 x 5 card is a help to focusing. Don't get carried away in unnecessary detail. Don't rush. You'll normally have plenty of time to make your case. The hearing officer may well ask you questions to help you explain your position. Make sure you present all documentary evidence and witnesses necessary to back up your contentions. Later, the hearing officer will give the tenant or his or her representative a chance to present his or her case and to ask you questions. Answer the questions quietly. It is almost always counterproductive to get into an argument. Even if you feel the tenant is lying or misleading, don't interrupt. You will be given time later to rebut the testimony. Direct all your argument to the hearing officer, not to the tenant or her representative.

When your witnesses are given the opportunity to testify, the normal procedure is simply to let them have their say. You may ask questions if the witness forgets something important, but remember, this is not a court and you don't want to come on like a lawyer. Very likely, the referee will also ask your witnesses questions. The tenant has the right to ask the witnesses questions as well.

In rare instances, you may get a hearing officer or rent-board chairperson who dominates the hearing or seems to be hostile to you, or perhaps to landlords in general. If so, you will want to stand up for your rights at the same time that you take care not to needlessly confront the hearing officer. Obviously, this can be a tricky business, but if you know your legal rights and put them forth in a polite, but direct way, you should do fine. If you feel that the hearing officer is simply not listening to you, politely insist that you be given your right to complete your statement and question your witnesses.

Just before the hearing is to end, the hearing officer should ask if you have any final comments to make. Don't repeat what you have already said, but make sure all your points have been covered and heard.

The final words from the hearing officer will usually be to thank everyone for coming and to tell you when you can expect the decision. Most put this in the mail within a few days (or weeks) of the hearing.

4. The Decision

Depending on the city and the hearing procedure, you may or may not end up with a written decision and an explanation of why it was so decided.

In most cities, where your application for an increase was heard by a hearing officer, you have the right to appeal to the full rent board if you are turned down (your tenant(s) have this same right if you prevail). To do this, you must file within a certain time and state your reason for the appeal. You may or may not have the opportunity to appear in person.

The rent board will probably take the facts as found by the hearing officer as being true and limit their role to deciding whether the referee applied the law to these facts correctly.* In addition, the board will not usually consider any facts you raise in your statement which you could have brought up at the referee's hearing, but didn't. If a new piece of information not known at the time of the first hearing has just been discovered, how-

---

* There is an exception to this general rule in some cities. If you arranged for a typed transcript of the original hearing at your expense or have paid to have the tape recording of the hearing made by the hearing officer typed, the rent board may review it.

ever, they will possibly consider it. (If it's your tenant(s) who is appealing and you are satisfied with the earlier decision, you will want to emphasize the thoroughness and integrity of the earlier procedure and be ready to present detailed information only if it seems to be needed.) On the other hand, the rent boards of some cities (including Los Angeles) will allow the entire hearing to be held all over again. (This is sometimes called a "de novo" hearing.)

The entire rent board may have more discretion to make a decision than does a single hearing officer. If your case is unique, the hearing officer may even decide to sidestep it and let the entire board consider the implications of establishing a new legal rule or interpretation. If you again lose your decision before the entire board, or if your city only permits one hearing in the first place and you have availed yourself of it, you may be able to take your case to court if you are convinced the rent board or hearing board failed to either follow the law or their own procedures. However, if yours is a situation where the hearing officer or board has broad discretion to decide issues such as the one you presented, you are unlikely to get the decision overturned in court. Speak to an attorney about this as soon as possible, as there is a time limit (usually 30 days) on how long you can take to file an appeal.

E. Rent Regulation Chart

The following chart provides a summary of the specifics of each ordinance of the cities discussed above in Section C. However, for more detail and specifics, and any recent changes not reflected in this book, you should obtain a copy of the appropriate ordinance.

RENT CONTROL CHART

BERKELEY

Ordinance Adoption Date: 6/3/80; latest amendment 6/8/82.

Exceptions: Units constructed after 6/3/80, owner-occupied single-family residences and duplexes. [Sec. 5.]

Administration: Appointed 9-member Rent Stabilization Board, 2180 Milvia Street, Berkeley, CA 94709, (415) 644-6128.

Registration: Required, or landlord can't raise rents, and tenants can withhold current rents (but may have to pay all or part of withheld rent to landlord after registration). Stiff penalties for noncooperation. [Secs. 8, 11.f.4, 11.g.]

Rent Formula: 6/3/80 freeze at 5/31/80 levels [7/1/82 freeze at 12/31/81 levels for 3-unit and 4-unit owner-occupied properties not covered by original 1980 ordinance], plus annual adjustments by Board after investigation and hearings. [Secs. 10, 11.]

Individual Adjustments: Landlord may petition for further increase based on increased taxes or unavoidable increases in utility or maintenance costs, and on costs of capital improvements necessary to bring property up to minimum legal requirements. Increase not allowed based on increased debt service cost due to recent purchase. (If tenant agrees to join in landlord's request, "fast track" petition method, under which a decision will be made within 30 days and without a formal hearing, may be used.) Tenant may apply for rent reduction based on poor maintenance. [Sec. 12.]

Notice Requirements: None in addition to state law.

Vacancy Decontrol: None. [Ordinance Sec 6.q allows for decontrol only if rental unit vacancy rate exceeds 5% and both Board and City Council agree; this is a virtual impossibility.]

Eviction: Landlord must show "just cause" to evict. For other restrictions, see Vol. 2.

Penalties: Violation of ordinance is misdemeanor punishable by maximums of $500 fine & 90 days imprison- ment (1st offense) and $3000 fine & one year imprisonment (2nd offense). [Sec. 19.] Tenant may sue for excess rent collected plus up to $750. [Sec.15.a]

Other Features: Landlord must place security deposits in interest-bearing Savings & Loan account and credit interest against rents each December, as well as when tenant vacates. [Sec. 7, Regulation Secs. 701, 702.]

BEVERLY HILLS

Ordinance Adoption Date: (Beverly Hills Municipal Code, Title 11) 4/27/79; latest amendment (12/7/82).

Exceptions: Units constructed after 10/20/78, units that rented for more than $600 on 5/31/78, single-family residences, rented condominium units [Sec. 11-1.02.]

Administration: Appointed 7-member Rent Adjustments Board 450 N. Crescent Drive, Beverly Hills, CA 90210, (213) 550-4939.

Registration: Not required.

Rent Formula: Except for specific "surcharges" which must be justified and the rent-increase notice (see below), rents may not be increased in any 12-month period by more than 8% or a percentage based on the "Urban All Items Consumer Price Index for Los Angeles," whichever is less. (The CPI-based figure is calculated by adding the monthly CPI figures for the most recently-published 12-month period, subtracting from that a second CPI sum based on for the 12-month period before that, and dividing the difference by the lesser of the two sums.) To this permitted increase, the landlord may add a "capital expenditure surcharge" so as to additionally increase the rent by up to 4% more (calculated by amortizing capital improvement costs), a "utility expense surcharge" based on owner-paid utility cost increases in excess of the allowed annual percentage increase, and a 10% surcharge for each adult tenant occupying the unit over and above any maximum number of adult occupants specified in the lease. The landlord may also pass through the amortized cost of any legally-required improvements. [Secs. 11-3.02 - 11-3.07.]

Individual Adjustments: Tenant who contests validity of any capital improvement surcharge or utility surcharge over and above the annual increase percentage may petition Board to request nonallowance of the surcharge. Landlord seeking increases above annual percentage increase and allowed surcharges may apply to Board for higher "hardship" increase. (Ordinance is silent on fcators to be considered, but does not preclude hardship increase based on high debt service costs due to recent purchase.) [Sec. 11-4.02.]

Notice Requirements: Landlord must post in the lobby, hallway, or other "public" location on the property a notice stating the name, address, and telephone number of the owner or authorized agent, and must give each tenant a copy of the notice; failure to comply with this requirement precludes increase of rents. Rent-increase notice must state the basis justifying the rent increase and advise the tenant that records and documentation verifying it will be made available for inspection by the tenant or the tenant's representative. [Sec. 11-3.09.] The justification should break down the increase into portions allowed under annual adjustment and individual surcharges.

Vacancy Decontrol: Landlord may charge any rent after a tenant vacates voluntarily, but not when landlord terminates tenancy. Once the property is rerented, it is subject to rent control based on the higher rent. [Sec. 11-3.10.]

Eviction: Landlord must show "just cause" to evict. For other restrictions, see Vol. 2.

Penalties: Violation of ordinance is a misdemeanor punishable by maximums of $500 fine & 6 months imprisonment. [Sec. 11-7.06.] Tenant may sue for three times any rent in excess of legal rent collected ($500 minimum), plus attorney's fees. [Sec. 11-7.05.]

CAMPBELL

Ordinance Adoption Date: 1983 (Campbell Municipal Code, Chapter 6.09)

Exceptions: Single-family residences, duplexes, and triplexes. [Sec. 6.09.030(l).]

Administration: Campbell Rent Mediation program, 1030 S. Winchester Blvd., Suite 100, San Jose, CA 95128, (408) 243-8570.

Registration: Not required.

Rent Formula: No fixed formula; rent increases must be "reasonable." [Sec. 6.09.150.]

Individual Adjustments: Tenants in 25% of the units (but at least 3 units) affected by an increase can contest it by filing a petition within 37 days, or lose the right to object to the increase. Disputes raised by tenant petition are first subject to "conciliation," then mediation. If those fail, either party may file written request for arbitration by city "Fact Finding Committee." Committee determines whether increase is "reasonable" by considering costs of capital improvements, repairs, maintenance, and debt service, and past history of rent increases. However, the Committee's determination is not binding. [Secs.6.09.050 - 6.09.150.]

Notice Requirements: On written request by a tenant, an apartment landlord must disclose in writing to that person the apartment numbers of all tenants receiving rent increases that same month. [Sec. 6.09.040.]

Vacancy Decontrol: None.

Eviction Features: Ordinance does not require showing of "just cause" to evict, so 3-day and 30-day notice requirements and unlawful detainer procedures are governed solely by state law.

Note: Because this ordinance does not provide for binding arbitration of any rent-increase dispute, it is not truly a rent-control ordinance. Compliance with any decision appears to be voluntary only.

COTATI

Ordinance Adoption Date: (Cotati Municipal Code, Chapter 19.19), 9/23/80; latest amendment 2/7/84.

Exceptions: Units constructed after 9/23/80 (Board has authority to remove exemption), owner-occupied single-family residences, duplexes, and triplexes. [Sec. 19.12.020.D.]

Administration: Appointed 5-member Rent Appeals Board, 201 W. Sierra, Cotati, CA 94928, (707) 795-5478.

Registration: Required, or landlord can't raise rents, and tenants can seek Board permission to withhold current rents (but may have to pay all or part of withheld rent to landlord after registration). [Sec. 19.12.030.O.]

Rent Formula: 9/23/80 freeze at 6/1/79 levels, plus annual "general adjustments" by Board after investigation and hearings. [Sec. 19.12.050.] Annual general adjustment is to be adequate to cover operating cost increases and to permit net operating income to increase at 66% of the rate of increase in the CPI (Consumer Price Index (all items) for urban consumers, San Francisco-Oakland). [Regulation Secs. 3000-3002.]

Individual Adjustments: Within 30 days after Board determines annual general adjustment, landlord may petition for further increase based on increased taxes or unavoidable increases in utility or maintenance costs, and on costs of capital improvements necessary to bring property up to minimum legal requirements. Increase not allowed based on increased debt service cost due to recent purchase. Tenant may apply for rent reduction based on poor maintenance. [Secs. 19.12.060, 19.12.070, Reg. Secs. 4001-4052.]

Notice Requirements: None in addition to state law.

Vacancy Decontrol: None. [Ordinance Sec. 19.12.030.P allows Board to decontrol only of a category of housing whose rental unit vacancy rate exceeds 5%; this is highly unlikely.]

Eviction: Landlord must show "just cause" to evict. See Volume 2.

Penalties: Tenant may sue for three times any excess rent collected ($500 minimum) plus attorney's fees, or tenant may simply credit any excess payments against future rent payments. [Sec. 19.12.110.]

Other Features: Landlord must place security deposits in interest-bearing Savings & Loan account and credit interest to tenant when she vacates. [Sec. 19.12.150.]

EAST PALO ALTO

Ordinance Adoption Date: 11/23/83; latest amendment 9/4/84.

Exceptions: Units constructed after 11/23/83, units owned by landlords owning 4 or fewer units in city, property rehabilitated in accordance with federal Internal Revenue Code Sec. 174(k). [Sec. 5.]

Administration: Appointed 7-member Rent Stabilization Board, 2415 University Ave., East Palo Alto, CA 94303, (415) 853-3100.

Registration: Required, or landlord can't raise rents, and tenants can apply to Board for permission withhold current rents (but may have to pay all or part of withheld rent to landlord after registration). [Secs. 8, 11.E.4, 15.A.1.]

Rent Formula: 11/23/83 freeze at 4/1/83 levels, plus annual adjustments by Board after investigation and hearings. [Secs. 10, 11.]

Individual Adjustments: Landlord may apply for further increase based on increased taxes or unavoidable increases in utility or maintenance costs, and on costs of capital improvements necessary to bring property up to minimum legal requirements. Increase not allowed based on increased debt service due to recent purchase. Tenant may apply for rent reduction based on poor maintenance. [Sec. 12.]

Notice Requirements: Notices increasing rent by more than that allowed under annual across-the-board adjustment must state that it is subject to appeal by tenant petition to Board, and must list Board address and telephone number. [Sec. 12.E.]

Vacancy Decontrol: None.

Eviction: Landlord must show "just cause" to evict. For other restrictions, see Vol. 2.

Penalties: Violation of ordinance is misdemeanor punishable by maximums of $500 fine & 90 days imprisonment (1st offense) and $3000 fine & one year imprisonment (2nd offense). [Sec. 19.] Tenant may sue landlord for excess rent unlawfully collected plus up to $500. [Sec. 15.A.4.]

Other Features: Landlord must place security deposits in interest-bearing Savings & Loan account and credit interest against rents each December, as well as when tenant vacates. [Sec. 7.]

HAYWARD

Ordinance Adoption Date: 9/13/83; latest amendment 12/11/84.

Exceptions: Units first occupied after 7/1/79, units owned by landlord owning 4 or fewer rental units in the city. [Sec. 2(l).]

Administration: Administered by city-manager-appointed employees of Rent Review Office, 22300 Foothill Blvd., Hayward, CA 94541, (415) 581-2345 ext. 214.

Registration: Not required.

Rent Formula: Annual rent increases limited in any 12-month period to 7%, plus increased utility costs if documented as specified. [Sec. 3(c),(d).]

Individual Adjustments: The tenant can contest an increase over 7% by first contacting the person specified in the notice (see notice requirements, below) for an explanation of the increase. Tenant then must file petition with the Rent Review Office before the increase takes effect (30 days) or lose the right to object to it. Disputes raised in tenant petition are heard by a 3-member mediation-arbitration panel; if mediation fails, arbitration is mandatory and binding on both parties. Landlord may be allowed to pass on increased utility and maintenance costs and "amortize" [spread out] capital expenditures. [Sec. 5.]

Notice Requirements: Landlord must give tenant a copy of ordinance or city-prepared booklet summary of it at the beginning of the tenancy, and with a document which gives the unit's rent history [Sec. 4(a)], lists improvements to the unit, and states that the previous tenant's security deposit was not used for any improper purpose [Sec. 7(d)]. Rent-increase notices must be accompanied by a blank tenant petition form and also by a second notice either stating that the increase is allowed under the 7%-increase limitation, or giving specific reasons for an increase above 7%. The notice must also include the name, address, and telephone number of the landlord or other person able to explain the increase. [Sec. 4(b).]

Vacancy Decontrol: Rent controls are permanently removed from each unit following a voluntary vacancy (without any legal action by or notices from the landlord, even for cause), the expenditure of $200 or more on improvements by the landlord afterward, and city certification of compliance with city Housing Code.[Sec. 8.]

Eviction: Landlord must show "just cause" to evict. See Vol. 2.

Penalties: Failure to provide required information to tenant is an infraction (petty offense) punishable on first, second, or third offense within 12-month period by fines of up to $50, $100, and $250, respectively. Fourth offense within 12 months is misdemeanor punishable by maximums of $500 fine & 6 months imprisonment. [Sec. 20.b.] Tenant may sue for excess rent collected, treble that amount or $500 (whichever is greater), and attorney's fees. [Sec. 20.a.]

Other Features: Ordinance requires landlords holding security deposits longer than a year to pay 6.5% interest, credited against the tenant's rent on his anniversary date; no requirement for separate account, however.

LOS ANGELES

Ordinance Adoption Date: (Los Angeles Municipal Code, Chapter XV), 4/21/79; latest amendment 5/29/85.

Exceptions: Units constructed (or substantially renovated with at least $10,000 in improvements) after 10/1/78, "luxury" units (defined as 0,1,2,3, or 4+ - bedroom units renting for at least $302, $420, $588, $756, or $823, respectively, as of 5/31/78), single-family residences, except where 3 or more houses are located on the same lot. [Sec. 151.02.G,M.]

Administration: Appointed 7-member Rent Adjustment Commission, 215 West 6th St., Los Angeles, CA 90014, (213) 485-4727.

Registration: Required, or tenants can withhold rents. (However, once the landlord registers the property, the tenants must pay all the rent withheld. [Sec. 151.11.B.] Tenant may also defend any unlawful detainer action on the basis of the landlord's failure to register the property [Sec. 151.09.F].

Rent Formula: Except with permission of Commission or Community Development Department, rents may not be increased by more than a 3%-to-8% percentage based on the "All Urban Consumers Consumer Price Index" for the Los Angeles/Long Beach/Anaheim/Santa Monica/Santa Ana areas. The figure is published each year by the Community Development Department on or before May 30th, and applies to rent increases to be effective the following July 1st through June 30th of the next year. The actual percentage is calculated by averaging the CPI over the previous 12-month period beginning the September 30th before that, but in any event cannot fall below 3% or exceed 8%. (For increases effective between 7/1/85 and 6/30/86, the figure is exactly 4%.) In addition, if the landlord pays for gas or electricity for the unit, she may raise the rent an additional 1% for each such type of utility service. [Secs. 151.06.D, 151.07.A.6.]

Individual Adjustments: Landlord may apply to the Rent Adjustment Commission for higher increase to obtain "just and reasonable return" (does not include "negative cash flow" based on recent purchase, but does include negative "operating expense" not counting landlord's mortgage payment).[Sec. 151.07.B] Also, landlord may apply to Community Development Department for permission to pass on to the tenant the cost of capital improvements not directly benefitting the landlord (e.g., new roof cost considered, but not cost of new swimming pool) spread out over 5 or more years [Sec. 151.07.A].

Notice Requirements: Landlord must give tenant a copy of current registration statement showing that the property is registered with Board. [Sec. 151.05.A.] Landlord who proposes to charge tenant rent higher than maximum is required to provide written justification for the difference. [Sec. 151.05.C.]

Vacancy Decontrol: Landlord may charge any rent after a tenant either vacates voluntarily or is evicted for nonpayment of rent, breach of a rental agreement provision, or to substantially remodel. Controls remain if landlord evicts for any other reason, fails to remodel after evicting for that purpose, or terminates or fails to renew a subsidized-housing lease with the city housing authority. However, once the new rent for a vacated unit is established by the landlord and the property is rerented, it is subject to rent control based on the higher rent. [Sec. 151.06.C.]

Eviction: Landlord must show "just cause" to evict. For other restrictions, see Vol. 2.

Penalties: Violation of ordinance, including failing to include proper information in eviction notices, is a misdemeanor punishable by maximums of $500 fine & 6 months imprisonment. [Sec. 151.10.B.] Tenant may sue for three times any rent in excess of legal rent collected, plus attorney's fees. [Sec. 151.10.A.]

LOS GATOS

Ordinance Adoption Date: (Los Gatos Town Code, Chapter 24), 10/27/80; latest amendment 12/5/83.

Exceptions: property on lots with 2 or fewer units; single-family residences; rented condominium units. [Sec. 24.20.015.]

Administration: Los Gatos Rent Mediation program, 1030 S. Winchester Blvd., Suite 100, San Jose, CA 95128, (408) 395-6350.

Registration: Not required. (However, a "regulatory fee" to pay for program is added to annual business license fee, when business license is required.)

Rent Formula: Rents may not be increased more than once within 12-month period (except to pass through regulatory fee), and are limited to 5% or 70% of the All Urban Consumers Consumer Price Index for the San Francisco-Oakland area. [Secs. 24.30.010, 24.70.015(3).]

Individual Adjustments: Tenants in 25% of the units affected by an increase above the formula above can contest it by filing a petition within 30 days, or will lose the right to object to the increase. Disputes initiated by tenant petition are first attempted to be resolved by "conciliation." If that fails, either party may file a written request for mediation, and, if that fails, binding arbitration. [Secs. 24.40.010 - 24.40.050.] Mediator/arbitrator may consider costs of capital improvements, repairs, maintenance, and debt service, and past history of rent increases. [Regulation Secs. 2.03 - 2.05.] (Landlord may also file petition to ask for rent increase over allowed percentage, but why bother if burden is on tenant to contest any increase?).

Notice Requirements: Rent-increase notice (or separate statement served with it) must state, "You have the right to use the Rental Dispute Mediation and Arbitration Hearing Process. For further information contact Los Gatos Rent Mediation Program," giving program's address and telephone number. On written request by a tenant, an apartment landlord must disclose in writing to that person the apartment numbers of all tenants receiving rent increases that same month. [Sec. 24.30.030.]

Vacancy Decontrol: Landlord may charge any rent after a tenant vacates voluntarily or is evicted following 3-day notice for nonpayment of rent or other breach of the rental agreement. Once the property is rerented, it is subject to rent control based on the higher rent. [Sec. 24.70.015(1).]

Eviction: Ordinance does not require showing of "just cause" to evict, but tenant has other defenses. See Vol. 2.

Other Features: Mediation/arbitration process applies not only to rent increases and evictions, but also to provision of "housing services". [Sec. 24.40.010.] Since ordinance deems every lease and rental agreement to include a provision to agree to binding arbitration under the ordinance Sec. 24.40.040], a party invoking the process can in effect keep a "housing services" dispute out of the courts, which will do nothing other than enforce any final binding arbitration award.

OAKLAND

Ordinance Adoption Date: 10/7/80; latest amendment 7/16/85.

Exceptions: Units constructed after 1/1/83, buildings "substantially rehabilitated" at cost of 50% of that of new construction, as determined by Chief Building Inspector. [Sec. 2.i].

Administration: Appointed 7-member Residential Rent Arbitration Board, 1421 Washington Street, Room 414, Oakland, CA 94612, (415) 273-3371.

Registration: Not required.

Rent Formula: Rents may not be increased more than 8% in any 12-month period for occupied units, and 12% in any 12-month period for units vacated after the landlord terminated the tenancy." [Sec. 5.]

Individual Adjustments: Tenant can contest an increase in excess of that allowed (but only if his rent is current) by filing a petition with the Board. The petition must be filed within 30 days. Hearing officer may consider costs of capital improvements, repairs, maintenance, and debt service, and past history of rent increases. [Sec. 5.c.]

Notice Requirements: Landlords are required to notify tenants of the Residential Rent Arbitration Board at outset of the tenancy, in an addendum to the lease or rental agreement. [Sec. 5.d.]

Vacancy Decontrol: Landlord may charge any rent after a tenant vacates voluntarily. Controls remain if tenant vacates "involuntarily," though 12-month rent-increase ceiling increases to 12% from 8%. Once the property is rerented, it is subject to rent control based on the higher rent. [Sec. 5.b] Controls may be permanently removed if landlord spends at least 50% of new-construction cost to "substantially rehabilitate" property.

Eviction: Ordinance does not require showing of "just cause" to evict, but there are other requirements. See Vol. 2.

Penalties: Violation of ordinance is infraction (petty offense) punishable on first, second, and third offenses within 12-month period by fines of up to $50, $100, and $250, respectively. A fourth offense within 12 months is a misdemeanor punishable by maximums of a $500 fine & 6 months imprisonment. [Sec. 9.1.]

PALM SPRINGS

Ordinance Adoption Date: (Palm Springs Municipal Code, Title 4), 9/1/79; latest amendment 1984.

Exceptions: Units constructed after 4/1/79; owner-occupied single-family residences, duplexes, triplexes, and 4-plexes; units where rent was $450 or more as of 9/1/79. [Secs. 4.02.010, 4.02.030.]

Administration: Appointed 5-member Rent Review Commission, 3200 E. Tahquitz McCallum Way, Palm Springs, Calif., (619) 323-8211.

Registration: Required, or landlord can't raise rents. [Sec. 4.02.080.]

Rent Formula: Rent as of 9/1/79, plus annual increases not exceeding 75% of the annual All Urban Consumers Consumer Price Index for the Los Angeles/Long Beach/Anaheim metropolitan area. (Step-by-step calculation procedure is set forth in ordinance.) [Secs. 4.02.040, 4.02.050.]

Individual Adjustments: Landlord may petition for further increases based on "hardship." Commission consent for increase is not necessary if tenant agrees in writing, but landlord may not coerce consent under threat of eviction or nonrenewal of lease, and may not include general waiver in lease or rental agreement. [Secs.4.02.060, 4.02.065.]

Notice Requirements: Before raising rent, landlord must notify tenant in writing of the base rent charged on 9/1/79, the present rent, and the date of the last previous rent increase. [Sec. 4.02.080(d)(2).] This information can be included on the rent-increase notice.

Vacancy Decontrol: None.

Eviction: "Just cause" to evict is not required, but there may be other restrictions. See Vol. 2.

Penalties: Tenant may sue for any excess rent collected, attorney's fees, and a penalty of up to $300. [Sec. 4.02.090.] Tenant may also seek the $300-plus-attorney's-fees penalty against landlord who coerces consent to rent increase. [Sec. 4.02.060(c).]

SAN FRANCISCO

Ordinance Adoption Date: (San Francisco Administrative Code, Chapter 37), 6/79; latest amendment 6/7/82.

Exceptions: Units constructed after 6/79; buildings over 50 years old and "substantially rehabilitated" since 6/79; owner-occupied single-family residences, duplexes, triplexes, and 4-plexes. [Sec. 37.2(o).]

Administration: Appointed 5-member Residential Rent Stabilization and Arbitration Board, [Sec. 37.4], 170 Fell St., Room 16, San Francisco, CA 94102, (415) 621-RENT.

Registration: Not required.

Rent Formula: Rents may not be increased by more than a 4%-to-7% percentage based on the "All Urban Consumers Consumer Price Index" for the San Francisco-Oakland Metropolitan Area. The figure is published each year by the Board, and in any event is between 4% and 7%. [Sec. 37.3.] Landlord may also pass through increased utility costs without permission from the Board [Sec. 37.3], and may apply to city Real Estate Department for certification of capital improvements the amortized cost of which may also be passed through to the tenant [Sec. 37.7.]

Individual Adjustments: Landlord may apply to Board for higher increase based on increased costs. Hearing officer decides case based on various factors, including operating and maintenance expenses, but not "negative cash flow" based on recent purchase. Hearing officer may also consider rent-increase history , failure to make repairs, or any decrease in services. Tenant may contest any claimed passthrough of utility costs, or to request rent reduction based on decrease of services or poor maintenance. [Secs. 37.8.]

Notice Requirements: Where rent increase includes utility or capital-improvement passthroughs or banked (accumulated) previous across-the-board increases (all of which may be applied without Board permission), landlord must give tenant written itemized breakdown of such increases, on or before the date of service of the rent-increase notice. [Regulation Sec. 4.10.]

Vacancy Decontrol: Landlord may charge any rent after a tenant vacates voluntarily or is evicted for good cause. Once the property is rerented, it is subject to rent control based on the higher rent. [Sec. 37.3(a).]

Eviction: Landlord must show "just cause" to evict. See Vol. 2.

Penalties: Violation of ordinance, including wrongful eviction or eviction attempts, is a misdemeanor punishable by maximums of a $2000 fine & 6 months imprisonment. [Sec. 37.10.]

SAN JOSE

Ordinance Adoption Date: (San Jose Municipal Code, Title 17, Chapter 17.23) 7/7/79; latest amendment 7/19/85.

Exceptions: Units constructed after 9/7/79, single-family residences, duplexes, and condominium units. [Sec. 17.23.150.]

Administration: Appointed 7-member Advisory Commission on Rents, 801 N. First Street, Room 200, San Jose, CA 95110,   (408) 277-5431.

Registration: Not required.

Rent Formula: Rents may not be increased more than 8% in any 12-month period, and may not be increased more than once within the 12 months. However, a landlord who has not raised the rent for 24 months is entitled to a 21% increase. [Secs. 17.23.180, 17.23.210.].

Individual Adjustments: Tenant can contest an increase in excess of that allowed by filing a petition before rent increase takes effect (30 days), or lose the right to object. Disputes initiated by tenant petition are heard by a mediation hearing officer, who may consider costs of capital improvements, repairs, maintenance, and debt service, and past history of rent increases. Either party may appeal mediator's decision and invoke binding arbitration. (Landlord may also file petition to ask for rent increase over allowed percentage, but why bother if burden is on tenant to contest any increase?). [Secs. 17.23.220 - 17.23.440.]

Notice Requirements: Where rent increase exceeds 8%, rent-increase notice must advise tenant of her right to utilize the Rental Dispute Mediation and Arbitration Hearing Process, giving the address and telephone number of the city's rent office. The notice must also indicate the time limit within which the tenant may do this. [Sec. 17.23.270.]

Vacancy Decontrol: Landlord may charge any rent after a tenant vacates voluntarily or is evicted following 3-day notice for nonpayment of rent or other breach of the rental agreement. Once the property is rerented, it is subject to rent control based on the higher rent. [Sec. 17.23.190.]

Eviction: Ordinance does not require showing of "just cause" to evict.

Penalties: Violation of ordinance by charging rent in excess of that allowed following mediation/arbitration, by retaliation against the tenant for asserting his rights, or by attempting to have tenant waive rights under ordinance is a misdemeanor punishable by maximums of a $500 fine and 6 months imprisonment. [Secs. 17.23.515 - 17.23.530.] Tenant may sue landlord for excess rents charged, plus treble damages or $500 (whichever is greater) [Sec. 17.23.540.]

SANTA MONICA

Ordinance Adoption Date: (City Charter Article XVIII), 4/10/79; latest amendment 11/4/84.

Exceptions: Units constructed after 4/10/79; owner-occupied single-family residences, duplexes, and triplexes; single-family dwellings not rented on 7/1/84. [Charter Amendment (C.A.) Secs. 1801(c), 1815, Regulation (Reg.) Secs. 2000+, 12000+.] However, rental units other than single-family dwellings not rented on 7/1/84 must be registered and the exemption applied for.

Administration: Elected 5-member Rent Control Board, 1685 Main Street, Santa Monica, CA 90401,   (213) 458-8751.

Registration: Required, or landlord can't raise rents, and tenants can request permission from Board to withhold rents. [C.A. Secs. 1803(q), 1805(h).]

Rent Formula: 4/10/79 freeze at 4/10/78 levels, plus annual adjustments by Board after investigation and hearings. [C.A. Secs. 1804, 1805(a),(b), Reg. Secs. 3000+.]

Individual Adjustments: Landlord may apply for further increase based on increased taxes or unavoidable increases in utility or maintenance costs, capital improvements, but not "negative cash flow" due to recent purchase. Tenant may apply for rent reduction based on poor maintenance. [C.A. Sec. 1805(c)-(h), Reg. Secs. 4000+.]

Notice Requirements: Rent-increase notice must state, "The undersigned [landlord] certifies that this unit and common areas are not subject to any uncorrected citation or notices of violation of any state or local housing, health, or safelty laws issued by any dovernment official or agency." [Reg. Sec. 3007(f)(3)]. Otherwise, tenant may refuse to pay increase and successfully defend unlawful detainer action based on failure to pay increase.

Vacancy Decontrol: None. [C.A. Sec. 1803(r) allows Board to decontrol any category of property only if the rental unit vacancy rate exceeds 5%; this is a virtual impossibility.]

Eviction: Landlord must show "just cause" to evict. See Vol. 2.

Penalties: Violation of the charter amendment is a misdemeanor punishable by maximums of a $500 fine and 6 months imprisonment. Tenant may sue landlord in court or in administrative hearing for violating ordinance in any way, and may recover attorney's fees; tenant may recover rents unlawfully charged, plus treble damages and attorney's fees. [C.A. Sec. 1809(a)-(d).]

Other Features: Landlord must place security deposits in interest-bearing Savings & Loan account, but landlord may use interest to "offset operating expenses"; in considering rent-increase petitions, Board may consider whether interest was actually so applied. [C.A. Sec. 1803(s).] Security deposits cannot be increased by notice of change of terms of tenancy. [Reg. Sec. 3000.]

THOUSAND OAKS

Ordinance Adoption Date: 7/1/80; latest amendment 12/6/83.

Exceptions: Units constructed after 6/30/80; "luxury" units (defined as 0,1,2,3, or 4+ - bedroom units renting for at least $400, $500, $600, $750, or $900, respectively, as of 6/30/80); single-family residences, duplexes, triplexes, and 4-plexes, except where 5 or more units are located on the same lot. [Sec. III.L.]

Administration: Appointed 5-member Rent Adjustment Commission, 401 W. Hillcrest Drive, Thousand Oaks, California, (805) 497-8611.

Registration: Required. [Sec. XIV.]

Rent Formula: Rents may not be increased by more than 7% in any 12-month period. [Secs. III.G,H, VI.]

Individual Adjustments: Landlord may apply to the Rent Adjustment Commission for higher increase based on capital improvement costs, or to obtain "just and reasonable return" (does not include "negative cash flow" based on recent purchase.) [Sec. VII.]

Notice Requirements: Landlord must prominently post in the apartment complex a listing or map of rental units, showing which are subject to the ordinance and which are not. [Sec. VI.C.] Landlord who proposes to increase rent more than 7% (thus requesting individual adjustment increases), is required to provide written justification for the difference. [Sec. V.]

Vacancy Decontrol: Property that becomes vacant after 5/1/81 due to tenant voluntarily leaving or being evicted for nonpayment of rent is no longer subject to any provision of the ordinance. [Sec. VI.]

Eviction Features: Landlord must show "just cause" to evict. See Vol. 2.

Penalties: Tenant may sue for three times any rent in excess of legal rent collected, plus a penalty of up to $500 and attorney's fees. [Sec. IX.]

WEST HOLLYWOOD

Ordinance Adoption Date: (West Hollywood Municipal Code, Article IV, Chapter 4), 6/27/85; latest amendment 9/85.

Exceptions: Units constructed after 7/1/79 ("just-cause" eviction requirements do apply, however). However, all exemptions (except the standard one "boarding" exemption) must be applied for in registration document (see below). [Sec. 6406.]

Administration: Appointed 5-member Rent Stabilization Commission, 8611 Santa Monica Blvd., West Hollywood, CA 90069, (213) 854-7400.

Registration: Required, or landlord can't raise rents. [Sec. 6407.]

Rent Formula: 11/29/84 freeze at 8/6/84 levels, plus annual adjustments by Board after investigation and hearings. Landlords who pay for tenants' gas and/or electricity may increase an additional 1/2 % for each such utility. [Secs. 6408, 6409.].

Individual Adjustments: Landlord may apply for further increase based on unavoidable increases in utility or maintenance costs or taxes, and for capital improvements. Tenant may apply for rent reduction based on poor maintenance. [Sec. 6411.]

Rent-Increase Notification: Rent-increase notice must contain statement to the effect that landlord is in compliance with ordinance, including filing and payment of required registration documents and fees. [Sec. 6409.G, Regulation Sec. 40000(f).]

Vacancy Decontrol: When tenant of property other than a single-family dwelling voluntarily vacates or is evicted for cause, landlord may increase rent by additional 10%; however, no more than one such increase is permitted within any 24-month period. When tenant of single-family dwelling voluntarily vacates or is evicted for cause (other than for occupancy by owner or relative), landlord can raise rent to any level; once the single-family dwelling is rerented, it is subject to rent control at the new higher rent. In either case, landlord must file "vacancy increase certificate" with city and show she has repainted and cleaned carpets within previous six months; certificate must be filed within 30 days after tenant vacates, or landlord cannot raise rent under this provision. [Sec. 6410.]

Eviction: Landlord must show "just cause" to evict. See Vol. 2.

Penalties: Violation of ordinance is misdemeanor punishable by maximums of $1000 fine and 6 months imprisonment. [Sec.6414.E.] Tenant may sue landlord for three times any rents collected or demanded in excess of legal rents, plus attorney's fees. [Sec. 6414.C.]

Other Features: Landlord must credit 5 1/2 % interest on security deposits against rents at least once every five years, as well as when tenant vacates. [Sec. 6408.B.]

WESTLAKE VILLAGE

Note: This small city (population 10,000) has a rent-control ordinance that applies to apartment complexes of 5 units or more (as well as to mobilehome parks, whose specialized laws are not covered in this book.) Because the city's only apartment complex of this size has undergone conversion to condominiums, there is therefore now no property (other than mobilehome parks) to which the ordinance applies, and we don't explain the ordinance here.

F. Attempted Evasion of Rent Control Ordinances

When rent control laws were first adopted in the 1970's, many landlords became very imaginative in inventing ways to circumvent ordinances. In cities with vacancy decontrol, landlords began terminating month-to-month tenancies so that they could raise rents. As noted above, this caused localities to enact "just-cause-for-eviction" protections. In response, a few landlords began inventing ways to fake having just cause, or to otherwise bully tenants into leaving. This, in turn, was followed by more amendments to close such "loopholes," and by more refined ways to avoid the new rules, and so forth.

To some extent, this game worked fairly well from a landlord point of view for several years. That is, many landlords did get rid of low-paying tenants and raise the rent. However, newer rent control ordinances have closed many of the original loopholes and, in some cases, now provide for heavy financial penalties against

landlords who try to circumvent a rent-control or just-cause-eviction ordinance. In addition, tenant and rent board sophistication in spotting and countering landlord maneuvers has improved. For example, a favorite landlord ploy to move out low-paying tenants is to claim that the landlord, or a close member of the landlord's family, is going to move in. This constitutes a "just cause for eviction" under most rent-control ordinances if there is no other unit available for the relative. As it turned out, however, many of the alleged landlord relatives were phony, or only moved in for a week or two, or the landlord had another suitable vacancy. At any rate, the result was the same--once the tenant moved out, the landlord promptly re-rented the place to a stranger, with a hefty rent increase. Similarly, in areas where the necessity of vacating the unit to make major repairs to the property was listed in an ordinance as a valid reason for eviction, some landlords used this reason to evict, but then made few, if any, repairs. Other landlords deliberately reduced services or adopted obnoxious behavior to encourage their tenants to "voluntarily" leave.

As noted, to combat this, ordinances were rewritten to provide severe financial penalties against landlords who attempted to circumvent the law. For example, the ordinances of Los Angeles and San Francisco (as well as Berkeley, Cotati, and Santa Monica) provide that a tenant may sue and recover actual and punitive damages against a landlord who uses a trick, such as the phony relative ploy, to evict a tenant in order to take advantage of vacancy decontrol under that city's ordinance.* In addition, the law allows a tenant to sue a landlord for having made her life miserable, under the legal theory of "intentional infliction of emotional distress" (see **Newby v. Alto Rivera Apartments** (1976) 60 Cal.App.3d 288, 131 Cal.Rptr. 547). Finally, all rent control ordinances (except that of Palm Springs) forbid lease or rental agreement clauses where the tenant supposedly gives up or waives her rights under the law.

Our advice concerning all this is simple. The best way to avoid the possibility of legal hassles is to forget about trying to circumvent the intent behind a rent control law, if indeed you ever thought about it. Save your energies for working toward a repeal or amendment of any rent control law you think is unfair. If you live in a strict rent control city and can

figure out a way to do it, consider selling your properties and buying others in areas which don't make it so difficult for you to operate. This may not be as difficult to do as you might imagine, given the number of groups of unrelated adults who are purchasing housing together as tenants-in-common and then signing a contract to control ownership details.

G. Rent Mediation

In a few cities where city councils have felt tenant pressure, but not enough pressure to adopt rent control ordinances, voluntary rent guidelines or landlord/tenant mediation services have been adopted. Voluntary guidelines, of course, do not have the force of law, and neither do exhortations to the effect that agreeing to mediation is a good idea. However, agreeing to comply with voluntary rent guidelines, or to handle a dispute by mediation, is often an excellent idea, particularly when the alternative may be hiring a lawyer to sue a tenant refusing to pay a rent increase and going to court to obtain a money judgment you may never collect. It's also good to keep in mind that several cities have rent control at least in part because some landlords completely ignored voluntary guidelines and mediation services, causing tenants to show up at polls and support rent control in record numbers. We discuss mediation in more detail in Chapter 7, as a useful device to try and settle many types of landlord-tenant disputes.

---

* See **Brossard v. Stotter** (1984) 160 Cal.App.3d 1067, 207 Cal.Rptr.108. The tenant was allowed to bring suit for damages even though the landlord had earlier won an eviction lawsuit on the basis that she didn't use the phony-relative ploy. The tenant successfully claimed that the landlord's use of the phony relative ploy didn't become obvious until after the tenant was evicted and the property rerented.

5

Deposits and Tenant's Insurance

A. Introduction

Most landlords quite sensibly ask for a deposit before entrusting tens of thousands of dollars worth of real property to a tenant. Not too many years ago, the details of what a deposit covered, how much could be charged, and when, and if, a deposit had to be returned, were pretty much controlled by the words the landlord put in the lease or written agreement. This has all changed. Now, deposits, including the maximum amounts that can be charged and what the deposit can be used for, are closely regulated by state law. It goes almost without saying that it is absolutely essential that you know what these rules are and that you follow them carefully.

The first thing to understand is that many terms, such as "cleaning deposit," "cleaning fee," "security deposit," etc., which used to be defined in a multitude of ways in leases and rental agreements, now all have the same meaning as far as the law is concerned. Today, California deposit law* very broadly defines a "security" deposit to include "any payment, fee, deposit, or charge," including last month's rent (but not first month's rent), paid by a tenant at the time she moves in. In other words, no matter what you call a deposit you collect from a tenant, the law calls it a "security deposit," and you can't limit your tenant's right to have this sort of up-front payment accounted for as a refundable deposit by calling it something else. (However, as we'll see in Section D of this chapter, you can mistakenly limit your own rights under California's deposit law by calling part or all of a deposit "last month's

---

* Civil Code Section 1950.5

rent.") To avoid confusion by your tenants, and to maximize your own flexibility, you should also use the term "security deposit" (see Section D, below). As a matter of good business practice, we also recommend that you insist on getting the first month's rent and any deposits in the form of a certified check. This will be a substantial amount of money, usually in the $2,000-$5,000 range, and you don't want to allow a tenant to move in and then have the check bounce.

NOTE: HOLDING DEPOSIT EXCEPTION: Security deposit rules do not apply to credit check fees or money paid to hold or bind a deal before a lease or rental agreement is signed and a tenant moves in. We discuss holding deposits and credit fees in more detail in Chapter 1, Sections E and F.

B. Dollar Limits on Deposits

Subdivision (c) of Section 1950.5 of the California Civil Code limits the amount you can collect as a deposit as follows:

● **Unfurnished Property:** The deposit (including last month's rent) can't exceed two month's rent.

● **Furnished Property:** The deposit (including last month's rent) can't exceed three month's rent.

Property is considered to be "furnished" if it contains at least essential furniture, such as a bed in each bedroom, a couch or chairs for the living area, and an eating table with chairs, in addition to a refrigerator and stove.

EXAMPLE 1: Lena Landlady rents her two-bedroom apartments for $500 per month. Since Lena's apartments are unfurnished, she can charge no more than two months' rent, or $1,000 total deposit, regardless of how the deposit is divided into "last month's rent,"

"cleaning fee," and so forth. In other words, if Lena charges a $200 "cleaning deposit," a $300 "security deposit," and $500 "last month's rent," she is just within the law. Remember, the rent Lena collects for the first month doesn't count for this purpose.

NOTE: In Section D of this chapter, we will see that it makes more sense to lump the payments together as a "security deposit" rather than to designate parts of it for specific purposes, such as "last month's rent," etc.

EXAMPLE 2: Lenora Lessor rents her three-bedroom furnished house for $650 a month. Since total deposits, etc. on furnished property can legally be three times the monthly rent, Lenora can legally insist on receiving up to $1,950 for last month's rent and deposits. This is in addition to the first month's rent of $650 that Lenora can (and should) insist on, in advance, before turning the property over to a tenant. Realistically, though, Lenora might not find any takers if she insists on receiving $1,950 in deposits plus the first month's rent, for a total of $2,600. In the case of furnished property, the market often puts a practical limit on the amount charged for deposits which is lower than the maximum allowed by law.

Since the amount of a deposit is tied to the rent, you may wonder how an increase in rent affects the amount of the deposit. As we saw in Chapter 2, the amount of rent for a month-to-month tenancy, as well as other terms of the agreement, can normally be changed by giving the tenant 30 days' notice in writing. (We discuss in detail the procedure for doing this in Chapter 14.) If this is done, the landlord can also legally increase the amount of the deposit because, as we have just discussed, the maximum deposit allowable is computed by multiplying the rent by three for furnished units and by two for unfurnished ones. It's important to understand, however, that to be legally entitled to the increased deposit, you must ask for it, using a 30-day notice.

EXAMPLE: A landlord who rents an unfurnished house or apartment to a tenant for $300 a month can charge total deposits (including anything called "last month's rent") of two times that amount, or $600. Let's assume the deposit is in this amount. If the landlord then raises the rent to $400, the only change regarding the deposit is the maximum deposit the landlord is allowed to charge, which is now $800. In other words, the tenant is not required to fork over the $200 difference. In order for this to be required, the landlord must also raise the deposit amount with a 30-day notice of "Change of Terms of Tenancy." We discuss how to do this in Chapter 14, "Raising Rents and Changing Terms of Tenancy."

One final note--some cities with rent control ordinances place further restrictions on deposit amounts and increases. Before attempting to raise a tenant's deposit in a rent-controlled city, be sure to obtain a copy of the applicable rent-control ordinance.

C. Record Keeping on Deposits

In most localities, you don't have to pay a tenant interest on deposits (for last month's rent), or put it in a separate bank account--unless your lease or rental agreement requires it. In other words, you can simply put the money in your pocket or bank account and use it, as long as you have it available when the tenant moves out (see Chapter 18, "The Tenant Moves Out").* Some local rent control ordinances (including those in San Francisco, Berkeley, and Santa Monica) require interest payments on deposits. Interest requirements are not limited to rent-controlled cities,

however; for example Santa Cruz, which does not have rent control, nonetheless requires landlords to pay interest on tenants' deposits.

Some landlords have found that it is good public relations to pay tenants interest on their deposits, even though no law in the area in which they rent requires it. This, of course, is up to you.

D. Last Month's Rent

In Section B above, we discussed the fact that there are limits on how much you can collect for deposits, no matter whether you call it a "security deposit," "last month's rent" or something else. It is important that you realize, however, that if you do use the term "last month's rent," you are stuck with its literal meaning. Thus, if you give your tenant a year's lease, from January 1 to December 31, the tenant's payment of a "last month's rent" pays the rent for December in advance. If you rent to your tenant from month to month, the tenant's "last month's rent" will take care of the rent for the last month, after you or the tenant give the other a 30-day notice. In other words, you can't use "last month's rent" as a security deposit for damage or cleaning charges.

All this adds up to an unpleasant reality. If you accept an up-front payment from a tenant, and call it "last month's rent," you are legally bound to use it for that purpose only. At the same time, you get no advantage, as the total amount you can charge (two or three times the rent, depending on whether the unit is unfurnished or furnished), does not increase. If, instead, you require your tenant to pay a "security deposit" and do not mention last month's rent, she will have to pay the last month's rent when it comes due and then worry about how to get the security deposit back when she moves out. In this situation, if she either damages the premises or fails to pay rent, you can hold on to the appro-

---

* The old case of **Ingram v. Pantages** (1927) 86 Cal.App. 41 seems to require the maintenance of separate bank accounts for each deposit. In practice, though, this case is generally ignored.

priate amount of the entire deposit.

EXAMPLE 1: After Leatrice Landlord learned that she couldn't charge nonrefundable cleaning fees when renting out her $300-a-month apartment, she decided to collect a total of $600--a $300 security deposit and $300 "last month's rent." Her next tenant, Dot Damage, applied this last month's rent when she gave her 30-day notice to Leatrice. This left Leatrice with the $300 security deposit. When Dot moved out, leaving $400 cigarette burns on the bathroom vanity, Leatrice was stuck with a $100 loss.

EXAMPLE 2: Learning something from this unhappy experience, Leatrice charged her next tenant a simple $600 security deposit, not limiting any part of it to "last month's rent." This time, when the tenant moved out (fortunately she had paid her last month's rent as legally required), the whole $600 was available to cover the cost of any repairs, cleaning, etc.

Another reason for a landlord to accept a "deposit" rather than a "last month's rent" is to avoid confusion over how the "last month's rent" is to be applied during the tenant's last month of occupancy if the rent has been increased, but the deposit for last month's rent was not increased. For example, consider a landlord who, when he begins renting to a tenant for $400 a month, accepts $400 "last month's rent," but over the years raises the rent to $500 without also raising the deposit for "last month's rent." (See Section B above on raising deposits concurrently with rents.) Some tenants take the position that the landlord, by accepting $400 as "last month's rent" implicitly agreed to accept the $400 as full payment for that month, even though the current rent is $500. There is no definitive legal answer, but the tenant has a pretty good argument that "last month's rent" means last month's rent. The potential disagreement can

easily be avoided by labelling all up-front payments as a "security deposit."

E. Non-Refundable Fees and Deposits

Simply stated, it is not legal to collect non-refundable fees or deposits instead of refundable deposits. Some older leases still provide for the payment of an automatic cleaning fee, or use some other language to characterize money that must be paid by a tenant in addition to the rent as something other than a refundable deposit or last month's rent. This is not legal.* Except for holding fees charged before a landlord-tenant relationship is established, all deposits and fees must be refunded, unless the tenant skips out owing rent or leaves the premises dirty or damaged. If this is the situation, the landlord can only keep that portion of the deposit necessary to clean or repair damages exclusive of "ordinary wear and tear" (CCP §1950.5). (See Chapter 18.)

When it comes to cleanliness, the landlord may use the deposit money to pay for putting the property into the condition a new tenant would insist on, if the outgoing tenant neglected to do this. The practice of routinely charging a fixed fee for cleaning drapes or carpets, whether essential or not (i.e., even if the tenant does her own reasonable level of cleaning before moving out), is simply not legal. If your tenant moves out, leaving the

---

* This includes charging a "hidden" nonrefundable deposit by insisting on an amount of rent for the first month that is considerably higher than for later months. Granberry v. Islay Investments (1984) 161 Cal.App.3d 382, 207 Cal.Rptr. 652. Also see People v. Parkmerced Co. (1988) 198 Cal. App. 3d 683, 244 Cal. Rptr. 22.

place less than perfect, you have to decide whether the problems can reasonably be seen as constituting normal wear and tear or whether they justify your making reasonable deductions from the deposit to pay for additional cleaning or repair work. If you do decide to keep a part of the deposit, you should prepare in advance to justify your decision. We discuss how to do this in detail in Chapter 1, "Renting Your Property" and Chapter 18, "The Tenant Moves Out."

As far as cleanliness is concerned, the tenant must leave the property in a condition that a reasonable person would regard as being clean. If she does not, you are entitled to use that portion of the deposit reasonably necessary to restore it to this condition. Unfortunately, if you are far more fastidious than the average American, you cannot legally hold your tenant to this standard. Of course, if it comes to a court fight, an acceptable standard of cleanliness will be decided by the judge who hears the case.

A different rule applies to damage to the property. You, as landlord, can't charge for "ordinary wear and tear," such as normal paint deterioration, wear and tear of drapes and carpets, and similar routine maintenance items. Obviously, if the tenant has disfigured, discolored, burned, or otherwise damaged the carpeting, drapery, or paint on the walls, or has damaged the unit in some other way, a reasonable charge is warranted. Again, as we discuss in detail in Chapters 1 and 18, the best way to do this is to insist on a detailed inspection, including filling out a landlord/tenant checklist when the tenant moves in and then again when she leaves.

NOTE ON PAINTING: Because responsibility for painting property is so often a problem between landlord and tenant, let's focus on it for a moment. Here are the basics. Repainting the walls is almost always a routine maintenance item that has to be taken care of every few years. However, it should not have to be done twice a year. Thus, if you paint a property and turn it over to a tenant who only stays a few months and leaves the walls significantly marred or defaced, you have every legal justification for charging the tenant to repaint. If the tenant's stay has been longer, say two years, any need for repainting that arises during that time is more likely due to ordinary wear and tear, and no charge for repainting is warranted. This is certainly true if the tenant has lived in the property five or six years or more, and you haven't repainted during his occupancy. The practice followed by some landlords of charging the tenant for the repainting costs based on a percentage of how long the tenant lived in a unit, as compared to how long the landlord estimates the paint job should last, is reasonable, but it must be applied with a degree of flexibility to take the facts of the particular situation into consideration. In other words, if a departed tenant files suit in small claims court to challenge the amount of her deposit you withheld to repaint, you, as the landlord, must be able to show that the damage was in "excess of the ordinary wear and tear" standard.

An attempt to charge a tenant for unnecessary cleaning, or for damage that really comes under the heading of ordinary wear and tear can, in theory, subject the landlord to liability for the amount of the deposit wrongfully withheld, plus interest of 2% per month (beginning two weeks after the tenant leaves) and up to $200 punitive damages if the tenant files a lawsuit and the judge finds that the failure to refund the deposit was in "bad faith."* However, as long as the landlord has made a reasonable effort to document

* Civil Code Section 1950.5(k).

dirt and damage by use of pictures and Landlord/Tenant Checklists, it is extremely unlikely that a judge will over-award punitive damages even if she concludes that the landlord retained more of the deposit than was justified by the facts of the situation.

NOTE ON MOVING OUT: We discuss moving out in detail in Chapter 18. It is appropriate to mention here, however, that under Civil Code Section 1950.5, a landlord has fourteen days to either return a tenant's entire deposit or give the tenant an itemized statement of deposit deductions and any deposit refund remaining.

F. Deposits and Selling the Rental Property

Suppose you own a number of rental units, collect deposits, and then sell the property? Sometime later, the tenant moves out and quite naturally wants her deposit back. Who owes her the money? You do, unless you have taken the steps set out in Subdivision (g) of Civil Code Section 1950.5 to shift the responsibility to the new owner. To do this, you must:

• Transfer the deposit to the new owner (less any lawful deductions for back rent, necessary cleaning, and damages in excess of ordinary wear and tear that exist at the time of transfer, provided the tenant is notified of them in an itemized statement); and

• Notify the tenant by first-class mail (preferably certified) or personal delivery of a written notice of the change of ownership, itemizing any lawful deductions and giving the new owner's name, address and phone number.
How do you actually transfer the money to the new owner? If you have established a separate account for each tenant's deposit, you can simply make the change at the bank. If you have no separate account and have mixed the money with your own, be sure to include

a provision in the real property sales contract for your property which says that part of the buyer's legal consideration for the sale is the buyer's specific agreement to take responsibility for the repayment of all deposits.

If you don't properly transfer the deposit to the new owner and notify the tenants as required, the new owner will still be liable (along with you) to the tenants for any untransferred portion. (One exception to this rule applies if the new owner can convince a judge that after making a reasonable inquiry when buying the property, she erroneously concluded that the deposits were in fact transferred or that the seller refunded them to the tenants before selling.) Also, the new owner can't increase the tenant's deposits to make up for your failure to transfer the money. The new owner, if stuck with this situation, will be able to sue you for any funds he's out by virtue of your failure to transfer and notify.*

SAMPLE CONTRACT PROVISION
TRANSFERRING TENANTS' DEPOSITS

As part of the consideration for the sale of the property described herein, Seller shall transfer to buyer all "security," as that term is defined by Section 1950.5 of the Civil Code, deposited with Seller by tenants of the premises, after making any lawful deductions from each tenant's deposit, in accordance with Subdivision (g) of Section 1950.5, after notifying Buyer and each tenant of the amount of deposit remaining on account for each tenant, and after notifying each tenant of the fact of such transfer to Buyer. Thereafter, Buyer shall assume liability to each tenant for the amount transferred after such lawful deductions.

---

* Civil Code Section 1950.5 (i).

G. Insurance (As a Back-up to Deposits)

This isn't a book on how to buy landlord's insurance, but because insurance can compensate you for some damages to your property caused by tenants, it is appropriate to mention it here. After all, the legal limits as to how much you can charge for deposits are so strict that you may want to get all the additional protection possible.

In the context of protecting yourself from damage caused by your tenant, there are basically two broad types of policies:

● Landlords' insurance, which is designed to cover you and your building generally. It should protect you from losses from fire and water damage, as well as personal liability for injury to a tenant or someone else, and illegal acts by you and your employees. You will need this sort of insurance for many reasons, which we will discuss in subsequent chapters.

● Tenants' insurance, often called a "Tenant's Package Policy," which covers the tenant's liability to third parties, as well as damage to his own property caused by fire, water damage etc. and certain types of damage to your building caused by the tenants' acts.

We strongly advise you to purchase landlords' insurance. You may also wish to require that your tenant purchase tenant's insurance as part of the lease or written rental agreement.*
One advantage of doing this is that, if there is a problem caused by a tenant which is covered by the tenant's policy, your premium rate won't be affected even though your landlord's policy also covers the damage. The provision in the lease or rental agreement should specify the broad type of coverage your tenant must purchase. This should include fire and water damage to the value of the house or apartment unit, as well as tenants' liability to third parties for negligence, as well as protection for the tenant's own property. You may want to look around and locate a broker or company who writes a good policy at a reasonable price and simply require it. Of course, if you do require that a tenant purchase this insurance, you will want to be sure you receive an official notice from the company that the policy has been purchased.

In addition, you may also want to ask the agent or company to provide notice to you if the tenant's policy is cancelled (i.e., for nonpayment of premiums) or otherwise terminated.

How does a tenant's policy help you if the place is damaged? Well, if damage is caused by fire or water (e.g., the tenant leaves something burning on the stove which causes a kitchen fire),

---

* We include a provision in the tear-out lease/rental agreement at the back of this book, which gives the tenant the option of obtaining such insurance or being held personally liable for damage caused by her acts of those of her guests, etc. If you absolutely wish to require insurance, here is a clause that will do the job: "Tenant, within 10 days of the signing of this agreement, shall obtain insurance which will reimburse Landlord for the cost of fire or water damage and vandalism to the premises and indemnify Landlord against liability to third parties for any negligence on the part of Tenant or his or her guests or invitees, and cover damage to the tenants' personal possessions to a maximum of $ _____ . Tenant shall provide Landlord with proof that this has been done."

his policy, not yours, will be responsible. But what if a tenant simply moves out and destroys your property? Will his policy pay off? Probably not, unless it covers vandalism (it's a good idea to require this) and the tenant's conduct qualifies as such.*

Of course, your prospective tenant may balk at buying insurance. However, since this type of policy isn't very expensive ($250 per year is about average), and is primarily designed to protect the tenant's personal property, finding a tenant who will purchase insurance should not be a big hurdle. And there may even be an advantage to eliminating tenants who don't understand why purchasing a basic renter's policy is a good idea, in favor of those who understand why it makes sense.

* The law isn't completely clear as to whether you can recover for vandalism should the property be damaged intentionally, but many companies will pay off, partially because it's often hard to know whether the tenant destroyed your property or a stranger entered and caused the damage.

6
Managers

A. Do You Need a Manager?

Many small landlords choose to manage their own rental property. If you are one, you can skim or skip the material in this chapter. If you have decided to turn over some or all of the day-to-day aspects of residential rental property, such as advertising, selecting tenants, collecting rents, doing maintenance and repair work, to a resident manager or property management company, or both, this chapter is for you. The law requires that there be a manager residing on the premises of any apartment complex containing sixteen or more units.*

Obviously, types of property managers vary widely, from the tenant who gets a rent reduction in exchange for collecting rents, doing yard work, making repairs, or relaying tenants' problems to you, to large corporate real estate enterprises managing thousands of units. Similarly, the duties which landlords commonly assign their managers are not uniform. For example, you may not want to be involved in advertising, interviewing, screening and selecting prospective tenants, and will delegate the responsibility for these tasks to your manager. Or, you may wish to have an on-site manager handy with tools to take care of routine maintenance, such as minor plumbing and electrical repairs, while arranging for more major repairs to be made by outsiders.

* California Administrative Code, Title 25, Section 42.

If you are new to the landlord business and decide to employ someone to help you run your properties, your first job is to decide what sort of manager you want and what his specific duties are. This is a practical decision that we can't help you with. Once you decide what you want your manager to do, however, there are a number of things you can do to protect both yourself and your manager from legal liabilities. We will look at these in this chapter.

B. Management Companies

Obviously, it's important to decide how you wish to pay your manager or management firm. Real estate management companies generally work on a fixed percentage (typically five to ten percent) of the total rent collected in exchange for carrying out all or most management functions, such as renting the units, collecting rent, providing for an on-site manager if necessary, and seeing to it that all ordinary maintenance needs are met. Unusual maintenance or repair items are generally not included in this percentage. The management company will bill you for these charges or ask you to pay them directly to the appropriate contractor or repair person.

To comply with California law, management companies will insist on an on-site manager if your building has more than sixteen units and, in many situations, even if it has somewhat less. If your rental property only has a few units, or you own a number of small buildings spread over a good-sized geographical area, the management company probably won't hire resident managers, but will simply respond to tenant requests and complaints from their central office.

One advantage of hiring a property management firm to manage your property is that they take care of the paperwork associated with owning rental property. Since you hire a property management firm as an independent contractor, and they in turn hire the people who actually do the work, you don't have to worry about the usual social security, unemployment, and workers' compensation paperwork that normally accompanies hiring people. All you need do is sign a management agreement (management companies have their own forms, which you should thoroughly read and understand before signing) and tell the firm where to mail you the rents (less their deduction of the management fee, of course) and how to contact you in case any problems arise.*

The primary disadvantage of hiring a management company is that the management fee consisting of a fixed percentage of the rents collected can amount to a fairly substantial figure. For example, ten percent of the $500 rents collected each month from tenants in a 20-unit complex amounts to $1,000, a sum you could certainly use, especially if you are in a negative cash flow situation and can't deduct the management commission from profit.

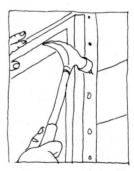

---

* It's important to understand whether the management company is charging you a fixed percentage of all rent collected or of the rental value of your property. This can be quite different if you have a lot of vacancies or turnover.

C. Hiring Your Own Manager

Because management company charges do add up, many landlords, particularly owners of small apartment complexes of five to thirty units, often find it advantageous to do much of the management work themselves, hiring their own resident managers as needed. A typical situation involves hiring a tenant who lives in a multi-unit building to act as manager. The tenant gets reduced rent in exchange for doing certain tasks, which may involve collecting rents, relaying complaints, and keeping the building and yard clean. In other situations, the landlord will require that the tenants pay rent directly to him, leaving the manager mostly in charge of low-level maintenance and seeing that the tenants don't do anything outrageous.

From a legal point of view, you can run into trouble hiring your own manager in three principal ways:

● If your agreement with your manager is not in writing, your relationship will often be so fuzzy that it will lead to legal problems between the two of you;

● If you avoid putting the manager on a formal payroll, you are likely to have problems with government agencies such as the IRS, the Franchise Tax Board, or Workers' Compensation;

● If your manager commits an illegal act, you may be responsible.

Let's look at each of these areas, and what you can do to limit your liability.

1. Put Your Agreement With Your Manager in Writing

Traditionally, landlords and resident managers arrive at oral agreements as to what the manager is supposed to do and how much she is to be compensated. Indeed, in your own earlier years, you probably lived in places managed rather informally by a student or retired couple in exchange for a cut in the rent. Even today, oral agreements such as this are not uncommon. Unfortunately, however, even though oral agreements are legal and binding, they are not advisable. If a dispute arises between you and the manager, oral agreements are difficult or impossible to prove. It is a far better business practice to put your understanding in writing.

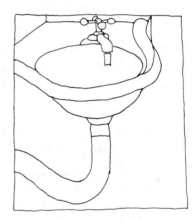

To take but one common example of how an oral agreement can go haywire, consider a tenant who rents a unit worth $450 for a reduced rent of $300 in exchange for his promise to collect your rents and do routine repairs. If this tenant-manager forgets about the repair part of the agreement and you decide to evict him, any legal action-- including an unlawful detainer lawsuit if necessary--will be fraught with issues that depend on who said what to whom. In other words, whether the manager is legally obligated to pay the unreduced $450 rent will depend not only on whether you specifically mentioned the repair duties and the manager agreed to them, but whether you can prove that this agreement took place.

Here is an example of a sound written agreement which spells out the relationship between the landlord and his manager:

NOTE: This sample agreement will probably not meet your needs exactly. Feel free to modify it, keeping in mind the discussion of legal do's and don'ts set out above.

RESIDENTIAL RENTAL PROPERTY MANAGEMENT AGREEMENT

Linda Landlady and Helena Handywoman agree as follows:

1. Linda Landlady is the owner of a dwelling, hereinafter the "four-plex," consisting of four separate residential units, located at 1234 Legal Street, Fresno, California. Helena Handywoman is currently renting Unit "A" of the four-plex on a month-to-month basis;

2. Helena is hereby employed by Linda as Linda's resident manager for the premises at 1234 Legal Street. Helena's duties as manager include:

    a. Collecting rents when due from each tenant of the four-plex, herself included. If any tenant has not paid his or her rent within five days after it is due, Helena shall promptly notify Linda of that fact;

    b. Maintaining the common areas, including lawns, shrubbery and driveways, in proper order and repair;

    c. Receiving complaints from any tenants in the four-plex with respect to any defects or needed repairs in any of the units;

    d. Making plumbing, heating, electrical, and other repairs of a minor nature in the residential units, in response to a tenant complaint or request from Linda. Minor repairs include (but are not limited to) replacement of faucet washers, unclogging of drains, replacement of light switches, and replacement of small window panes. Linda will reimburse Helena for the cost of materials, not to exceed $25 for any repair unless authorized in advance by Linda;

    e. Arranging for major repairs (e.g., repairs she is unable to complete herself and repairs costing more than $25) to be made by local repair companies. However, Helena will arrange for such repairs only after obtaining authorization from Linda;

3. Helena shall keep track of the total hours she has spent performing the above duties, and shall refrain from working more than ten hours in any one-week period without prior authorization and additional compensation from Linda;

4. This agreement may be terminated by Linda or Helena at any time by written notice to the other;

5. This agreement does not affect any provision of the rental agreement under which Helena occupies Unit "A" of the four-plex;

6. As compensation to Helena for the performance of her duties under this agreement, Linda will pay Helena the sum of $200 on the last day of each month. Helena's duty to pay rent under the rental agreement shall not be affected by the payment or nonpayment of this compensation.

Dated: January 1, 198_

                    LINDA LANDLADY

Dated: January 1, 198_

                    HELENA HANDYWOMAN

2. Compensating Your Manager

One reason many landlords prefer an arrangement by which the tenant-manager receives a reduced rent in exchange for services is that they believe this frees them from the hassle and expense of being an employer, which, of course, means dealing with the IRS, Social Security, Unemployment, Workers' Compensation, disability insurance, and so forth. Unfortunately, however, no matter what you call a manager and how you try to disguise the fact you are paying her, your failure to treat your manager as an employee and provide for these sorts of payroll deductions is illegal. Put simply, the IRS considers the compensation the manager receives in reduced rent as being taxable income, even though no money passes from the owner to the manager, and even though some money (rent less the reduction) is still paid to you by the tenant.

Failure to properly account for a tenant-manager's compensation and pay income tax and other contributions required under federal and state law can result in federal and state tax and other penalties, and even the imposition of criminal penalties if your actions are sufficiently flagrant. So please, if you compensate a manager in any way, contact the IRS, the Franchise Tax Board and other relevant agencies to learn the necessary reporting and deduction requirements. **Landlording: A Handy Manual For Scrupulous Landlords and Landladies Who Do It Themselves,** by Leigh Robinson, is an excellent source of specific information on how to do all this.

You should also realize that if a manager is injured on the job, say by falling down the stairs while going from one apartment to another to collect rent or perform maintenance, or even by a violence-prone tenant (it can and does happen), a landlord who has failed to provide for disability and

workers' compensation insurance will face serious legal problems. These include civil and criminal penalties and possibly a lawsuit by the injured manager. And, even worse, if the landlord loses the lawsuit, the court judgment probably will not be covered by any other kind of landlords' insurance, and will therefore have to be satisfied by the landlord out of her own pocket. Contact the California Employment Development Department about unemployment and disability insurance payments and your insurance agent regarding workers' compensation insurance.

One final problem is that a resident manager's compensation is subject to the requirements of minimum wage laws. Thus, if the total number of hours a manager works multiplied by the minimum hourly wage exceeds the rent reduction or other fixed rate of pay, you are in violation of these laws. For example, a landlord who employs a manager who puts in four 20-hour weeks during the month must pay $3.35 for each of those 80 hours, or $268, and will run afoul of the minimum-wage laws even with a $250 reduction in rent. You can avoid this problem by inserting a clause in the agreement with your manager which limits the total number of hours worked each month, or which provides for additional payment if the manager works more hours than anticipated.

Please do not get the idea from all of this that providing a resident manager with reduced rent in exchange for management services is illegal. It is not. As long as the necessary tax and insurance deductions and reporting requirements are met, and so long as the manager's rent reduction isn't less than that allowed under the minimum-wage laws, given the number of hours worked, you are acting legally.

There is, however, an important practical reason why reducing rent as a way to compensate your manager isn't a good idea. This is because an agreement, whether verbal or in writing, that a tenant receive reduced rent in exchange for services as a manager can lead to future problems if the manager doesn't properly perform his duties. If a manager doesn't measure up to the job, you may, of course, terminate the employment. Your next step will probably be to insist that the ex-manager go back to paying the full rent (perhaps retroactively, if he or she failed to do the work for a particular month but claimed the rent reduction).

But what happens if the manager refuses to go along with this? Unfortunately, your only means of enforcing your request is to initiate an eviction lawsuit. If your former manager resists, your lawsuit is almost sure to be complicated by the fact that the amount of rent due depends on whether the manager's employment was properly terminated and/or whether he owes any extra rent as a result of not performing his duties.

What is the best alternative to giving a tenant reduced rent in exchange for working as a manager? Simply to have the tenant-manager pay his full rent and to pay him a separate salary. Since you should be treating him as an employee anyway, and making the proper deductions, following this approach is no more difficult than using the rent-reduction method. Now, should there be a problem with the tenant-manager's

performance of her duties which leads you to terminate her employment, there's no question that she is obligated to pay the full rent, as she has done all along. If you refer back to the sample Residential Rental Property Management Agreement set out earlier in this chapter, you will see that this agreement follows the approach we suggest here.

D. Owner Liability for Manager's Acts

You can be sued by your tenants for the acts of your manager or management company. This is because your manager is considered to be an "agent" for you (the "principal") in your operation of your rental property. Generally, this means that whatever your manager does in the course of his or her employment is seen in the eyes of the law as being done by you.* This is another reason why many landlords hire management companies, a part of whose responsibility is to keep current on legal do's and don'ts.

Obviously, if you hire an on-site manager, you should either limit her responsibilities to carrying out very routine tasks, or insist that she be properly equipped to deal with more complex situations. This means making sure your manager is familiar with the basics of landlord-tenant law.

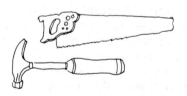

---

* Some outrageous criminal acts which have nothing to do with the manager's duties may be an exception to this rule in that they are so far outside the scope of your employment relationship with your manager that you have no liability.

EXAMPLE 1: Teresa Tenant complains to your manager, Larry Laidback, about a loose step on the stairway leading up to her apartment. Larry neither takes care of the problem, nor tells you about it. After having complained to Larry three times, Teresa (or a guest) slips on the step and breaks her leg. Even though you never knew about the loose step, and even though you had good reason to think Larry was a competent manager, you are liable for Teresa's medical bills and lost wages. Good thing your landlords' liability insurance is paid up! (See Chapter 11.)

EXAMPLE 2: Unbeknownst to you, your manager, Ura Uptight, to whom you've delegated the duty of selecting tenants, applies one of her own criterion to making these choices--that of skin color. She also refuses to rent to families with children. Imagine your surprise when a qualified tenant who happens to be a member of a minority group sues you (as well as Ura) on the basis of your responsibility for her action in refusing to rent to an Asian family with two children.

EXAMPLE 3: Your trusted manager, Pam Pocketeer, is responsible for itemizing cleaning and damage costs and for returning the balance of each tenant's security deposit after deducting $10 per hour for the damage repair and cleaning she performs. Unfortunately, Pam's pickiness leads her to charge for unnecessary cleaning of apartments which departing tenants left in immaculate condition. In addition, Pam is lax about returning deposits within the two weeks allowed by law. When six former tenants whose deposits Pam has pocketed sue you for return of their money and for punitive damages, you're liable.

As noted above, when you hire a manager to perform some or all your duties, you do not escape from legal responsibility to see that both California and local landlord-tenant laws are complied with. In other words, you remain responsible for your manager's failures, and even for her illegal acts, if they occurred in the course of her employment by you. This is true even if you are not at fault.

Fortunately, there is a way to protect yourself at least somewhat. You can do this by limiting the authority you delegate to your manager. If you do this in writing, you reduce (but do not eliminate) the possibility you will be liable for manager misconduct that exceeds the authority you delegated. For example, a landlord who instructs his manager in writing only to accept rental applications, but not to make the decisions on who to rent to (leaving that for the landlord), is less likely to be held liable if a manager goes ahead and rents an apartment in a discriminatory fashion.

And if you do choose to delegate certain authority to your manager, such as selecting tenants, you can also protect both yourself and the manager by supplying the manager with a list of guidelines as to how to carry out his duties legally. This not only educates the manager as to how to avoid legal trouble, but also demonstrates that you acted in good faith. As such, it can prove to be very useful should anyone sue you based on your manager's misconduct. Here's a sample set of instructions a landlord might give to a manager to whom he delegates fairly broad management authority. Obviously, if your manager is given more limited authority, your instructions should also be more limited.

MEMORANDUM

To: Manager, Shady Oak Apartments
From: Lena D. Landlady, Owner
Subject: Management Duties

Dear New Manager:

Welcome to your new position as resident manager of Shady Oak Apartments. In performing your duties under our management agreement, you are requested to keep the following in mind:

1. Discrimination in rental housing on the basis of race, religion, sex, sexual preference, marital or familial status, age, national or ethnic origin, and any other unreasonable or arbitrary basis is illegal. This is true whether you are accepting rent applications for vacant apartments or dealing with current residents. Your duties, in the event of a vacancy, are to advertise and accept rental applications in a nondiscriminatory manner. After you have collected all applications, please notify me at 555-2468 and I will arrange to sort through the applications and make the final decision as to who occupies units at Shady Oak.

2. You are not to issue any rent-increase or termination notices without my prior approval. When a tenant's rent is more than five days past due, and he or she is not withholding rent because of dissatisfaction with the apartment (e.g., the tenant has made no complaints in the previous six months), you may, without prior approval from me, serve the tenant a three-day notice to pay rent or quit, using the blank forms I have supplied you. However, if you have any reason to think that the tenant in question may assert that his or her failure to pay rent is based on the inhabitability of the premises, please contact me immediately. Do this even if you are convinced that the tenant's complaints are frivolous.

3. Treat all tenants who complain about defects, even trivial defects, or ones you believe to be nonexistent, with respect. You are to enter all tenant complaints into the log book I have supplied to you and respond to tenant complaints about the building or apartment units immediately in emergency situations, and within 24 hours in non-emergencies. If you cannot correct or arrange to correct any problem or defect yourself, please telephone me immediately.

4. Except in serious life or property threatening emergencies, do not enter a tenant's apartment without his or her consent or in his or her absence, nor permit anyone else to do so without proper notice. You may enter in the tenant's absence during ordinary business hours to effect repairs and/or maintenance, provided you have given the tenant a 24-hour notice (preferably in writing and delivered personally, but posted on the door if necessary) and the tenant hasn't objected. Please call me if you have any problem in this regard.

5. When a tenant moves in, and then again when he or she moves out, conduct an inspection of the unit. If possible, do this with the tenant. On each occasion, complete a Landlord/Tenant checklist form, having the tenant sign it if possible. In addition, if the unit appears to be dirty or damaged when the tenant leaves, take a series of polaroid pictures.

6. If you think a tenant has simply "skipped out" (abandoned the apartment), do not enter it. Telephone me first.

7. Once a tenant has vacated his or her apartment and given you the key, be sure to itemize all cleaning costs and costs necessary to repair damages in excess of ordinary wear and tear. This itemization, along with a notation of the amount of any back rent, are to be saved for me, along with the before and after Landlord/Tenant Checklist forms

and the departing tenant's forwarding address. Please make sure I see this material within a few days of the tenant moving out, and no later than a week after the tenant moves out. I will mail the itemization, along with any balance due on the tenant's security deposit, to the tenant within the required two-week period.

8. If you have any other problems or questions, please do not hesitate to call me, leaving a message on my answering machine if I am not at home.

Sincerely,

Lena D. Landlady

NOTE: One final word about your liability for your managers acts. As noted above, if you narrowly limit what your manager can and cannot do, you protect yourself to some degree from liability for your manager's illegal acts which are beyond the scope of the authority you have granted. However, it's important to realize that if your manager violates your instructions (e.g., rents a unit when you have told her not to), and commits an illegal act (e.g., discriminates against a qualified applicant), you may still be liable, because as far as the world is concerned, your manager had the apparent authority to act as she did. How can you make sure that your manager doesn't even have the apparent authority to screw up? You can't. This is where you have to rely on your landlord's insurance policy and make sure it covers the illegal acts of your employers (see Chapter 11, Section D).

E. Disclosure to Tenants

When you operate a structure of three or more rental units through a manager, California law requires you to notify your tenants in writing of the name and address of that manager. You must also notify your tenants of your own name and address, or of those of a person authorized to receive legal no-

tices on your behalf. (The tear-out lease/rental agreement form at the back of this book contains such a clause in Paragraph 20q.) This person and the manager can be the same person if you wish. Your disclosure must be available on demand to tenants renting under an oral rental agreement, and must be included in a written rental agreement or lease. It may also be posted in two conspicuous places on the property (and in every elevator, if there are any).*

---

* Civil Code Sections 1961-1962.5.

A typical disclosure, whether in a written rental agreement or posted in a conspicuous place, might look something like this:

DISCLOSURE OF MANAGER AND OWNER OF PREMISES

PLEASE TAKE NOTE that MARIA MANAGER, 1234 Market St., Apt. 1 San Jose, California, is authorized to manage the residential premises at 1234 Market Street, Apartments 1 through 4, San Jose, California. If you have any complaints about the condition of your unit or common areas, please notify Ms. Manager immediately. The above-named manager is authorized to act for and on behalf of the owner of the above-described premises for the purpose of service of process and for the purpose of receiving all notices and demands.

[OR]

LOUISE LANDLADY, 1234 Embarcadero Rd., Palo Alto, California, is the owner of the above-described premises. If you have any complaints about the condition of the unit or common areas, please notify Louise Landlady immediately.

There are no penalties for violating this law, but if you don't comply, the law deems your manager to be your agent for the purpose of service of legal notices--whether you like it or not. This means that if you are sued by a former tenant, she can serve the lawsuit papers on you by simply giving them to your manager.

EXAMPLE: Three of your tenants rented under written agreements that failed to name anyone to receive legal notices on your behalf. Three additional tenants rented units under a verbal agreement with your manager, Pam Pocketeer, who refused to disclose your name and address, which was not posted on the premises. All six tenants name you in a lawsuit based on substantial housing code violations, but serve the lawsuit papers (summons and complaint) on Pam, your agent for service of process by virtue of your noncompliance (or Pam's) with the disclosure law. Pam neither appears in court nor notifies you. All the tenants win default judgments against you because you were properly served--through your agent-- and didn't appear in court.

Obviously, this is an extreme example. Hopefully, however, it will encourage you to comply with the disclosure law.

Lawyers, Eviction Services and Mediation

A. Introduction

This book is designed to give you the basic information about California laws and legal procedures necessary to efficiently run your business. It is not designed to completely replace lawyers. Generally speaking, we believe you can deal with most routine legal services safely and efficiently without a lawyer. Just the same, there are times when good advice from someone who is thoroughly familiar with landlord-tenant law will be helpful, if not essential. And even if you are completely confident that you can handle most legal tasks yourself, you may still want to turn some of them over to a lawyer. After all, just because you know how to run a lawn mower, it doesn't mean you must always cut your own grass.

If you do need, or choose to work with, a lawyer, it obviously helps to know what you are getting yourself into. The first thing to keep in mind is this: Lawyers are in business to make money. They have to pay a lot of office overhead, as well as support themselves and their families in a style to which they are, or would like to be, accustomed. Thus, most attempt to charge fairly high fees, normally in a range of $75 to $150 an hour. Obviously, you will wish to adopt strategies designed to gain a maximum amount of quality legal services at a reasonable cost.

Okay, you're probably with us so far. But how do you minimize legal fees at the same time that you protect your legal rights? The broad answer is to adopt two, or sometimes three, strategies. First, carefully inform yourself about the laws that affect your business so that you can anticipate and avoid many legal problems. That's where this book comes in. Knowing landlord law and keeping current with it will take some time and attention to detail, but it's not really difficult.

Second, decide whether you really want to be your own lawyer most of the time, or whether you want to limit your role to being an informed consumer of legal services, by which we mean work with a lawyer but make the important decisions yourself. There is no right choice. Either can work well for you. Often landlords decide to either hire a lawyer or do most of their own legal work based on the scale of their operations and how much time they have. Obviously, if you are semi-retired and own two buildings with ten units, your decision might be much different than if you own 50 units and have a full-time job besides.

If you do decide that you want to work with a lawyer regularly, your next strategic decision is how to hire one. We discuss this in some detail in Section D of this chapter.

B. Legal Research Tools

As noted, any sensible landlord will take the time to inform himself about the laws that affect his or her business. This book is a good start, but it is not enough. You should absolutely have access to a current copy of the

California legal codes that pertain to the rights and responsibilities of landlords. These are primarily the California Civil Code and the California Code of Civil Procedure. See Section G of this chapter, "Legal Research Notes," for more detail on how to use these codes. We refer to both often, but do not have the space to reproduce all of the relevant laws. These codes are generally available in public libraries and all county law libraries, which are open to the public and paid for with your tax dollars. However, because having immediate access to the laws that affect your business is so important, we recommend that you purchase these code books. They are sold in a number of different editions by at least two publishers, and are available at any law bookstore. In addition, Nolo Press sells the least expensive paperback versions (see back of this book for order information).

If you are a landlord in a city with a rent-control ordinance, you must also have a copy of the ordinance, as well as all rules issued by the rent board having to do with rent increases, hearings, etc. And, even if you don't live in a rent-control area, you should have access to any local ordinances that affect your business. For example, if your city requires smoke alarms or dead bolt locks in all rental units, or requires that you pay interest on tenant's security deposits, you need to know about it.

C. When Do You Need a Lawyer?

In some cases, especially with tenants who won't pay their rent or move out, you may have no choice but to go to court in an eviction lawsuit. Although we show you in the second volume, the **Landlord's Law Book: Evictions,** how to do this in detail, you may wish to have a lawyer go to court for you. Or, if you start an eviction lawsuit yourself, and it becomes more than you can handle--either because the tenant contests the lawsuit and/or hires a lawyer, or for some other reason--you may want to have a lawyer take it over. If you get involved in other types of lawsuits in superior court, such as those based on claims of discrimination, or a personal injury suffered by a tenant because of what she claims was a defect on the property, it is even more likely that you will want and need a lawyer's help.

Whenever you think of using a lawyer, keep in mind this view of clients that is held by a lawyer-friend of ours: she imagines a client who has built a shack on some old railroad tracks in a high mountain valley. One day, when she puts her ear to the track, she hears a distant vibration. A few days later she can hear the sound of a train rumbling on a warm breeze that blows up the canyon, and soon the sound is distinctly audible. At this point, she can begin to see the smoke of the engine, and not much later the train is running down on her, spitting fire and belching smoke. When the thing is fifty yards away, she picks up the phone, calls her lawyer and asks her to get an injunction against the railroad company! What we mean to say is this--if you decide to use a lawyer, don't wait until it's too late.

EXAMPLE: Lorna Landlord ignores several complaints by Toni Tenant concerning a defective heater. When Toni withholds rent, Lorna first files a three-day notice demanding the entire amount of the rent, and then, when this is not forthcoming, an unlawful detainer lawsuit. Toni responds by claiming that the lawsuit is in retaliation for her legitimate complaint about the heater and that she doesn't owe the amount demanded because her apartment was uninhabitable. Lorna, suddenly concluding that she has several tick-

lish legal problems on her hands, calls a local lawyer, who she tells to get rid of Toni. Assuming Toni's original complaint was even arguably legitimate, however, Lorna has so screwed things up that it will very likely take the lawyer several months and a large chunk of cash to straighten things out. And chances are, the result, which will involve fixing the heater, cancelling the eviction suit, paying Toni's legal fees and allowing her to pay a reduced rent during the time the heater was broken, will not please Lorna. (See Chapter 10 for more on what constitutes a legal reason justifying a tenant's withholding rent for a habitability-related problem.)

There is no simple answer to the question of when you need a lawyer. This is because there are many possible areas of dispute between landlord and tenant, and many levels of landlord ability to deal with problems. Throughout this book we will point out specific instances when the advice or other services of an attorney may be useful. Here are a few general pointers:

● If the lease or written rental agreement between you and your tenant has an attorneys' fees clause, you are entitled to recover your attorneys' fees if you win a lawsuit based on the terms of that agreement. This sort of clause does not guarantee, however, that a judge will award attorneys' fees equal to the amount you end up paying your attorney, especially if your attorney charges high fees, or that you will ultimately be able to collect on the judgment from the tenant (or former tenant). Also, remember that an attorneys' fees clause in your lease or rental agreement works both ways. Even if it doesn't say so, you're liable for the tenant's attorneys' fees if you lose;*

● If your tenant either refuses to pay rent, or otherwise seriously violates the lease or rental agreement, and refuses to move, or correct the problem after you properly serve a three-day notice, or if a month-to-month tenant refuses to move after you've given her a 30-day notice, you should see a lawyer about bringing an eviction lawsuit if you don't want to do it yourself, following the instructions in Volume II, on evictions;

● If you handle an eviction lawsuit yourself, and the tenant contests it by filing papers in court, you may want to hire a lawyer to continue with it, especially if your tenant has a lawyer;

● If you are sued for a lot of money in a lawsuit that involves complicated issues, such as a tenant's allegations that you invaded her privacy, discriminated against her, or that some defect in your premises caused her injury;

● If you have any problem that you can't understand or solve by reading this book.

D. Finding a Lawyer

Finding a lawyer who charges reasonable prices and whom you feel can be trusted is not always an easy task. There is always the fear that by just picking a name out of the telephone book you may get an unsympathetic attorney, or one who will charge too

---

* Civil Code Section 1717.

much. You should realize that these are common fears and that you are not the only one who feels that hiring a lawyer is likely to be a no-win situation--the tenant cheats you if you don't get legal help and the lawyer cheats you if you do.

We believe that this sorry result is not inevitable. Just as you can competently handle much of your own legal work if you take the time to inform yourself on how to do it, there are lawyers who specialize in representing landlords, do a competent job, and charge fairly for their services.

If you don't know an attorney who can be trusted and can't get a reliable recommendation from a friend, you have a problem. While you might be lucky and randomly pick an attorney who matches your needs perfectly, you might just as easily wind up paying too much for too little.

To make your search a little easier, check with a local landlords' association to see if they can recommend someone. Some attorneys devote a large part of their practice to representing landlords. Many even charge reasonable flat fixed rates, such as $250 to $300, to prosecute and conclude eviction lawsuits, and don't charge extra if occasionally an eviction is heavily contested by a tenant. Chances are you'll be much better represented by a lawyer who specializes to some extent in landlord-tenant matters, and who appreciates the speed and attention to detail necessary to evict a non-rent-paying tenant within anything like a reasonable amount of time. Quite a few landlords have been burned by inexperienced attorneys who unwittingly treat an eviction lawsuit as just another civil case destined to languish in court for several months--all the while charging $90 an hour with no fee ceiling.

Once you get a referral to someone who sounds good, make an appointment and discuss your situation. It's always a lot better in the long run, and usually cheaper, to do this before you have an acute problem.

As you are probably painfully aware from watching all those soft-spoken actors pretending to be lovable lawyers in television commercials, lawyers can now legally advertise. Generally, however, we do not advise you to go to one of the heavily advertised legal clinics. Since you are a businessperson with a continuing need for legal help, you should be able to negotiate favorable rates and get better service from a landlord specialist who doesn't buy television time at thousands of dollars per minute.

Referral panels set up by local bar associations are also not high on our list of favorite ways to find a lawyer. Lawyers are sometimes given some minimal screening as to their expertise in landlord/tenant law before qualifying to be listed, but usually the emphasis is on the word "minimal." You may get a good referral from these panels, but all too often they are a haven for the inexperienced practitioner who doesn't have enough clients.

Instead, your best bet is to talk to other landlords in your area. Find out who they use and what it costs. then, call the various law offices that have been personally recommended. State your problem. Ask them how much it would cost for a visit. Try to talk to a lawyer personally to attempt to get an idea of how friendly and sympathetic she is to your concerns.

E. Paying a Lawyer

If you own a number of units, you will probably want to work out a continuing relationship with the lawyer. One way to accomplish this is by paying the attorney a modest yearly retainer to work with you and represent you in court as needed. Using this up-front payment approach, you can usually get a lot of service for a very reasonable rate. Another sensible approach is to negotiate a fee schedule for various kinds of routine services based on the lawyer handling all your work. As you will probably provide a fair amount of business over the years, this should be substantially below the lawyer's normal hourly rate. A third sensible approach is to routinely do the initial legal work involved in evictions and similar procedures yourself, but to be prepared to turn a case over to a lawyer if and when it becomes hotly-contested and/or complicated. After all, even if you delegate the whole job to a lawyer, she will probably have a secretary (who probably knows less than you do) accomplish most of the preliminary work. If this is your plan, you should look for a lawyer who doesn't resent your doing some of your own legal work and who won't sock you with a high hourly rate for picking up a case you began. Keep in mind that as a businessperson, you should have more than enough leverage to set up this sort of arrangement.

But what should you do if you are a very small landlord and you expect (and probably pray) that you will have little continuing need for a lawyer? What incentive does a lawyer have to represent you and charge fees you can afford when you do inevitably get into occasional legal hot water? Unfortunately, the answer is "Not much." Your best bet is to try and find a lawyer who specializes in landlord-tenant law who will charge you the same sort of prices he or she charges larger landlords. This is not impossible if a lawyer views your work as being similar to what she already does for others. And who knows, the lawyer may hope that you will expand your business and become a more profitable client in the future.

Finally, a few general hints. Lawyers whose office and lifestyles are reasonably simple are more likely to help you for less money than lawyers who feel naked unless wearing a $750 suit. You should be able to find an attorney willing to discuss your problems for $75. Beware of lawyers who advertise "free consultations." As your own business experience doubtless tells you, the world provides little or nothing of value for free. This is doubly true when it comes to buying legal help. Lawyers who will see you for nothing have every motive to think up some sort of legal action for which they can charge. If you insist on paying fairly for an attorney's time, you are far more likely to be advised that no expensive legal action is needed.

F. Non-Lawyer Eviction Service

The standardization of eviction procedures and the steady increase in lawyers' fees have given birth in recent years to a new industry known as "eviction services." These exist in most metropolitan areas. As we discuss in the second volume on evictions, filing and following through with an eviction lawsuit involves a fair amount of filling out of forms. And once the forms are filed with the court, they must then be served on the tenant--a task

that isn't always easy. For a fee that is usually much lower than what lawyers charge, eviction services prepare most of the initial paperwork, file the necessary papers in court, and have the tenant served with the summons, complaint, etc. Of course, if you read and understand the material in the second volume of the book, on evictions, you'll be able to handle all this yourself if you wish. But if you'd rather leave the initial steps in the eviction lawsuit to someone else, you may want to check with a landlords' association or look in the telephone book under "Eviction Services." Just as you would do with anyone else, be sure the eviction service is reputable and experienced, as well as reasonably priced. This means that you should ask for references and check them.

One problem, though, is that many non-lawyer eviction services are unable to do more than help people fill out legal forms and arrange for the appropriate filing and service of these forms. Should the tenant contest the eviction suit (which happens less than 10% of the time), the eviction service won't be able to help you in court, unless they have an attorney on their staff who you can retain to represent you. This, of course, will cost extra. At this point, of course, you can decide to represent yourself in court, or hire your own lawyer to take over.

G. Legal Research Notes

We don't have space here to show you how to do your own legal research in anything approaching a comprehensive fashion. **Legal Research: How To Find and Understand the Law,** by Steve Elias, is an excellent resource if you wish to learn basic legal research skills, something we highly recommend for anyone in the landlord business in the last part of the twentieth century. Our goal here is only to tell you how to find the basic laws that control your business. In addition, we show you how to locate the important judicial decisions (most of which are mentioned in this book) which interpret these laws.

Landlord/tenant laws and legal procedures are principally contained in two codifications (Codes) of California law--the Civil Code (C.C.) and the Code of Civil Procedure (C.C.P.). The Civil Code is divided into numerous sections, dealing generally with people's legal rights and responsibilities to each other. Most of California's substantive landlord-tenant law is contained in Sections 1940 through 1991 of this code. The Code of Civil Procedure is a set of laws which tell how people enforce legal rights in civil lawsuits. Eviction lawsuit procedures are contained in Sections 1161 through 1179 of the Code of Civil Procedure. Also of interest are the small claims court procedures mentioned in Sections 116 through 117.22.

Although these codes list the applicable laws passed each year by the legislature, they don't list any of the appellate court decisions which determine what those laws mean. Sometimes these case decisions are extremely important. For example, the case of **Green v. Superior Court** has interpreted Civil Code Sections 1941 through 1942 on minimum housing standards to allow tenants in substandard housing to withhold rent--without using it to make repairs themselves--even though no law specifically provides for this. (See Chapter 10, Section D.) To gain access to the printed reports of important court decisions, you have to go to a law library.

The best way to learn of the existence of written court decisions which interpret a particular law is to first look in an "annotated code." An annotated code is a set of volumes of a particular code, such as the Civil Code or Code of Civil Procedure, that contain not only all the laws (as do the regular codes), but also a brief summary of all court decisions interpreting each one. These annotated codes-- published by West Publishing Company (West's Annotated California Codes-- blue volumes) and by Bancroft-Whitney (Deerings's California Codes--brown volumes)--can be found in some public libraries and any county law library or law school library in the state. They have comprehensive indexes by topic, and are kept up to date each year with paperback supplements ("pocket parts") located in a pocket in the back cover of each volume. Don't forget to look through these pocket parts for the latest law changes or case decisions since the hardcover volume was printed.

Each brief summary of a court decision is followed by the title of the case, the year of the decision, and the "citation." The "citation" is a sort of shorthand identification for the set of books, volume, and page where the case can be found. The "official" volumes of cases are published by the California Supreme Court as the **Official Reports of the California Supreme Court** (abbreviated "Cal.," "Cal.2d," or "Cal.3d," respectively representing the first, second and third "series" of volumes, the third containing all cases decided since 1969) and by the California Courts of Appeal* as **Official Reports of the California Courts of Appeal** (similarly abbreviated "Cal.App.," "Cal.App.2d," and "Cal.App.3d"). The same cases are also reliably published in "unofficial volumes" by the West Publishing Company. These are **California Reporter** (abbreviated "Cal.Rptr.")

and **Pacific Reporter** (abbreviated "P." or "P.2d," respectively for the first and second series). The case is the same whether you read it in the "official" or "unofficial" reporter.

Here are some examples of case citations:

---

* The Courts of Appeal are California's "intermediate" level appeals courts, on a lower legal level than the California Supreme Court, but "higher" than the superior, municipal and justice courts of the counties. There are six appellate districts in the state, with courts in San Francisco, Los Angeles, Sacramento, San Diego, Fresno, and San Jose. (The California Supreme Court is headquartered in San Francisco.)

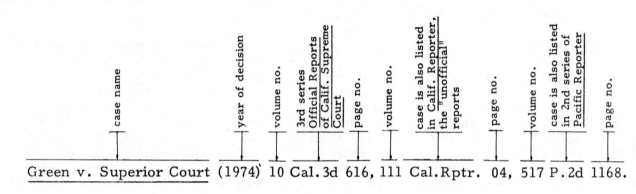

Green v. Superior Court (1974) 10 Cal.3d 616, 111 Cal.Rptr. 04, 517 P.2d 1168.

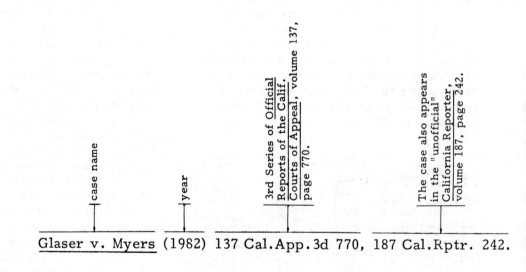

Glaser v. Myers (1982) 137 Cal.App.3d 770, 187 Cal.Rptr. 242.

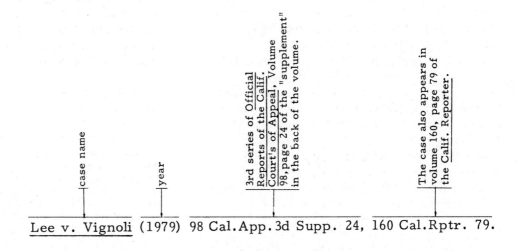

Lee v. Vignoli (1979) 98 Cal.App.3d Supp. 24, 160 Cal.Rptr. 79.

- case name
- year
- 3rd series of Official Reports of the Calif. Court's of Appeal, Volume 98, page 24 of the "supplement" in the back of the volume.
- The case also appears in volume 160, page 79 of the Calif. Reporter.

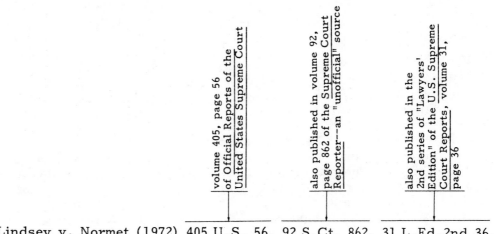

Lindsey v. Normet (1972) 405 U.S. 56, 92 S.Ct. 862, 31 L.Ed.2nd 36.

- volume 405, page 56 of Official Reports of the United States Supreme Court
- also published in volume 92, page 862 of the Supreme Court Reporter--an "unofficial" source
- also published in the 2nd series of "Lawyers' Edition" of the U.S. Supreme Court Reports, volume 31, page 36

The above examples should take some of the mystery out of legal research. If, in the course of your research, you still have questions, again we recommend Elias, **Legal Research: How To Find and Understand the Law** (Nolo Press).

H. Mediation

Mediation involves bringing in a neutral third party to help disputants settle differences. Generally, it works well in all situations where the parties want to settle their disputes in order to work together in the future. In a landlord-tenant context, mediation can be extremely helpful in a number of areas, such as disputes about noise, anti-social tenant conduct, the necessity for repairs, a tenant's decision to withhold rent because defects have not been repaired, rent increases, privacy and many more. Many large landlords, especially non-profit organizations which manage projects for low-income or elderly residents, find that an established meditation procedure is invaluable.

A mediator does not impose a decision on the parties, but uses her skills to facilitate a compromise. Mediation is most effective when procedures are established in advance. Typically, the landlord contacts some respected neutral organization, such as a city or county landlord-tenant mediation project, the American Arbitration Association, or a neighborhood dispute resolution center, such as San Francisco's Community Board Program, and arranges for this group to mediate legitimate landlord-tenant disputes, should the need arise. There are a great number of mediation programs in California, and if you ask around in your area, you should find one. The landlord then establishes a dispute resolution procedure which might work like this:

• The procedure for lodging complaints to the landlord is explained to every tenant;

• The fact that mediation is available if a dispute develops is emphasized. The tenant is told that if a dispute (whether over privacy, rent withholding because of allegedly defective conditions or whatever) escalates to the point where normal face-to-face compromise techniques prove to be of no avail, both landlord and tenant can request mediation. In this context, it's obviously important that the tenant feel the mediator is fair, so be prepared to explain any procedure you have established (and defend its fairness) in detail. If possible, it's best to split the cost of a mediation, if there is one. If this isn't acceptable to the tenant, and you decide to pay for all of it, make sure your tenant realizes that the mediator has no power to impose a decision;

• At the mediation session, each side gets to state their position. Just doing this often cools people off considerably and frequently results in a compromise. If the dispute is not taken care of easily, however, the mediator may suggest several ways to resolve the problem, or may even keep everyone talking long enough to realize that the real problem goes deeper than the one being mediated. For example, if a tenant has threatened rent withholding because of a defect in your premises, you may learn that the real problem from the tenant's point of view is that your manager is lazy and slow to make repairs. This may lead to the further discovery that the manager is angry at the tenant for letting his kids pull up his tulips and call him a "big dummy."

At any rate, mediation often works, and if it doesn't, you haven't lost much, especially if you make sure mediation occurs promptly and you limit its use to situations where tenants have some arguably legitimate complaint and are not cynically using it as an excuse to stay in your property without paying rent. If mediation fails, you can still fight it out in court.

8

Discrimination

There used to be a time when a land-lord could refuse to rent to anyone, for any reason. Similarly, a landlord could evict a month-to-month tenant on 30 days' notice because he didn't like the color of the tenant's skin, his religion, or national origin. In short, all sorts of groups, including Blacks, Asians, Jews, Hispanics, unmarried couples, families with children, women, and the disabled, were routinely subjected to discrimination. Fortunately, the days of legal discrimination are long gone. Today, there are a series of federal and California civil rights laws which provide severe financial penalties for landlords who discriminate on the basis of race, religion, sex, age and a number of other categories. And just to be sure all bases are covered, the California Supreme Court has weighed in with an opinion* which says that almost any unreasonable discrimination is illegal.

A. Forbidden Types of Discrimination

It is illegal for a landlord to refuse to rent to a tenant, or to engage in any other kind of discrimination (such as requiring more rent or larger deposits) on the basis of a

---

* Marina Point, Ltd. v. Wolfson (1982) 30 Cal.3d 72.

group characteristic, such as race or religion. It is legal to discriminate against people for reasons closely related to the landlord's legitimate business needs, as would be the case where a prospective tenant has a bad credit history or references (see Section B, below). In addition, state law, and in some cases federal law, absolutely forbid discrimination on the following grounds, regardless of a landlord's claim of a legitimate business need:

Race: This is forbidden by California's Unruh Civil Rights Act [Civil Code Sections 51-53] and Fair Employment and Housing Act [Government Code Sections 12900-12996], and by the U.S. Civil Rights Act of 1866 [42 U.S.C., Section 1982 - see **Jones v. Mayer Co.** (1968) 392 U.S. 409], and the Federal Fair Housing Act of 1968 [42 U.S.C. Sections 3601-3619];

Religion: This is forbidden by all the laws listed above, except the Civil Rights Act of 1866;

Ethnic Background and National Origin: Same as **Religion**, above;

Sex: Same as **Religion**, above;

Marital Status: Including discrimination against couples because they are unmarried. This is forbidden under California law by both the Unruh and Fair Employment and Housing Acts [see **Atkinson v. Kern County Housing Authority** (1976) 58 Cal.App.3d 89; and **Hess v. Fair Employment and Housing Comm.** (1982) 138 Cal.App.3d 232];

Age: This is forbidden by Civil Code 51.2;

Families with Children: Discrimination against families with children is forbidden by the Unruh Civil Rights Act [see Civil Code Section 51.2 and **Marina Point, Ltd. v. Wolfson** (1982) 30 Cal.3d 72], except in housing reserved exclusively for senior citizens.* In addition, San Francisco, Berkeley, Los Angeles, Santa Monica and Santa Clara County (unincorporated areas only) have local ordinances forbidding this sort of discrimination;

Physical Disability: It is illegal to refuse to rent to a person with a physical handicap on the same terms as if they were not handicapped. In addition, you must rent to an otherwise qualified blind, deaf or physically-handicapped person with a properly-trained dog, even if you otherwise ban pets. Discrimination on the basis of physical disability is forbidden by California Civil Code Section 54.1;

Sexual Orientation: This includes homosexuality. Discrimination on this basis is forbidden by the Unruh Civil Rights Act.** In addition, a number of California cities specifically ban discrimination for this reason;

Smoking: Discrimination against smokers has not been tested in California courts. It may be illegal;

Animals: It is legal to refuse to rent to people with pets, except for properly-trained dogs for the blind, deaf, and physically handicapped;

Public Assistance: Discrimination against people on public assistance is

---

* Civil Code Section 51.3 defines senior-citizen housing as that reserved for persons 62 years of age of older, or a complex of 150 or more units (35 in non-metropolitan areas) for persons older than 55 years.
** See **Hubert v. Williams** (1982) 133 Cal.App.3d Supp.1.

forbidden by the Unruh Civil Rights Act [see 59 Ops.Cal.Atty.Gen. 223 (1976)];

Other Lawful Discrimination: After reading the above list outlining the types of discrimination forbidden by California and federal law, you may assume that it is legal to discriminate for other reasons--say because a person owns a computer. Or, because none of the civil rights laws specifically prohibit discrimination against men with beards or long hair, you might conclude that such discrimination is permissible. This is not true. Although federal civil rights laws have

generally been interpreted by the courts to prohibit only those types of discrimination specifically covered by their terms (i.e., discrimination based on "race, color, religion, national origin, or sex"), California's Unruh Civil Rights Act has been construed by various appellate courts to forbid **all** forms of "arbitrary" discrimination which bears no relationship to a landlord's legitimate business concerns. So, even though the Unruh Act contains only the words "sex, race, color, religion, ancestry, or national origin" to describe types of discrimination that are illegal, the courts have ruled that these categories are just examples of types of arbitrary and illegal discrimination. On this basis, the California

Supreme Court has ruled that landlords can't discriminate against families with children, and has stated that discrimination against other groups, such as "Republicans, students, welfare recipients," or "entire occupations or avocations, e.g., sailors or motorcyclists"* is also illegal. Similarly, if you refuse to rent to a person because you don't approve of unmarried people living together, you are guilty of unlawful discrimination.

Although the most common forms of illegal discrimination in rental housing consists of refusing to rent to prospective tenants for an arbitrary reason, or offering to rent to one person on tougher terms than are offered to others with no good reason for making the distinction, these aren't the only ways a landlord can be legally liable for unlawful discrimination. A landlord's termination, or attempt to terminate a tenancy, for a discriminatory reason, or discrimination in providing services, such as the use of pool or meeting-room facilities or other common areas, is illegal and can provide the discriminated-against tenant with a defense to an eviction lawsuit as well as a basis for suing the landlord for damages (see Section C, below).

EXAMPLE 1: Osgood Owner rents apartments in his six-unit apartment building without regard to racial or other unlawful criteria. His tenants include a Black family and a single Latina woman with children. When Leo Lessor buys the building from Osgood, he immediately gives only these two tenants 30-day notices. Unless Leo can come up with a valid non-discriminatory reason for evicting these tenants, they can defend an eviction lawsuit Leo brings on the basis of unlawful discrimination. The tenants can also sue Leo for damages in state or federal court.

---

* See Marina Point, Ltd. v. Wolfson (1982) 30 Cal.3d 72, 180 Cal.Rptr. 496.

EXAMPLE 2: Now, let's assume that Leo, having lost both the eviction lawsuits and the tenants' suits for damages against him, still tries to discriminate by adopting a less blatant strategy. One way he does this is by adopting an inconsistent policy of responding to late rent payments. When his caucasian tenants without children are late with the rent, he doesn't give them a three-day notice to pay rent or quit until after a five-day "grace period," while non-white tenants receive their three-day notices the day after the rent is due. In addition, when non-white tenants request repairs or raise other issues about the condition of the premises, the speed of Leo's response mimics a turtle's walk after waking from a snooze in the sun. These more subtle (or not so subtle, depending on the situation) means of discrimination are obviously also illegal, and Leo's tenants have grounds to sue him, as well as to defend any eviction lawsuit Leo brings against them.

B. Legal Reasons to Discriminate

The fact that all forms of arbitrary discrimination in rental housing are illegal does not mean that you are required to rent to people who have bad credit references or a history of failure to pay rent or other bills, or who are noisy, obnoxious, or who would otherwise be terrible tenants. Refusing to rent to prospective tenants with bad credit histories, or even to those with an income you honestly feel is insufficient to afford the rent you charge, is perfectly legal. Why? Because these reasons for tenant selection are reasonably related to your legitimate business interests. And, if a person from a minority group also happens to fit one or more obvious "bad

tenant risk" criteria, you are on safe legal ground as long as you can legitimately document your legal reasons for not renting. Other legitimate reasons for refusing to rent to a person would include a criminal record for a violence-related act and a person who wants to run a business from their home, whether it be typesetting or prostitution.

But pay attention to the fact that judges, tenants' lawyers, and fair housing groups are well aware of the fact that some landlords try to make up legal reasons to discriminate, when the real reason is that they just don't like people with a particular racial or religious background. So, if you refuse to rent to a Black, a gay person, a woman, or a family with children, or someone who speaks only Spanish, but you have a legitimate business reason for doing so (such as bad credit references or a history of eviction for nonpayment of rent), be sure you document your reason.

1. Credit and Income Criteria

The most obvious examples of legitimate business reasons for refusing to rent to a particular prospective tenant include those related to the tenant's past history of nonpayment of rent, or to his ability to pay rent in the future. Many landlords routinely have a credit-reporting agency run a check on a prospective tenant's credit history. Assuming this is your practice, the best way to protect yourself against an accusation that you're using a bad credit history as an excuse to illegally discriminate against certain prospective tenants is to do a credit check on every prospective tenant and to make your selection based on the results of that credit check. In this regard, some landlords use a point system, giving each prospective tenant a certain number of points at the outset, with deductions for bad credit and other references and extra points added for extremely good ones. Points are also awarded based on length of employment, amount of monthly income, etc. They then rent to the person with the highest score.

One landlord we know uses the following system: For each year a tenant has rented from the same previous landlord, he awards one point, up to a maximum of three. He does the same for each year the tenant has worked for his employer. He then adds one point for each $100 of the tenant's monthly income above $1,200 (0 points for $1,200, 1 point for $1,300, etc.) Finally, he gets a credit report from a local credit-reporting agency, and based on his somewhat subjective impression of whether this report is "poor," "fair," "good," or "excellent," he gives 0, 1, 2, or 3 points.

Many landlords also have a rule that they won't rent to a tenant evicted by a previous landlord for nonpayment of rent. This is sensible. However, if you have such a rule, be sure you apply it to all tenants, and that your decision not to rent to someone for that reason is based on reliable information.

A few final words about credit checks. Make sure you don't discriminate against married couples by counting only the husband's income.* This long-practiced form of discrimination, though disappearing, still can be found among people who haven't realized that

* Civil Code Section 1812.30.

married women today seldom permanently leave the labor force after bearing children. Also, be sure to treat unmarried couples the same as married couples. This means that when a working couple, married or not, applies to rent, always consider both persons' incomes.

State and federal laws prohibiting discrimination against women do allow you to consider one spouse's income alone if only that spouse signs the credit agreement, contract, lease, etc. By now you should realize it's in your best interest to have both spouses or mates sign your lease or rental agreement. This way, if you have to bring an eviction suit for nonpayment of rent, you can get a judgment for rent against both, which means you can try to collect from two people rather than just one.** (See Chapter 9.) Assuming, then, that you insist that both spouses or unmarried persons sign the lease or rental agreement, you should consider the combined income of both persons living together as a couple, married or unmarried, in order to avoid the accusation of marital status or sex discrimination.

A few landlords apply a fixed-income standard to prospective tenants by requiring that their income be three or four times the monthly rent. This

** The law does allow a provider of a "necessity of life" (such as housing), in collecting a judgment against a married individual, to look to the community property of both spouses, or even the separate property of the non-signing spouse. Civil Code Sections 5120.110 and 5120.140. Still, it's easier to collect, and to avoid complex post-judgment proceedings, by getting a judgment against both spouses based on their both having signed the lease or rental agreement.

practice is legal. A person who must spend more than about 40% of her income for rent each month is much more likely to fail to meet this obligation than is a person whose income is large enough that they only spend 20% of it on rent.

EXAMPLE: Loni Landlord rents her one-bedroom apartments for $500 a month. Based on her experience that a person with a low income will have trouble meeting her rent payments, Loni requires that a person renting these apartments have a gross monthly income equal to four times the rent, or $2,000.* Loni also applies the same income criteria to her two-bedroom apartments, which rent for $600. This means that Tina Tenant, who earns $1,200 each month, and her husband Tom, who earns $800, qualify for the one-bedroom apartment because their combined monthly income of $2,000 equals four times the rent.

WARNING: If you do use income criteria to choose your tenants, be certain that you apply the same standard to all prospective tenants without exception. And, keep your paperwork on prospective tenants you have rejected and accepted.

2. Families with Children and "Overcrowding"

The fact that discrimination against families with children is illegal does not mean you have to rent your one-bedroom apartment to a family of five. In other words, it is legal to establish reasonable space-to-people ratios. It is not legal to use "overcrowding" as a euphemism justifying discrimination because a family has children if

you would rent to the same number of adults.

A few landlords, realizing they are no longer able to enforce a blanket policy of excluding children, have now adopted criteria that for all practical purposes forbid children under the guise of preventing "overcrowding." These include allowing only one person per bedroom, with a married or living-together couple counting as one person. This rule would allow renting a 2-bedroom unit to a husband and wife and their one child, but would allow a landlord to exclude a family with two children. The courts are beginning to make this practice illegal where the effect of its use is to keep all (or most) children out of a landlord's property.**

Until the courts spell out just what type of overcrowding standards a landlord can legitimately apply, we suggest you apply a fairly liberal rule towards children rule, so as to avoid any possible legal trouble. One criteria is the Uniform Housing Code, which has been adopted by most cities. Because the code allows a fair amount of crowding and makes only extreme overcrowding illegal, basing your occupancy policy

---

* This is legal despite the fact that it is illegal to discriminate against people who receive public assistance. The point of this prohibition against discrimination is only that, if you set your income criteria at a level that people on public assistance can meet, you must consider them equally.

** One court has already ruled against a landlord who did not permit more than four persons to occupy three-bedroom apartments, **Zakaria & Lincoln Property Co.**, (1986) ___ Cal.App. ___, 229 Cal. Rptr. 669. In Smith v. Ring Brothers Management Corp. (1986) ___ Cal.App. 3rd ___, 228 C.R. 525, another court held that a rule precluding a two-child family from occupying a two-bedroom apartment violated a local ordinance similar to state law.

on it should pretty well guarantee that you have a good defense to any claim that you discriminate against children.

The Uniform Housing Code (Section 503(b)) states that a unit is considered overcrowded if any bedroom has an area of less than 70 square feet for one or two occupants, plus 50 additional square feet for each additional occupant. When you think about it, this means that bedrooms can be fairly crowded. Many landlords may conclude that the code in fact allows too much crowding, and will want to adopt a somewhat stricter standard. Although it's impossible to be sure, we suspect that requiring somewhat more space per tenant will stand up should it be challenged in court. For example, if you require a sleeping area of 90 square feet for the first two occupants and 70 square feet for any additional occupant in the same bedroom; or you restrict occupancy of studio apartments to one person, one-bedroom apartments to two people and two-bedroom apartments to four people, no matter what the square-foot-to-people ratio, you would probably be on safe legal ground; but we can't, of course, guarantee it.

EXAMPLE 1: A single woman and her five-year-old son apply to rent your studio apartment, which has a

sleeping area of about 10' x 14,' for total sleeping area of 140 square feet, more than enough to accommodate the mother and son in the first 70 square feet. This occupancy would be legal under the Uniform Building Code, so your refusal to rent on the basis of overcrowding might arguably leave you open to a charge of discrimination. However, this is a situation where you can probably keep out the child legally if you have a firm policy of only allowing one person to rent your studio apartment.

EXAMPLE 2: A married couple and their three children seek to rent your small house. You have a policy of requiring 90 square feet sleeping space for a couple and 70 square feet for any additional person in the same bedroom. The house has two bedrooms, one measuring 12' x 14' (168 square feet), and a smaller one measuring 10' x 10' (100 square feet). Under even your more strict standards, three persons (the couple and one child) could share the larger bedroom, with 90 square feet required for the couple and 70 more, for a total of 160 square feet, for the child. The other two children could share the 10' x 10' bedroom, since its 100 square feet accommodate two people. Therefore, you probably cannot legally claim overcrowding as an excuse not to rent to them. However, if there were only two small bedrooms, overcrowding would be a legitimate criterion for refusing to rent. If this is your situation, it is not legal for you to inquire as to the age and sex difference of the two children who will be sharing the same bedroom. This is their parents' business, not yours.

EXAMPLE 3: A couple with one child applies to rent your apartment containing one small 10' x 10' bedroom (100 square feet). As the Uniform Housing Code requires 70 square feet for the first two persons and 50 more square feet for the child, for a total of 120 square feet, you can legitimately refuse to rent to them, particularly if your locality has adopted the Uniform Housing Code. You can claim that if you did rent the unit to three people, the city might prosecute you for permitting overcrowding. Again, you could probably legally set your crowding standards somewhat higher than the UHC, as long as they are reasonable and consistently applied.

Maintaining a consistent policy in this area is extremely important should you ever be faced with legal action on the basis of over-crowding. If you allow three adults to live in a two-bedroom apartment, you better let a couple with a child live in the same type of unit or you can obviously face a charge that you are illegally discriminating.

NOTE ON AFTERBORN CHILDREN: Often a child will be born after your tenants have already resided on your property for some time. Are you entitled to evict them if the birth of the new child would result in an overcrowded situation? Legally, yes, if your lease or rental agreement reasonably provides that your property can only be occupied by a set number of people, and the baby is one too many. (We discuss how to do this in Chapter 2.) However, you should realize that, psychologically, people who are expecting a child are extremely protective (sometimes paranoid) about their new family and are likely to be upset if you ask them to move. This will probably lead to them closely scrutinizing your rental policies vis-a-vis families with children. Make sure that your rental policy can bear this scrutiny. Specifically, this means that:

1. You do allow children in all units where there is enough room for them;

2. The unit in question would be clearly overcrowded by the addition of another child. If the new situation does not create a clear case of overcrowding, you are probably better off letting the family stay to avoid the possibility of lawsuit.

You are within your rights to insist on a reasonable increase in the rent after the child is born, however, if your lease or rental agreement specifically limits occupancy to a defined number of people.* On the other hand, if you lease to "Philip and Madelaine Saroykin and Family" or "The Saroykin Family" or "Philip and Madelaine Saroykin and their minor children," you are stuck with the existing rent until the lease runs out. Or, if you rent under a month-to-month tenancy, until you send a 30-day notice increasing the rent. If you do increase the rent, however, make sure your increase is reasonable. Should you double a tenant's rent when a child is born, you are almost sure to be charged with discrimination against children.

C. Legal Remedies for Discrimination

Because of the number of different laws forbidding and punishing discrimination, a tenant or prospective tenant who believes a landlord has unlawfully discriminated against her can seek redress in several different ways. It's important that you, too, know how this works.

Because discrimination on the basis of race, sex, religion, or national origin is prohibited by both state and federal laws, a tenant who feels she has been discriminated against on one

---

* Cities covered by rent control handle the questions of whether rent can be raised if a child is born differently. Check locally.

of these grounds may take her complaint to federal court, state court (including small claims court), the Federal Department of Housing and Urban Development (HUD), or the California Department of Fair Employment and Housing (FEHA). Commonly, the federal courts require the tenant to have filed a complaint with the Department of Housing and Urban Development first. Similarly, HUD usually, but not always, requires that a complaint have been made with the state agency first. As these procedures are obviously tenant remedies, we do not go into detail here. If you wish to know more, contact the HUD or FEHA. Discrimination on other grounds, such as marital or family status, disability, or sexual orientation, can generally be taken only to the state court or to California's Department of Fair Employment and Housing.

If they find that discrimination has taken place, state and federal courts have the power to order a landlord to rent a particular piece of property to the discriminated-against person. In addition, the court can award damages to compensate the tenant for humiliation, emotional distress, embarrassment, etc., and can also award punitive damages and attorneys' fees. Under the Federal Fair Housing Act, which covers discrimination based on sex, race, religion, and national or ethnic origin, punitive damages are limited to $1,000. For racial discrimination, however, higher punitive damages are allowed under the Civil Rights Act of 1866.* Under Cali-

---

* Morales v. Haines (7th Circ., 1973); Lee v. Southern Home Sites Corp. (5th Circ., 1970) 429 F.2d 290.

fornia's Unruh Civil Rights Act, triple actual damages may be awarded for a violation of discrimination laws, and at least $250 must be awarded. Small claims courts can award damages of up to their maximum jurisdictional amounts of $1,500. For more information on small claims courts, see Everybody's Guide to Small Claims Court, by Ralph Warner (Nolo Press).

The California Department of Fair Employment and Housing can also order a landlord to rent a particular unit to a certain tenant, as can HUD, but its power to award monetary damages is limited to $1,000. With the exception of a suit brought in small claims court, you should see an attorney if a tenant sues you or files an administrative complaint against you for discrimination. Showing you how to defend a housing discrimination lawsuit is beyond the scope of this book.

D. Landlord-Occupied Premises

Although this book is intended primarily for landlords who rent entire apartments or homes exclusively for occupancy by their tenants, a few words should be said about situations where an owner rents (or a tenant sublets) part of a house or apartment in which he or she resides, sharing common kitchen and bathroom facilities. You've undoubtedly seen roommate or house-sharing ads containing all sorts of restrictions, like, "Young, female, non-smoking vegetarian who reads Asimov, wanted to share house," etc. Is this legal? Yes, because the California and federal civil rights laws apply only to housing rental operations that are considered to be a "business." Although the renting of a single apartment or house (or even one half of an owner-occupied duplex*) constitutes the operation of a "business" to which these laws apply, renting out a **portion** of a dwelling in which the owner (or a tenant seeking a roommate) continues to reside normally does not. Or, in other words, an owner (or tenant) occupant who will be sharing common kitchen or bathroom facilities with the tenant (sub-tenant) may, if he or she wishes, discriminate arbitrarily in renting a portion of the property, without violating any civil rights laws. One exception, however, is where the owner-occupant (or tenant) rents **two** rooms or portions of a dwelling (such as in a single-family house with three or more bedrooms). In this situation, California's civil rights laws do apply to make discrimination illegal,**although we haven't heard of any lawsuits challenging people's rights to choose only non-smoker, vegetarian, single mothers or some other narrowly-restricted group in this situation. Obviously, if a landlord in this situation discriminates on the basis of race or religion, there could well be cause for legal action.

E. Managers and Discrimination

If you hire a manager to manage all or part of your rental property for you, particularly if the manager selects tenants, make certain that she fully understands that any sort of arbitrary housing discrimination is illegal and will subject her and you to

the possibility of a lawsuit or an administrative complaint by the tenant or prospective tenant, or even by a local fair-housing group or district attorney. (See Chapter 6, Section D on landlord liability for a manager's conduct.) Unfortunately, however, even properly instructing and warning your manager about illegal discrimination will not necessarily protect you if she violates the law. In short, it's up to you to take precautions to ensure that your manager doesn't discriminate.

One way to do this is to prepare a written policy statement as to the law and your intention to abide by it. Require that your manager post this in the building office if there is one and give it to all prospective tenants. It might look like this:

FROM: Shady Dell Apartments

TO: All Tenants and Applicants

It is the policy of the owner and manager of Shady Dell Apartments to provide equal opportunity in housing. We comply with all federal, state and local laws prohibiting discrimination. In short, we rent our units without regard to a tenant's race, ethnic background, sex, religion, marital or family status, physical disability, or sexual orientation. If you have any questions or complaints regarding our rental policy, the following agencies will provide you with information on fair-housing laws:

| California Dept. of Fair Employment and Housing | U.S. Dept. of Housing & Urban Development |

[FILL IN ADDRESS AND PHONE NUMBER OF OFFICE NEAREST YOU]

If despite the preparation of an equal opportunity statement and your own honest determination not to discriminate you think your manager may

---

* An owner-occupant of a duplex or triplex, etc. is governed by civil rights laws in the renting of the other unit(s) in the building, even though he or she lives in one of the other units, because that person is renting out property for use as a separate household, where kitchen or bathroom facilities aren't shared with the tenant. See **Swann v. Burkett** (1962) 209 Cal.App.2d 686 and 58 Ops. Cal.Atty.Gen. 608 (1975).
** Government Code Section 12927(c).

use unlawful discriminatory practices to select tenants, you should immediately resume control of tenant selection yourself. Remember, if there is trouble, you will end up paying for it. If you aren't sure what your manager is doing, you might even wish to do some investigating. When you have a vacancy, have someone you suspect the manager might discriminate against apply for a vacancy. How does your manager treat them? Would you want to defend a lawsuit brought by the prospective tenant?

INSURANCE NOTE: Your landlords' policy will protect you for suits based on claims of illegal discrimination only if it covers illegal acts by you and your employees beyond the standard fire and personal liability protections.*

---

* Even then, there's some uncertainty over whether the law requires insurance companies to cover you for your own intentional acts. In other words, if you set out to intentionally discriminate and someone you illegally discriminate against successfully sues you, your insurance company may resist paying the judgment.

9

Sub-Tenants, Co-Tenants, Roommates, Live-Ins and Guests

A. Introduction

When you rent a small apartment or a house to a single tenant, there's no question about who is responsible for paying the rent--it is the person whose name is at the bottom of the lease or rental agreement. If you rent a larger place to two, three or more people, and all of them sign the rental contract, it is still fairly easy to understand the legal rules involved (see Section B of this chapter). But what happens if after you rent, other people move in and do not sign the lease or rental agreement? And, what, if any, are your rights and duties vis-a-vis the friends, lovers and family of your tenants? The answers to those questions can vary from the unclear to the just plain hopeless, unless you estab-lish clear rules before this sort of problem arises and stick to them.

The way to do this is simple. Include a clause in all your leases or written rental agreements to accomplish the following four things:

1. Establish the number of people who can live in the property;

2. Establish that the person (or people) whose names appear on the lease or rental agreement, along with their minor children, are the only ones who can live there;

3. Require that any sub-lease, assignment of the lease or rental agreement, or the right for any additional people living in the unit, requires your written consent in advance;

4. Limit the right of tenants to stay in a unit without your consent. One good way to do this is to include a clause in your lease or rental agreement saying that no visitor can stay overnight more than 10 (or 14, 21, or 28) days in any six-month period.

B. Tenants and Co-Tenants

A tenant is usually a person who rents from a landlord under a written or oral lease or rental agreement. In some situations, which we will discuss later in this chapter, people who move into your property with no contract with you, but pay rent, gain the status of tenants. Assuming you follow our advice and use a written lease or agreement, a tenant is normally the person whose signature is on the bottom line of one of these agreements, next to yours. We don't even discuss your situation here if you rent under an oral agreement, except to reiterate that your legal position is so compromised from the beginning by the failure to have any written requirement governing who can live in the property, that no advice we can give will be of much help.

When two or more people rent property together, and all sign the agreement or lease, they are co-tenants. Co-tenants each have the following obligations:

● Unless you agree otherwise, each co-tenant is responsible to you for performing all the obligations under the lease or rental agreement, including paying all of the rent, regardless of what they agree among themselves. For example, if Laura Landperson rents to two roommates (Ted and Carol), who both sign the rental agreement and agree between themselves to split the rent, they are each responsible to pay Laura the entire rent amount. If one

doesn't pay her half, the other must make up the difference, unless Laura has agreed otherwise in the lease or rental agreement, or she specifically rents different parts of the premises to each tenant under separate rental agreements. And, if Laura doesn't receive all the rent (this may require one tenant to cover the other's share), she has the right to file an unlawful detainer (eviction) lawsuit against both, even if one person paid what they believed was their half.

● Both Ted and Carol are likewise independently liable to Laura for all damage to the property (except ordinary wear and tear). Just as it legally makes no difference who failed to pay the rent, it makes no legal difference to the landlord who (or whose friends) caused the damage.

Let's look at several common situations.

EXAMPLE 1: Ted and Carol both sign a written rental agreement providing for a total monthly rent of $800. They agree between themselves to each pay one-half. After three months, Ted refuses to pay his half of the rent (or simply moves out without notice to landlord Laura or roommate Carol). As one of two co-tenants, Carol is legally obligated to pay all the rent. Ted, as the other co-tenant, is equally liable, but if he is unreachable, or out of work, Laura can properly sue Carol for the whole amount. Since she and Ted rented under a month-to-month written rental agreement, Carol can cut her losses to one month's rent by giving Laura a 30-day written notice of intention to move. (Ted could also have cut off his liability for future rent this way.) Carol can do this even if Ted is lying around the place refusing to pay or get out. We discuss the details of tenancy termination in Chapter 17.

EXAMPLE 2: Assume the same fact situation as in Example 1, except that this time there is a lease for one year. Both co-tenants are independently liable for the whole rent for twelve months. If one refuses to pay, the other is still liable, unless a third person can be found to take over the lease. If the lease forbids subletting or assignment, Laura's consent to this is required, but if she unreasonably refuses, she may be seen as failing to mitigate damages and this will probably cut off her right to recover the rest of the rent due under the lease. We discuss this aspect of sublets, assignments and mitigation of damages in detail in Chapter 17.

C. Sub-Tenants

In the simplest sense, a sub-tenant is a person to whom a tenant rents all or part of the property. This can occur where the tenant moves out temporarily (e.g., for a couple of months in the summer) and rents the entire dwelling to someone else, or where she rents one or more rooms while continuing to live there. Typically, a sub-tenant does not have a separate agreement with the landlord. Their right of occupancy depends on:

● The continuing existence of the tenancy between the landlord and the tenant; and

● Whatever implied, oral or written rental agreement the sub-tenant has with the tenant, who functions as the sub-tenant's landlord.

In one word, a landlord who allows a tenant to rent to a sub-tenant without his consent is foolish. This is because the sub-tenant is not liable to the landlord for the rent because there's no agreement between the landlord and the sub-tenant. Instead, the sub-tenant is supposed to pay the tenant/sub-lessor the rent under whatever agreement they have, and the tenant, in turn, is supposed to pay the landlord. The law does allow the landlord to terminate the tenancy of the main tenant if the rent isn't paid, or the lease or rental agreement is otherwise broken, and subsequently to evict the sub-tenant, as his or her right to stay depends directly on the existence of the tenant's right to stay.* Even this isn't easy, as the landlord must sue and serve separate papers on both the tenant and the sub-tenant, if any (see Chapter 15 and Volume II on evictions). At the very least, this requirement means that a landlord who allows subletting should know the names of any sub-tenants.

---

* As we will discuss further in Volume II on evictions, the landlord's unlawful detainer lawsuit must name the tenant, sub-tenant and any other adult occupant of the property. Arieta v. Mahon (1982) 31 Cal.3d 381.

By this time you should be getting a pretty good idea of why allowing sub-tenants is unwise. Because a sub-tenant is liable under the lease or rental agreement only to the tenant, and not to the landlord, the landlord gains nothing by the presence of the sub-tenant. At the same time, the landlord is stuck with someone the tenant selected, and who, if an eviction is ever necessary, the landlord must sue, serve papers on and get a judgment against. Obviously, it is better to have your property occupied by people who you or your manager have screened, and who are directly liable to you under a written agreement. To be sure this occurs, you should provide in your leases or rental agreements that subletting part or all of the premises is forbidden without the land-lord's consent.* Most printed rental agreements and lease forms, including the ones at the back of this book, contain this provision. If, despite this clause, the tenant goes ahead and sublets anyway, you now have grounds for eviction (see Volume II, on evictions), provided you act promptly.

You should also think about the problems which can develop if a tenant

---

* This consent cannot be unreasonably withheld if you wish to try and collect damages against a tenant with a lease/rental agreement who leaves early. See Chapter 17.

sublets part of the property by taking in a roommate. You can control this if your lease or written rental agreement limits occupancy of the dwelling to a specific number of people. This gives you a legal ground to object to the new person if you wish. We discuss this in detail in Section D, just below.

Suppose that a good tenant who has been with you for years wants to sublet a unit for six months while she is out of the area. Or, imagine that for some other sensible reason, a tenant you like comes to you and asks your permission to sublet. As long as you have a provision in your lease or rental agreement which says that the tenant can't sublet without your permission, you are in control of the situation.

Assuming you wish to accommodate the tenant, and you approve of the proposed sub-tenant, your best bet is usually to directly lease the unit to the new person for the period that the original tenant plans to be away. Then, when the first tenant returns and the second leaves, you can again rent to the first. Obviously, if you don't like the sub-tenant, or have some other problem with the arrangement, simply refuse to agree.

What happens if the original tenant becomes uneasy about your plan to rent to the sub-tenant directly rather than letting him do it? He may ask you how he will get the unit back if the new tenant is reluctant to leave when he returns. As long as your lease or rental agreement contains a prohibition against subletting, your answer should be a very polite version of, "That's your problem." Think of it this way. By asking you the question, your tenant admits that he doesn't completely trust the new tenant, even though he selected him. This is not a situation where you want to be in the middle. It's far better that the original tenant bear the brunt of any problem--if there is one--than you.

SPECIAL NOTE ON SAN FRAN-
CISCO'S MASTER TENANT CONCEPT:
San Francisco has a somewhat bizarre
ordinance recognizing the concept of a
"master tenant" in shared housing situations. A master tenant (or tenants)
is the person who signs the lease with
the landlord and is responsible to her.
That tenant then has the legal authority to rent to others. Oddly, the
master tenant can charge the other
tenant more rent than he himself pays
(up to the rent control level) and can
evict them whenever he pleases, with no
need to demonstrate "just cause" for
eviction under the city rent control
ordinance. We do not believe that it's
wise for a San Francisco landlord to
get into a "master tenant/sub-tenant"
situation, at least in part because the
law in this area is complicated by
conflicting rent board rules. Your
best bet is to follow the general advice set out in this chapter. Insist
that all co-tenants sign a lease or
rental agreement with you, and if one
or more leaves, deal directly with
their replacements.

D. Roommates

Suppose love (or loneliness) strikes
your tenant and she proposes to move in
a roommate? Assuming your lease or
rental agreement restricts the number
of people who can occupy the unit,
unless you give written permission for
additional tenants, you can decide
whether to say "Yes" or "No." Obviously, you should make your decision based
on whether you believe the new person
will be a decent tenant. Assuming the
person the tenant proposes to move in
has a good credit record and isn't
otherwise objectionable, and there is
enough space in your unit, you may want
to say "Yes." If you do, we recommend
that you insist that the new tenant
become a full co-tenant instead of
allowing the original tenant to sublet.

You do this by preparing a new lease or
rental agreement for signature by both
(or all) tenants. If you don't insist
on doing this as soon as you learn of
the new occupant, you may inadvertently
give up your right to object (especially if you accept rent from this person), no matter what kind of clause is
contained in your written agreement.

What about charging more rent if a
roommate moves in? It is perfectly
reasonable for you to raise the rent
(or the security deposit) if another
person is going to live in your property, unless this is prohibited under
local rent control laws. Obviously,
more people living in a residence means
more wear and tear on carpets, drapes,
walls, and so forth, and higher maintenance costs in the long run. Also, a
rent increase at the time when an additional tenant moves in should cause
little hardship to the current occu-
pant(s), who will now have someone else
to pay part of the rent. But any higher rent charged because of an extra
person moving in later shouldn't be out
of line with rents for comparable units
occupied by the same number of persons.

But what if the existing tenant has
a lease, with a fixed rent, that
doesn't expire for some time? As long
as the lease is based on a set number
of tenants and it requires the tenant
to get your permission for more to move
in, you are within your legal rights to
withhold permission until the lease is

changed to provide a reasonable rent increase in exchange for permission to have another person occupying the premises.*

Now, let's assume your tenant simply moves a roommate in on the sly, despite the fact that your lease or rental agreement prohibits this. Since this constitutes a breach of your agreement, you may want to use it as grounds to end a lease or a written rental agreement. If the tenant is obnoxious, this may be a good chance to end a long term lease. Of course, if your tenant has a month-to-month tenancy in an area where there is no rent control, and the rent is not part of a federal housing program, you can always give the tenant a 30-day notice to leave, without the legal requirement of establishing any reason. We discuss terminations of tenancy in Chapter 17. If you live in a rent control area requiring just cause for eviction, see Chapter 4. Generally, moving in an illegal tenant should qualify as "just cause" to get rid of the tenant under most rent control ordinances, because it is a significant violation of the terms of the tenancy. However, you can't evict a tenant until you first give him notice of the problem (i.e., the additional tenant) and a chance to cure it (i.e., get that person to leave).

But now, let's go back to our example of Laura the landlord and her tenants, Carol and Ted, which we discussed in Section B of this chapter, above. Now, suppose Ted originally rented the apartment and Carol moved in later. For some reason, Laura the landlord tacitly accepted the situation (maybe she was mesmerized by young love). What is the relationship between Carol, Ted and Laura? Is Carol obligated to pay rent to Laura if Ted fails to pay?

What if Ted moves out, but Carol wants to remain? If Ted ruins the paint or breaks the furniture, does Carol have any obligation to pay Laura for the damage?

The answer to these questions is that Carol starts with no legal rights or obligations to Laura (although she possibly has obligations to Ted, as his sub-tenant, depending on their agreement) regarding the rent, or the right to live in the apartment. She has entered into no contract with Laura.** Ted is completely liable for 100% of the rent and also for all damage to the premises, whether caused by Carol or himself, because he has entered into either a lease or written rental agreement with Laura.

In this situation, if Ted leaves almost immediately after Carol moves in, Carol has no right to take over the lease without Laura's consent. However, if Ted stays and Carol shares the unit for any considerable period of time, pays rent, and otherwise acts like a tenant, she gains a tenant's legal protections. Thus, if Ted leaves at this point and Laura wants to get rid of Carol, she would have to bring a formal eviction action.

To avoid the possibility of a legally confused situation, Laura should take some decisive action as soon as she realizes that Carol is more than a

---

* In addition, if the property is subject to strict or moderate rent control (see Chapter 4, Part C), you may have to petition the rent-control board for permission to increase the rent based on an increased number of occupants.

** Of course, if she damages the property, she is liable just as a visitor, a trespasser, or a thief who causes damage would be liable.

casual visitor.* If Carol seems like a suitable tenant, Laura should invoke the clause in the lease or rental agreement restricting occupancy to one person, Ted, and require that both Carol and Ted enter into a new lease or rental agreement. The point of Laura doing this is to obligate Carol directly to her. Again, assuming the lease or rental agreement is properly drafted in the first place to establish the number of people allowed to live in the unit and to require the landlord's approval of any additional tenants and long-term visitors, Laura may want to ask for an increase in the rent as a condition allowing Carol to live on the premises.

Should Laura fail to make Carol a full-fledged tenant and the situation arise that Ted wants to move out and Carol remain, it is crucial that the legal relationship between Carol, Ted and Laura be clarified. This could be done as follows:

Laura and Ted: Laura should first insist that Ted give her a written notice of what he intends to do at least 30 days before he leaves. If he does this, he is off the hook completely in a written rental agreement situation. Even if a lease is involved and Ted is leaving before it runs out, he is very likely free of his responsibility to pay rent, because Laura has a legal duty to take steps to limit her loss as much as possible, i.e., to mitigate damages (see Chapter 17). This means looking for a new tenant to pay the rent. As long as Carol is a reasonably solvent and non-destructive person, Laura would suffer no loss by

accepting Carol as a tenant to fill out the rest of the term of Ted's lease. And, if Laura refuses Carol without good reason, Ted will probably be legally absolved for future responsibility (again, see Chapter 17 for details).

Laura and Carol: If Laura is willing to accept Carol as a tenant, she should insist that Carol sign a rental agreement or lease before Ted leaves. If Carol refuses, she should be asked to leave. If she refuses to do this, it would be a mistake for Laura to physically remove her, even though Laura has never received rent from her and does not consider her to be a tenant. The reason for this is that a court might well rule that self-help actions undertaken by Laura were illegal, which would give rise to a hefty damage settlement. In other words, even though it's more immediate trouble, Laura would be well advised to use legal proceedings to evict Carol if she has any claim at all to being a tenant.

E. Assignment to a New Tenant

In Section C, above, we said a subtenancy might occur when the main tenant "temporarily" re-rents her apartment to someone else, presumably with an intent to come back before the lease

---

* We suggest including a clause in all leases and rental agreements limiting a tenant's right to have overnight visitors. One way to do this is to say that no visitor shall be allowed to stay overnight for more than ten (or 14, 21 or 28 days) in any six-month period without your written permission. The value of this requirement is that if a tenant does try and move someone in for a longer period, they have violated the lease or rental agreement and you can take action.

expired. But, what about the tenant who has no intention of returning, such as a tenant with a year lease who stays six months and sublets to someone else for the remaining six months of the lease term? According to technical legal jargon, this is not a sublet, but an "assignment," under which the tenant has legally "assigned" all her rights to the property to someone else. From a landlord's point of view, this arrangement has most of the disadvantages of a sublet, namely that she cannot assert any reasonable control over who lives in the premises. We distinguish the term "assignment" from "sublet" in part because lawyers often do, and to explain why the lease and rental agreement at the back of this book forbid both assignments and sublets without the owner's consent.

There is one important technical difference between assignment and subletting as far as the landlord's rights are concerned. This is that where an assignment is involved, the new occupant (the "assignee") is responsible to the landlord for everything the original tenant was liable for--even in the absence of an agreement between that person and the landlord (Civil Code Section 822). This should be distinguished from the situation in which a tenant sublets to a second tenant who is responsible to the first tenant, not the landlord (see Section B, above). Nevertheless, if in the unlikely event you sign a lease agreement which allows a tenant to leave early, and to accept the new tenant he or she produces, it's advisable not to let the old tenant assign her lease to the new tenant, but rather, to enter into a new lease or written rental agreement with the new occupant. If you do this, your legal relationship with the new tenant will be clear.

F. Guests

There is no contractual relationship between a landlord and a guest or visitor of a tenant or sub-tenant. That sounds simple, doesn't it? The prob-
116

lem, as you probably know all too well, is that there's no precise legal line between guests and roommates, the latter being legal sub-tenants allowed in by the tenant, until and unless they sign a lease with the landlord. For example, a person may be a frequent overnight visitor--four or five times a week---but still qualify as a guest, whereas a roommate might only be in residence a few nights each week, as is common with airline flight attendants.

Unfortunately, some landlords become overly concerned with what they see as immoral overnight behavior between the tenant and the guest. This is a mistake. It is specifically illegal to discriminate against unmarried couples in California including gay or lesbian couples. In addition, the California Supreme Court cases of Marina Point v. Wolfson and In Re Cox* makes any unreasonable discrimination illegal. Despite your own religious or moral views, discriminating against people on the basis of who they go to bed with is illegal. In short, landlords should not involve themselves with tenants' private lives. However, it is wise to become concerned where it appears a "guest" has moved in clothing and furniture and begun to receive mail at your property. Assuming that the lease or rental agreement prohibits subletting, restricts the occupancy to a set number of persons, or calls for an increase in rent if more people move in, and limits the number of days guests can stay, this is the point at which you can legally intervene. As discussed earlier in this chapter, a landlord is well advised to insist that a guest-cum-sub-tenant, as well as the tenant, sign a new lease or rental agreement, and as part of doing this perhaps request an increase in the rent or a larger security deposit. Or, in the alternative, the landlord should make it clear that he or she does not want to rent to the new tenant and that

---

* Respectively 30 Cal. 3d 72 (1982) and 3 Cal. 3d 205 (1972).

if the person remains on the premises, an eviction action based on breach of the occupancy terms of the lease will ensue.

G. Co-Tenants' Contracts With Each Other

Usually, co-tenants will orally agree between themselves to split the rent (even married and unmarried couples often have informal, or sometimes formal, agreements to this effect) and to occupy certain parts of the property, i.e., separate bedrooms. Not infrequently, this sort of agreement will go awry. Whether the co-tenants are a married or unmarried couple, or just two or more people sharing rent and space under the same roof, problems may arise as to who should leave if a dispute gets bad enough. Disputes can also develop over whether one co-tenant can keep the other out, who is responsible for what part of the rent, etc.

The best advice we can give to landlords who face serious disagreements between co-tenants is to not get involved in these disputes, as a mediator or otherwise. If approached by one or more co-tenants about a dispute, you should explain that any disagreements between them are to be resolved by themselves, and that so long as the current lease or rental agreement remains in effect, each and all co-tenants are legally obligated to pay all the rent due, and abide by the other terms of the agreement, whether they live on the premises or not. Make sure the tenants clearly understand that you as the landlord are not legally affected by any agreement between the tenants or co-tenants.

For example, if co-tenants Ted and Carol agree to pay Laura Landlady $700 rent each month, and Ted and Carol between themselves each agree to pay $350, Laura's only concern in the face of a dispute between Ted and Carol is to receive $700, whether $350 comes from each, or $700 from Carol or Ted alone. If Ted doesn't come up with his $350, it's up to Carol to pay the whole $700 and convince Ted to pay his share, perhaps taking him to small claims court as a last resort.

If Carol approaches Laura with a plea to accept only $350 because Ted won't pay his share, Laura can legally accept the part rent payment but should politely but firmly tell Carol that she is responsible for the entire rent, and that Laura might as well rent to another couple that doesn't have such disputes. We discuss accepting partial payments of rent in detail in Chapter 3, Section D.

The same sort of rule applies when one of several co-tenants violates one of the other terms of the lease or rental agreement other than non-payment of rent. For example, if one co-tenant moves in an extra roommate or brings in a pit bull contrary to the lease or rental agreement, the landlord may hold all co-tenants responsible, even those who objected or weren't consulted by the prime offender. If you wind up having to evict on this basis, it's up to you whether to bring suit against only the offending co-tenant, or against all of them.

Even in the case of acrimonious or even violent disputes between co-tenants, a landlord must allow each co-tenant access to the property, unless one of the co-tenants has obtained a restraining order (or other court order) against the other. You may change the locks and give a key to the remaining co-tenant, so as to keep the other one out, only if the other co-tenant terminates his tenancy and voluntarily leaves, or if a court has issued an order that he stay out. In years past, when it was difficult for unmarried couples to get restraining orders under California law, landlords were sometimes tempted to bend this rule to protect a tenant they were friendly with, or sympathetic to, from the other. No matter what the merits of doing this in the past, it is unwise today. Restraining orders are now available in domestic partner situations, and if one co-tenant is abusing the other, ask that person to complain to a judge, not to you.

Should one of several disputing co-tenants leave, and the remaining co-tenant(s) wants to bring in someone else (who would otherwise be a sub-tenant), you should insist on drawing up a new lease or rental agreement, assuming you approve of the new tenant. Otherwise, you can give the remaining tenants a 30-day notice, as long as you rent under a month-to-month tenancy and your property is not covered by a rent-control ordinance with a "just cause" for eviction provision. Even if your tenants had a fixed-term lease, you can insist on a new lease if the original lease specified (as does the one at the back of this book) that it is only valid for the named tenants.

Should it happen that one tenant named in the lease wants to remain by herself after the other moves out, you are probably required by law to let her do so. You may be worried that the remaining tenant doesn't have enough income to pay the rent and you may wish to discuss this and even suggest her getting an acceptable roommate. However, you should not subject yourself to the possibility of a discrimination lawsuit by giving a 30-day notice or even pressuring her to move; it's safer to see if she really can go it alone, and to begin eviction proceedings only if she can't.

H. Co-Signers

Some landlords require co-signers on rental agreements and leases, especially when renting to students who depend on parents or on other persons for much of their income. The co-signer signs a separate agreement or the rental agreement or lease, under which she agrees to pay any rent or damage-repair costs the tenant fails to pay.

In practice, a co-signer's promise to guarantee the tenant's rent obligation often has little value. This is because the primary factor that motivates a tenant otherwise reluctant to pay the rent is the knowledge that he may be quickly evicted, if he doesn't pay. However, you cannot sue a co-signer along with the tenant in an eviction suit. The co-signer must be sued separately in either a regular civil lawsuit or in small claims court. This means that as far as going after the co-signer on the tenant's rent obligation is concerned, your best weapon-- the possibility of an eviction lawsuit-- is unavailable.

Another legal obstacle to enforcement of a co-signer's promise is that the promise is not enforceable if the lease or rental agreement has been changed without the co-signer's written approval.* Even the simple renewal of a lease involving the signing of a new document by the landlord and the tenant--but not by the co-signer-- will eliminate the co-signer's liability. So may a rent increase or other change in the terms of tenancy. Taking this one step further, a court might refuse to hold a co-signer liable for any period beyond that of the original lease term, where the tenancy has since become one from month to month. Since lease expirations, renewals and rent increases usually occur over the life of a residential tenancy, a landlord who foregoes the nuisance of getting the co-signer's signature every time the tenancy somehow changes may wind up with a worthless promise.

Thus the benefits of having a lease or rental agreement co-signed by someone who won't be living on the property are almost entirely psychological. A tenant who thinks you can look to the co-signer--usually a relative or close friend of the tenant--may be less likely to default on the rent. Similarly, a co-signer asked to pay the tenant's debts may persuade the tenant to pay.

---

* See Civil Code Section 2818; **Wexler** v. McLucas (1975) 48 Cal.App.3d Supp.9.

10

The Landlord's Duty to Repair and Maintain the Property

A. Introduction

It used to be that the tenant's duty to pay rent, and the landlord's right to receive it, were unaffected by how dilapidated or run-down the property had become. In fact, under English common law, tenants still had to pay all the rent due under the lease even if the property had been destroyed through no fault of the tenant. As you know, however, today's laws and court decisions condition the tenant's duty to pay rent on the landlord's fulfillment of his duty to maintain the property and keep it in good repair. In addition, a number of state and local laws having to do with health and safety require that a landlord keep residential property in good condition.

B. The Landlord's Responsibilities

California's "State Housing Law," contained in Health and Safety Code Sections 17900 through 17995, lists a property owner's general obligations to the state, in terms of keeping residential property in livable condition. This law, in turn, refers to very specific housing standards contained in a book called the "Uniform Housing Code," available from the International Conference of Building Officials, 5360 South Workman Mill Road, Whittier, California 90601, and in most libraries. Section 17995 of the Health and Safety Code makes repeated serious violations of the State Housing Law a crime (misdemeanor) punishable by a fine of up to $500 and imprisonment of up to six months in jail. In addition, quite a few cities and counties have enacted local housing codes that are at least as strict as state law. Check with the building inspection or health department of the city or county in which your property is located to see if any local laws apply to your property.

In addition, Civil Code Section 1941.1 lists the minimum legal requirements for a rental dwelling to be "tenantable." This is important because if rental property isn't tenantable, a tenant may well be excused from paying all or part of the rent (see Section D, below). These Civil Code requirements are more general than the specific requirements of the Uniform Housing Code, and were originally intended to be enforced by the tenant through the withholding of rent and other remedies, as opposed to the Housing Code requirements which were to be enforced by state or local government. However, as a result of a series of pro-tenant court decisions, tenants' rights have been expanded well beyond what past legislatures seemed to intend.* And, in any event, many of the Civil Code requirements have always overlapped those of the State Housing Law and local rules. Put these two facts together, and our conclusion is that it normally doesn't make sense to try to distinguish housing law requirements enforceable by state or local government from the tenantability requirements which can be enforced by the courts if the tenant withholds rent and the landlord tries to evict him for nonpayment of rent. To sum all of this up, landlords are increasingly finding that state and/or local housing code violations once thought much too minor or technical to sensibly render the property untenantable or "uninhabitable" are being recognized by courts as a legal excuse for tenants not to pay all or part of the rent.

According to the State Housing Law and Civil Code Section 1941.1, a landlord must make sure the house or apartment unit she rents out has the following:**

● A structure which is weatherproof and waterproof (1941.1); this means there must be no holes or cracks through which wind can blow or water can leak in;

● A plumbing system in good working order (free of rust and leaks), connected to both the local water supply and sewage system or septic tank (1941.1); the landlord is not responsible for low pressure, contamination, or other failures in the local water supply, and her obligation is only to connect a working plumbing system to it;

---

* For example, in Secretary of HUD v. Layfield (1979) 88 Cal.App.3d Supp. 28, an appellate court ruled that a tenant could withhold rent if the landlord failed to provide adequate security patrols, even though Civil Code Section 1941.1, the part of the law enforceable by the tenant, says nothing about a requirement for security guards.

** The State Housing Law is the enforcement tool used by cities and counties that use the Uniform Housing Code (UHC), whereas Civil Code Section 1941.1 lists the defects that the law specifically allows tenants to take action on. Accordingly, each requirement we list just below is followed by either "UHC" or "1941.1" to indicate the source of law. However, courts are likely to run the two together by allowing the tenant to withhold rent for UHC violations as well, to the extent such requirements are adopted by the applicable city or county.

• A hot water system capable of producing water having a temperature of at least 120 degrees Fahrenheit (1941.1 and UHC);

• A heating system that was legal when installed (1941.1), and which is maintained in good working order so as to be able to heat every room to at least 60 degrees Fahrenheit (UHC);

• An electrical system that was legal when installed, and which is in good working order and without loose or exposed wiring (1941.1); there must be at least two outlets, or one outlet and one light fixture, in every room but the bathroom (in which only one light fixture is required), and common stairs and hallways must be lighted at all times (UHC);

• A lack of insect or rodent infestations, rubbish or garbage in all areas (1941.1); the landlord's obligation to the tenant with respect to the living areas is only to rent out units that are initially free of insects, rodents, garbage, etc., so that if the tenant's housekeeping habits attract pests, that's his problem. However, the landlord is obliged to the state and local government to keep all areas clean and free of rodents, insects, etc. at all times;

• Enough garbage and trash receptacles in clean condition and good repair to contain tenants' trash and garbage without overflowing before the refuse collectors take it away each week (1941.1); and,

• Floors, stairways, and railings kept in good repair (1941.1).

In addition to the above requirements, each rental dwelling must, under the State Housing Law, have the following:

• A working toilet, wash basin, and bathtub or shower; the toilet and bathtub or shower must be in a room which is ventilated and allows for privacy;

• A kitchen with a sink, which cannot be made of an absorbent material such as wood;

• Natural lighting in every room through windows or skylights having an area of at least one-tenth of the room's floor area, with a minimum of 12 square feet (three square feet for bathroom windows); the windows in each room must be operable at least halfway for ventilation, unless a fan provides for mechanical ventilation; and

• Safe fire or emergency exits leading to a street or hallway; stairs, hallways, and exits must be litter-free, and storage areas, garages, and basements must be free of combustible materials.

NOTE: PAINT, DRAPES AND CARPET: Very often a tenant will complain about faded or unsightly interior paint, or about old or decrepit carpets or drapes. Contrary to anything you may have heard, there is no law that requires a landlord to repaint the interior every so often. So long as the paint isn't actually flaking off, it should comply with the law. (Flaking interior paint, particularly lead-based paint, presents a danger to young children--the flakes have a sweet taste but are toxic. The paint should be removed, not just painted over, and replaced with a new coating of non-lead-based paint. If you fail to do this and an injury results, you may be found to be negligent and therefore liable. We discuss negligence in Chapter 11.) As for carpets and drapes, so long as they're not sufficiently damp and/or mildewy to constitute a health hazard, and so long as carpets don't have dangerous holes that could cause one to trip and fall, the landlord isn't legally required to replace them.

As a general rule, the landlord's duty to keep her rented property in good repair and properly maintained makes sense. And to make sure a landlord doesn't try to avoid this duty, Civil Code Section 1942.1 makes any lease or written rental agreement provision by which a tenant agrees to give up his rights to a habitable home illegal and unenforceable.*

One exception to this rule is that the tenant and landlord can agree that the tenant is solely responsible for repairs and maintenance "as part of the consideration for the rental." This rule has been interpreted narrowly by the courts to include only agreements to lower rent in exchange for the tenant's obligation to make repairs. In other words, courts have not permitted landlords to present tenants with form leases or rental agreements containing standard take-it-or-leave-it clauses under which the tenant allegedly pays less than the normal rent in exchange for assuming the landlord's duties of maintenance and repair. Let's look at an example to illustrate how the burden of repair can legally be shifted to the tenant, and then a second where the landlord's effort to do this is plainly not legal.

EXAMPLE 1: Langley Landlord normally rents his two-bedroom apartments at $400 a month. One of these apartments, recently vacated by Mel

---
* Also see **Green v. Superior Court** (1974) 10 Cal.3d 616.

Moose, is a shambles. Along comes Holly Handyperson, who asks Langley to lease the unit to her for only $200 a month in exchange for her agreement to repair and maintain the place. Although this sort of agreement can easily go bad if all the specific details aren't worked out in advance and written down, it is legally sufficient to remove Langley's duty to Holly to keep the property repaired and maintained. However, if Holly falls down on the job and doesn't fix the problems, Langley is still liable to comply with all government-imposed housing laws and regulations.

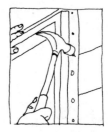

EXAMPLE 2: Lilly Landlord's pre-printed rental agreements all say "Tenant agrees, as part of the consideration for the rental, that he/she will be responsible for all repairs and maintenance." She presents these forms on a take-it-or-leave-it basis to all tenants, but charges them the going rent for the property. Lilly's rental agreement is a sham which, under state law, any judge is required to see through and refuse to honor. Lilly, whether she knows it or not, is still responsible to her tenants for taking care of repairs and maintenance.

And let us repeat one important point. Even if a landlord offers reduced rent in fair exchange for a tenant's undertaking of responsibilities for repair and maintenance, the landlord is still responsible to the state, county or city government to keep her property in compliance with applicable housing laws.

EXAMPLE 3: In exchange for a year's lease at only $200 a month, Herb Handy agrees to repair, maintain and remodel a charming rickety old Victorian house owned by Ladonna Landlady. Six months later, Ladonna learns from the county building department that Herb hasn't fixed any of the many problems. The next day, she gets a letter from Herb saying he has decided not to pay any rent at all because the place is so decrepit. Herb obviously can't excuse his non-payment of rent by pointing to the defects he agreed to fix but didn't. But, although Ladonna probably has grounds to sue or even evict Herb, the city can still penalize her for not making the repairs Herb was supposed to make.

C. The Tenant's Responsibilities

The same section of the Civil Code that requires the landlord to keep her property tenantable also requires the tenant to use the premises properly and keep them clean. Specifically, Civil Code Section 1941.2 requires the tenant to:

• Keep the premises as "clean and sanitary as the condition of the premises permits";

• Properly operate gas, electrical and plumbing fixtures (examples of abuse include electrical outlet overloading, flushing large, foreign objects down the toilet, and allowing bathroom fixtures to become filthy);

• Refrain from damaging or defacing the premises or allowing anyone else to do so;

• Use living and dining rooms, bedrooms, and kitchens for their proper

respective purposes (e.g., no regular use of living or dining room as makeshift bedrooms).

As you can see, these rules simply require that a renter show a minimum of common sense. The reason the law lists the obvious is that the tenant's failure to comply with these requirements is said by the law to excuse the landlord from her responsibilities to the tenant (but not state or local government) to keep the property in good repair. Or, in other words, where the tenant's violation contributes substantially to the existence of the dilapidation or interferes substantially with the landlord's obligation, the tenant can't hold the landlord responsible for the fact that the unit is untenantable. As we will see in Section D below, this is important because Civil Code Sections 1942(c) and 1929 prevent the tenant from deducting rent on account of a condition caused by a tenant's "want of ordinary care," i.e., negligence.

EXAMPLE 1: Odette Odoriferous complains to her landlord about a defective heater. When the landlord's repair person goes to fix the heater, she is confronted by an essence of rotting garbage and mildewed laundry that is so powerful she is unable to enter on a full stomach. Odette's landlord isn't responsible to Odette for fixing the heater until and unless she cleans house, even though the foul smell didn't cause the heater to break. Under the law, Odette's failure to keep the place clean and sanitary obviously "interferes substantially" with her landlord's attempt to fix the heater.

EXAMPLE 2: By his own sorrowful admission, Terry Tantrum, angry over the loss of his job, puts his fist through a window. As as result, a cold wind blows in, cooling off Terry, if not his temper. Terry can't withhold rent to make his landlord fix the window, since Terry caused the problem in the first place by intentionally damaging the property. However, Terry's landlord is still responsible to the state and/or local government to fix the window, after which he can and should bill Terry for the repair--as well as tell Terry to cool it.

EXAMPLE 3: Here we have the same situation as above, but it also happens that the heater in Terry's apartment is inoperable--through no fault of his own. Although Terry is responsible for the window he intentionally broke, his landlord is responsible for fixing the heater, since Terry's act of breaking the window obviously didn't "contribute substantially to the existence of the dilapidation" of the defective heater.

Examples 2 and 3 above deal with a common and frequent area of misunderstanding in this area--windows. Quite a few landlords think a tenant is responsible for all broken windows. This is not true. The tenant is responsible only if he or she intentionally or carelessly broke the window.* If the damage was outside the tenant's control, however, for example because a burglar, vandal or neighborhood child

---

* Section 1941.2(a)(4) conditions the landlord's duty to repair on the tenant's not causing or allowing damage to the property, and Sections 1929 and 1942(c) prevent the tenant from withholding rent for defects caused by his own carelessness.

broke a window, the landlord is responsible for fixing it. Where the tenant or his friends and/or family cause the damage, it's his responsibility to have it fixed or to reimburse you for doing so. This same rule applies to other types of tenant-caused damage, such as toilets clogged with large objects (children's toys, sanitary napkins, etc.), broken kitchen equipment (e.g., a refrigerator that no longer works because the tenant defrosted with a carving knife), and so forth. As to the landlord's remedy against a tenant who refuses to arrange for the repair or reimburse the landlord for its cost, the landlord can bring a suit against the tenant, perhaps in small claims court, for the cost of the repairs. If the tenancy is from month to month in a non-rent-controlled area, the landlord may also want to consider a 30-day termination notice. (If the damage is very severe, such as numerous broken windows, holes in the wall, etc., the landlord can sue for eviction on the basis that the tenant has "committed waste" to the property, i.e., severely damaged it. See Volume II, The Landlord's Law Book: Evictions.)

In all situations, the landlord's best protection is a lease or rental-agreement provision that requires the tenant to reimburse the landlord for repairs necessitated by the tenant's carelessness. If the tenant refuses to reimburse the landlord for the cost of such repairs, the landlord can sue for eviction based on the tenant's violation of that clause. (The landlord, however, must be able to establish that the damage was truly caused by the tenant's neglect, or he will lose the case and have to pay the tenant's court costs and attorney's fees.)

CAUTION: When landlords are confronted by tenants asking that repairs be made, they sometimes--especially when they feel the particular tenant is unreasonable or otherwise unpleasant-- look around for some tenant misconduct to justify not making the repair. This is probably a mistake, unless the tenant's failure to maintain the property is fairly outrageous. Why? Because it can result in legal problems which are out of proportion when compared to the maintenance problem. This is because a landlord's tit-for-tat response may escalate into rent withholding on the part of the tenant, necessitating a nasty eviction action. Even if a landlord is morally right and is judged so in court, the time and expense involved are unlikely to be worth it. The better response is usually to fix the problem and try to work out a better maintenance plan with the tenant for the future. If this fails, you may want to think about trying to get rid of the tenant. This is fairly easy to do, unless you are in a jurisdiction containing a rent control law with a "just cause for eviction" provision, or have a long-term lease. Still, you must be careful that your move to end the tenancy cannot be legally interpreted as retaliating against the tenant for making a legitimate complaint. See Section F, below, for rules on retaliatory evictions.

D. The Tenant's Remedies, or "Forewarned is Forearmed"

Now that you know the landlords' and tenants' responsibilities as far as keeping the property in livable condition, you should also know that a tenant has several very powerful remedies to enforce his rights against a landlord remiss in her duty to repair and maintain the property.

1. The "Repair-and-Deduct" Remedy

Civil Code Section 1942 says that under certain circumstances a tenant can, witnout the landlord's permission, contract to have the defect repaired herself and withhold the cost of the repairs from the following month's rent. This is commonly called the "repair-and-deduct" remedy. In order for the tenant to do this, the following must be true:

● The defect must be related to "tenantability." In other words, it must be a serious (or at least somewhat serious) problem directly related to health or safety;

● The defect or problem must not have been caused by the tenant's careless or intentional act;

● The cost of the repair (or at least the amount withheld) must be no more than one month's rent, and the tenant can use this remedy no more than twice in any 12-month period; and

● Before having the repair done, the tenant must give the landlord or manager "reasonable" notice of the problem, either verbally or in writing.

NOTE: Although the law used to require written notice to the landlord, and although tenants are best advised to give notice in writing, verbal notice is legally sufficient.

Of all the above requirements that a tenant must meet in order to exercise the repair-and-deduct remedy, the rule that the tenant give "reasonable" notice is the one most open to interpretation. According to Subdivision (b) of Civil Code Section 1942, "reasonable notice" is presumed to be 30 days, but can be a lot less for an urgent problem, such as a defective heater in winter, a leaky roof during the rainy season, or a stopped-up toilet any time.

EXAMPLE 1: Phil Phussbudget complains to Linton Landlord that the kitchen sink faucet drips water slightly. In this rental agreement, the landlord has the responsibility to pay the water bill. Since Linton pays for the water, and since Phil can close his bedroom door at night to block out the noise, this isn't a serious problem, and Phil must give Linton 30 days to change the faucet washer before he can have a plumber do it and deduct the cost from the rent.

EXAMPLE 2: In July, Ted Tenant tells Larchmont Lessor that he was treated to some April showers in his living room three months before. Unless it suddenly starts raining regularly in the middle of summer, this problem, though serious, isn't urgent, and Ted must wait at least 30 days before he can take the repair into his own hands. The fact that Ted took his time reporting the leak contributes to the conclusion that Larchmont is within his rights in taking his time to respond.

EXAMPLE 3: On January 15th, Frank Frozen tells his landlord, Regina Rentor, that the heater no longer works. Regina doesn't fix it that day or the next, even though they are weekdays. In the meantime, Frank and his family must sleep in an unheated 45-degree apartment. So, after only two days, Frank has the heater fixed at a cost of $100. In February, Frank deducts this amount from his rent. Regina sues to evict Frank for nonpayment of rent. The judge decides that two day's notice was reasonable under the circumstances, and Regina loses, doubly so as she must pay not only her court costs and attorney's fees, but Frank's as well.

As you can see from the preceding example, it doesn't mean much that a landlord thinks a tenant's use of the repair-and-deduct remedy happened too soon after the complaint was made and that the landlord wasn't given a reasonable time in which to fix the problem. Why? Because if it comes to a fight, "reasonable notice" will be defined by a judge, not the landlord. And going to court over this sort of dispute, unless the tenant's behavior was truly outrageous, is not a productive way to arrive at a decision. A landlord's best bet is to set up a good responsive maintenance system and stick to it. We discuss this in more detail below. And remember, in deciding whether the tenant acted unreasonably, consider how much it would have cost you to make the same repair. If the tenant paid $200 for a $40 job, you have a lot more incentive to do something than if she paid $80 for a repair you could have accomplished for $50.

WARNING: RETALIATORY EVICTION IS ILLEGAL: One final note about the repair-and-deduct remedy. Occasionally, a landlord, faced with a troublesome tenant who seems to be unreasonably asserting his legal remedies to the letter of the law, whether it be in the form of a complaint to local officials or the deduction of repair costs from the rent, is tempted to give the tenant a 30-day notice terminating the tenancy or raising the rent. A tenant can defend against this sort of eviction or rent increase on the basis that the landlord is illegally retaliating against him for exercising his rights. This is true whether the 30-day notice was served by the landlord one day or several months after the tenant's complaint. The tenant isn't automatically "immunized" against a 30-day-notice eviction by virtue of having made a complaint prior to receiving the 30-day notice, but still must prove the landlord's intent was to retaliate. Similarly, it's also true that the tenant can cry "retaliation" in response to a 30-day notice long after having made the original complaint. Of course, the more time that has elapsed from the time of the tenant's complaint to the landlord's 30-day notice, the harder it is for him to convince a judge the notice was retaliatory.

In addition, the tenant can even sue the landlord for "retaliatory eviction," although this type of suit is still fairly rare.* Put simply, it isn't wise for a landlord to retaliate against a tenant who asserts the repair-and-deduct remedy. If you feel your tenant has improperly deducted the costs of repairs from the rent, say because you were not given enough notice, or were given no notice, try working things out with the tenant. Failing that, if you feel strongly enough about it, the proper recourse is to file suit against the tenant for the deducted part of the rent, whether in small claims court (see Chapter 18, Section C), or in a municipal court eviction lawsuit (see Volume II on evictions).

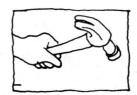

2. Other Rent-Withholding Remedies

The repair-and-deduct remedy isn't the only legal way a tenant can withhold part or all of the rent from a landlord who doesn't properly maintain residential property. In 1974, the California Supreme Court decided the most famous (or infamous, depending on how you look at it) landlord-tenant case in the state's history. Known as **Green v. Superior Court** (10 Cal. 3d 616), the Court ruled that a tenant can also legally withhold rent, aside from the repair-and-deduct remedy, if the landlord is in serious violation of the minimum requirements for a habitable dwelling. The Court based this decision on the conclusion that the law recognizes that a landlord impliedly promises that a dwelling will be fit for human habitation when he rents it. If it is not, the landlord is said, in legalese, to have "breached" the "implied warranty of habitability."

In order for a tenant to legally withhold rent under the rationale of the **Green** case, the following must be true:

● The defect(s) must be serious ones that may adversely affect the tenant's health or safety;

● The problems must not have been caused by the tenant; and

● The tenant must have given the landlord reasonable notice of the problem.

---

* See **Schweiger v. Superior Court** (1970) 3 Cal. 3d 507, 90 Cal. Rptr. 729, **Aweeka v. Bonds** (1971) 20 Cal. App. 3d 278, 97 Cal. Rptr. 650, and **Glaser v. Meyers** (1984) 137 Cal. App. 3d 770, 187 Cal. Rptr. 242.

Except for the absence of any limitation on how much or how often the tenant can withhold rent, these **Green** case requirements are similar to those we discussed above under the repair-and-deduct remedy, with one important exception. The repair-and-deduct remedy can be used to fix minor defects so long as the tenant has actually had them repaired after proper notice to the landlord, while rent withholding is limited to serious problems that result in uninhabitability. Extreme dilapidations justifying the withholding of rent would probably include a bathroom ceiling that has collapsed and not been repaired, rats, mice and cockroaches infesting the building, a number of rooms lacking heat in the winter, etc.

In making their decision, the Court in the **Green** case concurred with a New Jersey court decision that said: "One cannot be expected to live in a multi-storied apartment building without heat, hot water, garbage disposal or elevator service." It's important to realize, however, that fairly trivial defects, such as leaky water faucets or cracked windows or plaster, aren't enough to allow the tenant to withhold rent on the basis that the landlord has violated the implied warranty of habitability.

Before a tenant can withhold rent, claiming a breach of the implied warranty of habitability, she must notify the landlord (or manager) of the problem. There are, however, no precise notice requirements (e.g., that the notice be in writing or served in a certain way), as this remedy was established somewhat vaguely by the California Supreme Court, not by the legislature. There is also no definite rule as to how long the landlord has to fix the problem after receiving notice of it, except that 60 days is too long under any circumstances, even for minor defects. In other words, the tenant can give the notice verbally or in writing, but before withholding rent on account of a defect, she must give the landlord a "reasonable" time to respond. Again, as with "repair-and-deduct" rent withholding (Section D, above), what's "reasonable" can only truly be defined by a judge.

Under new Civil Code Sections 1942.3 and 1942.4, a tenant may withhold rent and sue a landlord who takes more than 60 days to fix any defect that a local health or building-inspection department official insists be repaired following an inspection. This doesn't mean, though, that a landlord always has two full months to correct the problem. Instead, it means that the chances of a landlord's suffering several financial penalties increase greatly if she waits more than 60 days to repair a defect of any kind, following an official notice that she do so.

EXAMPLE: On December 23, Fred asked Sam, his landlord, to fix the broken heater in his apartment. Sam said he'd "get around to it in a few days." On the 26th, Fred complained again to Sam, who said, "we'll see about it next week." Tired of freezing, Fred called the local health department. On December 28, a health department inspector checked out the property and sent Sam a letter insisting he fix the heater. On January 2, Fred told Sam he was withholding the rent until the heater was repaired. As it wasn't reasonable for Fred to go for more than a day or two without heat, Fred was within his rights to withhold the rent. This is true even though it hasn't been 60 days since the health department sent the notice to Sam.

EXAMPLE 2: Assume that in the previous example Fred grudgingly paid the rent in January and February. Come March 1, Fred refuses to pay the rent because the heater still isn't fixed. Because it's now more than 60 days since the health department told Sam to fix the heater, Fred has (a) a much greater chance of winning any rent-nonpayment eviction lawsuit brought by Sam, and (b) a right to sue Sam and recover damages for having gone without heat for over two months, plus $1000 and attorney's fees.

In some situations, where a tenant simply cannot get a landlord to pay attention to the need for serious repair, rent withholding is justified. Most of the time it isn't, being little more than an after-the-fact ploy to avoid paying rent the tenant is unable or unwilling to pay. In this situation, the tenant is often cynically trying to set up a defense to your future court action for eviction and non-payment of rent. Perhaps the tenant doesn't really even expect to win in court, but thinks that if she tosses enough sand in the air, she will get away with a few months free rent before being evicted. In this connection, some tenants will go to great lengths to notify local authorities of the existence of supposed defects and sometimes will even create them in the first place.

3. Vacating Property

According to Civil Code Section 1942, the existence of a problem that qualifies a tenant to use the repair-and-deduct remedy (Subsection 1, above) also allows the tenant to simply pack up and leave without further notice if the landlord fails to fix the problem in a reasonable time. In this situation, the tenant is not responsible for payment of any rent from the time the repair should have been made, even if due under a long-term lease. In addition, the tenant is entitled to a pro-rated refund of any rent he's paid in advance, which covers the time during which the unit was in disrepair.

EXAMPLE: On January 1st, Lionel Lessor leases his house to Lisa Lessee for a year, and Lisa pays the first month's rent of $600. On February 1st, Lisa pays the rent again, but the day after that, the hot water heater springs a leak. Lisa tells Lionel about the problem, but Lionel does nothing. Several more anguished calls from Lisa, who has no hot water, produce no action. After fifteen days-- which Lisa thinks is reasonable under the circumstances--she simply packs up and leaves. She is probably acting reasonably and legally under the circumstances. And not only is Lisa relieved of any further obligation under the lease, but she's also entitled to a refund of $300, representing the prorated rent for the rest of the month, plus her security deposit (less any lawful deductions--see Chapter 18, Section B).

4. Lawsuits by Tenants for Defective Conditions

A landlord who fails to maintain property can also be sued by a tenant. In other words, the tenant isn't limited to passive remedies, such as moving out and/or refusing to pay the rent. The theory on which a tenant's suit is based is that by failing to repair defective conditions, the landlord breaches an "implied" term of the lease or rental agreement--that is, to provide a habitable dwelling. The tenant, whether he remains on the property or moves out, can sue the landlord, in small claims or regular court, for the following:

● Partial or total refund of rent paid in earlier months while conditions were substandard;

● The value, or repair costs, of property lost or damaged as a result of the defect--like furniture ruined by water leaking through the roof;

● Compensation for personal injuries--including "pain and suffering"--caused by the defect;

● Attorney's fees, if the lease or rental agreement has an attorney's fees clause.

WARNING: Under Civil Code Section 1942.4, a landlord who fails to correct a defect of the type mentioned in Civil Code Section 1941.1 (weatherproofing, plumbing, heating, infestations, etc.-- see Section B) within 60 days after receiving written notice to repair from a public agency (such as a health or building department) may be sued by the tenant for up to $1000, plus other damages. Also, the tenant can recover attorney's fees in this type of suit, even if the agreement has no attorney's fees clause.

A list of the types of housing defects which can theoretically expose a landlord to liability, as well as the different types of damages and/or injuries for which the tenant could recover, are virtually endless. We discuss this subject in more detail in Chapter 11. As with other legal remedies having to do with defective housing conditions, it is not legal for a tenant to waive the right to sue the landlord for damages as the result of the landlord's neglect of the property by a provision in a lease or rental agreement. This is true even though some standard-form leases and rental agreements used by landlords contain a clause by which the tenant purports to give up the right to sue the landlord. In other words, these clauses are void and will not be enforced by courts. One "exception" to this is the situation where the tenant legitimately agrees to repair and maintain the property himself in exchange for reduced rent; if the tenant is injured by a defect he could have foreseen and remedied, the landlord will not be liable. (This isn't really an exception to the rule that a tenant can't waive the right to sue for the landlord's neglect, since in this situation, the tenant, not the landlord, is guilty of neglect.)

Finally, a landlord may not retaliate against a tenant who files a lawsuit and stays in the property. It may seem inconsistent for a tenant to take the extreme step of suing his landlord and expecting to remain on the property, presumably on good terms with the landlord. Nevertheless, a tenant who sues and stays is exercising a legal right, and retaliation, such as with a 30-day rent-increase or termination notice, is illegal and will give the tenant yet another ground on which to sue.*

---

* See Civil Code Section 1942.5; **S.P. Growers Assn. v. Rodriguez** (1976) 17 Cal.3d 719 and **Vargas v. Municipal Court** (1978) 22 Cal.3d 902.

E. How Much Rent Can a Tenant Legally Withhold?

Assuming there is a serious problem with a rental unit and the landlord does not fix it in a reasonable time, how much rent can a tenant withhold? Unfortunately, the answer to this question is imprecise. It comes down to this; the tenant can withhold as much rent as the landlord--or a judge, if the case gets to court--will let her get away with under the specific circumstances.

The criteria the judge will use to make this determination on account of habitability-related defects are varied. For example, where a particular defect makes one or more rooms unlivable (such as a bad roof leak during rainy season), the judge will probably pro-rate the rent based on the reduced number of livable rooms or floor space. In other situations, the judge might base a decision on the testimony of a person in the real estate industry who is knowledgeable about what the property, with all defects, would rent for to an informed tenant. Or, a judge may more or less offhandedly guess at an amount due the tenant as compensation for the inconvenience or annoyance of putting up with the problem each month, and subtract that from the monthly rent. Hopefully, your system of expressing your intention to keep your unit habitable and following up with prompt repairs when necessary will mean you never have to face a court argument over this issue. If you do, however, be ready to prove the following:

● The claimed defect did not make the unit uninhabitable; or

● Even if it did, you were never given adequate notice and a chance to fix it. (It is at this point that you should present your detailed complaint procedure to the court and show, if possible, that the tenant didn't follow it.); or

• Assuming there was a major defect that wasn't fixed within a reasonable time (perhaps you were away and your manager screwed up), this defect only justifies the withholding of a small amount of rent.

F. Court Response to Rent Withholding

Rent withholding almost always comes before a judge in the context of an unlawful detainer (eviction) lawsuit. That is, in response to the tenant's failure to pay rent, the landlord has served a three-day notice to quit the premises or pay up, and when the tenant fails to do either, has filed suit. Depending on the facts, the possible range of judicial responses is as follows:

• If the judge in an eviction suit based on nonpayment of rent rules that the tenant had no right to withhold any rent at all, she will give a judgment to the landlord for the unpaid rent and possession of the property, ordering the tenant's eviction.

• If the judge decides that the tenant withheld the right amount, she will enter judgment for the tenant, who will be able to stay in the property. In addition, the landlord will be responsible for paying the tenant's court costs, and his attorney's fees if the lease or rental agreement has an attorney's fees clause.

• If the judge takes a middle ground, namely that the tenant has a right to withhold rent, but not as much as he did, so that he owes the landlord

the difference, it's a little more complicated. The judge will normally order the tenant to pay the difference, sometimes giving the tenant a few days to do so. If the tenant does pay the landlord within the time the judge allows, he gets to stay, wins the lawsuit, and can even get a judgment against the landlord requiring him to pay court costs.* (This is because the tenant had a valid complaint, even if he did withhold too much rent, and the tenant shouldn't be penalized for having been unable to guess the right amount of rent to withhold.) On the other hand, if the tenant doesn't pay this difference, the landlord normally wins a judgment for that amount, possession of the property, court costs, and attorney's fees, if the lease or rental agreement has an attorney's fees clause and the landlord was represented by an attorney.

Here is an example of how all of this works:

EXAMPLE 1: Wilbert Whiner rents a two-bedroom apartment from Leonardo Landlord for $400 a month. Because the toilet makes an occasional "running" sound until Wilbert jiggles the handle, Wilbert withholds an entire month's rent. Leonardo Landlord gives Wilbert a three-day notice and follows this with an eviction lawsuit. The judge decides that Wilbert has no right to withhold the rent and gives Leonardo a judgment for the $400 rent, court costs, and possession of the property. (Since Leonardo handled his own suit, he is not eligible for attorney's fees.) fees.)

EXAMPLE 2: When the November rains came in through the roof of one of the two bedrooms in Tim Tenant's

---

* See C.C.P. §1174.2 and Strickland v. Becks (1979) 95 Cal. App. 3d Supp. 18, 157 Cal. Rptr. 656. This rule also applies to attorney's fees if the applicable lease or rental agreement has an attorney's fees clause. See Civil Code Section 1717(a).

apartment, he asked Lulu Landperson to fix it. Come December, Lulu still hasn't fixed the leak and the bedroom is cold and unusable. Based on the reduced usable floor-space of his unit, Tim pays Lulu only $300 of the $400 rent. Lulu then gives Tim a three-day notice demanding the other $100, and sues Tim when he doesn't pay. The judge decides Tim withheld the right amount and owes Lulu nothing. Tim gets to stay, and Lulu must pay Tim's court costs and attorney's fees because the written rental agreement under which Tim signed provides for attorney's fees for the owner if she wins a suit (see Chapter 2, Section E).

EXAMPLE 3: For $900 a month, Lou Landlord rents a two-bedroom house to Ken Kool. The house is heated by two wall heaters, one in the kitchen and one in a bedroom, which is somewhat isolated in the "bedroom wing." In late November, the bedroom heater stops working. This leaves one end of the house, including one of the two bedrooms and a bathroom, chilly and uncomfortable. On December 1st, the heater is still not fixed, so Ken refuses to pay Lou any rent. Lou finally fixes the heater on December 15th and demands the rent. Ken claims he only owes $450, half the rent for December. Lou takes the $450, but insists on the other $450, giving Ken a three-day notice to pay up or get out, followed by an unlawful detainer (eviction) lawsuit when Ken doesn't respond. After hearing the case, the judge decides that since half the house was livable for the first half of December, Ken should also pay half of that half-month's rent, or $225, in addition to what he already paid. However, as Ken was correct in withholding rent, he wins the suit and can stay in his apartment, and Lou must pay the court costs. However, if Ken doesn't pay the additional $225, Lou wins, getting a judgment for the $225, possession of the property, and court costs.

NOTE: SANITY SAVES: No one in her right mind wants to get involved in a court fight if it's humanly possible to avoid one. The psychic and monetary costs of the American court system usually result in losing, even if you win. Armed with this knowledge, it makes sense to compromise with a tenant even if this involves your accepting somewhat less than you might end up with in court. See Chapter 7, Section H for a discussion of how landlord-tenant mediation can help in this area. See Section G of this chapter for more on a landlord's remedies.

One final word--as with the repair-and-deduct remedy, it is illegal for a landlord to retaliate against a tenant for legitimately asserting a right to withhold rent. A landlord's 30-day termination or rent-increase notice that follows a tenant's withholding of rent is a sure sign of retaliation, unless the landlord has other, very legitimate, reasons for giving the notice. Of course, this doesn't preclude a three-day notice for nonpayment of rent, followed, if need be, by an eviction suit on that basis, since the landlord's motive in that situation is simply to get his rent.

G. How to Protect Yourself in Advance Against Rent-Withholding Schemes

What can you do to head off a tenant who tries to use rent withholding or the repair-and-deduct remedy for the wrong reasons? Outside of picking tenants wisely, your best bet is to establish a clear, easy-to-follow procedure for tenants to ask for repairs and to respond quickly when complaints are made. In this connection, we recommend that you:

• Give every tenant a copy of your complaint procedure when they move in, as part of the written "Landlord/Tenant Checklist" (see Chapter 1, Section G);

• Remind tenants of your policy to keep your building in good repair as part of every written communication. Be sure to include a brief review of the complaint procedure;

EXAMPLE: At the bottom of all routine notices, rent increases and other communications, Lew Landperson might remind the tenants of his 12-unit apartment building of the following: "It is the policy of the management to properly maintain your apartment unit. If you have any questions or complaints regarding your unit, or the building, please direct them to Moe Manager between 9:00 a.m. and 6:00 p.m., Monday through Saturday, either by calling 555-9876 or by coming to the office to fill out a Request for Repairs form. In case of emergency during non-business hours, call 555-6789."

• Post your complaint procedures if you have a multi-unit building;

• Log all complaints in a ledger or other book so that you have a record of when they were made. Respond quickly to all complaints about defective conditions. This doesn't mean you have to jump through hoops to fix things that don't need fixing or to engage in heroic efforts to make routine repairs when fixing them in the normal course of business would be adequate. It does mean prompt action under the circumstances;

• Tell the tenant in writing if repairs will take more than 48 hours, excluding weekends;

STATELY MANOR APARTMENTS

Time Estimate for Repair

October 10, 198_

Terry Tenant, Resident
123 Main Street, Apt. 12
San Jose, California

Dear Resident:

Thank you for promptly notifying us of the following problem with your unit:

Fixing the pilot light on your gas stove.

We expect to have the problem corrected on October 13, 1985, due to the following: new pilot light element is out of stock locally, but has been ordered and will be delivered then. We regret any inconvenience this delay may cause. Please do not hesitate to point out any other problems that may arise.

Sincerely,

Moe Manager

• If a tenant threatens to withhold rent, respond promptly in writing, telling her either:

a. When the repair will be made and the reasons why it is being delayed; **or**

b. That you do not feel there is a legitimate problem and that the complaint is simply a ploy to justify rent withholding. At this point, you might also consider suggesting that you and the tenant mediate the dispute. (We discuss mediation in Chapter 7, Section H.)

Leonardo D. Landlord
123 Da Vinci Place
Venice, California

July 21, 1985

Wilbert Whiner
456 Springsteen Square
Apartment 7
Los Angeles, California

Dear Mr. Whiner:

This is in response to your letter of July 19th in which you suggested the possibility of withholding your next month's rent if the bathroom toilet is not repaired.

Please be advised that I have ordered the replacement parts necessary to prevent the stopper from improperly seating and allowing water to run from the tank to the bowl. An order was necessary through ABC Plumbing Supply because I have been assured that the part is not available locally. I expect to receive the part within one week. Until then, the toilet still flushes and is usable, despite the "running" sound it makes.

As you will recall, I came to check the toilet on three occasions and found it perfectly operable. I suspect that the stopper only occasionally does not seat properly into the hole separating the toilet tank from the bowl. In any event, a jiggle on the flush handle when the toilet makes a "running" sound will correct the problem on the few occasions when the stopper fails to seat. The problem is a minor one which does not result in your unit being considered uninhabitable, and therefore does not justify rent withholding under California law. Accordingly, should you withhold rent on this basis, I will have no choice but to respond with three-day notice to pay rent or leave the premises, followed by an unlawful detainer suit if you fail to comply.

Sincerely,

Leonardo D. Landlord

Why should a landlord bother to establish this type of procedure? Isn't it a lot of trouble for nothing? No. Most of the notices as to how and when to make complaints can be incorporated into your existing forms. And the benefits of establishing a clear paper trail as to your good intentions are great. Specifically, it helps you communicate with tenants who do have legitimate problems and creates a climate of cooperation and trust that can work wonders in the long run. And at least as important, it provides you with an excellent defense when it comes to those few unreasonable tenants who seek to withhold rent for no adequate reason other than their disinclination to pay. (In addition, if you need to establish that the repair problem is bogus, you may want to have the repair-person who looked at the "defect" come to court to testify about it.) You may still have to go to court to evict them (if so, see the second volume of this book, on eviction procedures), but your carefully-documented procedures will help you accomplish this with a minimum of time and expense.

NOTE: In Chapter 11, we emphasize that this same sort of responsive repair policy can pay big dividends in helping to limit your liability to your tenants in lawsuits based on injuries suffered as a result of allegedly defective conditions on your property. This is both because there are less likely to be tenant injuries in the first place if your property is well maintained, and because in most situations an injured person must prove not only that they were hurt, but that you were negligent. This can be difficult to do if you adopt an extremely responsive repair scheme and stick to it.

WHILE YOUR'E HERE, I WAS WONDERING IF YOU COULD DO SOMETHING ABOUT THE ANTS.

H. The Landlord's Remedies if Tenant Withholds Rent

When confronted with a tenant who withholds all or part of the rent, whether justifiably or not, most landlords almost reflexively turn to a lawyer to bring an eviction lawsuit. This often results in a scenario in which papers are filed, a court date is set, and testimony is taken. Even if the landlord eventually gets the tenant evicted, it is often only after considerable cost. Indeed, in most eviction suits, the lawyers are the only clear winners. Even if the landlord gets a judgment for unpaid rent and attorney fees, these amounts often turn out to be uncollectible. In addition, the landlord must pay his attorney.

Fortunately, there are sometimes better and more creative ways to deal with tenants who threaten to withhold rent or use the repair-and-deduct remedy. These include:

• **Strategic Retreat:** If your analysis of the situation tells you the tenant is wrong, but sincere, and is not simply trying to make up an excuse for non-payment of rent, you may want to go along with the tenant's withholding or repair-and-deduct proposal. If, for example, the tenant uses the repair-and-deduct remedy, but you feel you were never given adequate notice, and could have had the problem fixed for $50 less than the tenant did, it may make sense to go along with the tenant's action. Trying to evict the tenant will cost far more and you may or may not win the suit.

But this isn't the same thing as saying you should roll over and accept any silly scheme your tenants invent. Set up a meeting with the tenant in question to review your repair procedures. Listen to any grievance the tenant has, and make sure that the next time there is a problem, you will be notified promptly. Obviously, if a particular tenant persists in being unreasonable, you will eventually have to get more assertive.

• **Compromise:** Short of agreement that a tenant's withholding of rent is proper, a landlord faced with what the tenant believes is a legitimate withholding of rent (as opposed to a mere inability to pay, where a minor defect is used as an excuse) should try to work the problem out with the tenant, considering the possibility of some sort of compromise. A compromise would certainly include repairing any defect having to do with any of the "tenantability" criteria listed in Section B of this chapter, and might also include a pro-rated reduction in rent for the period between the time the tenant notified the landlord of the defect and the time the landlord corrected the problem. For example, if the tenant didn't give the landlord proper notice of the problem until the rent was due, but the defect is still a

serious one, a compromise might be reached where the tenant bears part of the burden for failing to notify the landlord within a reasonable time before withholding rent.

The first step in trying to work out a compromise with the rent-withholding tenant might be to give him a call. Dropping over unannounced to talk face-to-face isn't usually a good idea, as it may threaten the tenant and put him in a defensive posture. If you're reluctant to call, you might want to try a letter. Let's take an example. Assume our friend Lenny Landlord is confronted one day by Terrence Tenant, who suddenly announces on May 1st that he's withholding his May rent in its entirety because Lenny has refused to repair several minor defects, including peeling paint, a leaky water faucet, a running but otherwise operable toilet, a small hole in the carpet, and a cracked window. Lenny's letter to Terrence might look something like the one on the following page.

• **Mediation:** Mediation involves bringing in a neutral third party to help disputants settle their differences. It can be extremely helpful in resolving disputes over the condition of premises, the need for repairs, the amount of rent (if any) it is reasonable to withhold, etc. We discuss mediation in some detail in Chapter 7, Section H.

May 3, 198_

Terrence Tenant
123 Main Street, Apt. 4
Monterey, California

Dear Mr. Tenant:

I am writing you in the hope we can work out a fair compromise to the problems which have led to your decision to withhold rent. You have rented a unit at the Villa Arms for the last three years and we have never had this sort of problem before. Let's try to put it behind us.

To review briefly, on May 1st, Mr. Marvin Manager, my resident manager at the apartment complex in which you reside, indicated to me that you stated to him that you were refusing to pay your rent as the result of several defective conditions in your apartment, which you had asked to have corrected a week ago, but which haven't as yet been attended to. Mr. Manager states that you listed these defects as some peeling paint on the interior wall of your bedroom, a leaky kitchen water faucet, a running toilet, a small hole in the living room carpet, and a cracked kitchen window.

I have instructed Mr. Manager to promptly arrange with you for a convenient time to allow him into your apartment in order to perform repairs as to all the problems you mentioned. I am sure these repairs would already have been accomplished except for the fact that Hank Handy, our regular repairperson, has been out sick for the last ten days.

Because of the inconvenience you have suffered as a result of the problems, I am prepared to offer you a pro-rated rebate on your rent for ten days, this being the estimated length of time it will have taken Mr. Manager to remedy the problems from the day of your complaint. As your monthly rent is $450, equal to $15.00 per day, or $105.00 per week, I am agreeable to your paying only $400 rent this month. If this is not acceptable to you, please call me at 555-1234 during the day. If you would like to discuss any aspect of the situation in more detail, I would be pleased to meet with you at your convenience. I will expect to receive your check for $400, or a call from you, before May 10th.

Sincerely,

Lenny Landlord

11

Landlord's Liability for Injuries to Tenant Due to Defective Housing Conditions

When we talk about personal injuries, we get into an area that lawyers call "torts." A great many (we believe **too** many) lawyers make a nice living filing lawsuits on behalf of people who have been injured as a result of the "negligent" or "intentional" actions of others. While we don't have the space here to show you how to fight a lawsuit brought by a tenant who claims she was injured as a result of some sort of defect in your property, or illegal act perpetrated by you or any of your employees, we can give you an overview of the legal and practical issues involved. It is our belief that by understanding the law in this area, you should be able to take a number of positive steps to reduce the likelihood that you will be found to be liable.

Let's start with the basics. Landlords may be liable for physical injuries caused by faulty premises (e.g., a broken stair, inadequate lighting, substandard wiring). A tenant may even recover against the landlord for maintaining a legal nuisance (i.e., a serious and persistent illegal condition that adversely affects the tenant's enjoyment of the property), even though no physical injury occurs. For example, an apartment tenant, plagued by the stench of nearby garbage scattered about because the landlord hasn't provided enough garbage cans, can sue the landlord for whatever a judge or jury may determine to be the value of the annoyance and inconvenience of putting up with the smell.

NOTE: We discuss a landlord's liability for intentional acts, such as discrimination, invasion of privacy and illegal evictions, etc. in Chapters 8, 12 and 16, respectively.

A. Landlord Liability in General

A number of years ago, a landlord wasn't liable for a tenant's injury from any kind of housing defect, the theory being that the tenant was entirely responsible for repairing and maintaining the property. Even after this rule gave way to one holding a landlord liable for defects that she knew or should have reasonably known about, a landlord could still protect herself from most suits brought by their tenants. This was accomplished by putting a clause in all leases and rental agreements which freed the landlord of responsibility for injuries suffered by a tenant, even if the injury was a direct result of the landlord's negligence. This type of clause is no longer legal or enforceable.*

Basically, the law is now that a landlord must act towards her tenant as a reasonable person would, considering all the circumstances. If a landlord acts in an unreasonable way and an injury occurs, she can be held financially responsible.* Put more concretely, a landlord who fails to repair or otherwise remedy a defect or dangerous condition on her rental property, which she knows about or should have known about, will be liable to a tenant or other person injured as a result of the defect or condition.

Note: A landlord may also be fined if conditions are bad enough. The owners of an apartment building in East Palo Alto were fined $25,000 after police repeatedly raided the building because of notorious drug-dealing there. The owners also agreed to reimburse police for the cost of the raids, and had to pay $13,000 to relocate eight families who were not involved in the drug dealing. This arrangement was approved by a court after local officers sued the owners in 1988.

Here are just a few cases in which courts have held that a landlord can be liable for a tenant's injuries:

• Tenant falls off stairway due to a defective handrail [Brennan v. Cockrell (1973) 35 Cal.App.3d 796, 111 Cal.Rptr. 122];

• Tenant falls over a rock on a common stairway not properly maintained by the landlord [Henronille v. Marin Ventures (1978) 20 Cal.3d 512, 143 Cal.Rptr. 247];

• Tenant injured or property damaged by fire resulting from defective heater or wiring [Evans v. Thompson (1977) 72 Cal.App.3d 978, 140 Cal.Rptr. 525, and Golden v. Conway (1976) 55 Cal. App.3d 948, 128 Cal.Rptr. 69];

• Tenant robbed and assaulted in dimly-lit common area. [Penner v. Falk (1984) 153 Cal.Appl 3d 858, 200 Cal.Rptr. 661]; Isaacs v. Huntington Memorial Hospital (1958) 38 Cal. 3d 112, 211 Cal.Rptr. 356.

• Tenant raped as a result of poor security or lighting in common areas, or after complaining of defective locks in apartment [Kwaitkowski v. Superior Trading Corp. (1981) 123 Cal.App. 3d 324, 176 Cal.Rptr. 494, and O'Hara v. Western Seven Trees Corp. (1977), 75 Cal.App. 3d 798, 142 Cal.Rptr. 487].

---

* California Civil Code Section 1953.
** Civil Code Section 1714.

• A tenant's vicious dog bites another tenant's visitor. Although the tenant owning the dog was held to be liable to the other tenant's visitor, the landlord was also found to be liable for doing nothing about the dog, even though he knew it was vicious. [Ucello v. Landenslayer (1975) 44 Cal.App.3d 504, 118 Cal.Rptr. 741.]

• Tenant's guest is injured when she trips on a tool left on an apartment building stairway by an independent contractor hired by the landlord. Cordet v. Robert Christopher Co. (1985) __ Cal.Rptr. __ .

NOTE ON DEADBOLT LOCKS: The ordinance of many cities and counties require all rental units to be equipped with deadbolt locks. Even if this isn't required, it's a good idea. Quite simply, your chances of being held liable to a tenant who suffers either a loss of property or a physical attack are greatly increased if the property you rent is equipped with substandard locks. In this connection, you should also be sure that all windows close properly and can be securely locked.

You'll notice that most of these cases involved situations that the landlord might have guarded against, such as dimly-lit common areas, rocks on unkempt stairways, or vicious dogs owned by other tenants. However, even a landlord who acts reasonably is not immune from liability for a hidden defect in the property that injures the tenant. The idea that a landlord can be held liable to a tenant even for certain unavoidable injuries arising from defects in the property is known as "strict liability," which we discuss in Section B(2) of this chapter. Despite the "strict liability" rule, most tenants' lawsuits are still based on landlords' negligence or fault, and every honest attempt by a property owner to repair defects and minimize danger will certainly minimize the risk of liability.

B. Legal Standards for Liability

You'll be relieved to know that a landlord isn't always liable to a tenant whose property or person is injured. For example, a landlord isn't responsible for fire damage to a tenant's belongings or person unless a defect in the property or the landlord's carelessness caused the fire. If another tenant's neglect caused it, the tenant must look either to that person or her own insurance company. This, after all, is the purpose of renter's insurance.

Almost all the situations in which a landlord was held to be liable for an injury that occurred on or in the premises involved landlords who were either careless or made a specific promise (e.g., "maximum security building") about the property, which turned out not to be true. For example, in the two cases where landlords were held liable to tenants who were assaulted by a third person, one involved a landlord who failed to respond to tenant complaints about poor lighting in common areas, while the other involved a landlord who advertised his property as a "security" apartment complex. Here is an example of a situation in which a landlord would be legally liable on account of her negligence.

Now, here is an example of a situation for which a landlord would probably be found to be negligent.

EXAMPLE: Frances Fussenfume

complains--once in writing--to Sylvia Slumlord about a gas leak that seems to be coming from a wall heater. Sylvia does nothing. One day, while Frances is gone, the fumes build up and are ignited by the water heater pilot light across the room, causing a fair-sized explosion and destroying much of Frances' property. Sylvia will be held liable for the value of the property, since she received plenty of notice to correct an obviously dangerous problem and did nothing about it.

1. What Constitutes Negligence?

A technical definition of what constitutes negligence could easily fill the next few pages. Indeed, whole law texts have been written on the subject. Here is a one-sentence definition: If, as a result of your conduct (or failure to act when the law implies a duty or responsibility to act), someone's person or property is injured because you didn't act with reasonable care to prevent the harm, you're liable for the damages. A landlord who fails to exercise "reasonable care" is liable for an injury or loss occurring on the property whether the victim is a tenant or a visitor, whether she suffered the harm in her own apartment or on a common area, such as a stairway or courtyard, or whether the harm was caused by a pure accident or someone else's intentional act.

Obviously, the landlord's duty to exercise reasonable care depends on the circumstances. For example, a tenant who trips over a rock on a common

stairway improperly maintained by the landlord will likely be more successful in a lawsuit against the landlord than would be a tenant who tripped over a rock in the middle of her living room, an area over which she's responsible for keeping free of debris. On the other hand, a tenant injured by a fall caused by a hole in the linoleum floor in an apartment kitchen might well recover if the problem had been called to the landlord's attention and she had failed to fix it.

It is important to understand that in addition to being held liable for defects in the physical premises, a landlord can also be held liable for negligently failing to use reasonable care to protect her tenants and their visitors from intentional and criminal acts by other persons, such as muggings, robberies, burglaries, rapes or worse. This isn't to say that a landlord is always liable for whatever injuries a tenant or visitor suffers, but only that she is liable when the exercise of reasonable precautions might have prevented the attack. (On the other hand, as we'll see in Section B(2), neither is the landlord always free from liability even if he's exercised all reasonable precautions. Still, doing so will certainly reduce the risk of liability. Here are a few examples to illustrate this point.

EXAMPLE 1: Mal Manager is the on-site manager of Shady Hall apartments, a luxury apartment complex which, unfortunately, has several long corridors through which the tenants and their guests must pass in order to get to their apartments. After a number of bulbs in ceiling light fixtures burn out, several tenants ask Mal to replace them. Despite repeated complaints to Mal about the lighting, as well as several recent muggings in nearby buildings, Mal doesn't get around to remedying the situation. One evening, Vinny Visitor walks through a poorly lit hallway on his way to his friend's apartment and is severely beaten and robbed. Mal, as well as the owner,

Layne Landlady, will almost surely be held liable for the full extent of Vinny's injuries (including medical bills, lost earnings, pain and suffering, etc.) because, having been informed of the problem, they might have prevented or at least discouraged the attack with proper maintenance of the lighting system. Had there been no complaints preceding the attack, they would still probably be found liable, on the theory that it was negligent under the circumstances not to make regular inspections and remedy the problem.

EXAMPLE 2: Tom Tenant, a resident of a small apartment complex, goes downstairs to the well-lit and locked laundry room accessible only by keys issued to each tenant. Tom does not lock the door. While he is loading his wash, a stranger bursts in, followed by another person wielding a gun. A gunfight ensues in the laundry room and Tom is injured by a stray bullet. Because the owner took the security precaution of keeping the laundry room locked, because the lighting was good, and because no similar events or other violent incidents had occurred in the past, Tom's landlord will probably not be held responsible for Tom's injuries.

EXAMPLE 3: Lisa Lessee rents an older single-family house from Len Landperson. Despite complaints to Len about defective window locks, Len does nothing. One day, Lisa comes home from work to find one of the windows with the defective locks open and her color TV and stereo missing. Because Len ignored Lisa's complaints about the locks, whose defects contributed to the burglary, Len will very likely be held liable for the value of the missing property.

To summarize, a landlord, as well as a manager, can be held liable for harm done to a tenant or guest due to any unsafe situation which the landlord or manager might have prevented by taking reasonable precautions. This liability can extend to the acts of outside contractors if they result in common areas being maintained in an unsafe condition. If the landlord or her manager or other agent was given notice, particularly written notice, of the problem beforehand, the chances that legal liability will be found is greatly enhanced. However, even if no complaints are made, the landlord isn't off the legal hook, especially if the defects should have been discovered in the normal course of building maintenance.

NOTE ON SMOKE DETECTORS: Traditionally, landlords were not liable to tenants if a fire broke out on the premises, unless it was caused by a landlord's obvious negligence (e.g., old wiring that a landlord knew was dangerous wasn't replaced). More recently, however, a number of cities and counties have begun to require smoke detectors in all rental units. This is obviously a good idea. If you live in an area with this requirement and don't comply, your lack of compliance could be a factor in deciding whether you are liable for any property loss or injury suffered by a tenant. If you install smoke detectors, make sure you follow reasonable maintenance procedures to see that they keep working.

Even if a landlord has been negligent in failing to correct a particular problem which later caused harm to a tenant or guest, there are still a few defenses and partial defenses available in some situations. Let's look at them.

a. Comparative Negligence

If the injured tenant or visitor was also guilty of negligence--for example, by being drunk, or just not watching his step when he tripped over a rock on the landlord's poorly-maintained common stairway--the landlord's liability is proportionately reduced. For example, if a judge or jury ruled that a tenant who had suffered $10,000 in damages was equally (50%) as negligent as the land-

lord, the tenant would recover only
$5,000.

b. Assumption of Risk

Another defense is called "assumption of risk." Assumption of risk
means that a person who knows the possible danger of a certain action and
decides to take the chance anyway is
not entitled to recover anything, even
if the other person is also arguably
negligent. An example would be a tenant who takes a shortcut to an apartment building through a dimly-lit path-
way where there have been several recent muggings and who his himself ac-
costed by muggers may not be able to
win a lawsuit against a landlord based
on the fact that he didn't install
floodlights to illuminate the entire
property surrounding his building.

c. Breach of Warranty and "Fraud"

A landlord's negligence in failing
to correct a problem through which a
tenant or visitor is injured isn't the
only basis by which she can be held
liable for that person's injury. If a
landlord makes an express promise in a
lease or rental agreement, such as to
provide heightened security, or even
without such a written provision, if
she advertises or represents to tenants
or prospective tenants some special
feature of the property, she is very
likely to be held liable to any tenant
injured if the representation turns out
to be untrue.

For example, a landlord who advertises an apartment complex as having
elaborate security measures, such as
special locks, private security-guard
patrols, or 24-hour television monitor-
ing in halls and lobby, will probably
be liable to a tenant whose home is
burglarized or who is attacked, if in
fact the security precautions really
aren't as good as advertised. This
will be true even in situations where
the landlord would probably not be held
to be liable had she never claimed to

have installed any special security
devices in the first place. Similarly,
if security becomes lax because there
has been a complete absence of problems
or injuries, such as previous violent
incidents or burglaries in a building
that advertises "state-of-the-art" security systems, liability will almost
surely be found.

NOTE: BROKEN SECURITY SYS-
TEMS: Security systems, such as garage
doors that open on electronic signal,
television monitors in lobbys and hallways, etc., are sure to suffer periodic
breakdowns. During these periods, your
legal liability is heightened. For
example, if a tenant is attacked in
your garage the day after the automatic
door breaks (and before you can get it
fixed), you may well be legally liable.
The moral is clear. If a security system breaks, have it fixed immediately.
If this isn't possible, consider having
a security company provide a guard during the hours when problems are most
likely to occur.

2. Strict Liability

"Strict" liability means liability
without fault. In other words, to
prevail in a case based on strict liability, a plaintiff (person suing)
does not have to prove that the defendant (person sued) was negligent. This
doctrine is often applied in "products
liability" cases, where a manufactured
appliance, automobile or other device
breaks for no apparent reason and
causes injury or property damage. For
example, if the steering mechanism on a
new car fails (or an elevator falls),
causing an accident, the people injured
are entitled to recover damages from
the manufacturer without having to

prove the manufacturer was negligent, i.e., didn't do all it could to avoid the defect. Although there are a number of reasons for applying "strict liability" in this situation, it comes down to a conclusion that steering mechanisms on new cars are supposed to work (and elevators are not supposed to fall), and if they fail, the manufacturer is legally responsible without the injured people having to mount an elaborate case proving negligence.

Strict liability has recently been held applicable to landlords. In May 1985, the long-standing rule that only a negligent landlord is liable for injury to her tenant was, in effect, changed by a ruling of the California Supreme Court. The court, in a case known as **Becker v. IBM Corp.,** * ruled that, in addition to being liable to tenants and anyone else injured as a result of the landlord's negligence, a landlord can still be liable for injuries suffered by a tenant even if the injury occurs through no fault of the landlord whatsoever.

In the Becker case, the court ruled that the owner of a 36-unit apartment complex was liable to a tenant seriously injured by a shower door made of dangerous untempered glass, even though that type of glass appears no different from tempered safety glass used in modern shower doors, and even though the landlord could not have known about the untempered glass. When the apartment was purchased, shower doors in only five of the apartment units contained safety glass, while those in the other 31 units contained the dangerous untempered glass--which no one but a glass expert could tell was unsafe. Under standard negligence rules, the landlord could not be considered negligent in having failed to replace the regular glass doors with safety glass. The landlord never knew about the kinds of glass; the previous owner didn't tell him, and no tenant had ever

complained--until, of course, one was seriously injured in the accident that made this hidden defect apparent.

The Becker ruling means, in essence, that landlords may be held liable for all injuries suffered by tenants--and others--as a result of defective housing conditions. If the defect is "latent," or hidden, the landlord will still be liable under the strict liability theory announced in the Becker case. If the defect is not hidden, i.e., fairly apparent to the casual observer, it is one which a reasonably vigilant landlord should know about, and application of ordinary negligence principles will render the landlord liable.

This does not mean that a landlord is liable every time a tenant is injured. In a previous example illustrating negligence, we saw that a landlord sued by a tenant injured by a gunfight in the laundry would not be liable, where the gunfighters broke into the locked laundry room, the lighting was good, and no similar events or violent incidents had occurred in the past. This is still true, because the Becker case applies only to <u>defects</u> in the property. On the other hand, the application of strict liability in landlord-tenant cases would mean, for example, that a landlord would be liable to a tenant injured by a stranger who was able to enter the apartment due to a defective lock-- even if the tenant never complained about the lock.

Among the defenses that may, in certain circumstances, be available in a lawsuit based on strict liability theory are, again, assumption of risk and misuse of the product. Thus, if the tenant has somehow overloaded or otherwise misused the appliance which caused the fire, the landlord may not be liable.** The full ramifications of the

---

* 38 Cal.3d 454, 213 Cal.Rptr.213 (1985).

** In strict liability cases against manufacturers, liability has been found when the consumer misused the product in a way that the manufacturer should have foreseen. The same rule will probably be applied to landlords.

Becker case are not yet fully known, and may not be for several years as the appellate courts fill in the details. Although it remains to be seen whether landlords will be held liable in virtually every case in which a tenant is injured by defective housing conditions, hidden or not, it is clear that fine distinctions about what a "reasonable" landlord would do under similar circumstances will become less important, and tenants who have suffered injury as a result of defective housing conditions will find it more easy to recover.

3. Punitive Damages

In certain extreme cases, where a person's acts were either intentional or reckless, the law allows a judge or jury to award "punitive" damages--extra money over and above the amount required to compensate the victim. In this context, punitive damages are designed to punish a person guilty of extremely negligent conduct, with an eye toward preventing similar conduct in the future.* The fact is that in situations where the landlord has been actually aware of a long-existing and dangerous defect, but neglected to correct the problem, the landlord is guilty of more than ordinary carelessness. Although punitive damages are rarely awarded in lawsuits based on negligence, they can be awarded in extreme cases if the conduct is outrageous enough. And, if this is the case, the tenant may even be able to recover under another legal theory, namely intentional or negligent infliction of emotional distress, and obtain compensation for whatever the jury decides a tenant's emotional upset and mental suffering is worth.**

---

* Civil Code Section 3294.

** See **Stoiber v. Honeychuck** (1980) 101 Cal.App.3d 903.

C. Avoiding Liability for a Tenant's Injury

As you've seen from Section B, above, the most common legal theory under which tenants and their guests suffering injury or damage due to a housing defect recover settlements from landlords (and landlord's insurance companies--see Section D) is negligence. The most common way landlord negligence is demonstrated is where a landlord ignores tenant complaints as to dangerous conditions which subsequently cause injury. Second on the list when it comes to proving negligence is the situation where even absent tenant complaints, a landlord does not notice and fix defects which he could have discovered from a reasonable inspection.

Obviously, the best way to avoid liability for this kind of actual or supposed negligence is to adopt a conscientious policy of soliciting and responding quickly to tenant complaints about potential safety problems. In Chapter 10, where we discuss tenants' rent-nonpayment defenses based on a supposed breach by the landlord of the implied warranty to provide habitable premises, we suggested a detailed system of repeatedly asking for, and responding to, tenant feedback as to the existence of any defects on the property. Conscientiously following this sort of system will go a long way toward protecting you from suits based on negligence, at the same time it makes your tenants' lives safer and hopefully happier.

Let's review the basic principles discussed in Section B of Chapter 10 here. As a conscientious landlord, you should:

• Tell tenants when moving in, and repeatedly during their tenancy, that you want to be immediately notified of any defects or other safety problems, both in their particular units and in common areas. Do this in writing, both by placing conspicuous notices in several places about your property and routinely including notice of your repair policy and procedures in communications to the tenant;

• Document all tenant complaints and your response. In this connection, you may want to adopt a policy that if time allows, tenants' requests for repairs, maintenance and added security, etc. should be made in writing on a form provided by you or your manager;

• If oral complaints are made (and you shouldn't discourage this, especially when time is of the essence in fixing a truly dangerous problem), you should create your own record by sending a brief note to the tenant acknowledging receipt of the complaint, with a copy for your records;

• Whenever a complaint is received, enter it in a log book. List the date and time of the complaint and how and when you responded. If there's ever a question about whether you had notice of a defect, and there's no entry in a concientiously-maintained log book of a complaint ever being made, it should go a long way towards showing that no complaint was made;

• Adopt a policy under which complaints are responded to promptly. If safety is involved, be particularly sensitive to doing what is necessary to remedy the situation promptly. Always note your action in the log book;

• Establish a policy of frequently inspecting any common areas on your property. Be particularly sensitive to safety in halls, parking areas, laundry rooms, etc. If you have a pool, your fencing, signs, maintenance techniques and emergency equipment should be checked by an expert in the field at regular intervals. It is probably unwise to insist on frequent inspections of your tenants' individual apartments or homes. What you gain in making frequent inspections to make sure things are safe must be balanced against your tenants' likely feelings that their privacy is being invaded. Still, every property should be carefully checked for potential safety problems periodically (often this can be done when a tenant moves out).

NOTE: Many insurance companies will help you inspect your property with an eye to eliminating hazards. Insurance company staff engineers can be of particular help in areas such as pool fencing and locks, location of fire extinguisher, etc. This service is usually free to policyholders. Take advantage of it.

In addition to ordinary negligence, however, we mentioned in Section B above that a landlord may also get into legal hot water if she promises some level of care or safety and doesn't deliver. The best way to protect yourself in this area is to be very careful about your advertisements and other representations. Thus, even if your building has a security system or your pool has special safety systems, you may well not want to brag about them in any advertisements or other promotional material you circulate. As noted earlier in this chapter, if you claim a 24-hour security system, but only provide a 23-hour system, and someone is injured by a mugger during the hour without security, you are likely to be found legally liable. However, if you never claimed or guaranteed the existence of a security system in the first place, your chances of avoiding legal liability are enhanced. Obviously, all of this is a matter of degree and there are no hard and fast rules, except the more you brag, the more you better be able to back up your promises.

D. Insurance

As is obvious from Sections A and B of this chapter, a landlord can suffer financial ruin as the result of a tenant's or guest's injury. The financial ruin can result not only from having to pay judgments and settlements to tenants, but also from the heavy legal fees involved.

The best way to minimize your potential for financial loss is obviously to purchase appropriate liability insurance. This type of insurance provides for payment of any judgments, up to the policy limits, arising out of the insured activity, e.g., the leasing of residential real property. It is usually combined with a fire insurance policy and various other rental property owners protections, such as protection from illegal acts by you or your manager or employees. Such insurance not only protects you against having to pay court judgments, but also against incurring legal fees to defend any lawsuit brought by tenants or visitors for injuries suffered on the premises.

Insurance policies, however, do not and cannot cover liability for either punitive damages awarded in a lawsuit, or for intentional acts, such as beating up a tenant. However, keep in mind that punitive damages are almost never

awarded in landlord-tenant cases based on accidental injuries, and that as a general rule, a landlord won't be liable for any punitive damages if he refrains from extreme neglect and intentional wrongs against his tenants and others.

Your next question is probably, how do you know if you have a good liability policy? Probably your best bet is to deal with insurance agents and brokers with good reputations in your community. Talk to people who own property similar to yours, or to real estate people with several years experience-- they will know who comes through and who doesn't. In the meantime, here are a few rules of thumb:

• Purchase high levels of liability coverage. Personal injury damage awards, especially in large metropolitan areas, can be, and often are, very high, and a million dollars' coverage does not cost a great deal more than a hundred thousand dollars' coverage;

• Make sure the liability section of the policy covers libel, slander, unlawful eviction, wrongful arrest and invasion of privacy, as well as protecting you from personal injuries suffered by tenants and guests;

• Make sure you have non-owned auto liability insurance to protect yourself from liability for your manager or other employee's bad driving of their own automobile while running errands for you;

• Your bank or mortgage company will protect its interest in the property by requiring you to purchase fire insurance. But, they won't pressure you into buying more than enough insurance to protect their interest. This means you should review your policy annually to make sure your policy limits continue to meet the appreciation of the property;

• Depending on where your property is located, you may want extended coverage for damage caused by earthquake, flood, wind and hailstorms, and so forth;

• If your property is damaged or destroyed, your tenants, of course, will stop paying rent. Make sure your fire/damage policy provides that you will be compensated for lost rents while the property is being rebuilt or repaired;

• If you hire any management or other employees, be sure to obtain workers' compensation insurance to protect yourself from liability to an employee injured on the job. We discuss this in Chapter 6;

• If your manager will handle money, it's a good idea to add a manager's bond provision to the policy to protect yourself if the money ends up in the manager's pocket instead of yours.

12

Landlords' Right of Entry and Tenants' Privacy

Next to disputes over rents or other money matters, the most emotional misunderstandings between landlord and tenant commonly involve conflicts between a landlord's right to enter the property to maintain, repair, show for sale or rent, or just plain inspect it, and a tenant's right to be left alone to enjoy his home. What is so unfortunate about these kinds of problems is that many of them can be avoided if both landlord and tenant understand and follow both existing legal rules and common sense. Unfortunately, we can't do anything to help you if one of your tenants is completely devoid of the latter and turns paranoid every time you want to inspect the furnace or fix the plumbing. The best we can do is make sure you know your legal rights and responsibilities, as well as offer-

ing you several common sense tenant management suggestions that have worked well for other landlords.

Traditionally, a tenant was entirely responsible for maintaining and repairing his rented abode. This being true, landlords of old had few occasions to ever come onto the property--other than to forcibly evict the tenant for failing to pay the rent or for otherwise violating the lease. In fact, a tenant who paid his rent and otherwise abided by the terms of the lease was completely within his legal rights to treat a nosy landlord as a trespasser and order him off the property, or even bodily remove him if he refused to leave. Today, however, as we learned in Chapter 10, the law conditions the tenant's duty to pay rent on the landlord's proper repair and maintenance of the premises. This means that, of necessity, a landlord must keep fairly close tabs on the condition of her property. For this reason, and because it makes good sense to allow a landlord reasonable access to their own property, the law now clearly recognizes the right of a landlord to enter the premises under a number of defined circumstances.

This doesn't mean a landlord can enter a tenant's home at any time for any reason. Once you rent residential property in California, you must respect it as your tenant's home. If you wish to enter, you should strictly follow the legal rules.

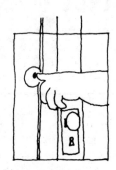

A. The Landlords' Right of Entry

Section 1954 of the California Civil Code establishes the circumstances under which a landlord can enter his tenant's home, and Section 1953(a)(1) provides that these circumstances cannot be expanded, or the tenant's privacy rights waived or modified, by any lease or rental-agreement provision. The first thing to realize is that there are only four broad situations in which you may legally enter while a tenant is still in residence. They are:

1. To deal with an emergency;

2. To make needed repairs (or assess the need for them);

3. To show the property to prospective new tenants or purchasers; and

4. When you are invited in by the tenant.

In most instances (emergencies and tenant invitations excepted), a landlord can only enter during "normal business hours" and then only after "reasonable notice," presumed to be 24 hours. Normal business hours, customarily, are 9 a.m. to 5 p.m., Monday through Friday, but the statute doesn't say specifically.

1. Entry in Case of an Emergency

Under Civil Code Section 1954, a landlord or manager can enter the property without giving advance notice in order to respond to a true emergency which threatens injury or property damage if not corrected immediately. For example, a fire, gas, or serious water leak is a true emergency which, if not corrected, will result in damage, injury, or even loss of life. On the other hand, a landlord's urge to make even needed repair of an important but non-life-or-property threatening defect, say of a stopped-up drain, isn't a true emergency for which the law allows no-notice entry by the landlord. To facilitate this right, a landlord is entitled to have a key to the premises, including any locks the tenant may add. To avoid misunderstandings in this area, it is a good idea to state this right in the lease or rental agreement, as we do in the one in the tear-out lease/rental agreement form in the Appendix. (See Chapter 2, Section E on lease and rental-agreement provisions.) But what about security systems, burglar alarms, etc. which are installed by the tenant? Some landlords feel they should always know how to disarm these. We generally disagree. Keeping track of all this information is difficult, if not impossible, when you think about the ideosyncrasies of all the alarm systems on the market. In addition, if a tenant's goods are stolen and the alarm doesn't function, you may wish you did not know the code or have the key.

But what if an emergency occurs and you have to enter and shut off the alarm? All you really need to know is the name and phone number of the alarm company. This is commonly printed on the alarm box itself. Call the alarm company as soon as you enter and tell them what the situation is. They may still call the police to check things out, but the tension inherent in the situation should be diffused.

2. Entry to Make Repairs

Section 1954 allows you and your repairperson, contractor, etc. to enter to make and assess the need for and cost of routine repairs or alterations. In this situation, however, you must enter only during normal business hours (9:00 a.m. to 5 p.m., Monday-Friday) and must give "reasonable notice." As we noted above, Civil Code Section 1954 contains a presumption that a 24-hour notice period is reasonable. Accordingly, it is always wise to give your tenant at least 24 hours' notice if possible. However, if there is a good reason for it, giving a reasonable but shorter notice is legal. This is because under the wording of the statute, the 24-hour notice period is only a presumption of reasonableness, not an absolute requirement.

EXAMPLE: If Lexington Landlord arranges to have a repairperson inspect a wall heater at 2 p.m. on Tuesday, he should notify Lenora Lessee on or before 2 p.m. on Monday. But if Lexington can't reach Lenora until 6 p.m. (e.g., she can't be reached at home or at work), less than 24 hours' notice is probably okay. Of course, if Lenora consents to Lexington's plan, the notice period is not a problem (see Section 4, below).

If you can't reach the tenant at home or at work to give 24 hours' notice of your intention to enter, and you are worried that the particular tenant is concerned about her privacy, it is a good idea to post a note detailing your plan on the tenant's front door, keeping a copy for your own records. Now, if the tenant doesn't receive the notice, it's because she didn't return home and you couldn't reach her at work, in which case, a 24-hour notice would have been impracticable anyway.

In many situations, the 24-hour notice period will not be a problem, as your tenant will be delighted that you are making needed repairs and will cooperate with your entry requirements. However, as every long-time landlord knows, some tenants are completely unreasonable when it comes to cooperating with you to see that you have reasonable access to make repairs, at the same time that they are extremely demanding that repairs be made. If you must deal with a tenant who is a stickler for her legal right of privacy, your best bet is to give at least 24 hours' notice of your intent to enter and not to try and shorten this period.

Here is a sample notice:

November 19, 198_

Terrence Tenant
123 Parker Street
Apartment 4
Berkeley, CA

Dear Mr. Tenant:

Pleased be advised that in response to your complaint regarding the heater in your apartment, the management has arranged to have it repaired tomorrow, on Tuesday, November 20, at 2:00 p.m. We attempted to give you telephoned notice to this effect today between 9:00 a.m. and 5:00 p.m. Because we were unable to reach you at home or work, I am leaving this note on your door.

Sincerely,

Melba Manager

WARNING: A landlord can't use his right to limited access to harass or annoy the tenant. Repeated inspections, even when 24-hour notice is given, are an invitation to nonpayment of rent, a lawsuit or worse.

Problems may arise in situations where the repairperson shows up a few hours or more late, for example, where she's supposed to come at 4 p.m. and doesn't show up until 8 a.m. the next morning. If the tenant has been seriously inconvenienced, they are likely to be hostile and to stand on their rights. You or your manager can avoid this sort of problem if you can get the repairperson to come on time in the first place, or if this isn't possible, to always call the tenant and explain the problem and ask the tenant's permission to enter later on. If the tenant says, "No," the repairperson should not enter anyway, but should contact you so that a second 24-hour notice can be given.

3. Entry to Show Property

Section 1954 also allows you to enter your property to show it to prospective tenants toward the end of a tenancy and to prospective purchasers if you wish to sell it, as long as you comply with the "business hours" and "reasonable notice" provisions discussed in Section A, above. Here is a sample fill-in-the-blank notice that can be used for this type of situation, as well as for entry to make repairs.

152

Shady Dell Apartments
123 Market Street
Los Angeles, CA

January 5, 1986

Renee Renter
123 Market St., Apt #4
Los Angeles, CA

Dear Mr./Ms. _____ :

    Please be advised that the management of Shady Dell Apartments would like to enter your apartment on _____ , 19__ at 2:00 a.m./p.m. for the following reason(s):

    ( ) To make or arrange for the following repairs(s) and/or improvement(s): _____

_____

_____

    ( ) To exhibit the premises to: ( ) a prospective tenant, ( ) workers and/or contractors regarding the above repair or improvement,

    ( ) Other: _____

_____

    If you wish to be present, or have a friend or associate be present, at that time, you may, of course, make the appropriate arrangements. If you have any questions, please call me at 555-5555 or come to the Manager's Office between 9:00 a.m. and 6:00 p.m.

    This notice is given in accordance with the provisions of Section 1954 of the California Civil Code.

Sincerely,

Marlene Manager

For example, a landlord who doesn't plan to renew a tenant's about-to-expire lease, or who has given or received a 30-day notice terminating a month-to-month tenancy, may show the premises to prospective new tenants during the last few weeks of the outgoing tenant's stay. However, it is not a good idea to show property if a dispute exists over whether the current tenant has a right to stay. A landlord's insistence on showing the property in this situation not only causes unnecessary friction, but is obviously of little practical use, since the landlord is unable to tell the new tenants when they can move in.

EXAMPLE: Tired of receiving his rent two or three weeks late each month, Owen Owner gives Renfrew Renter a 30-day notice on October 1, terminating Renfrew's month-to-month tenancy, effective October 31. Renfrew says he has a right to stay because he claims Owen is retaliating against him for having made a minor complaint to the manager. Although Owen knows this is nonsense, and that he has a right to terminate Renfrew's tenancy, and will prevail in court if it comes to that, he may be better off not insisting on his right to show the place. In any case, it won't do him much good as he won't be able to tell any prospective tenant when the apartment will be available. Why? Because Renfrew is likely to argue his theory of retaliatory eviction in court as part of his defense to Owen's eviction action. This will take at least three weeks, and probably more if Owen wins. Also, if Owen shows the premises, as if Renfrew's leaving is a foregone conclusion, Renfrew is likely to become more hostile, thus eliminating the possibility that he will give up his court fight and go quietly.

As noted, you may also show the property to prospective buyers or mortgage companies. This situation often arises when a property that is for sale is a rented single-family house or condominium unit, but can also occur where a multiple-unit building is placed on the market. Again, remember that under Section 1954, 24 hours is presumed to be reasonable notice to your tenant. Problems usually occur when a real estate salesperson trying to sell the property shows up on the tenant's doorstep without warning or calls on very short notice and asks to be let in to show the place to a possible buyer. In this situation, the tenant is within his or her right to say politely but firmly, "I'm busy right now--try again in a few days after we've set a time convenient for all of us." Naturally, this type of misunderstanding is not conducive to good landlord-tenant relations, not to mention a sale of the property. Make sure the real estate salespeople you deal with understand the law and respect your tenant's rights to advance notice.

Selling a house occupied by a tenant isn't easy on anyone. At times, you will want to show the place on short notice. And you may even want to have an occasional open house on weekends. Your tenant, on the other hand, is liable to feel threatened by the change in ownership. From her point of view, any actions you take to show the house to strangers may seem like an intolerable intrusion.

Obviously, the best way to achieve your ends is with the cooperation of the tenant. With a little advance planning, this may not be so difficult to arrange. One good plan is to meet with the tenant in advance and offer a reasonable rent reduction in exchange for cooperation. However, you should realize that this type of agreement is enforceable only so long as the tenant continues to go along with it. Indeed, this may be one situation when an informal understanding that the rent be lowered so long as the tenant agrees to the frequent showings (e.g., two open houses a month and showing the unit on 2-hour notice, as long as it doesn't occur more than three times a week) may be better than a written agreement. Why? Because, technically, any written agreement changing the rent is really an amendment to the rental agreement, and rental agreement clauses under which tenants give up their privacy rights are void and unenforceable if it comes to a court fight.

LOCK BOX NOTE: Under no circumstances should an owner of occupied rental property which is listed for sale allow the placing of a key-holding "lockbox" on the door. This is a metal box that attaches to the front door and contains the key to that door. It can be opened by a master key held by area real estate salespeople. Since a lockbox allows a salesperson to enter in disregard of the 24-hour notice requirement, it should not be used--period. If the tenant claims any of his belongings are missing because of the "open-door" policy promoted by a lockbox you authorized, you could face a lawsuit.

4. Entry With the Agreement of the Tenant

Of course, a landlord can always enter rental property even without 24 hours' notice, if the tenant agrees without pressure or coercion. As we noted earlier when we talked about the special problems associated with selling rental property, it is often wise to work out a sensible understanding with the tenant if circumstances necessitate. For example, if you have a maintenance problem that needs regular attending to (e.g., a fussy heater or temperamental plumbing), you might want to work out a detailed agreement with the tenant covering entry.

If problems are only occasional and you have no special needs of entry, you can probably rely on a friendly telephone call to the tenant asking for permission to enter. (Don't be too insistent, lest the tenant claim you coerced this permission out of him.)

If the tenant agrees, but has been difficult and not always reliable in the past, you might even want to cover yourself by documenting his apparent willingness--sending him a confirmatory thank-you note afterwards, keeping a copy for yourself. If this is met with unease or outright hostility, you will be wise to stick to the 24-hour notice procedure outlined in Section B, above.

5. Entry After the Tenant Has Moved Out

To state the obvious, a landlord may also enter the premises at any time after the tenant has moved out, whether voluntarily after giving back the key, or involuntarily after the sheriff or marshall conducts an eviction pursuant to a court order following a successful eviction lawsuit. In addition, a landlord who believes a tenant has abandoned the property (skipped out without giving any notice or returning the key) may legally enter. However, before you do this, read Chapter 17, which contains the legal procedure for entry if you are not absolutely sure your tenant has permanently departed.

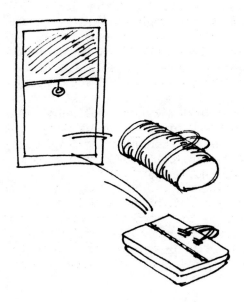

B. A Landlord Cannot Demand to Enter at Will

Many leases or written rental agreements say that the landlord can enter the rental unit and inspect any time he wants. Quite simply, these kinds of provisions are not legally enforceable. As we saw earlier, Section 1953(a)(1) of the Civil Code says that any agreement where the tenant gives up or modifies his or her right to privacy is of no effect. Given this, it's just plain counterproductive to include obviously illegal and unenforceable provisions in your written agreements. Indeed, we believe it's a good idea to have a lease or rental agreement clause that sets forth the tenant's obligation to allow the landlord legally-required access under Civil Code Section 1954. If you do this, and if the tenant then adamantly refuses you access, assuming you have a legal reason and have given proper notice, he has breached the lease or rental agreement. This means that if all attempts at compromise fail, you can use this breach by the tenant as a basis for eviction. In addition, if you have a lease that very specifically states your right to access under Civil Code Section 1954, denial of that right should be sufficient legal reason to send a three-day notice telling the tenant to shape up or leave. (We discuss this in Chapter 15). Complete denial of legal access also qualifies as a just cause for eviction under even strict rent control ordinances, but in some cities you must first send the tenant a notice giving him a chance to mend his ways (see Chapter 4, Section B).

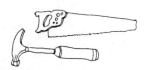

C. Landlords' Remedies when Faced With Unreasonable Tenants

Occasionally, a landlord who gives reasonable notice of her intent to enter the tenant's home for legitimate purposes is still faced with an adamant refusal by the tenant to allow entry, even though she has included a summary of the entry requirements of Civil Code Section 1954 in the lease or written rental agreement. If you encounter repeated unreasonable refusals to let you or your employees enter the premises during normal business hours for one of the legitimate reasons listed earlier in this chapter, you can legally enter anyway. However, for practical reasons, a wise landlord faced by a tenant who is unreasonably asserting her right to privacy will not enter alone. It's just common sense to bring someone along who can later act as a witness in case the tenant claims some of her property is missing.

Another problem faced by landlords is that some tenants have their locks changed. No statute or case law addresses whether a tenant is within her rights to change the locks without giving the landlord an extra key. Again, as noted earlier, we suggest that you require landlord key access in your lease or written rental agreement, as well as notice of any change of locks or the installation of any burglar alarms, along with the name and number of the alarm company.

But what should you do if you have a serious conflict over access with an otherwise satisfactory tenant? A meeting with the tenant to see if the problem can be resolved is a sensible first step. If this doesn't work, mediation by a neutral third party may work. See our discussion of how to set up a mediation in Chapter 7, Section H. If all else fails, your best bet is probably to give the tenant a 30-day notice to leave if you rent under a month-to-month tenancy in a non-rent-control rental area, or to evict the tenant on the basis of their failure to abide by your written right-of-entry provision if you rent under a lease or in an area requiring just cause for eviction.* If you contemplate a formal court action to get rid of the tenant, make sure you can document your position.

NOTE: It is unwise to have a lock installed by a tenant changed even if you immediately provide the tenant access. This invites a lawsuit and false claims that you stole the tenant's possessions, etc.

---

* As we explain in Volume II, on evictions, you're much better off giving a month-to-month tenant a 30-day termination notice stating no reason (at least in non-rent-controlled cities where you don't need "just cause" for eviction), rather than using a three-day notice that gives the tenant the chance of contesting the reason for eviction stated on the notice.

D. The Tenant's Remedies if a Landlord Acts Illegally

It's appropriate to say a few words about what happens if you do violate your tenant's right of privacy. Obviously, as a conscientious landlord, you should be receptive to a tenant's complaint that her privacy is being violated and try and work something out that will meet both of your needs. However, there are some tenants who are just plain paranoid when it comes to their privacy. At the same time they want you to maintain the property perfectly, they don't want to give you a reasonable chance to do it. In this situation, it's easy for you or your manager to make a technical mistake that at least theoretically invades a tenant's privacy. If so, a tenant may respond by claiming you have violated her right to quiet enjoyment of the property** and withhold a portion of the next month's rent. If this occurs, it's up to you either to accept a tenant's nonpayment of whatever sum of the rent she felt she deserved as compensation, or to bring an eviction suit based on nonpayment of rent. In addition, you should know that repeated abuses by a landlord of a tenant's right of access gives a tenant under a lease a legal excuse to break it by moving out, without liability for further rent.

** "Quiet enjoyment" of rental real property is the name lawyers give to the fairly straightforward concept that a tenant has the same right to enjoy her home free from interference by her landlord (or anyone else) as does a homeowner.

A tenant faced with a landlord or manager who won't respect her privacy can also bring a lawsuit based on trespass and invasion of privacy, and can ask for money damages* And remember, an owner can be held liable for his property manager's disrespect of the tenant's right of privacy even if the owner never entered, or never even knew about the manager's conduct.

E. Other Types of Invasions of Privacy

Entering a tenant's home without his knowledge or consent isn't the only way a landlord can interfere (however unintentionally) with the tenant's privacy. Here are a few other commonly-encountered situations, with advice on how to handle them.

1. Letting Strangers into the Premises

Occasionally a landlord or resident manager will be faced with a very convincing stranger who will tell a heart-rending story: "If I don't get my heart medicine which I left in this apartment, I'll die on the spot," or "I'm Nancy's father and I just got in from the North Pole, where a polar bear

ate my wallet and I have no other place to stay." The problem arises when you can't contact the tenant at work or elsewhere to ask whether it's okay to let the desperate individual in.

Keep in mind that although perhaps nine out of ten stories such as the above are legitimate, it doesn't make sense to expose yourself to the potential liability involved should you get taken in by a clever con artist. There is always at least a chance that the stranger is really a smooth talker who your tenant has a dozen good reasons to want kept out. So, take our advice, never let a stranger, including the police (unless they have a search warrant, or say they need to enter to prevent a catastrophe, such as an explosion) into your tenant's home without your tenant's permission. If you do, you can be sued for any damage or loss incurred. Even if you have been authorized to allow a certain person entry, it is wise to ask the stranger for identification. Although this no-entry-without-authorization policy may sometimes be difficult to adhere to in the face of a convincing story, stick to it. You have much more to lose in admitting the wrong person into the tenant's home than you would have to gain by letting in someone who's "probably okay."

2. Putting "For Sale" or "For Rent" Signs or Lock Boxes on the Property

Occasionally, friction is caused by landlords who put "For sale," or "For rent" signs on tenants' homes, such as a "For sale" sign on the lawn of a rented single-family house. Although a

---

* It's easy for a tenant to press her claim for $1,500 or less in small claims court without a lawyer. See Warner, **Everybody's Guide to Small Claims Court** (Nolo Press).

landlord may otherwise be very conscientious about respecting the tenant's privacy when it comes to giving 24 hours' notice before showing property to prospective buyers or renters, the erection of a sale or rental sign on the property is a virtual invitation to prospective buyers or renters to disturb the tenant with unwelcome inquiries. This is particularly true with "For sale" signs, since existing tenants who like where they are living often justifiably feel a little bit threatened and insecure when a house they're renting is being sold to a new owner, who may raise the rent or evict them to move in herself. In this situation, if your tenant's privacy is completely ruined by repeated inquiries, the tenant may resort to rent withholding or sue you for invasion of privacy, just as if you personally had made repeated illegal entries.

Even worse are "lock boxes" that some multiple listing real estate salespersons insist on installing on the tenant"s door. These little boxes, containing the keys to the property, can be opened by any of numerous real estate salespeople at any time. This will leave you wide open to a tenant's lawsuit for invasion of privacy, and possibly liable for any property the tenant claims to have lost.

Keep in mind that in the age of computerized multiple-listing services, many real estate offices can, and commonly do, sell houses and all sorts of other real estate without ever using a lock box, and without placing a "For Sale" sign on the property, except during the hours when an open house is in progress. If you or your real estate office must put up a sign advertising sale or rental of the property, make sure it clearly indicates a telephone number to call and warns against disturbing the occupant in words like, "Inquire at 555-1357--Do Not Disturb Occupant." If your real

estate office refuses to accommodate you in this regard, find a new one that will respect your tenants' privacy and keep you out of a lawsuit.

3. Giving Information to Strangers

As a landlord, you may be approached by strangers, including creditors, banks and perhaps even prospective landlords, to provide credit or other information on your tenant. Resist your natural urge to be helpful, unless the tenant has given you written permission to release this sort of information. As with letting a stranger into the tenant's home, you have nothing to gain, and possibly a lot to lose, if you give out information that your tenant feels constitutes a serious violation of her privacy. And if you give out incorrect information--even if you believe it to be accurate--you can really be in a legal mess if the person to whom you disclose it relies on it to take some action that negatively affects your tenant.

Some landlords feel that they should communicate information to prospective landlords, especially if the tenant has failed to pay rent, maintain the premises, or has created other serious problems. If you do give out this information, make sure you are absolutely factual and that the information you provide has been requested. If you go out of your way to give out negative information (e.g., you try and blackball the tenant with all other landlords in your area), you definitely risk legal liability for libelling your tenant and interfering with her contractual rights, even if the tenant deserves blackballing.

NOTE: BEWARE OF GOSSIPY MANAGERS: A number of landlords we know have had serious problems with on-site managers who have gossiped about tenants who, for example, paid rent late, or were served with a three-day notice, or had overnight visitors, etc. This sort of gossip may seem innocent, but if flagrant, can be an invasion of privacy for which you can be liable. So, impress on your managers their duty to keep confidential all sensitive information about tenants.

4. Calling or Visiting the Tenant at Work

Should the need arise for you to call your tenant at work (say when his Uncle Harry shows up and asks to be let into his apartment), try to be sensitive to whether it's permissible for him to receive personal calls. While some people work at desks with telephones and have bosses who don't get upset about occasional personal calls, others have jobs that are greatly disrupted by any phone call. A general rule seems to be that the more physical the type of the work, the more tyrannical employers are about prohibiting personal phone calls at work. Under no circumstances should you continue to call a tenant at work who asks you not to do so. This is especially true when calling about when the rent will be paid, etc. And never leave specific messages with your tenant's employer, especially those that could reflect negatively on her. A landlord who leaves a message like "Tell your deadbeat employee I'll evict her if she doesn't pay the rent" can expect at least a lot of bad feeling on the part of the tenant, and, at worst, a lawsuit for slander and/or invasion of privacy. As for visiting the tenant at work--say to collect late rent--this is something you should absolutely avoid unless invited by her. What it boils down to is that no matter what you think of your tenant, you should respect the sensitive nature of the tenant's relationship with her employer.

5. Unduly Restrictive Rules on Guests

A few landlords, overly concerned about their tenants moving new occupants into the property, go a little overboard in keeping tabs on the tenants' legitimate guests who stay overnight or for a few days. Often their leases, rental agreements, or rules and regulations will require a tenant to "register" an overnight guest. While landlords should be concerned about persons who begin as "guests" becoming permanent unauthorized residents of the property (see Chapter 9, Section F), it is overkill to require a tenant to inform his landlord of a guest whose stay is only for a day or two. Keep in mind that just because you rent your tenant her home, you don't have the right to restrict her social life or pass upon the propriety of her visitors' stays. As with other subjects we mention in this chapter, extreme behavior in this area--whether by an owner or a management employee--can be considered an invasion of privacy for which you may be held liable.

6. Spying on the Tenant

As a result of worrying too much about a tenant's visitors, a few landlords have occasionally attempted to interrogate tenants' visitors, knocking on their tenants' doors at odd hours or too frequently, in order to see who answers, or just gaze inside, and even peeking through windows. Needless-to-say, even only a little bit of this sort of conduct can render a landlord liable for punitive damages in an invasion-of-privacy suit. As far as talking to tenants' guests is concerned, engaging in anything more than pleasant hellos or non-threatening small talk is legally out of bounds. If you think your tenant's activity with respect to guests-cum-residents, or anything else, is a problem, make an appointment with the tenant and ask to talk about it.

13

How to Avoid Making Illegal Rent Increases and Retaliatory Evictions

A. Introduction

This chapter is primarily written for landlords in non-rent-control areas. Those of you in areas with rent-control laws which contain "just cause for eviction" provisions should refer to Chapter 4. This is not to say that retaliatory rent increases and terminations are legal in rent-control areas. It's just that the question of whether rent increases and terminations are retaliatory, and therefore illegal, seldom comes up in most rent-control areas, where more stringent local laws restrict rent increases and terminations of every kind, retaliatory or not.

Unfortunately, this chapter is essential reading for all landlords, even those of you (the great majority, certainly) who have no intention of ever illegally retaliating against any tenant for exercising her legal rights. The problem is that the laws have been written so broadly that all sorts of innocently-motivated landlord conduct can form the basis for either a lawsuit against the landlord for damages, or a successful defense against a landlord's unlawful detainer action. In other words, a well-meaning ignorance of the law can cause you as many problems as if you cynically disregard it, especially if you are dealing with a dishonest tenant who is determined to misuse the law to try and avoid paying rent.

Our goal in this chapter is twofold. First, we want you to clearly understand how the law defines retaliatory evictions and retaliatory rent increases. Second, and more important, we want you to know how to anticipate and avoid the legal problems that can be created by the few tenants who will try to maneuver you into the position of appearing to violate their rights. This really isn't as difficult as you might imagine. Think of it this way. You want to take the same precaution against the possibility of a tenant cheating you as you would against being bitten if you were walking in rattlesnake country. When it comes to rattlers, if you wear boots, know how to recognize the critters, and watch your step, it's unlikely that you will be bitten. There is normally no need to anxiously arm yourself with a load of weapons. As long as you are prepared, you usually have plenty of time to avoid any snake that happens along. Indeed, it may even be counterproductive to arm yourself, especially if you stumble and shoot your foot. Similarly, when dealing with the occasional dishonest tenants, if you know your legal rights and learn to take sensible advance steps to nullify and counter their hostile urges, you should have few legal problems.

B. Retaliatory Evictions

As we've discussed in the preceding chapters, residential tenants have a number of legal rights and remedies. For example, we saw in Chapter 2 that a tenant on a fixed-term lease has a right to refuse to pay a rent increase before the end of the lease term (unless the lease calls for periodic rent increases), and that a month-to-month tenant can insist on a written notice of 30 days before submitting to any change in terms of tenancy.

Similarly, in Chapter 8, we reviewed the tenant's right to be free from arbitrary or discriminatory treatment based on factors such as her race, religion, sex, disability, marital status, etc., and to complain to administrative agencies, or even courts, when she feels her rights are being violated, and in Chapter 10, we discussed the tenant's right to live in premises free of defects that might endanger her or her family's health or safety, including the right to complain to local authorities or to withhold rent in appropriate cases, or even to file a lawsuit against a landlord who fails to keep the premises in proper repair. Finally, in Chapter 12, we discussed the tenant's right to privacy and freedom from having the landlord enter the property when he feels like it.

However you may feel about many of these tenant's rights and remedies, one thing is clear. Tenant protection laws are meaningless if a landlord can legally retaliate against a tenant who asserts her legal rights. For example, the right of a month-to-month tenant to complain to the local fire department about a defective heater is worth little if the landlord, angry about the complaint, is free to retaliate against her with an immediate 30-day termination or rent-increase notice. Recognizing this, the California legislature and courts have made it illegal for a landlord to attempt to penalize a tenant in any way simply because she has attempted to vindicate a legal right that works to the landlord's disadvantage.

The principal statute in this area is Section 1942.5 of the Civil Code. It would be wise to read it. This section makes it illegal for a landlord to retaliate against the tenant "for having exercised any right under the law," whether by reducing services, by giving a 30-day rent-increase or termination notice, or even threatening to do so, or doing anything else that works to the tenant's disadvantage.

This legal rule has come to be known, somewhat inaccurately, as "the defense of retaliatory eviction." We say inaccurately, because it is often used to refer to situations where the tenant is not actually evicted, but faces only the legal prerequisites to an otherwise legal eviction, i.e., a three-day or 30-day notice. In other situations, this defense isn't raised in the context of an eviction at all, but is advanced by a tenant as part of resisting a rent increase claimed to be retaliatory. To be fair, we should emphasize that the defense of retaliatory eviction is sometimes properly raised by a tenant when the landlord, in order to "get even," gives the tenant notice to vacate the premises or pay a rent increase after the tenant has asserted one or more legal rights. If this occurs, the landlord is legally in the wrong and deserves the consequences.

Often, however, a retaliatory eviction defense by a tenant is little more than a smokescreen created to justify the failure to pay rent or to prevent a landlord from proceeding with a legal eviction. If this occurs, your job as a landlord is fundamentally different. You must not only know the law, you should use your knowledge to develop a coherent strategy in advance so that you can quickly and efficiently deal with the tenant's illegal conduct. Fortunately, this is not as difficult as you might imagine.

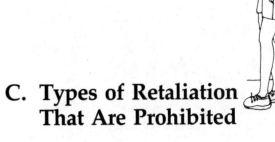

C. Types of Retaliation That Are Prohibited

In the previous decade, a landlord could give a month-to-month tenant a 30-day termination notice, raise the rent, or do anything else that was otherwise legal, so long as she wasn't doing it to "get back" at a tenant who had made a complaint or withheld rent because of a tenantability-related problem. Today, however, the law forbidding retaliation against tenants who assert certain rights is much broader. Civil Code Section 1942.5(c) makes it illegal for a landlord to increase a tenant's rent, decrease services, terminate the tenancy, or even threaten to do any of these things "for the purpose of retaliating" against the tenant on account of her having "lawfully and peaceably exercised any rights under the law." Unfortunately, there is no time limit to this rule, and, at least in theory, a tenant could claim that a 1988 rent increase was in retaliation for a 1986 complaint. In addition, courts now commonly rule that it's against the law for the landlord to retaliate against the tenant for engaging in any legal conduct, not just the things mentioned in Civil Code Section 1942.5.

One common tenant misconception about the "retaliatory eviction" defense is that once a tenant exercises a legal right, there is a certain time period (60 or 180 days) during which it is illegal for the landlord to raise the rent or terminate the tenancy under any circumstances. This is wrong. A landlord can legally do this at any time, provided she does so for a legitimate non-retaliatory reason. Of course, the practical problem with this is that a landlord who suddenly raises a tenant's rent, or gives her an eviction notice, immediately after the tenant asserts a legal right, opens herself up to a charge of illegal retaliation, even if her real reasons for evicting the tenant are legitimate.

A tenant who asserts the defense of retaliatory eviction is generally required to establish the following things if the case goes to court:

• That she [the tenant] exercised a legal right, or at least did something perfectly legal in a lawful and peaceful manner;

• Her tenant's exercise of the right was adverse to the landlord;

• The landlord (or manager) knew that the tenant had exercised the right; and

• The landlord responded with her own action against the tenant (i.e., an eviction or rent increase) so quickly, or in some other way, as to suggest her motive was to retaliate against the tenant.

Here are a few examples of situations where landlords are commonly accused of retaliating against the tenant. We list them here under the theory that to be forewarned allows you to be forearmed:

• The tenant has made a complaint about housing conditions, either to the landlord or to a health or building inspection department. (Retaliation is illegal in this situation, no matter how unfounded or frivolous the tenant's complaint to governmental authorities may be.)

• The tenant has withheld rent to protest bad housing conditions, or makes use of the "repair-and-deduct" remedy. (NOTE: It is considered a form of illegal retaliation to follow this with a 30-day termination or rent-increase notice; however, if the landlord disagrees with the right of the tenant to withhold rent, he can give the tenant a three-day notice to pay rent or quit, with an eye toward suing the tenant on the basis of rent nonpayment. We discuss this in detail in Chapter 15.)

• The tenant has engaged in political activity of any kind. A tenant who actively campaigns for local candidates whom property owners find obnoxious, or who campaigns for a rent control ordinance, has an absolute right to do so without fear of intimidation.

• The tenant has participated in, or organized, a meeting of tenants or a tenants' organization.

The above list is for illustration only. There are many more situations in which a tenant can assert a particular right and the landlord's subsequent efforts to evict the tenant or raise the rent on account of it will be considered illegal. This is true no matter how unpleasantly conveyed, ill-founded, or just plain wrong the tenant's gripe is. After all, the issue isn't whether the tenant had a good reason to act as he did, but whether his act was the exercise of a legal right and whether the landlord wanted to strike back at him with a 30-day notice, a rent increase, or other form of retaliation. Thus, tenants have prevailed on "retaliatory eviction" grounds in situations as unusual as the tenant's refusal to lie for the landlord at a trial, the tenant's calling the police for a crime committed by a manager, or even the tenant's refusal to submit to the landlord's romantic advances. Instead of trying to keep track of all the situations where it's illegal for a landlord to evict the tenant or raise the rent, it's better to assume that even if local rent control or just-cause-eviction laws don't apply:

1. Just and legitimate cause is required to terminate a month-to-month tenancy; and

2. Any rent increases or other changes in the conditions of the tenancy must be reasonable and done for legitimate business reasons.

This leads to two pieces of advice which we believe will serve you well:

• First, if a tenant withholds rent or makes a complaint for even an arguably legitimate reason at about the time you were going to raise the rent or give the tenant a 30-day notice, wait. First take care of the complaint. Next, let some time pass. Then, do what you planned to do anyway. The delay may cost you a few bucks, or result in some inconvenience, or even cause you to lose some sleep while you gnash your teeth, but all of these are preferable to being involved in litigation over whether or not your conduct was in retaliation for the tenant's complaint.

• Second, even though the law (in non-rent-control areas) says that a landlord doesn't need a reason to terminate a tenancy, be prepared to demonstrate that you do have a good reason to evict the tenant. In other words, in anticipation of the possibility that a tenant may claim that you are terminating her tenancy for retaliatory reasons, you should be prepared to prove that your reasons were valid and not retaliatory. When you think of it, this burden isn't as onerous as it might first appear. From a business point of view, few landlords will ever want to evict an excellent tenant. And assuming there is a good reason why you want the tenant out, you only need document it.

EXAMPLE: Suppose a tenant makes a legitimate complaint to the health department about a defective heater in an apartment she rents from you. Even though she does so without having had the courtesy to tell you first, she's still within her legal rights to make the complaint. Suppose further that about that same time, this tenant's neighbors complain to you, not for the first time, about her loud parties that last into the wee hours of the morning, and threaten to move out if she doesn't. Now suppose further that in response to the neighbors' complaints, you give the noisy tenant a 30-day notice. This results in the tenant refusing to move and your having to file an unlawful detainer complaint. To this, the tenant responds that the eviction was in retaliation for the complaint to the health department. A contested trial results. Perhaps you win in court, but in this situation, there is a good chance you won't.

Now, let's look at how you might better handle this problem:

STEP 1: Fix the heater;

STEP 2: Write the tenant, reminding her of your established complaint procedures (see Chapter 10). Tell her that you consider this sort of repair a routine matter which didn't necessitate a complaint to a public agency;

Here is a sample letter:

February 1, 198_

Tammy Tenant
123 State Street, Apt. 15
San Diego, CA

Dear Ms. Tenant:

As you know, Ms. Melba Manager, my resident manager at Sunny Dell Apartments, repaired the heater in your unit yesterday, on January 31.

Ms. Manager informs me that she never received a complaint from you nor any request to repair the heater, and that she learned about the problem for the first time when she received a telephone call to that effect from one Inez Inspector of the San Diego County Health Department. Apparently, you notified the Health Department of the problem without first having attempted to resolve it with Ms. Manager.

While you certainly do have a legal right to complain to a governmental agency about any problem, you should be aware that the management of Sunny Dell Apartments takes pride in its quick and efficient response to residents' complaints and requests for repairs.

In the future, we hope that you will avail yourself of our complaint procedure if you have a problem with any aspect of your apartment. Simply fill out a Request for Maintenance form, available from Ms. Manager during her office hours of 9:00 a.m. to 6:00 p.m., Monday through Saturday. In case of an urgent request during the evening or on Sundays, you may call me at 555-1234.

Sincerely,

Lily Landlord
Owner

STEP 3: Carefully document the noise complaints of the neighbors. If possible, get them in writing. Feel out the neighbors about whether they would testify in court if necessary;

STEP 4: Write the tenant about the neighbors' complaints.* The first letter should be conciliatory. Offer to meet with the tenant to resolve the problem, but also remind the tenant of the rental agreement (or lease) provision banning illegal conduct, and that excessive noise after a certain hour is a violation of city or county ordinances. If the letter doesn't work, follow up with another, even though you are sure this will not do any good either. These letters will help you greatly should a court fight develop later;

Here are some sample letters:

---

* In several cities with rent-control ordinances that require just cause for eviction, you are required to give the tenant a written 30-day notice to cease whatever conduct you claim violates the lease or rental agreement. Only if they fail to comply can you legally give them a 30-day notice to terminate the tenancy. If you rent in one of these areas, you will need to modify the following letters to comply with the requirements of your ordinance.

February 15, 198_

Tammy Tenant
123 State Street, Apt. 15
San Diego, CA

Dear Ms. Tenant:

I am writing this letter to inform you that several of your neighbors have complained to Ms. Melba Manager, Sunny Dell Apartments' resident manager on several occasions during late January and early February, when you apparently hosted several parties in your apartment. In addition to complaints regarding shouting and the playing of loud music until 2:00 a.m., it appears that several party guests littered beer cans and other debris in the balcony outside the entrances to your apartment and those of several other units.

It is very important to the management of Sunny Dell Apartments that our residents be able to enjoy the peace and serenity of their homes. While we have no objections to our residents hosting occasional parties, we would hope that such events would be conducted with due regard for other residents, some of whom are elderly people quite easily agitated by excessive noise and litter.

Accordingly, we request that when you host parties in your apartment, you keep the noise within reasonable levels, particularly after 10:00 p.m., as is required by your rental agreement and that you restrain your guests from littering the common areas. Thank you for your cooperation.

Sincerely,

Lily Landlord
Owner

February 25, 198_

Tammy Tenant
123 State Street, Apt. 15
San Diego, CA

Dear Ms. Tenant:

On February 15, I wrote to inform you that several of your neighbors had complained about loud music emanating until the early hours of the morning from frequent parties you have in your apartment. I also called your attention to complaints regarding litter scattered about by your party guests.

Since then, I have received several more similar complaints regarding parties given within the past two weeks. Some of the persons complaining have indicated their intention to move should this conduct continue. You appear intent on ignoring both my warnings to you and complaints made directly to you by your neighbors. For example, I am told that on February 20, you refused to reduce the volume of very loud music played at 1:30 a.m. until the police were called to ask you to do so, and that the next morning your neighbors discovered 15 empty beer cans and bottles scattered about the entrance to your apartment.

Please be advised that paragraph 8 of your rental agreement makes illegal conduct in and about the premises a violation of the agreement and that the making of excessive noise during late hours is rendered unlawful by city ordinance. Accordingly, this sort of behavior is of the type for which your tenancy may be terminated. Should I receive any more complaints of similar conduct by you or your guests, I will have no choice but to have Ms. Manager give you a 30-day notice of termination of tenancy.

Sincerely,

Lily Landlord
Owner

STEP 5: If possible, wait a few months, during which you should carefully document any more complaints before giving the tenant a 30-day notice.

This sort of preparatory work may influence the tenant not to claim you are guilty of retaliatory conduct. However, even if it does not, and you do end up in court, you should win easily.

NOTE: One common landlord misconception is that a tenant cannot prove a landlord's retaliatory state of mind unless the landlord foolishly makes an admission about her true reason for acting against the tenant. To the contrary, a landlord's state of mind can be proved by his or her conduct, just as a defendant's state of mind in a criminal case is inferred from testimony about that person's conduct. In deciding whether a landlord acted with a retaliatory motive, judges look at such things as:

• How soon the landlord responded with a rent increase or termination notice after the tenant exercised a legal right;

• How the landlord treated the complaining tenant as compared to other tenants who didn't exercise their rights in the same way;

• The overall reasonableness of the landlord's conduct; and

• Whether the landlord appears to have had a legitimate reason for doing what she did.

D. Legitimate Reasons for Terminating a Month-to-Month Tenancy

Okay, enough paranoia. There are a number of legitimate reasons which traditionally justify a landlord in terminating a tenancy. It is always wise to be able to assert one of these if a month-to-month tenant refuses to leave after you've given her a 30-day notice. Of course, you may have other, more pressing, concerns, but when faced with the possibility of going to court, it is wise to use the magic words and formulas they are used to hearing. So, if you want to get rid of a tenant because you simply can't stand him, you would be wise to scrutinize the following list to see if one or more of these reasons to end the tenancy also applies:

• The landlord wants to use the property for some purpose of his own, such as moving in himself, renting to a close friend or relative, or remodeling the unit;

• The tenant repeatedly pays his rent late;

• The tenant repeatedly disturbs other tenants or neighbors with, for example, loud music or frequent domestic disturbances;

• The tenant is violating the law or a legitimate provision of the rental agreement or lease, such as allowing too many people to live on the premises, or keeping an animal, or using a waterbed, if any of these are prohibited;

• The tenant has damaged the property and/or has housekeeping habits so awful as to cause a problem, such as attracting rodents or roaches;

• The tenant uses very insulting language to you, your manager, or other tenants, or is just generally a very disagreeable person. (Be sure you are able to articulate exactly what behavior offends you.)

E. Retaliatory Rent Increases

The same rules that apply to retaliatory evictions apply to rent increases. You can't legally raise a tenant's rent in response to a legitimate complaint or rent-withholding action. And, as you should now clearly understand, it's almost equally important that you not appear to do so. One way to protect yourself from charges that ordinary rent increases are retaliatory is to adopt a sensible rent-increase policy and stick to it. For example, many landlords raise rents once yearly in an amount that reflects the increase in the Consumer Price Index. Other landlords use a more complicated formula which takes into account other rents in the area, as well as such factors as increased costs of maintenance or rehabilitation. They make sure to inform their tenants about the rent increase in advance and apply the increase uniformly with all their tenants. Usually, this protects the landlord against any claim of a retaliatory rent increase by a tenant who has coincidentally made a legitimate complaint about the condition of the premises. Of course, any rent increase given to a tenant who has made a complaint should be reasonable both in relation to the previous rent, what you charge other similarly-situated tenants, and rents for comparable property in the area, or you are asking for legal trouble.

EXAMPLE 1: Lois Landlord owns two multi-unit complexes. In one of the complexes, Lois raises rents uniformly, at the same time, for all tenants. In the other apartment building (where she fears tenants hit with rent increases all at once will organize and generate unrest), Lois raises each tenant's rent in accordance with the Consumer Price Index on the yearly "anniversary" of the date each tenant moved in. Either way, Lois is safe from being found guilty of making a retaliatory rent increase, even if a rent increase to a particular tenant follows on the heels of a complaint.

EXAMPLE 2: Lem Landperson has no organized plan for increasing rents in his 20-unit building, but simply raises them at random, depending on his mood. On November 1, he raises Teresa Trouble's rent, without remembering her recent complaint about her heater. Teresa was the only one to receive a rent increase that month. In this situation, Teresa has a strong retaliatory rent-increase case against Lem, simply because an increase which seemed to single her out happened to coincide with her exercise of a legal right. If the increase made her rent higher than those for comparable units in the building, she will have an even better case.

F. Liability for Illegal Retaliation

Here are the methods by which a tenant can assert that a landlord is guilty of unlawful retaliatory conduct. We believe you need to know what they are so you can avoid being accused of such conduct.

1. The Tenant's Defense to an Eviction Lawsuit

A tenant who believes her landlord has illegally retaliated against her for having exercised a legal right can use what is called an "affirmative defense" in an eviction lawsuit.* This means that when a landlord goes to court to enforce a 30-day termination notice after the tenant refuses to move out, or to sue for nonpayment of rent because the tenant refuses to pay a rent increase she claims is retaliatory, the tenant says in effect, "even if the landlord serves me with the proper 30-day notice or an otherwise valid termination of tenancy (or rent increase), the landlord's action is invalid because she was retaliating against me for exercising a legal right."

Let's take two examples to show how this works.

EXAMPLE 1: On March 1, Lily Landlord gives Tammy Tenant a 30-day notice to move, effective April 1. Come April 1, Lily refuses to accept Tammy's offer of another month's rent of $400, telling her she expects her to move. Tammy refuses, claiming that Lily's notice was motivated by Tammy's January 31 complaint about the heater. If Lily wants to make Tammy move, she'll have to bring an eviction lawsuit, serving Tammy with a "summons" and "complaint" stating that the tenancy was from month-to-month, that a 30-day notice was served, and that the 30 days are up and Tammy hasn't moved. Tammy will then file an "answer" which states the "affirmative defense" that the notice was retaliatory. In this situation, the case will go to trial about May 10.

If Lily can convince the judge her real reason for giving Tammy the 30-day notice was her repeated loud parties that other tenants complained about, and that her motive wasn't to retaliate against Tammy, the judge will award Lily the pro-rated rent through May 10 ($400 for April, plus $133.33 for May 1-10), possession of the property, court costs, and attorney's fees if Lily hired an attorney and the lease or rental agreement contains an attorney's fees clause. Only then will Tammy have to move.

If the judge thinks Lily's excuse is just that, and that her motive was to retaliate, Tammy can stay, getting a judgment against Lily for court costs and for attorney's fees (if either party is entitled to them in the written agreement). However, once it's settled that Tammy stays, her rent for April and May ($800 total) will come due. If Tammy doesn't pay it, Lily can legitimately serve her a three-day notice to pay rent or quit, and sue again if it still remains unpaid.

EXAMPLE 2: On September 1, Luther Landperson gives Tom Tenant a three-day notice increasing Tom's rent from $500 to $550 per month. On October 1, Tom hands Luther a check for $500, refusing to pay the $50 increase on the basis that it was retaliatory. Tom, who began organizing a building tenants' union in July, is convinced the increase is Luther's way of striking back. Luther accepts the $500, but then gives Tom a three-day notice to pay the $50 or vacate. When Tom does neither, Luther files suit based on nonpayment of rent, Tom answers with a retaliatory rent increase defense, and the case goes to trial about November 15.

---

* In an eviction lawsuit, the tenant has the burden of proving that the landlord's motive was to retaliate against her. Western Land Office v. Cervantes, 175 Cal.App.3d 724 (1985) 220 Cal.Rptr. 784. However, the opinion suggests that if a tenant exercises a right under the law, and the landlord serves her with a termination or rent increase notice within six months, the landlord must state on the notice a justification or reason for the termination or rent increase.

If Luther wins, the judge will award him the unpaid $50 for October, plus the pro-rated rent of $275 through November 15, court costs, attorney's fees, if appropriate, and of course, possession of the property; Tom will have to move.

If Tom wins, the judge will order Luther to pay Tom's court costs and attorney's fees, if applicable. Since the decision is in Tom's favor, the judge has clearly decided the rent increase was retaliatory; thus, the proper rent is $500 after all. Of course, now that it's November, and the case is over, with Tom staying on, he'll owe Luther the $500 rent in November.

NOTE: Although the above examples show both the tenants and the landlords fighting bitter court battles to the very end, they are intended only to show what the law provides for when taken to this extreme. This isn't to say that both parties can't try to compromise at any stage. Always keep in mind that a landlord's "victory" can sometimes be hollow. If after spending hundreds of dollars on lawyers and filing fees and going without rent while the lawsuit is pending, the landlord winds up with an empty apartment and a court judgment that is uncollectable because the tenant who skipped town or is judgment proof (has no assets), the landlord has not gained much.

2. Tenant Lawsuits Against the Landlord

It's also important for all landlords to realize that a tenant who feels the landlord has illegally retaliated against her doesn't have to sit back and wait for the landlord to take the matter to court. The tenant can initiate a lawsuit. Many tenants' attorneys advise their clients to do just this in order to put the landlord at a psychological disadvantage. In effect, the tenant asks the court to rule that the landlord's conduct was retaliatory, and to bar the landlord from bringing an eviction suit.

Preventing an eviction in advance isn't the only kind of relief that California tenants have won. In addition to being a defense to prevent an eviction, "retaliatory" landlord conduct can be a valid legal basis for the tenant suing the landlord for money. A tenant who sues a landlord and convinces a judge or jury that the landlord illegally retaliated against her for exercising a legal right can obtain a judgment for damages for emotional distress, mental pain and suffering, punitive damages, court costs and attorney's fees, even if the lease or rental agreement doesn't have an attorneys' fees clause. Potential liability in retaliatory eviction suits can and does reach tens of thousands of dollars. The defense of this sort of lawsuit is well beyond the scope of this book, and a lawyer is strongly advisable. If you have a good landlord's insurance policy which protects you from so-called "illegal acts," this will cover you in this situation (except for the deductible amount and punitive damages), and you can turn your legal defense over to the insurance company. See Chapter 11 on landlord liability or tenantability-related defects, where landlord insurance is discussed in more detail. If you have no insurance, see Chapter 7 on how to

find, compensate and work with a lawyer. The point we want to make here
is, of course, that with a little common sense, a landlord need never get in
this situation in the first place.

It's also important to realize that
a tenant doesn't have to bring a lawsuit before the landlord does in order
to be able to obtain money damages. If
the landlord brings an eviction suit,
and the tenant defends on the basis of
retaliation and wins, the tenant, bol-
stered by her victory, can bring another suit for damages. In fact, the
tenant who won the preceding eviction
suit on the basis that the landlord
illegally retaliated, may be able to
apply that finding from the first eviction lawsuit to the second one, so as
to prevent the landlord from again
denying and litigating the issue of
retaliation. In other words, the only
issue in the second suit will be how
much the landlord owes the tenant.
This is obviously one more illustration
of how important it is to win or settle
any eviction suit where the tenant
defends on the basis of retaliatory
eviction.

G. Phony Tenant Claims of Retaliation

Sometimes it seems that every time a
tenant can't or won't pay a legitimate
rent increase, they try and justify
their own failure by claiming that you
were guilty of some retaliatory misconduct.
The same sort of phony reliance
on tenant protection laws can occur
when you seek to terminate a tenancy
for a perfectly legitimate reason and
the tenant doesn't want to move. How
do you cope with this sort of cynical
misuse of the law? As with most things
legal, there is no one answer. However, if you are prepared to plan
ahead, you should be able to minimize
any legal problems.

Viewed sensibly, you start with a
great advantage when faced with a tenant who attempts to throw up a sand-
storm of phony retaliation claims to
defeat your legitimate rent increase or
tenancy termination. As a business
person, you have an opportunity to plan
ahead, anticipate that some tenants
will adopt these tactics and prepare to
meet them. The tenant, on the other
hand, must react on an ad hoc basis and
sometimes has no more than a superfi-
cial knowledge of the law.

But how exactly do you plan ahead?
First, you realize that people affected
negatively by any course of action you
plan--no matter how legal and justi-
fied--are likely to strike back, often
mindlessly. Second, try to anticipate
what they will do and be prepared to
avoid or counter their tactics. Here
are a number of proven landlord tech-
niques--several of which we emphasize
throughout this book:

•Set up a complaint procedure and
publicize it to tenants at every opportunity. If a tenant raises any problem, respond promptly. If there is any
necessary delay, tell the tenant in
writing. This sort of policy will go a
long way toward demonstrating that if a

tenant faced with a rent increase or tenancy termination suddenly complains to an outside agency about some defect in the premises they rent, without talking to you first, the complaint is phony;

• As discussed in Section E of this chapter, raise rents according to some reasonable policy or formula, and make sure any tenant who has lodged a complaint is treated the same as other tenants;

• If you want to evict a troublesome tenant, be sure you can come up with one or more good reasons to justify your action. We discuss several possible reasons in Section D above. If other tenants share your enthusiasm to get rid of the tenant in question, get their objections in writing. A letter or petition signed by other tenants is a big help;

• Do not announce your intention to terminate a tenancy in advance unless you genuinely want to work things out with the tenant. Telegraphing your intentions gives the tenant a chance to lodge a complaint. For example, suppose you tell the tenant on the 25th that you're going to give him a 30-day notice on the 31st. His complaint to the health department on the 28th--over a trivial defect--will be followed by your written notice dated the 31st. The short timespan between his complaint and your 30-day notice will appear to substantiate the tenant's claim of your supposed retaliatory intent. Similarly, if you and a tenant are at loggerheads, and no compromise seems possible, move quickly. Don't let the tenant have time to create a raft of phony retaliatory eviction defenses;

• If a tenant who you want to get rid of has made a legitimate complaint--or even one which appears to be honest--wait until the dust settles. After you fix the problem and a number of months have passed, you are probably on good legal ground to proceed if--and only if--you can document a legitimate reason to terminate the tenancy (again, see Section D, above).

14

Raising Rents and Changing Other Terms of Tenancy

As we saw in Chapter 2, there is a fundamental difference between a lease and a rental agreement, whether written or oral, for a month-to-month or other periodic tenancy. For the most part, a lease fixes the terms of tenancy for the length of the lease, while the terms of a periodic tenancy can be changed by giving the tenant proper written notice. Here we provide you with the rules for raising rents and changing other terms of a month-to-month or other periodic tenancy. The material included here is primarily of interest to landlords who rent month to month, except for Section D, which deals with changing the set terms of a lease when the lease ends.

A. Basic Rules to Change or End a Tenancy

If you rent using a rental agreement (whether oral or in writing) for a month-to-month or other periodic tenancy, you or your tenant can terminate the tenancy by giving written notice to the other (except, of course, in some cities which have rent-control ordinances requiring the landlord to have "just cause" to evict. See Chapter 4, Section B). A month-to-month tenant may terminate her tenancy by giving the landlord 30 days' notice, the landlord can terminate a week-to-week tenant with a week's written notice to the tenant, and so on.

The length of the notice period is normally determined by the interval between rent payments (one month, two weeks, etc.), unless the rental agreement specifics a longer or shorter notice period necessary to terminate the tenancy. In other words, a landlord can normally terminate a month-to-month tenancy on 30 days' written notice, a week-to-week tenancy on seven days' notice, etc. The same rule applies to a situation in which the landlord wants to change the terms of a tenancy.* So, in order to increase the rent or otherwise change the terms of the tenancy, the landlord must normally give a month-to-month tenant 30 days' written notice.**

B. Rent Increase Rules

In areas without rent control, there is no percentage limit to the amount a landlord can increase the rent of a month-to-month or other periodic tenant. Similarly, there is no restriction on the period of time between rent increases. In other words, you can legally raise the rent as much and as often as good business dictates. Of course, common sense should tell you that if your tenants do not perceive your increases as being fair, you may end up with vacant rental units or a hostile group of tenants looking for ways to make you miserable.

Of course, if your property is located in a city with rent control, you should check that city's ordinance to see whether it applies to your property. (It might not, since quite a few cities exempt single-family homes, duplexes, and so forth; some cities with "vacancy decontrol" provisions in their rent-control ordinances exempt a previously-controlled rental after the tenant voluntarily leaves or is evicted for cause, etc.) If a rent-control ordinance does affect your property, check it for the following facts:

• The maximum yearly rent increase. This is either specified in the ordinance itself by including a certain allowable percentage or other increase formula, or it is established by a local rent board each year, in which case you will have to inquire;

• Whether the landlord must obtain permission from a rent board for a higher increase than set out by the ordinance or board.*** (This is generally required in "moderate" and "strict" rent-controlled cities. See Chapter 4, Section C.) In some cities with moderate rent control, a landlord can raise rents as much as she wants, with the tenant having the burden to object to increases above the approved formula increase;

• Whether the ordinance requires that a rent increase notice contain specific information, such as a reason for the increase, in addition to normal state law notice requirements.

You may also want to contact a local landlords' association, or perhaps a lawyer who routinely represents landlords and is familiar with requirements of the locality's rent-control law.

---

* Civil Code Section 827.
** This period can be reduced to as low as seven days if there's a clause to that effect in the rental agreement (see Chapter 2, Section E). It is also fairly common for a rental agreement to call for a notice period of 60 or even 90 days.

*** In cities that keep track of permissible rent control levels by requiring the landlord to register the property. Civil Code Section 1947.8 requires the rent board on request, to notify the landlord and tenant of the permissible rent.

1. When Can You Raise Rent?

We discuss general legal rules involving rent in detail in Chapter 3, and rent control laws in particular in Chapter 4. We do not repeat all this information here. Accordingly, you may want to reread these earlier chapters in connection with the material that follows.

One of the many legal misconceptions tenants are prone to make is the belief that a rent increase must take effect at the beginning of a rental term. This is not true. For example, in the case of a month-to-month tenancy, where the rent is paid in advance on the first day of each month, a 30-day notice can increase the rent effective May 10, if served 30 days earlier on April 10, even though the rent is due on the first day of the month. However, if you increase rent in the middle of a month, the rent for that month must be pro-rated, and pro-ration calculations are a little tricky. For this reason, many landlords find it easier to raise the rent as of the first of the full month after the notice is properly given.

However, if you do wish to pro-rate, here is the proper way to do it. Assume you wish to raise the rent of a tenant who has a written rental agreement with rent payable on the first of each month by giving notice on the 10th of the month. Assuming you, in fact, give the tenant a notice on the 10th of May, increasing the rent from $500 to $550, the rent increase is effective June 9 (May has 31, but it's best to use a 30-day month, no matter how many days the month has). This would mean that the tenant would owe rent pro-rated at $500/month from June 1 through June 8, plus rent pro-rated at $550 per month from the 9th through the 30th. Remember, the rent is due on the first of the month, because rent is payable in advance. This works out to $537.10. Again, it may be more trouble figuring

out how this number is calculated than it's worth. You can simplify the whole procedure by making your rent increase effective at the beginning of the month (or other rental period), even though you give more than 30 days' notice in order to do so. To return to the facts of the above example, this would mean giving your tenant notice on April 10, and having it take effect on June 1.

2. Informal Rent Increases

In practice, rents are often increased by a simple agreement between the landlord and tenant, or even a simple acquiescence on the tenant's part, even though this rent increase procedure does not comply with legal requirements. Many landlords do not give tenants proper written notice, but merely tell them verbally of the increase. In other situations, where they do send a notice, they don't follow legal service technicalities, but use ordinary mail. In either situation, if the tenant responds by paying the higher increased rent, for even a month, he has given up the right to object to the increase. This is true even if he has second thoughts later. In effect, the tenant's failure to

177

assert his right not to pay the increase is an implied agreement that the rent has been increased.

Even if you know your tenants well and believe they will go along with an increase, we believe it is a poor business practice to rely on verbal notice alone. You may wish to extend your tenant the courtesy of telling him of the increase personally, perhaps giving several reasons--although this isn't legally necessary, except in areas covered by rent control (see Chapter 4). However, you should also follow up with a proper written notice. This isn't because you don't trust your tenant, but because good business practice requires written notice and documentation of all important decisions.

C. Preparing a Notice to Raise Rent

A notice raising the rent (or changing some other term of the tenancy) of a tenant who occupies a unit under an oral or written rental agreement with a periodic tenancy (e.g., month to month, week to week, etc.) must be in writing and must clearly state the following:

• The full address of the property;

• When the change is to go into effect. This can normally be no sooner than 30 days for a month-to-month tenancy, unless a rental agreement clause allows for a shorter time. But it can be longer, even if the lease or rental agreement doesn't require this. In other words, you can give a tenant 60 or more days notice if you wish; and

• The amount of the new rent.

On the next page you will find a sample rent-increase notice prepared on a form we call "Notice of Change of Terms of Tenancy." (A tear-out, fill-in-the-blanks version of this form can be found in the Appendix at the back of the book.)

NOTE ON DEPOSITS: We noted in Chapter 5 that if you wish to raise the amount of a tenant's deposit when you raise the rent, you must specifically state that you are doing this. To accomplish this, check the box marked "other" on the Notice of Change of Terms of Tenacy form and indicate the amount of the new deposit. We discuss the maximum amount you can charge for a deposit for furnished and unfurnished units in Chapter 5.

D. How the Notice Is Served on the Tenant

The law is very strict on how a notice changing the terms of tenancy must be served on a tenant. It is not enough that you mail the notice or simply post it on the door, unless the tenant admits to receiving it--something you can never count on. Here are the three legal methods of service for a 30-day notice.

1. Personal Service

The best type of service of the 30-day notice is to simply hand your tenant the notice. Handing the notice to any other person, such as someone who lives with your tenant but is not listed as a co-tenant on the written rental agreement, is not sufficient, except as described next under the heading "Substitute Service."

NOTICE OF CHANGE OF TERMS OF TENANCY

TO _____Regina D. Renter_____ ,
                    (Name)

TENANT(S) IN POSSESSION OF THE PREMISES AT:

___1234 Market Street, Apartment #5_____
                (Street Address)

City of __San Jose__ , County of __Santa Clara__ , California.

YOU ARE HEREBY NOTIFIED that the terms of tenancy under which you occupy the above-described premises are changed as follows:

(XXX)   The monthly rent will be increased to $350.00, payable in advance.

(XXX)   Other: ___The amount of the security deposit is___

___raised to $700.00._____

_____ .

YOU ARE FURTHER NOTIFIED that the said change in terms of tenancy shall be effective,

(XXX)   On ___March 1, 1985___ .
              (Date)

(   )   On the 30th day following service on you of this notice. If the above-described change of terms of tenancy is an increase in rent, the amount due on the next following due date, pro-rated at the current rental rate prior to the said 30th day, and pro-rated at the increased rate thereafter, is $ _____ .

DATED: __January 17, 1985__

                                    _____
                                          OWNER/MANAGER

In order for "personal service" to be legally effective, it is not necessary that your tenant accept the notice in her hand, and you or your manager (or whoever will serve the notice) should not attempt to force the tenant to do this. It is enough that you make some sort of personal contact with your tenant and offer her the notice. If your tenant refuses to accept it, simply lay it down at her feet and walk away. Service is legally effective.

2. Subtituted Service on Another Person

If the tenant to whom you're attempting to give the notice never seems to be home, and you know where he is employed, you might try to personally serve him at the place of employment. If you are unable to locate the tenant at his workplace, the law allows you to use "substituted service" in lieu of personally giving the notice to the tenant.

"Substitute service" simply means that you give the 30-day notice to a "substitute" adult at your tenant's home or business, with instructions to that person to give the notice to the tenant. This must be followed with a mailed notice to the tenant's home to be effective. In order to serve the notice this way, you must:

● Try to personally serve the tenant at his home, but not succeed;

● Try to personally serve him at work, but not succeed;

● Leave a copy of the notice with an adult at home or work; and

● Mail another copy to the tenant at home by ordinary first-class mail.*

---

* C.C.P. Section 1162(2).

WARNING: Service of the notice is not legally complete until you both leave a copy with the "substitute" and mail a second copy to the tenant at home.

EXAMPLE: In late November, Lola Lowrent, having rented to Lucy Luckedout on a month-to-month basis for the past three years at a rent of $650 a month (payable on the first day of each month), wants to raise the rent to $725, effective January 1 of the following year. This means Lola's rent-increase notice must be served on or before December 1 (30 days before January 1). On November 30, Lola gives up trying to personally serve the notice on Lucy, who never seems to be home, at least according to Lucy's daughter, who always answers the door. Lola then simply posts a copy of the notice on the door. Come January, Lucy ignores the notice, claims she never received it, and refuses to pay the increased rent. Lucy is right (technically, at least), as she was never properly served. However, had Lola given the notice to Lucy's daughter in late November and promptly followed through by mailing a second copy of the notice to Lola, the rent increase would have been legally effective.

3. Posting and Mailing Service

If you can't find a tenant on whom you wish to serve the notice, and you can't find anyone else at home or work (or if you don't know where the tenant is employed), you may serve the notice using a procedure known as "posting and mailing." (People in the business call it "nail and mail".) To do this, you tack or tape a copy of the notice to the front door of the rental unit and mail a second copy to the tenant at that address. In order to serve the notice this way, you must do the following, in the order indicated:

• Try to personally serve the tenant at home, and find no one there;

• If you know where the tenant works try to serve her at work and find no one there;

• Post a copy of the notice on the front door of the property; and

• Mail another copy to the tenant at home by first-class mail.*

Again, service of the notice is not complete until you have followed through by mailing a second copy of the notice.

EXAMPLE: Although Lem Landlord wants to give Tom Tenant a notice increasing Tom's rent by $50 a month, Lem can never find Tom (or anyone else) at home, and doesn't know where he works. Since that leaves no one on whom to personally or substitute-serve the rent-increase notice, Lem is left with the "posting-and-mailing" alternative. To accomplish this, Lem can tape one copy to the door of the property and mail a second copy to Tom at that address by regular first-class mail.

---

* C.C.P. Section 1162(3).

4. Service by Other Methods

Although notices raising rent or otherwise changing terms of a month-to-month or other periodic tenancies are not technically legally effective unless served in one of the ways specified above, many landlords nevertheless routinely mail such notices or post them on their tenant's doors, thinking they have properly served their tenant. Actually, this often works in practice, because many tenants will admit receiving the notice or will simply pay the increased rent. This is especially true if the increase is reasonable and the landlord is on good terms with the tenant. As we mentioned in Section 2 above, once the tenant acknowledges receiving the notice, or pays the increased rent, she gives up the right to complain about any legal insufficiency in the manner the notice was served, and the rent increase becomes effective, even if the service of the notice is technically improper. This is true regardless of the tenant's reason for acquiescing to the increase, and it doesn't matter if she didn't know the notice had to be served a certain way, was too concerned about maintaining good relations with her landlord to raise the issue, or simply didn't care.

EXAMPLE: On May 25, Renee Rent-raise prepares a notice telling her tenant, Linda Luckless, her rent will be increased from $775 to $875 a month, effective July 1. Not having read this book, Renee mails the notice by ordinary first-class mail. Linda pays the increased rent on July 1, and every month after, but learns in December that the law requires the notice to have been served by personal, substituted or posting and mailing service. Linda demands that Renee give her back the $100 increase she paid during each of those months. Renee doesn't have to, since Linda, by paying the increase, gave up her right to insist on technically-legal service of the notice.

As we mentioned above, notice of a rent increase is legally effective if the tenant actually admits receiving it, even if the notice wasn't served as required by law. For example, a rent increase is effective for a tenant who admits receiving a notice (at least 30 days before a rent increase, in the case of a month-to-month tenancy) that was only posted on his door and not mailed. This also means in effect that when a landlord serves a rent increase notice using certified mail with a return receipt (to be signed only by the tenant receiving the letter), the tenant's signature on the return receipt makes the increase effective.* This is true even though certified mail is not mentioned in Civil Code Section 827 as a legal way to serve such a notice.

Here is a checklist which should help you follow correct procedures when you are about to raise your tenant's rent:

_____

* This type of service can result in problems if someone other than the tenant signs for the certified letter and the tenant later claims he never received the notice.

CHECKLIST TO RAISE RENT

• Determine that your tenancy is from month-to-month or some other shorter period. As part of doing this, make sure your agreement doesn't require a 60- or 90-day notice period. Of course, no increases are allowed during the term of a lease unless specified in the lease.

• Find out if any local rent control laws prevent or limit your proposed increase.

• Decide when you want the increase to take effect. (At least 30 days' notice is required for month-to-month tenancy, unless your rental agreement calls for a shorter notice period.) As noted above, having the rent increase take effect on the day rent is payable eliminates the need to pro-rate rent.

• Fill out the blank Notice of Change of Terms of Tenancy at the back of this book. You will need to include the tenant's name, an identification of the premises, its address, the new rent amount, and the date it is to be effective. Then, sign the notice and make a copy for your files.

• Give the notice personally to the tenant or use substituted or posting-and-mailing service, or mail it by certified mail, return receipt requested (allowing a week for delivery), as discussed above.

E. Changing Terms Other Than Rent

As noted, if you rent to tenants under a periodic tenancy, the law allows you to change the terms of the agreement other than the amount of rent. Any rental agreement provision can be modified or even added in this way. For example, a landlord who originally allowed her month-to-month tenant to have a pet could give her a 30-day notice imposing a new provision forbidding them. Similarly, the landlord could impose a pool fee, change the rules or fees for parking, or reduce the number of people allowed to live in a unit in this way. The form of notice required to accomplish this is the same as for raising the rent, except that instead of reading "Rent is hereby increased to $ _____ per month," the notice should state the change you wish to make, such as one of the following:

• Tenant is prohibited from keeping pets in or on the premises;

• Tenant may only park one motor vehicle in the parking lot behind 111 Navelier St.;

• Tenant must pay $25 per month for use of the swimming pool. Payment to be made with the monthly rent;

• Tenant may not allow more than __ person(s) to reside in Apartment 6, at 111 Navelier St., without the landlord's written permission.

Just as some cities' rent-control ordinances regulate the amount by which landlords can raise rents, some ordinances also prevent a landlord from otherwise changing the terms of the tenancy, particularly by reducing services while keeping the rent the same. For example, San Francisco's rent-control ordinance was interpreted to prevent several landlords from taking back their tenant's rights to park in previously allowed parking spaces or begin charging parking fees. If your property falls under a rent-control ordinance, check to see if it restricts changes in terms other than rent. Also prohibited by local rent-control laws, as well as by state law,* are changes in rental-agreement terms that purport to have the tenant give up legal rights. In other words, the illegal and unenforceable rental agreement and lease terms discussed in Chapter 2, Section E, on leases and rental agreements, are no more effective if accomplished by a Notice of Change of Terms of Tenancy than they would be if in the original lease or rental agreement. The Notice Changing Terms Other Than Rent can be prepared on the same tear-out form in the back of this book used for raising rents. Again, the notice should specify the tenant's name, the address of the property, when the change of terms is effective (giving at least 30 days' notice in the case of a tenancy from month to month) and of course, the change itself, spelled out as carefully as if you were inserting it as an additional clause in a rental agreement for the first time. Here's a sample notice changing terms other than rent:

---

* Civil Code Section 1953(b).

NOTICE OF CHANGE OF TERMS OF TENANCY

TO: _____Thomas Tennant_____ ,
                                    (Name)

TENANT(S) IN POSSESSION OF THE PREMISES AT:

_____456 Main Street, Apartment 7_____ ,
                    (Street Address)

City of ___Los Angeles___ , County of ____Los Angeles____ , California.

YOU ARE HEREBY NOTIFIED that the terms of tenancy under which you occupy
the above-described premises are changed as follows:

   (   )   The monthly rent will be increased to $_____ , payable
              in advance.

   (XXX)   Other: Tenant shall not allow more than three persons to
                   reside in the premises without owner's written
                   permission.

YOU ARE FURTHER NOTIFIED that the said change in terms of tenancy shall
be effective,

   (   )   On _____
                (Date)

   (XXX)   On the 30th day following service on you of this notice
               If the above-described change of terms of tenancy is an
               increase in rent, the amount due on the next following
               due date, pro-rated at the current rental rate prior to
               the said 30th day, and pro-rated at the increased rate
               thereafter, is $ _____ .

Dated: ___July 31, 1985___

                       _____
                                OWNER/MANAGER

Finally, the notice should be served in the same manner as a notice increasing the rent, namely by personal service (or substituted or posting-and-mailing service, if necessary), or by certified mail, return receipt requested.

F. Rent and Leases

Once you lease a place to a tenant for a period of time, you are stuck with the amount of rent provided for in the lease, right? Not necessarily. These days, more and more landlords are building some rent-rate flexibility into their leases. How can you do this? Simply by tying the amount of your rent to some government index, such as the Consumer Price Index (CPI) (see Chapter 2, Section C). For example, if you lease a place for three or five years at $600 per month, you might provide that at the first of each year, the rent is to go up by the same percentage as the CPI has increased during that same period of time. For this sort of rent increase, no formal notice is required. Simply send the tenant a letter reminding them of the lease term calling for the increase and demonstrating how you calculated the amount.

G. When a Lease Ends

What happens when the lease ends? Unless a new one is signed, the tenancy becomes a periodic one with the rent due at the same interval as called for under the lease (usually once a month). You can now raise the rent, change one or more of the terms of the tenancy, or terminate the tenancy by giving a written notice and serving it to the tenant, as discussed in Section B, above. If rent is paid once a month, you must give 30 days' notice. Why do you have to change the terms of the lease by written notice if the lease has run out? Because Section 1945 of the Civil Code provides that when a lease ends, all its terms continue in effect except those which have to do with the lease term itself.

EXAMPLE: Les Lessee rents a house from Owsley Owner under a one-year lease that runs from January through December. The lease provides that the $900 monthly rent is payable on the first day of the month, and that no pets are allowed. The lease expires on December 31, and Owsley elects to continue the tenancy by accepting another $900 from Les in the next month of January. The tenancy is now month to month, with all other terms the same, the rent still being $900, with no pets allowed. If Owsley wants to raise the rent or change the terms of what is now essentially a written month-to-month rental agreement, he'll have to give Les a 30-day notice to that effect.

15

The Three-Day Notice to Pay Rent or Quit

A landlord who is serious about having tenants pay their rent on time must be prepared to utilize the tools the law provides for enforcing payment. Ultimately, the landlord's most powerful weapon to assure payment of rent is her right to file an eviction lawsuit against tenants who don't pay. Although we reserve discussion of how to bring an eviction lawsuit for the second volume, there is one preliminary aspect of a rent-nonpayment suit which must be outlined here. This is the requirement that a landlord give the tenant three days' written notice to pay the rent or leave. The purpose of this chapter is to show you how to efficiently accomplish this.

But before we do this, here are a few words on our view of when a three-

day notice is appropriate. Many landlords resist handing out these documents. After all, preparing a three-day notice involves at least a little bit of trouble, and it's easy to conclude that it is the first step in what is sure to be a nasty court eviction battle, something almost every landlord dreads.

First, you should realize that serving a three-day notice notice to pay rent or quit does not necessarily lead to a lawsuit. Properly understood, a three-day notice is a tool designed to get the tenant to pay rent, not to evict her. Remember, an eviction lawsuit is generally something the tenant wants to avoid at least as much as you do. In fact, most tenants who receive a three-day notice do pay up within the three days. In a few cases, tenants don't pay, however, which means the three-day notice becomes the first step in a court action. If this occurs, the notice is likely to be scrutinized carefully. In other words, even though a three-day notice doesn't necessarily lead to an unlawful detainer suit, you should take pains to be sure all notices you prepare and serve are legally correct.

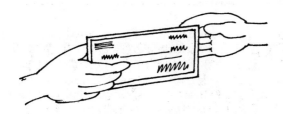

NOTE: It is a poor idea to let your bank redeposit rent checks that bounce, something they will normally do unless you request that bad checks be returned to you immediately instead. Why would you want to do this? For two excellent reasons. The first is that it alerts you to the fact that the rent is unpaid much sooner than if the check is resubmitted and returned for non-payment a second time. You can use this time to contact the tenant to ask that the check be made good immediately. If it is not, you can promptly serve a three-day notice.

The second reason that you want to get the check back quickly is that, if it is resubmitted, and again there are insufficient funds to cover it, the normal bank procedure is to punch holes in it. If this is done, the check can never again be presented for payment. If it's returned to you before it is punched, however, you can hold on to it. If the tenant doesn't make the check good, you can periodically call her bank over the next six months to see if enough funds have been deposited to cover it. In a surprising number of

instances, a tenant will eventually put more money in the account, often giving you the chance of collecting your money by cashing the check. In some instances where the tenant has moved out owing you money, this may save you the trouble of filing a lawsuit, getting a judgment and attaching the tenant's wages.

In the discussion that follows, we show you how the three-day notice to pay rent or quit is prepared. Pay close attention. Any mistake in the notice, however slight, may give your tenant (or her attorney) an excuse to contest or delay any eviction lawsuit you may ultimately bring if the tenant doesn't pay up in response to your notice. At worst, a mistake in the three-day notice may render your unlawful detainer lawsuit "fatally defective"--which means you lose, pay the tenant's court costs and attorney's fees, and have to start all over again with a correct three-day notice.

A. How to Determine the Amount of Rent Due

Your first job is to be sure you ask for the correct amount of rent in your three-day notice. While this seems an easy task, it often isn't. Indeed, the most common type of defect in a three-day notice involves the landlord demanding more rent than is due, or demanding improper extras, such as late charges, check-bounce fees, interest, utility charges, or even past due installments promised by the tenant towards a security deposit. Keep in mind that in order to win an eviction lawsuit against a tenant who fails to pay rent, the judge has to rule that the tenancy was properly terminated. A tenancy isn't legally terminated unless the three-day notice to which a tenant fails to respond stated the proper rent amount and is legally correct in other respects. For example, a three-day notice demanding $1,450 from a tenant who owes only $1,400 isn't legally sufficient to terminate the tenancy, even though the tenant does owe the $1,400, and a judge won't allow an eviction based on it.

In order to avoid making a mistake in your three-day notice, you should keep the following rules in mind:

• Do not demand anything other than past due rent in a three-day notice. In other words, you should not include late charges, fees of any kind, interest, utility charges, or anything else in a three-day notice—even if a written lease or rental agreement says you're entitled to payment for such items. Does this mean that you cannot legally collect these charges? No. It simply means you can't legally include them in the three-day notice or recover them in an eviction lawsuit. You can deduct these amounts from the security deposit or sue for them later in small claims court. (See Chapter 18);

• Rent is almost always due in advance for the entire rental period (see Chapter 3, Section B). For example, rent is due in advance on November 1 for the period November 1 through November 30. In other words, the amount of rent due is not apportioned on the basis of the date the three-day notice is served, but is due for the whole month, on the first or other rent payment date. The only time rent must be apportioned as part of a three-day notice is when the tenancy terminates in the middle of the rental period, usually because of an earlier 30-day notice. For example, if the landlord gives a 30-day notice on November 15, the tenancy should terminate on December 15. This means that on December 1, only 15 days' rent is due if the rental period begins on the first of the month. If the tenant fails to pay on the first,

the landlord should serve a three-day notice demanding only pro-rated rent for the 15-day period. To do this, you must first arrive at a daily rental amount. This is easy. The daily rental is always taken to be the monthly rental divided by 30, even in 28, 29 and 31-day months.

• If the tenant has paid you part, but not all, of the rent due, your demand for rent must reflect the partial payment;

• You do not have to credit any part of a security deposit (even if you call it last month's rent) to the amount of rent you ask for in the three-day notice. In other words, you have a right to wait until after the tenant has moved, to see if you should apply the deposit to cover any necessary damages or cleaning (see Chapter 18).

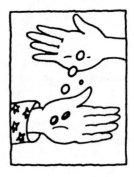

Here are a few examples of how rent is calculated in various situations:

EXAMPLE 1: Richard Renter has been paying $500 rent to Loretta Landlord on the first of each month, as provided by a written rental agreement. On October 6, Richard still hasn't paid his rent, and Loretta serves him with a three-day notice to pay the $500 or leave. (Although Loretta has, in effect, given Richard the benefit of a five-day grace period, she didn't have to, and could have given Richard the notice on October 2.) Even though the rental agreement provides for a $10 late charge after the second day, Loretta should not list that amount in the three-day notice.

EXAMPLE 2: Dan Deadbeat's rent of $450 is due the 15th of each month for the period of the 15th through the 14th of the next month--in advance of course. Dan's check for the period from October 15 through November 14 bounces, but Len Lessor doesn't discover this until November 15. Now, Dan not only refuses to make good on the check, but also refuses to pay the rent due for the November 15 through December 15 period. It's now November 20. What should Len ask for in his three-day notice? Dan owes Len $450 for October 15 - November 14 (the rent which was to have been covered by the bounced check), plus $450 for the period October 15 - December 14. The three-day notice should demand payment of $900. Len should not add check-bouncing charges or late fees to the amount in the three-day notice. And even though Len promises to leave "in a few days," Len should demand rent for the entire period of November 15 through December 14.

EXAMPLE 3: Because of repeated late rent payments by Dan's twin brother Dean, his landlord, Larry Lessor, gives Dean a 30-day notice on June 10, after Dean paid his June rent (due on June 1) nine days late. Because the 30-day notice will terminate Dean's tenancy on July 10, Dean will only owe rent for the first ten days of July due on the first day of that month. In this type of situation, rent should be apportioned if it is necessary to send

a three-day notice. In other words, if Dean doesn't pay up on July 1, the three-day notice he receives on July 2 should demand this 10 days' rent, or 1/30th of the monthly rent ($350/30 = $11.66/day) for each of these days, a total of 10 x $11.66, or $116.60.

EXAMPLE 4: Renee Renter is a month-to-month tenant who pays her landlord $300 rent on the first of each month. On June 30, she gives her landlord a 30-day notice saying she'll be leaving at the end of July. Her letter also says "Please consider my $300 security deposit as the last month's rent for the month of July." Renee's landlord has no obligation to let Renee do this, and can serve her a three-day notice demanding July's rent of $300 on July 2, the day after it's due. As a practical matter, however, he might be wiser to ask Renee for permission to inspect the property to see if it is in good enough condition to justify the eventual return of the security deposit. If so, there is little to be gained by filing a three-day notice and then suing for unpaid rent, since by the time the case gets before a judge, the need to return the security deposit (this must be done within 14 days after Renee leaves) will cancel it out.

To summarize what you've learned so far, to issue a correct three-day notice, demand only rent, due in advance and not pro-rated (except where the tenancy terminates in the middle of a rental period because of the service of an earlier 30-day notice), and give credit for partial rent payments, but not for any part of the security deposit.

NOTE ON HABITABILITY DEFENSES: In arriving at the amount of rent due, there is no requirement that you anticipate and adjust for the fact that you know your tenant is likely to claim that she doesn't owe the entire rent because the property was "untenantable" (see Chapter 10) for all or portion of the time for which you claim rent. In other words, ask for the entire amount due under the terms of the lease or rental agreement. If the tenant doesn't pay (or the two of you don't work out a compromise settlement and you file an unlawful detainer), it's up to the tenant to assert her habitability defense in court.*

B. Other Requirements of a Three-Day Notice

In addition to stating the correct amount of past due rent, your three-day notice must also contain all of the following:

• Your tenant(s)' name(s);

• A description of the property--a street address and apartment or unit number is sufficient;

• A demand that the tenant(s) pay the stated amount of rent due within three days or move. If you just demand the rent and do not set out the alternative of leaving, your notice is fatally defective;

• A statement that you will pursue legal action (or declare the lease/rental agreement "forfeited") if the tenant does not pay the entire rent or

move; and

• An indication--such as your signature--that the notice is from you. You don't need to date the notice, but it doesn't hurt.

C. How to Fill Out a Three-Day Notice

A sample three-day notice to pay rent or quit appears below, and a blank tear out three-day notice form is included in the forms section in the back of this book. You may tear out the form or use a photocopy.

Step 1: Fill in the Tenant's Name

The first blank is for the name(s) of the tenant(s) to whom the three-day notice is addressed. Although this is technically not required, it is so customary to put the tenant's name on a three-day notice that to omit it could invite a delaying tactic from a tenant's attorney on the theory that the tenant might not have known it was for her. Be sure to list the names of the tenant(s) whose names are listed on a written lease or rental agreement, or with whom you orally entered into a rental agreement, plus the names, if known, of any other adult occupants of the property.

Step 2: Fill in the Address

List the street address, city and county. In addition, be sure to list the apartment number if your tenant lives in an apartment complex or in a condominium unit. In the unlikely event the unit has no street address,

---

* However, if you expect a tenant to raise a habitability defense in court, we strongly urge you to read Chapter 10 before proceeding.

THREE-DAY NOTICE TO PAY RENT OR QUIT

TO _____ Tyrone Tenant _____

TENANT(S) IN POSSESSION OF THE PREMISES AT

123 Market Street, Apartment 4
_____(Street Address)_____

City of San Diego _____, County of San Diego _____, California

YOU ARE HEREBY NOTIFIED that the rent on the above-described premises occupied by you, in the amount of $ 400.00 ___, for the period from _____ to _____, is now due and payable.

YOU ARE HEREBY REQUIRED to pay the said rent within THREE (3) days from the date of service on you of this notice or to vacate and surrender possession of the premises. In the event you fail to do so, legal proceedings will be instituted against you to recover possession of the premises, declare the forfeiture of the rental agreement or lease under which you occupy the premises, and recover rents, damages and costs of suit.

DATE: __August 5, 1987__ 　　　　　　_Len Landlord_
　　　　　　　　　　　　　　　　　　OWNER/MANAGER

you use the legal description of the premises on the deed to your property, along with an ordinary understandable description of where the place is (e.g., "the small log cabin behind the third hill going north on River Road from Pokeyville"). You will have to retype the notice to make room for the legal description.

Step 3: Fill in the Rent Due

The next space is for you to fill in the amount of rent due. Although it is not legally required to indicate the rental period(s) for which the rent is due, it is customary, and some judges who are used to seeing it may question, or even reject, notices that don't include the dates.

Step 4: Sign and Date the Notice

The "ultimatum" language--that the tenant either pay the rent within three days or move out, or you'll bring legal action--is already included in the printed form. All you need to add are your signature and the date you signed it. The date should not be the same day the rent was due, but at least one day later.

NOTE: Be sure to make several photocopies for your records (the original goes to the tenant).

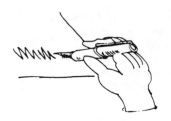

D. Serving the Three-Day Notice on the Tenant

The law is very strict about when and how you give the three-day notice to your tenant(s). Even a slight departure from the rules may result in your losing any eviction lawsuit you bring if it is contested.

1. When the Notice is Served

The three-day notice to pay rent or quit can be given to your tenant on any day after the rent was due, but not on the day it is due. For example, if the rent is due on the first day of each month, and you give the notice to the tenant on that day, it will have no legal effect. Of course, if you allow a three-day grace period (remember, you don't legally have to before serving the notice), you will have no problem.

If the rent comes due on a Sunday or holiday, rent is due on the next business day (Saturday is a business day). And the three-day notice cannot be given until the next day after that. If you make a mistake and give the notice to the tenant too soon, you face the risk that a sharp tenant's attorney will use that mistake to delay or defeat your eviction lawsuit. This is one of the many technicalities of eviction law that is not corrected by the passage of time after the lawsuit is filed. Bizarre as it sounds, if you gave the notice the notice only a day prematurely, but the tenant still didn't pay the rent during the two to three weeks he contested the lawsuit, you may still lose the case anyway. The moral is simple --count your days carefully.

EXAMPLE: When Tara Tardy didn't pay her $400 rent to Helga Hurried on Saturday, January 1, Helga prepared a three-day notice to pay rent or quit, giving it to Tara the next day. Unfortunately for Helga, the rent wasn't actually due until January 3, even though Tara's lease said it was due on the first, because January first, New Year's Day, was a legal holiday, as was January 2, a Sunday. Oblivious to all this, Helga waited the three days, and, as Tara still hadn't paid the rent, Helga filed her eviction lawsuit on January 6. Tara contested it, and the case finally went to court on February 5. Even though Tara clearly owes Helga the rent for January, and now February, Helga loses the lawsuit because Helga gave Tara the three-day notice before the rent was legally past due. Now Helga will have to pay Tara's court costs as well as her own, and will also be stuck with a very cocky tenant, buoyed by her victory on a technicality. Assuming Tara has still not paid the rent, Helga can, of course, serve a new three-day notice and begin the eviction procedure again.

2. Who Should Serve the Three-Day Notice

Anyone over the age of eighteen can legally give or "serve" the three-day notice on the tenant. However, please realize that if you have to bring an eviction lawsuit against the tenant, that person may have to come to court to testify that he or she gave the tenant the notice, so make sure you pick someone who will be available. You can legally serve the notice yourself, but it's often a better business practice to have it served by someone else. That way, if the tenant refuses to pay the rent and contests the resulting eviction suit by falsely claiming he didn't receive the notice, you will not have to rely on your own testimony that you served the notice, but can present the testimony of someone not a party to the lawsuit who is more likely to be believed by a judge. Of course, you must weigh this advantage against any time, trouble or expense you must expend to get someone else to accomplish the service and, if necessary, appear in court.

3. Who to Give the Notice To

If you rented your property to just one tenant, whose name alone appears on any written rental agreement or lease, you should serve that person the three-day notice. (However, as we'll see shortly, you can sometimes give the notice to a co-occupant of the property who isn't listed on the lease, if you can't locate the tenant who is on the lease.)

If you rented to more than one tenant, it's a good idea to serve separate copies of the three-day notice on each, even though service of the notice on one of several co-tenants who are all listed on a written lease or rental agreement is legally sufficient.* We recommend serving everyone to minimize the possibility that the non-served tenant will try to defend against any subsequent eviction lawsuit on the ground that he didn't receive the notice. You normally have no obligation to serve the three-day notice on occupants who are not named in the written rental agreement or lease and with whom you've had no dealings in renting the property.** However, if the person has been living in your property for some time (e.g., the lover or roommate of one of your tenants) and you have had contact with the person and treated them as a tenant (perhaps you even accepted rent from them), your best bet is to serve them with a three-day notice as well. We discuss who is and who is not a tenant in Chapter 9.

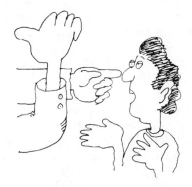

4. How the Notice Is Served on the Tenant

The law is very strict on how the three-day notice is served on the tenant. It is not enough that you mail the notice or simply post it on the

* University of Southern California v. Weiss (1962) 208 Cal.App.2d 759, 769, 25 Cal.Rptr. 475.
** Chinese Hospital Foundation Fund v. Patterson (1969) 1 Cal.App.3d 627, 632, 8 Cal.Rptr. 795.

door. Here are the three legal methods of service for a three-day notice:

• **Personal Service:** The best type of service of the three-day notice is to simply hand your tenant the notice. Handing the notice to any other person, such as someone who lives with your tenant but is not listed as a co-tenant on the written rental agreement, is not sufficient, except as described next under the heading "Substituted Service."

• **Substituted Service On Another Person:** If the tenant to whom you're attempting to give the three-day notice never seems to be home, and you know where he or she is employed, you should try to personally serve him or her at the place of employment. If you are unable to locate the tenant at either place, the law allows you to use "substituted service" in lieu of personally giving the notice to the tenant.

"Substituted service" rules are contained in Chapter 14, Section D.

Service of the notice using the substituted service method is not completed, and the three-day period does not start running, until you have both left the copy with the "substitute" and mailed the second copy to the tenant at home. The first day of the notice's three-day period is the day after both these steps are accomplished.

EXAMPLE: Dean Deadbeat should have paid his rent on the first of the month. By the fifth, you're ready to serve him with a three-day notice to pay rent or quit. When you try to personally serve it on him at home, a somewhat hostile buddy of Dean's answers the door, saying Dan's not home.

You can't serve the notice on him yet because you still have to try Dean's workplace—the one listed on the rental application Dan filled out when he moved in. You go there only to find that Dean called in sick that day. You could either give the notice to one of Dean's co-workers, or go back and give it to his friend at home, with instructions to give it to Dean when they see him. After that, you mail another copy of the notice to Dean at home by ordinary first-class mail. "Substituted service" is complete only after all this has been done.

• **"Posting-and-Mailing" Service:** If you can't find the tenant on whom you wish to serve the three-day notice, and you can't find anyone else at home or work (or if you don't know where he or she is employed), you may serve the three-day notice through a procedure known as "posting and mailing."* To do this, attach a copy of the three-day notice to the tenant's front door, following the instructions in Chapter 14, Section D.

EXAMPLE: Lana Late's rent is due on the 15th of each month, but she still hasn't paid you by the 20th. You can never find her (or anyone else) at home, and you don't know where she works. Since that leaves no one whom to personally or substitute serve the

_____

* An appeals court in Santa Clara County has ruled that posting-and-mailing service isn't effective, and the notice's three-day period doesn't begin running until the first day after the tenant actually receives the notice. **Davidson v. Quinn** (1982) 138 Cal.App.3d Supp. 9, 188 Cal.Rptr 421. The reasoning of this could cause problems where the tenant claims she never received the notice or received it several days after the posting and mailing. Although this ruling defies common sense, it is legally binding in Santa Clara County. However, judges in other counties may follow the ruling, so avoid posting-and-mailing service if other methods are possible. Otherwise, try to talk to the tenant—before you file an eviction lawsuit—and pin her down as to having received the notice. (Don't ask, "Did you get my three-day notice?" Ask, "When are you going to pay the rent I asked for in the three-day notice I left you?")

three-day notice, that leaves you with the "posting-and-mailing" alternative. You can tape one copy to the door of the property and mail a second copy to her at that address by regular first-class mail. Begin counting the three days with the next day after both of these tasks are accomplished.

E. If the Tenant Still Won't Pay (or Leave)

Although one of the main purposes behind a three-day notice to pay rent or quit is to get the tenant to pay, you may be faced with a tenant who still won't or can't pay the rent within the three days. As we'll see in Chapter 16, it is illegal to harass the tenant in any way, even if she has no valid reason for not paying. Threatening or physically evicting a tenant or cutting off his or her utilities is illegal and may subject you to severe liability. The only legal way to evict a nonpaying tenant who won't move voluntarily is to file an eviction lawsuit, go to court, and obtain a judgment that the sheriff or marshal evict the tenant. Eviction lawsuits are discussed in detail in the second volume.

16

Landlord No-No's: Self-Help Evictions, Utility Terminations and Taking Tenants' Property

As any experienced landlord will attest, there are occasional tenants who will do things so outrageous that the landlord will often be tempted to bypass normal legal protections and take direct and immediate action to protect his property. For example, as a result of numerous broken promises to pay rent, a landlord may consider changing the locks and putting the tenant's property out in the street. Or, in a situation where the landlord is responsible for paying the utility charges, he may be tempted to simply not pay the bill in the hopes that the resulting lack of water, gas, or electricity will hasten the tenant's departure. When you realize how long a legal eviction can sometimes take, these actions can almost seem sensible.

If you are tempted to take the law into your own hands to force or scare a troublesome tenant out of your property, heed the following advice: **Don't do it!** Only the sheriff, marshal, or constable (in justice court districts) are legally allowed to physically evict a tenant, and then only after the landlord has obtained a court order allowing the eviction to take place.* (We show you how to do this in Volume II, on evictions.) Evictions, or attempted evictions, by anyone else are illegal and may result in arrest, a lawsuit by the tenant for a great deal of money, or both. Obtaining such a court order and having the appropriate law enforcement officials carry out the eviction certainly entails some trouble, expense and delay. This is a cost of the prop-

---

* Civil Code § 1946.5 and Penal Code § 602.3 allow an owner-occupant of a house who is renting to one roomer or lodger, to insist--without going to court--that the local police evict the lodger for nonpayment of rent or for refusing to leave after expiration of a notice of

erty rental business that can be minimized by proper selection of tenants and good management techniques, but can never be completely eliminated.

Finally, please pay attention to this. If you are sued by a tenant who you forcibly evict, or try to evict, the fact that the tenant didn't pay rent, left your property a mess, verbally abused you, or otherwise acted in a fairly outrageous way will not be a valid defense. You will very likely lose the lawsuit and it will cost you far more than evicting the tenant using normal court procedures.

Below we discuss the rules regarding forcible evictions, other coercive attempts to get tenants out, and the taking of tenants' belongings, all of which are illegal. Let's look at each of these areas briefly, if for no other reason than to convince you to avoid this kind of behavior in the first place.

A. Forcible Evictions

Sections 1159 and 1160 of the California Code of Civil Procedure make it illegal for a landlord (or anyone else) to forcibly enter a tenant's residence, or even to peaceably enter the residence and then force or threaten the tenant out. So, it's just as illegal for a landlord to knock on the tenant's door, be invited in, and then threaten to bodily evict the tenant as it is for a landlord to kick down the door or break a window to enter the property. Or, to take another example, if a landlord simply tells a tenant: "I want you out," while accompanied by sufficiently numerous or large persons apparently capable of accomplishing the task, the landlord is courting serious legal trouble. A landlord foolish enough to evict, or try to evict, by

force or threat can be sued by the tenant under all sorts of legal theories, including trespass (yes, even though he breaks into his own property), assault, battery (if physical force is used against the tenant), and even intentional infliction of emotional distress. Enough said, we hope.

B. Locking or Driving the Tenant Out Without Force

Section 789.3 of the California Civil Code makes it illegal for a landlord to use the following nonviolent methods to evict or drive out a tenant:

• Locking the tenant out by changing the locks in his absence, attaching a "bootlock" to the door, or even nailing the door shut;

• Removing doors or windows in the hope that the tenant will move out because of the resulting drafty and unsecured dwelling;

• Removing any of the tenant's property, or even the landlord's furniture rented as part of furnished premises;

• Shutting off any of the utilities (including gas, electricity, water or even elevator service), or causing them to be shut off by nonpayment in cases where the landlord pays for the utilities.

NOTE: Remember, Section 1953 of the Civil Code, which we discussed in

Section E, Chapter 2, renders ineffective any lease or rental agreement provision by which the tenant agrees to give up the right to be evicted under normal court procedures, or agrees not to sue the landlord for any illegal conduct by him. In other words, even if your lease or rental agreement form contains a provision that purports to allow the landlord to break into the tenant's home, change the locks, recover property, shut off the utilities, or otherwise legally forego the requirements of a lawful eviction, it is completely void and of no effect.

Where utilities are concerned, it's possible that not all utility cut-offs violate this law. For example, suppose a landlord who pays for the tenant's utilities properly gives a month-to-month tenant a 30-day notice of change of terms of tenancy which requires the tenant to put the utilities in his own name and pay for them. (This may not be permissible in certain rent-controlled cities.) If the tenant refuses and the landlord stops paying the utilities, so as to result in a shutoff, the landlord's intent is not to illegally evict the tenant, but to enforce a proper change in terms. Still, this course is risky, since a judge may feel differently. Also, if it turns out that for any reason the change in the terms of the rental agreement is not effective (e.g., the 30-day notice was defective or found to be retaliatory in a later court action), the utility shutoff is at least a breach of contract for which the landlord can still be held liable. Thus, Civil Code Section 789.3 allows a court, in a lawsuit by a tenant against a landlord accused of unlawful lock-out, property removal, or utility shutoff, to award the tenant all of the following:

● The tenant's "actual damages"; this can include damages for inconvenience, emotional distress, humiliation, etc., loss of property illegally removed by the landlord (or stolen or damaged by third persons after the landlord put the property outside), and loss of use of the premises;

● Punitive damages of up to $100.00 for each day, or fraction of a day, that the tenant is unable to stay in the premises or goes without utilities or property removed by the landlord, with a minimum punitive damages liability of $250.00;

● Additional punitive damages that may be allowed if the landlord's conduct is especially outrageous, such as beating up the tenant or taking his property;

● A court-ordered award of attorney's fees, even if the lease or rental agreement has no attorney's fees clause; and

● A restraining order, injunction, or other court order preventing the landlord, under penalty of contempt of court, from using any other illegal means to attempt to get the tenant out.

As with suits for forcible eviction, a landlord cannot defend a suit for wrongful lock-out, property removal, or utility shutoff on the basis that the tenant didn't pay the rent, promised to leave but didn't, or did something else even more outrageous. The legal system takes the view that a landlord (or a tenant, for that matter), when faced with the tenant's (landlord's) wrong, cannot take the law into his own hands and later excuse himself because of the other's original misconduct. The place for the landlord to complain is in a separate suit against the tenant.

C. The "Baggage Lien Law"

You may have heard of the "Baggage Lien Law"--a California statute that allows a landlord to take and sell a tenant's personal belongings if she fails to pay the rent. First of all, California's Baggage Lien Law (Civil Code Sections 1861 - 1861a) applies mainly to persons residing in hotels and motels. Second, the part of the law that applies to ordinary residential tenancies (Section 1861a) allows you to take temporary possession of a tenant's property only after first obtaining a court order.

In order to obtain such an order, you must convince a judge that your tenant is about to destroy or remove your property from the premises. Even then, the law requires that the tenant be afforded a hearing in court, separate and apart from any hearing on the impending eviction case. Needless to say, the trouble and expense of doing this (not to mention the problems of getting a judge to sign the order) by far exceed any benefit you could obtain from being able to take the tenant's property. And, even if you get the property, it's not likely to benefit you much.

If the tenant can't pay the rent, he probably owes money on most of the valuable property in his possession and, assuming the creditor has a security interest in the property, as is usually the case with furniture and electronic equipment, you would be obligated to pay off that amount. In addition, most of the tenant's household goods, and quite a bit of other property as well, are exempt from a landlord's lien under California debtor exemption laws.* In other words, even

---

* All the exemption laws are listed in Sections 704.010 through 704.210 of the Code of Civil Procedure and are fully discussed in **Billpayer's Rights** by Honigsberg and Warner (Nolo Press).

if the landlord does take possession of the belongings under the Baggage Lien Law, the tenant can get it back. What all this boils down to should be obvious--forget about the Baggage Lien Law.

D. Effect of a Forcible Eviction on a Tenant's Liability for Rent

Quite a few years ago, almost nothing affected the tenant's liability to the landlord for the rent. Landlords didn't even have to worry about keeping their rented property habitable in order to collect the rent (see Chapter 10). But even then, the one thing that did excuse the tenant from paying the rent was if her landlord evicted her from the property or otherwise interfered with her right to "quiet enjoyment" of the premises. This is still true today, and a landlord who interferes with his tenant's use of the property by forcibly evicting her, locking her out, removing her property, or shutting off her utilities will find that, in addition to facing a tenant's suit for actual and punitive damages, the uncertainty which results around just how much rent the tenant owes him will greatly benefit the tenant in any eviction lawsuit that follows. This is because, if the tenant gets a lawyer and goes to court, she is almost sure to regain possession of the unit. The

199

landlord must then try to figure out how much the tenant owes him. As the following example illustrates, this isn't always easy.

EXAMPLE: Albert Apartment-Owner, exasperated at Rosie Renter's repeated excuses for not coming up with the $425 monthly rent for July and August, enters Rosie's apartment on August 6, changes the locks, puts Rosie's property and furniture in the hallway and shuts off the utilities. Rosie and her two children stay with friends until her lawyer gets a court order letting Rosie move back in on August 10. Rosie's lawyer got the court order as part of a lawsuit against Albert for actual and punitive damages (including punitive damages of $100 per day for each of the five days when she was locked out). Albert sees a lawyer, who advises him to do what he should have done in the first place-- file an unlawful detainer suit after service of the proper three-day notice to pay rent or quit.

On August 12, Albert prepares and serves the three-day notice, which demands the full $850 rent for July and August. Rosie defends on the basis that the lock-out reduced the rent actually due by an amount equal to five days' pro-rated rent, so that only $779 was due. At the unlawful detainer trial a month later, the judge rules that the three-day notice was defective because it erroneously demanded $850. Since it was defective it didn't legally terminate Rosie's tenancy. Accordingly, Rosie wins, getting judgment against Albert for attorney's fees under the attorney's fees clause in her rental agreement. Albert has to start all over again with a new and correct three-day notice and unlawful detainer. He eventually gets Rosie out in October. Rosie, of course, hasn't paid any rent all this time and Albert still has to defend against Rosie's lawsuit. In the end, Albert loses a few thousand dollars, when you add up the judgment against him, attorney's fees and lost rent.

NOTE: This example is based on an actual case handled by one of the authors, so please take it seriously and act accordingly.

17

Termination of Tenancies

As we learned in Chapter 2, the general rule is that neither the landlord nor the tenant has the legal right to terminate a tenancy based on a lease before the lease term expires, unless one or more terms of the lease is violated.* We also learned in Chapter 2 that where the tenancy is from month to month, either the landlord or the tenant can terminate the tenancy, or the landlord can change the terms by giving 30 days' written notice, unless the rental property is located in an area with a rent-control ordinance which requires just cause for eviction.

The purpose of this chapter is not to review the basic rules concerning leases or month-to-month tenancies in detail. Here we discuss how tenancies are terminated by a landlord or tenant, and how a tenant may "break a lease" by moving out before the end of the term.

---

* There is, in practice, one major exception to this rule which favors the tenant. This is the mitigation of damages rule, which has the effect of allowing the tenant to "break the lease" by skipping out before the end of the lease term. If this happens, the "mitigation of damages" rule requires that the landlord try to rerent the property. If he does, or even if he doesn't but could have if he had tried harder, a court will hold that the tenant's obligation to pay for the rest of the lease terms is at an end.

A. Termination of Month-to-Month Tenancies by the Landlord (except in cities requiring just cause for eviction)

It used to be that a landlord could give a tenant a 30-day termination notice for any reason, or for no reason at all.* Even if the landlord did have a particular reason for wanting to end the month-to-month tenancy, she didn't have to list the reason on the notice or explain it in court. This is still the general rule in California, but there are some big exceptions, including:

• A "Just-Cause" Requirement: A few cities, including San Francisco, Los Angeles, Berkeley, Santa Monica, Beverly Hills, Cotati, Palm Springs, Santa Monica, and West Hollywood, have rent-control ordinances which allow landlords to terminate a month-to-month tenancy only for reasons stated in the ordinance, such as the desire of a relative of the landlord to live in the property. Cities requiring "just cause" for eviction also require that a landlord state the cause they are relying on in the termination notice (landlord-initiated terminations of tenancies in rent-controlled cities are discussed in Section D, below);

• Subsidized Housing: A similar "just-cause" requirement exists for terminating tenancies where the landlord receives rent or other payments from the federal, state, or local government as part of a program to assist low-income tenants. Acceptable reasons for termination are usually listed in

---

* As noted in Chapter 2, Section E, if a rental agreement so specifies, or rent is paid at a shorter interval, a periodic tenancy can be ended with less than 30 days' notice.

the form lease drafted by the government agency. You must state one of these reasons explicitly in the 30-day notice when terminating housing-authority-assisted ("Section 8") tenancies or Housing and Urban Development (HUD)-assisted ("Section 236") tenancies;

• Discrimination: Even in areas where just cause for eviction isn't required, you can't evict for the purpose of excluding anyone because of race, religion, sex, marital status, having children, sexual preference, etc. (see Chapter 8 on discrimination);

• Retaliatory Evictions: You can never legally terminate a month-to-month or other periodic tenancy to retaliate against a tenant for exercising any right under the law, including the tenant's right to complain about perceived problems with the property, to organize other tenants into a "tenant's union," or even to withhold rent in the circumstances for which this is allowed (see Chapter 13 on illegal retaliation for details).

WARNING: Your tenant can sue you for illegal discrimination or retaliation. Laws protecting tenants in these areas are broad. Make sure your reason for evicting any tenant is related to the smooth and peaceful operation of your rental business and cannot possibly be construed as either discriminatory or retaliatory.

Examples of valid reasons to give a 30-day notice include:

• Your tenant is repeatedly late with her rent. You've given her three-day notices several times, but she has come through with the rent before the end of the third day. Your warnings to pay rent on time in the future have had no effect;

• The tenant has given you a number of bad checks. You've used three-day notices and the checks were made good, but it keeps happening;

• Your tenant continues to have loud and boisterous parties and play her stereo at unreasonable levels. She also has loud arguments with housemates, and other tenants are complaining to you;

• The tenant has caused damage to the property, e.g., holes in the wall, cigarette burns, damaged carpets or drapes, etc.;

• The tenant is extremely obnoxious or vulgar to you or your manager or to other tenants;

• Your tenant repeatedly violates the "no pets" or some other clause of your rental agreement;

• You want the property vacant to remodel it;

• You're selling your rental property (a single-family dwelling, for example) and the new buyers want the tenants out before escrow closes;

• You want to move in a close friend or relative to whom you promised to rent the property. (In some rent control areas, only parents and children count as close relatives, while in others, the definition is considerably broader--see Chapter 4 and Section D of this chapter.)

As we discuss in more detail in Section C of this chapter, it's important to realize that some reasons for eviction--such as making too much noise or damaging the property--also justify evicting with a three-day notice, because the tenant is in violation of a clause in your lease or rental agreement. This may cause you to ask a question along these lines: "If I can evict a tenant by using a three-day notice, why give the tenant with a month-to-month tenancy a break by using a 30-day notice?" The answer is, because it's good business. A tenant is

far more likely to defend against an eviction lawsuit which specifically accuses her of misconduct (and in which she was only given three days to get out or stop the behavior) than one in which 30 days' notice was given. And if a tenant does force you to go to court, remember that if your tenancy termination is based on a 30-day notice, you don't even have to list the reason in the lawsuit papers, or prove your reason for evicting in court (unless you are in a rent-control area calling for just cause for eviction or if you must rebut a tenant's defense to your lawsuit based on your supposed retaliation or discrimination). Finally, people with experience in the area know that judges are more reluctant to allow a tenant to be evicted using a three-day notice for breaching the rental agreement or causing a nuisance or damage than they are if you use a 30-day notice.

Once you've determined that the tenancy is periodic (e.g., from month to month), that your eviction is neither retaliatory nor discriminatory (and that just cause for eviction is not required under any applicable rent-control ordinance in your area), follow the steps outlined below to prepare and serve your 30-day notice. Because many of the steps in a 30-day notice eviction lawsuit are very similar, or even identical, to those in a nonpayment of rent case, parts of this chapter will refer back to Chapter 15 on three-day notices for nonpayment of rent.

1. Prepare the 30-Day Notice

As you can see, filling in this notice normally requires little more than the name of the tenant, the address of the property and the date and your signature. (You will find a blank tear out version of this form in the Appendix.)

If your rental agreement reduces the notice period required to terminate a tenancy to as low as seven days (see Chapter 2, Section E), you will have to change our form slightly. Simply white out the "30" and fill in the lesser number of days. However, if you collect your rent once a month, be sure that any seven-day notice doesn't terminate the tenancy during a period for which you've already collected rent in advance. For example, if you collected the rent for August on August 1, serving a seven day notice any sooner than August 24 would be an illegal attempt to end the tenancy before the end of the paid-for rental period (August 1-31).

NOTICE OF TERMINATION OF TENANCY

TO _____ Tyrone Tenant _____ ,

TENANT(S) IN POSSESSION OF THE PREMISES AT:

_____ 123 Market Street, Apartment 4 _____ ,
(Street Address)

City of __San Diego__ , County of __San Diego__ , California

YOU ARE HEREBY NOTIFIED that effective 30 DAYS from the date of service on you of this notice, the periodic tenancy by which you hold possession of the above-described premises is terminated, at which time you are required to vacate and surrender possession of the said premises. In the event you fail to do so, legal proceedings will be instituted against you to recover possession of the said premises, damages and costs of suit.

[If you are in a rent-control city which requires that you state a reason for terminating a tenancy, insert it here.]

DATED: November 14, 1986 _____
OWNER/MANAGER

---

2. Serving the 30-Day Notice

a. When the 30-Day Notice Should Be Served

A 30-day notice can be served on the tenant on any day of the month. For example, a 30-day notice served on March 17 terminates the tenancy effective 30 days later, on April 16. (Simply count 30 days, regardless of whether the month has 28, 29, or 31 days.) This is true even though rent is paid for a period running from the first to the last day of each month. Where a 30-day notice is served to terminate the tenancy in the middle of a month or rental period, the rent due for that period is pro-rated based on the final notice date.

EXAMPLE 1: Because of her constant loud parties, you serve your tenant, Rhoda Rockenroll, with a 30-day notice on August 13. The last day of the tenancy should be the 30th day after that, or September 12. On September 1, Rhoda owes you rent only for those first 12 days of September. The rent for each day is $450 divided by 30, or $15, so the rent for the first 12 days of September is 12 x $15, or $180. If you accept even one dollar more than this amount, Rhoda will be able to claim successfully that you accepted rent for a period beyond the 30-day period, thereby canceling the 30-day notice.

EXAMPLE 2: Because of her frequent late rent payments, you gave Sally Slowpoke a 30-day notice on January 22, terminating her tenancy effective February 21. The rent is $1,200 per month, due on the first of the month. When Sally moved in, you accepted her $1,200 "last month's rent." If you had called this a "security deposit" instead, the rent she'd owe on February 1 would be $40 per day (pro-rated based on $1,200 per month and a 30-day month) for each of the 21 days, or $840. But since you already have the $1,200 you called "last month's rent," this rent (and more) is already paid. If you accept any rent at all on February 1, Sally will be able to claim that you voided the 30-day notice by accepting rent beyond the notice period. Your best bet is to hold onto the "last month's rent" of $1,200, of which $840 is the actual rent for the first 21 days in February. The remaining $360 is handled like a security deposit, which you would have been wiser to call it in the first place (see Chapter 5, Section D, on deposits).

Many tenants served with a 30-day notice in the middle of a month or rental period who will owe rent for part of the next month will not be eager to pay that rent, even though they're living on the premises. Their attitude may be, "You're evicting me anyway, so I'm not giving you anything." If you anticipate this reaction, it's a good idea to try to talk to your tenant in advance in an effort to settle the issue amicably. If your efforts fail, you have two choices:

• You can either take the pro-rated rent for that last portion of the month out of the security deposit; or

• You can wait until the second day of the new 30-day period (the next day after the tenant should have paid his rent) and serve the tenant with a three-day notice to pay or quit, for the pro-rated rent due. If the tenant refuses to pay or leave after the three days, you can file an unlawful detainer lawsuit based on nonpayment of rent. (You can't sue for this pro-rated rent in an eviction lawsuit based on the 30-day notice unless you also use a three-day notice to pay or quit.)

EXAMPLE: In Example 1 above, Rhoda owed $180 in pro-rated rent for the first 12 days of September. On September 1, Rhoda refuses to pay, saying, "You're evicting me anyway, so forget it." On September 2, you serve Rhoda a three-day notice demanding that she pay the $180 rent or leave. If she ignores it, you can file a lawsuit based on her refusal to pay on September 6 without having to wait until the day after the 30-day period, September 13, to sue. If you decide to do this, refer to Volume II, **The Landlord's Law Book: Evictions.** If you give the 30-day notice on the last day of the month, so that the tenancy expires neatly at the end of the following month, you can avoid calculating pro-rated rent. Unfortunately, this requires that you give the tenant the 30-day notice a few days before the rent for the entire last month is due, and gives the tenant an opportunity to refuse to pay for an entire month. If the security deposit more than covers this amount, you may want to risk this. However, if it doesn't, your best bet is to give the tenant the 30-day notice shortly after you receive and cash the month's rent check. Assuming the tenant paid rent on time, this assures that the 30-day notice will be given

toward the beginning of the month or rental period, meaning that the last day of legal tenancy will fall only one or two days into the next month.

EXAMPLE: Linda Lately is habitually late with her rent, usually paying on the third day after receiving your three-day notices. You decide it's time for a change of tenants. On October 2, you knock on Linda's door and ask for the rent. If you luck out and get her to pay, cash the check. (You may even want to do it at her bank so that you get your money immediately.) In any event, after the check clears, promptly serve Linda her 30-day notice. This means the last day of her tenancy will be in early November and on November 1, she'll only owe you a few days' rent. Since you can't sue for this amount without a three-day notice (which really isn't worth the trouble for several days' rent), you can deduct this amount from the deposit when she leaves.

NOTE: Of course, if Linda doesn't pay her rent on the second day of October, you can use a three-day notice. If she still doesn't pay within three days, you can sue for nonpayment of rent as indicated in Volume II, on evictions. If Linda does pay before the end of the three-day period, serve your 30-day notice immediately after you get paid. You'll still lose only a few days pro-rated rent that you can't recover in the judgment, but your deposit should be big enough to cover that much.

b. Who Should Serve the 30-Day Notice?

As with the three-day notice (see Chapter 15), the 30-day notice may be served by any person over age 18, including you.

c. Who to Serve

As with three-day notices, you

should try to serve a copy of the 30-day notice on each tenant to whom you originally rented the property. However, service of the notice on one of several co-tenants who are listed together on a written lease or rental agreement is legally sufficient.

d. How the Notice is Served on the Tenant

A 30-day notice may be served in any of the three ways a three-day notice to pay rent or quit can be served (see Chapter 15, Section D):

• By personal delivery;

• By substituted service on another person, plus mailing; or

• By posting and mailing.

In addition, the 30-day notice may be served by certified mail, return receipt requested.* If you wish to use one of the first three methods, turn to Chapter 15 for how-to details.

B. Termination of Month-to-Month Tenancies by the Tenant

You will probably face tenant-initiated terminations of month-to-month

tenancies more often than any other type of termination. As we saw in Chapter 2, Section C, a month-to-month tenancy is properly terminated by you or your tenant giving the other a written notice of 30 days or more, unless the rental agreement specifically allows for a shorter notice period. This part of the chapter discusses the tenant's liabilities and responsibilities both when a proper 30-day notice is given and when a tenant skips out without following the legal notice requirements.

1. When the Tenant Gives 30 Days' Notice

Ideally, your tenant will give you the required notice. The notice should be in writing, and should be personally served on you or your manager or mailed by certified mail.* In practice, many tenants mail the notice by ordinary first-class mail, which is still legally effective so long as the landlord receives it 30 or more days before the termination date.

2. Insisting on a Written Notice

If the tenant simply phones or otherwise tells you verbally that he will be leaving in 30 days or more, it's good business to insist that the notice be in writing. If the tenant doesn't do this, you should prepare and serve your own written 30 days' notice on the tenant. Why bother doing this if they plan to leave anyway? Because if you don't, you may be caught between the proverbial rock and hard place if you sign a rental agreement for a new

---

* Unlike 30-day notices changing terms of tenancy, certified mail service is specifically allowed for 30-day termination notices. See Civil Code Sections 827 and 1946.

---

* Civil Code Section 1946.

tenant to move in immediately after the old tenant's promised date of leaving and the existing tenant does not move as promised. Because an oral promise to leave isn't legally binding, you can't sue to force the existing tenant to leave, except perhaps by three-day notice followed by an unlawful detainer suit if the rent has not been paid. But if you signed a lease or rental agreement, or even orally promised your new tenant that she could move in, you will be liable to that person for the full cost of temporary housing until the first tenant leaves.

EXAMPLE: On the basis of your tenants' telephoned promises to leave in 30 days, you sign a rental agreement beginning the day after you expect them to depart. They later inform you (or you discover) that they won't leave as planned. Because you received no written 30-day notice from the tenants, you cannot sue to evict them. The best you can do is serve them with a 30-day notice. If the tenants-to-be must stay in a motel until the present tenants leave in 30 days, you are responsible for the cost, which is certain to be more than the rent you will realize from your tenants.

If, on the other hand, your tenants gave you a written 30-day notice, but failed to abide by it, you can sue to evict them as soon as the 30 days are up. So, the moral is clear--if your tenants won't put the notice in writing, do it for them.

3. Application of Deposit to Last Month's Rent

In many instances, a month-to-month tenant will properly put a 30-day notice in writing, but will improperly insist that you apply the security deposit toward the last month's rent, which the tenant tells you he won't be paying. Although this is legal where you've called all or part of the tenant's initial payment "last month's rent," it isn't legal for the tenant to apply a "security" or other deposit in this way. Why should you care if a tenant doesn't pay last month's rent if the deposit amount, no matter what it's called covers the rent and the tenant leaves the property clean and undamaged? You shouldn't. The problem is that you can't know in advance in what condition the property will be left. If the tenant leaves the property a mess and has already applied the security deposit to last month's rent, you will obviously have nothing left to use to repair or clean the property. Again, it is precisely for this reason that you should make it clear in any rental agreement or lease that the tenant's up-front payment is a "security deposit" and not "last month's rent" (see Chapter 5, Section D).

You have two choices if you are faced with a tenant who tries to use a security deposit for last month's rent. Your first is simply to do nothing. In some circumstances, if you have good reason to believe that the particular tenant will in fact leave the property clean and undamaged, this may be the best thing to do. Your second choice is to treat the tenant's nonpayment (or partial payment) of last month's rent as an ordinary case of rent nonpayment. You are entitled to do this. If you follow this course of action, serve a three-day notice to pay rent or quit on the tenant as set out in Chapter 15, and file an eviction lawsuit as outlined in Volume II. Unfortunately, since it takes a minimum of three weeks to evict even in uncontested cases, this probably won't get the tenant out much sooner than he would leave anyway. However, it will result in your getting a court judgment for the unpaid last month's rent. This means you may apply the security deposit to pay for any necessary cleaning and damage costs, with any remainder applied to the judgment for non-payment of rent. If the deposit is not large enough to cover both, you can first take care of the cleaning and damages and then collect the judgment by garnisheeing the departed tenant's wages or bank account. We discuss how to do this and how to prepare a proper legal notice explaining your actions to the departed tenant in Chapter 18.

EXAMPLE 1: You've been less than thrilled with the way Moe and Maureen Messe have been taking care of the house you rented to them, and you suspect you'll need the bulk of their $900 security deposit to pay for cleaning and repairs. You've also grown accustomed to the rent being a few days late. You've thought about giving Moe and Maureen a 30-day notice, but to your pleasant surprise, they give you one--on January 4, about the time you expected the rent--except that instead of the $450 rent, they tell you to "take the rent out of their deposit." If you stand still for this, you may be out some money, as this will leave you only $450 with which to clean and fix the place.

EXAMPLE 2: The alternative to passively accepting Maureen and Moe's plan to have you take last month's rent out of the deposit, is to immediately serve them with a three-day notice to pay the remaining $450 rent or quit. Four days later, on January 8, you may bring suit (see Volume II) and have the unlawful detainer summons and complaint served. If your suit is uncontested, you can get a default judgment on the January 14 and perhaps get the sheriff or marshal to evict as soon as January 20. The money part of the judgment, assuming you can collect it, will compensate you for the rent, and you'll be free to use the deposit for its proper purpose--payment of repair and cleaning costs.

4. Acceptance of Further Rent After 30-Day Notice Is Given

Your acceptance of any rent for any period beyond the termination date in effect cancels the notice and creates a new tenancy. This is true whether you or your tenant terminate the tenancy. In other words, it's okay to accept rent from the tenant, but only in an amount that keeps the tenant paid up through the termination date. Acceptance of any more rent than this cancels the 30-day notice.

EXAMPLE: On April 15, Tom Tenant serves you a notice to terminate his month-to-month tenancy effective May 15. A few weeks later, however, he changes his mind and decides to stay. Too embarrassed to tell you this, he simply pays the usual $500 monthly rent on May 1. If he were intent on leaving on May 15 as promised, he should be paying only 15 days pro-rated rent of $250. Unwittingly, you cash the $500 check for the rent for all of May, even though you've already re-rented to a new tenant who hopes to move in on the

16th. Not only will you be powerless to evict Tom, but you'll also be liable to the new tenant for failing to put her in possession of the property as promised.

The way to avoid this sort of problem is simple. If the tenant offers you any rent that logically would apply for any period--no matter how short--beyond the termination date, you should accept it only if you want the tenancy to continue just as if you'd received no notice. This includes not accepting rent for the last month, if you've already accepted "last month's rent." If you don't want to continue the tenancy as before, but are agreeable to giving the tenant a few days or weeks more, you should prepare a written agreement to that effect and have the tenant sign it.

5. What to Do When the Tenant Gives Less Than 30 Days' Notice

Quite often your tenant will give you less than the full 30 days' notice to which you're entitled. She may mail the notice 30 days before vacating, meaning you will receive it only 28 days before,* she may give you two weeks' notice, or she may just say goodbye as she hands you the keys to the apartment. The important thing to know is that a tenant's written termination notice isn't ineffective just because it gives you less than the full 30 days' notice. It is still a valid notice of termination. You, however, are entitled to rent for the entire 30 days from the date of the notice. Indeed, most of what you learned earlier in this section about the necessity for

---

* As you saw in Section A of this chapter, a 30-day notice is properly served by certified mail, with ordinary first class mail constituting valid service only if and when it reaches its destination.

a written 30-day notice, etc. also applies to notices that give less than 30 days' notice. To review:

• A tenant's termination notice is of no effect unless it's in writing, even if the terms of the tenancy were not written down to start with;

• It isn't legal for the tenant to refuse to pay part or all of the last month's rent and insist that you apply the security deposit towards the last months' rent, unless the deposit specifically says it's for "last month's rent;"

• Your acceptance of any rent for any period beyond the termination date may void the notice.

The main effect of your tenant's failure to give you the full 30 days' notice is to allow you, under some circumstances, to charge--most likely from the tenant's deposit--additional pro-rated rent, beyond the termination date, for the number of days by which the notice was short. You are entitled to rent for 30 days from the date of the notice. If a tenant pays the rent for the full 30 days, she has the right to stay for that time.

EXAMPLE 1: On August 25, Tricia Transient gives you a handwritten note saying she'll be moving out in ten days, on September 4. Because you're entitled to rent for 30 days from the date of the notice, you're entitled to rent through September 24. So, on September 1, when Tricia tries to get

210

by with paying pro-rated rent for her four remaining days in September, you should remind her that you're entitled to 24 days' pro-rated rent. Of course, if Tricia pays it, she'll have the right to stay through the 24th if she wishes. If Tricia doesn't pay, which is likely, since your threat of an eviction suit for rent non-payment isn't likely to phase a tenant about to leave anyway, you can deduct the rent not paid from her deposit. (We discuss how to do this in Chapter 18.)

EXAMPLE 2: On May 29, Don Drifter gives you two hours' notice of his intent to leave, handing you the keys with a chummy, "Well, we'll be on our way." You're entitled to 30 days' rent from that date through June 28. Assuming the $600 rent for May was paid, but June's wasn't, you are entitled to subtract 28 days' pro-rated rent (28 x $20/day = $560) from Don's deposit. If the deposit won't cover this plus cleaning and damage costs, you'll have to take Don to small claims court for the balance.

One exception to the general rule that you are entitled to collect 30 days' rent whether or not the tenant gives you proper notice is that you can't "collect double" by charging your outgoing tenant extra rent beyond the date she left, while at the same time collecting that rent from a new tenant who moves in immediately. In other words, if you very quickly find a new tenant to replace the outgoing one who didn't give you the full 30 days' notice, and therefore suffer no loss as a result of the inadequate notice, you can't charge the outgoing tenant that extra rent. However, if there was a gap of a few days, during which time you had no paying tenant, you would be entitled to the pro-rated rent for the unrented days, plus any costs of advertising the property. You may deduct these amounts from the outgoing tenant's deposit, as discussed in detail in Chapter 18.

If you can't collect double rent, both from the outgoing tenant who didn't give sufficient notice, and from the new tenant, why should you bother getting a new tenant so quickly? In theory at least, because the law requires you to "mitigate damages" in this way. If you don't, and instead sit back and let the property lie vacant between the day the tenant vacates and the 30th day from the date of the notice, hoping to charge the rent for that period against the outgoing tenant's deposit, you may be in for an unpleasant suprise. Not only does the law require you to credit any rent received from an incoming tenant against the outgoing tenant's liability, but it also limits that liability to the extent you could have, but didn't, "mitigate damages" by finding a new tenant.* Of course, if this sort of lawsuit went to court, the burden of proving your failure to mitigate damages would be on the tenant and this would be difficult to do if you made even reasonable efforts to find a new tenant within the 30-day period.

EXAMPLE: On June 25, Rick Rideaway, who rents from you on a month-to-month basis, says he'll be leaving on June 30. Because Rick gives you only five days' notice, he's liable for the rent for another 25 days, through July 25. You charge him $500 for 25 days of pro-rated rent, or $375 (his monthly rent is $450), and because the property was clean and undamaged, return $125 to Rick. Because this covered the rent through July 25, you made no effort to re-rent the place until July 26, almost

* Civil Code Section 1951.2.

four weeks after Rick left. Rick takes you to small claims court, suing for the $375. The judge may find that even though Rick should legally have given you more than five days' notice, you should have made some reasonable effort to locate a new tenant. Based on the local housing market, which is extremely tight, the judge concludes that you probably could have found a new tenant within ten days if you listed the vacancy in the papers and with rental location agencies. The judge therefore allows you to keep only ten days' pro-rated rent, or $150, giving the tenant a judgment for the difference.

To summarize, where your month-to-month tenant gives you less than the required 30 days' written notice, you're still entitled to:

1. Thirty days' rent pro-rated from the date of the written notice, less

2. Any rent you reasonably could have collected from a new tenant for the period between the day the outgoing tenant left and the end of the 30-day period, plus

3. Any reasonable advertising expenses incurred in finding that new tenant. You can deduct this amount (less credit for any rent the tenant did pay for this period), plus repair and cleaning charges (see Chapter 18), from the tenant's security deposit.

C. Termination by the Landlord With a Three-Day Notice (except in cities requiring just cause for eviction)

As we discussed in Part A above, there are some situations in which a landlord may use a three-day notice to terminate a tenancy for cause in cities that do not have a rent-control ordinance requiring just cause for eviction (we discuss rent control in Section D of this chapter), including:

• Nonpayment of rent;

• Violation of a lease or rental agreement provision;

• Causing serious damage to the property;

• Causing a nuisance; and

• Using the premises for an unlawful purpose.

This is true whether the tenancy is for a fixed term or from month to month. As also indicated in Part A, however, a landlord in a non-rent control area who wants to evict a month-to-month tenant (whose rent is paid) will be better off using a 30-day notice, since she will not have to show just cause to evict the tenant or even have to accuse him of misconduct.

Nevertheless, there are circumstances in which a landlord may want to use a three-day notice. For example, the tenancy may be one for a fixed term, rather than from month to month (so that a 30-day notice can't be used), and, therefore, a three-day notice specifying the reason for termination may be the only way to evict without waiting until the lease expires. Or the tenant may have failed to pay rent, in which case the three-day notice to pay rent or quit discussed in Chapter 15 is not so much to terminate the tenancy, but to give the tenant an ultimatum that, if she doesn't comply with the lease or rental agreement within three days, the tenancy will be terminated. Or the tenants' conduct may be so outrageous that the landlord wishes to lay the groundwork for an eviction in the fastest way possible. We devoted a separate chapter to the three-day notice to pay rent or quit in Chapter 15, simply because this is the most frequent device used by landlords to force reluctant tenants to pay rent. Now, we briefly discuss three-day notices given for reasons other than nonpayment of rent. Since some of these notices don't have to give the tenant the choice of correcting his or her behavior instead of leaving, and since tenants generally fail to respond to three-day notices that do give this option--other than three-day notices to pay rent or quit--we view the following notices as being primarily a means for terminating a tenancy, with an eye toward initiating an eviction lawsuit (covered in the second volume).

1. The Three-Day Notice for Violation of the Lease

Section 1161(3) of the Code of Civil Procedure allows a landlord to give a tenant who violates a lease clause a three-day notice demanding that the tenant leave or (in most cases) correct the violation. However, the language of the notice depends on whether the tenant's violation of the lease can be corrected within a reasonable period of time, or whether the breach is not correctible. Examples of lease violations that can't be corrected include subletting all or part of the premises (if the lease prohibits this), extensively damaging the premises, or causing a nuisance.

When your tenant has violated a provision of the lease or rental agreement that is capable of being corrected, your three-day notice must give the tenant the option of either correcting the violation or moving out within three days. This kind of notice is technically called a "Three-Day Notice to Cure Covenant or Quit." How do you know which lease violations are "correctible" and therefore subject to this kind of three-day notice? The answer is simply that most lease violations, with the exception of subletting, extensively damaging the premises, or causing a nuisance (repeatedly disturbing other tenants or neighbors) are considered correctible. The tenant who violates a "no-pets" clause can correct the violation by getting rid of the pet. A tenant who refuses to pay an installment toward a security deposit he or she agreed in the lease to pay can correct the violation by paying the installment. Always give the tenant the benefit of the doubt on this one. If the tenant refuses to leave after getting your three-day notice, and you have to file an eviction lawsuit, you don't want your case thrown out of court because you should have given the tenant the option in the notice but didn't. Your three-day notice to perform covenant or quit should contain all of the following:

- A description--the street address and apartment number if any--of the property;

- A very specific statement as to how the tenant(s) violated a particular provision of the rental agreement or lease; this should be phrased in the language that the tenant(s) failed to "perform the covenant" (abide by a provision) of the lease.

- A demand that the covenant be "performed" (e.g., by getting rid of the pet) within three days or that the tenant(s) leave the premises within three days;

- A statement that you will pursue legal action (or declare the lease or rental agreement "forfeited") if the tenant does not cure the violation or move within the three days; and

- An indication such as your signature--or your manager's--that the notice is authorized by you; the date is optional.

- A proof of service that states how the notice was served on the tenant. The proof of service doesn't need to be filled out on the original notice that goes to the tenant; it's only necessary on the copy you file with the court if you bring an unlawful detainer suit.

Two sample three-day notices to perform covenant or quit appear on the following pages, one for violating a no-pets clause, and the other for failure to make agreed payments toward a security deposit which was to be paid off over a period of time. A blank tear out form is included in the Appendix. You may tear out this form or use a photocopy.

THREE-DAY NOTICE TO PERFORM COVENANT OR QUIT

TO _____ Lester D. Lessee _____ ,

TENANT(S) IN POSSESSION OF THE PREMISES AT

_____ 123 Main Street, Apartment 4 _____ ,
(Street Address)

City of __San Jose__ , County of __Santa Clara__ , California

    YOU ARE HEREBY NOTIFIED that you are in violation of the lease or rental agreement under which you occupy the above-described premises in that you have violated the covenant to:

_____ refrain from keeping a pet on the premises _____

_____

in the following manner:

_____ by having a dog and two cats on the said premises _____

YOU ARE HEREBY REQUIRED to remedy the said violation and perform the said covenant within THREE (3) DAYS from the date of service on you of this notice or to vacate and surrender possession of the said premises. In the event you fail to do so, legal proceedings will be instituted against you to recover possession of the said premises, declare the forfeiture of the said rental agreement or lease under which you occupy the same premises, and recover damages and court costs.

DATED: November 6, 1986   *Larry Landlord*
                                         OWNER/MANAGER

THREE-DAY NOTICE TO PERFORM COVENANT OR QUIT

TO _____ Ronald R. Renter _____ ,

TENANT(S) IN POSSESSION OF THE PREMISES AT

____ 1234 Market Street, Apartment 5 _____ ,
              (Street Address)

City of __ Oakland __ , County of __ Alameda __ , California

YOU ARE HEREBY NOTIFIED that you are in violation of the lease or rental agreement under which you occupy the above-described premises in that you have violated the covenant to:

pay agreed installments of the security deposit, in the amount of $50.00

per month on the first day of each month (in addition to rent) until paid

in the following manner:

failing to pay the said $50.00 on the first day of the month of December,

1983

YOU ARE HEREBY REQUIRED to remedy the said violation and perform the said covenant within THREE (3) DAYS from the date of service on you of this notice or to vacate and surrender possession of the said premises. In the event you fail to do so, legal proceedings will be instituted against you to recover possession of the said premises, declare the forfeiture of the said rental agreement or lease under which you occupy the same premises, and recover damages and court costs.

DATED: December 7, 1986   *Marty Manager*
                                         OWNER/MANAGER

215

2. The Three-Day Notice to Quit — Noncorrectible Violations, Damage to Premises, Nuisance, or Unlawful Use of Premises

There are several situations in which your three-day notice doesn't have to give the tenant the choice of correcting the problem or leaving. In this situation, a three-day notice to quit can just tell the tenant to leave in three days. The idea behind this kind of unconditional notice is that the tenant's conduct is so extreme, for example severely damaging the property or using the premises for an illegal purpose, that this harsher remedy is justified. Another basis for not re-quiring that a three-day notice give the tenant the option of correcting the problem is that it can't be corrected within three days. For example, a tenant who has sublet part or all of the property contrary to the lease or rental agreement can't correct this breach in three days because he, in turn, couldn't necessarily evict his own tenant, the sub-tenant, within that time.

The unconditional three-day notice to quit can be used only in one of the following situations:

• The tenant has sublet all or part of the premises to someone else, con-trary to the rental agreement or lease;

• The tenant is causing a nuisance on the premises, repeatedly annoying neighbors;

• The tenant is causing a great deal of damage to the property; this would be extreme problems such as holes punched in the wall, numerous windows broken, etc. Do not rely on this ground for ordinary run-of-the-mill damage caused by carelessness, in which case the tenant must at least be given a chance to correct the problem;

• The tenant is using the property for an illegal purpose--like running a house of prostitution, dealing drugs or even operating a legitimate business in violation of local zoning laws. You can't evict for minor transgressions such as smoking marijuana on the prem-ises.

The unconditional three-day notice to quit must contain the following:

• A description of the premises;

• A specific statement as to how and approximately when the tenant illegally sublet, caused a nuisance, damaged the premises, or illegally used the prem-ises. This is the most important part of the notice, and must be drafted very carefully to clearly tell the tenant what he or she is doing wrong. The slightest omission of necessary infor-mation could void the notice--another reason why a 30-day notice may be preferable;

• A demand that the tenant leave the premises within three days;

• An unequivocal statement that the lease is forfeited and that you will take legal action to remove the tenant if he or she fails to vacate within the three days;

• An indication, such as your or your manager's signature, that you authorized the notice.

A blank tear-out form is included in the back of this book, and can be used in any of the four situations (improper subletting, nuisance, waste, or illegal use) for which an unconditional three-day notice can be used. This form is filled out in much the same way as the three-day notice to cure covenant or quit, and you must be very specific as to the conduct you're complaining about. The following are four sample forms, one for each situation.

THREE-DAY NOTICE TO QUIT

(Improper Subletting, Nuisance, Waste, or Illegal Use)

TO _____ Theresa D. Tenant _____ ,

TENANT(S) IN POSSESSION OF THE PREMISES AT

_____ 1234 Frisco Street, Apartment 5 _____
(Street Address)

City of _San Francisco_ , County of _San Francisco_ , California

YOU ARE HEREBY NOTIFIED that you are required within THREE (3) DAYS from the date of service on you of this notice to vacate and surrender possession of the said premises by reason of your having committed the following nuisance, waste, unlawful use, or unlawful subletting:

You have unlawfully sublet a portion of the premises contrary to the

provisions of your lease, to another person who now lives on the

premises with you.

As a result of your having committed the foregoing acts, the lease or rental agreement under which you occupy the said premises is terminated. In the event you fail to vacate and surrender possession of the said premises, legal proceedings will be instituted against you to recover possession, damages, and court costs.

DATE: May 1, 1986   _____ Ollie Owner _____
                              OWNER/MANAGER

THREE-DAY NOTICE TO QUIT

(Improper Subletting, Nuisance, Waste, or Illegal Use)

TO _____ Ronald Rockenroll _____ ,

TENANT(S) IN POSSESSION OF THE PREMISES AT

1234 Diego Street, Apartment 5
_____
(Street Address)

City of _San Diego_ , County of _San Diego_ , California

YOU ARE HEREBY NOTIFIED that you are required within THREE (3) DAYS from the date of service on you of this notice to vacate and surrender possession of the said premises by reason of your having committed the following nuisance, waste, unlawful use, or unlawful subletting:

You committed a nuisance on the premises by reason of loud boisterous parties at which music was played at an extremely loud volume, and at which intoxicated guests milled about outside the front door to the premises and shouted obscenities at passersby every night from February 26th through 28th, 1986

As a result of your having committed the foregoing acts, the lease or rental agreement under which you occupy the said premises is terminated. In the event you fail to vacate and surrender possession of the said premises, legal proceedings will be instituted against you to recover possession, damages, and court costs.

DATE: March 1, 1986   _Freda Fedupe_
                           OWNER/MANAGER

THREE-DAY NOTICE TO QUIT

(Improper Subletting, Nuisance, Waste, or Illegal Use)

TO _____ Leslie D. Lessee _____ ,

TENANT(S) IN POSSESSION OF THE PREMISES AT

2468 Alameda Street
_____
(Street Address)

City of _San Jose_ , County of _Santa Clara_ , California

YOU ARE HEREBY NOTIFIED that you are required within THREE (3) DAYS from the date of service on you of this notice to vacate and surrender possession of the said premises by reason of your having committed the following nuisance, waste, unlawful use, or unlawful subletting:

You committed or allowed to be committed waste on the said premises

in that you or your guests have punched holes in the doors and walls

of the premises and broken the front living room window.

As a result of your having committed the foregoing acts, the lease or rental agreement under which you occupy the said premises is terminated. In the event you fail to vacate and surrender possession of the said premises, legal proceedings will be instituted against you to recover possession, damages, and court costs.

DATE: March 3, 1986 _____
OWNER/MANAGER

THREE-DAY NOTICE TO QUIT

(Improper Subletting, Nuisance, Waste, or Illegal Use)

TO _____Betty B. Better_____ ,

TENANT(S) IN POSSESSION OF THE PREMISES AT

369 Main Street, Apartment 12
(Street Address)

City of Los Angeles , County of Los Angeles , California

YOU ARE HEREBY NOTIFIED that you are required within THREE (3) DAYS from the date of service on you of this notice to vacate and surrender possession of the said premises by reason of your having committed the following nuisance, waste, unlawful use, or unlawful subletting:

You have used the premises for an unlawful use by using them to

operate and house a bingo parlor in violation of state law and local

zoning laws, between April 1, 1986 and the present.

As a result of your having committed the foregoing acts, the lease or rental agreement under which you occupy the said premises is terminated. In the event you fail to vacate and surrender possession of the said premises, legal proceedings will be instituted against you to recover possession, damages, and court costs.

DATE: April 10, 1986 _____
OWNER/MANAGER

3. Serving the Three-Day Notice

a. When the Three-Day Notice Should Be Served

Like the 30-day notice, a three-day notice can be served on a tenant on any day of the month. The only requirement is that the tenant's violations of the lease or rental agreement already have occurred. For example, if the tenant's third loud and boisterous party in a month occurred on April 15, and you're using the three disturbances as a basis for eviction, you can serve your three-day notice to quit on April 16.

If the tenant's violation of the lease or rental agreement involves a failure to pay money or do something else on a certain date--for example, a failure to pay a security deposit installment which the lease or rental agreement says is due (along with the rent) on the first day of the month, the same rules that apply to three-day notices to pay rent or quit (see Chapter 15, Section C) apply. So, if the day for the tenant to pay the money or otherwise perform the act falls on a Sunday or holiday, he doesn't legally have to do it until the following business day and the notice should be served the day after that.

It doesn't matter that you've accepted the rent for a particular month when it comes to giving a tenant a three-day notice for a reason unrelated to rent. For example, if Rhoda Rockenroll paid you the $500 rent for her apartment on October 1, then had four loud and wild parties (that lasted to 2.a.m. despite protests from other tenants) on October 5, 6, 13, and 14, your three-day notice could be given on the 15th, asking Rhoda to leave by the 18th, even though you've accepted her rent through October 31.* This is be-

_____
* This would be a situation in which you would probably want to give the three-day notice in the alternative--that is, tell the tenant to cease the offending conduct or leave.

cause Rhoda, in creating a nuisance after having paid her rent, has legally forfeited her right not only to continue under the lease or rental agreement, but also to live there for the rest of the period for which she paid rent in advance. After that, your service of the three-day notice on her, plus waiting the three days, allows you to file an eviction lawsuit to enforce the forfeiture by having her evicted. Again, we discuss the procedures involved in such lawsuits in Volume II, on evictions.

b. Who Should Serve the Notice?

As with the three-day notice to pay rent or quit (see Chapter 15), this three-day notice may be served by anyone over 18, you included.

c. Who to Serve

As we discuss in Chapter 15 on three-day notices to pay rent or quit, as well as in Section A(2) above on 30-day notices, you should try to serve a copy of the notice on each tenant to whom you rented the property. With three-day notices, you are also required to serve any sub-tenants with the notice.

d. How the Notice is Served

Again, as with three-day notices to pay rent or quit, a three-day notice to quit "or notice to perform covenant or quit" may be served as follows:

- By personal delivery;

- By substituted service on another person, plus mailing; or

- By posting and mailing.

See Section D of Chapter 15 for more detail on serving three-day notices. The rules for service are identical for all types of three-day notices.

D. Termination by the Landlord in Rent-Controlled Cities Requiring Just Cause for Eviction

As we saw in Chapter 4 on rent control, quite a few cities with rent control (most notably, Berkeley, Los Angeles, San Francisco, Santa Monica, and Cotati) require a landlord to have what is called "just cause" for terminating a periodic (e.g., month to month) tenancy. Some of these cities also require that the landlord's reason for terminating the tenancy, as allowed under the ordinance, be specified in the 30-day notice. As you can see from the sample 30-day notice in Section A of this chapter, there is a space where this information can be inserted. If your property is located in a rent-controlled city, you should first determine whether your property is subject to the ordinance. If it is, obtain a copy of the ordinance and look for a heading entitled "Eviction," "Good Cause for Eviction" or words to that effect (usually found toward the end of the ordinance), which lists the

reasons for which a landlord may terminate a tenancy.

The steps for terminating a tenancy in accordance with both state law and any applicable rent-control ordinance can require several important steps, including giving the tenant one, or even two, detailed written notices, depending on the basis for termination.

1. Reasons Allowed for Termination with a Three-Day Notice

Although the reasons for which a landlord can evict a tenant vary in the different rent-controlled cities, they all allow evictions for:

- Nonpayment of rent;

- Violation of a lease or rental agreement provision;

- Causing serious damage to the premises;

- Causing a nuisance;

- Illegal use of the premises.

As we just saw in Section C of this chapter, and also in Chapter 15, tenancy terminations based on any of these grounds can be accomplished under state law using a three-day notice which states the basis for the termination. We generally recommend using a 30-day notice to terminate a tenancy (except when the rent is not paid, or the tenant has violated the lease or rental agreement in a particularly outrageous way, in which case a three-day notice to pay rent or quit is appropriate, see Chapter 15), because under this procedure, there is normally no need to prove a reason for the eviction. However, we believe that rent-controlled cities requiring just cause for eviction constitute an exception to this general rule. The reason for this exception is simple: In these cities you must have good cause to evict (even if the tenancy is one from month to month), whether you use a three-day or 30-day notice. This being true, there is no advantage to using the 30-day notice.*

a. **Nonpayment of rent:** In rent-controlled cities, a three-day notice to pay rent or quit is not much different than in areas without rent control: although local ordinances generally require that eviction notices specify the reason for termination and that the tenant be given a chance to correct the problem, state law already requires a three-day notice to pay rent or quit to do this (see Section C, above), and the three-day notice to pay rent or quit in the back of the book is designed to do this. Some ordinances, however, including San Francisco's, require all eviction notices to note that tenant assistance is available from the local rent-control board. Check any ordinance applicable to your property for this requirement.

---

* Perhaps it could be said that there is a slight advantage to using a 30-day notice. A tenant receiving this much notice might more readily move, having more time within which to do so, than if only three days' notice is given. On the other hand, anti-landlord sentiment (which may encourage tenants to fight their landlords whenever possible) in rent-controlled cities is so strong, and low-cost legal help to tenants so readily available from tenants' groups and other sources, that even tenants who receive the full 30 days' notice are likely to stay and fight it out anyway.

b. **Violation of a Lease Provision:** As with the three-day notice to pay rent or quit, a "three-day notice to cure covenant or quit," specifying the tenant's lease or rental agreement violation and giving her a chance to correct it, satisfies ordinance requirements that the tenant's misconduct be specified and that she be given a chance to correct it. So, with the possible exception of a requirement that the local rent-control board's name, address and phone number be listed on the notice, a three-day notice based on a tenant's lease violation is no different in a rent-controlled city than in areas without rent control. (Again, see Section C of this chapter, above.)

A few words should be mentioned here about a particular kind of tenant violation of the lease. Many leases and rental agreements, including the form in the back of this book, contain a clause requiring the tenant to provide the landlord access to the property (see Chapter 12) as required by law. Just-cause eviction provisions of most rent-control ordinances allow eviction both for lease violations and specifically for the tenant's refusal to allow the landlord property access. As we discussed in Chapter 2 on leases and rental agreements, the importance of having an "access" clause in the lease or rental agreement is to allow you to evict, if necessary, a tenant who refuses to allow you legitimate access for repairs, etc., using a three-day notice to enforce this right. The three-day notice to perform covenant or quit would include language like, "you are in violation of the lease . . . in that you have violated the covenant to: allow Landlord access to the property as required by Civil Code Section 1954, following the giving of reasonable notice by the Landlord that he would conduct repairs to the premises on December 1, 1986, in the following manner: you refused to allow such access on December 3, 198_."

Three days later, if the tenant still refuses you access (following your again giving proper advance notice, of course--see Chapter 12), you may want to begin an eviction lawsuit.

c. **Damage and Nuisance:** Although the just-cause-for-eviction part of rent-control ordinances typically allows eviction of tenants for excessively damaging the property or causing a nuisance, as does state law, the ordinances differ from state law in one important respect. State law allows the use of a three-day notice to quit--that is, a notice which simply tells the tenant to move in three days, without the option of correcting the problem and staying. Rent-control ordinances, however, typically require that the tenant be given a chance to correct the problem, no matter what it is. For example, Berkeley's ordinance allows eviction of a tenant for damaging the property (in excess of ordinary wear and tear) only if she "has refused, after written notice, to pay the reasonable costs of repairing such damage and ceasing damaging said premises," whereas state law requires only that the tenant be given an unconditional three-day notice to quit (see Section C, above).*

_____

* This raises some interesting legal issues regarding how far a city may go in essentially altering state procedural laws governing three-day notices. However, see Birkenfeld v. City of Berkeley (1976) 17 Cal.3d 129, 148-151, which stated, essentially, that a more extensive digression from state law (requiring that an eviction certificate be issued by the rent board) was improper, while a less serious digression (requiring a 30-day notice to specify the reason for termination) was okay.

The ordinances, of course, give no indication, and no case law as of this writing answers this question, so here's an educated guess: One way is to simply use a three-day notice to perform covenant or quit. This gives the tenant an option to correct. Although this procedure is more than is required by state law, your tenant can hardly complain that under state law you shouldn't have given him the option to correct the problem. However, we prefer another method, in which two notices are used: first, a written notice, in letter form, which demands that the tenant correct the problem, pay to repair the damage or stop having loud parties, etc., and then, should the tenant fail to correct the problem, an unconditional three-day notice to quit. Let's look at an example to illustrate how these notices would be used.

EXAMPLE: After paying the rent on December 1, Paul Partier holds some wild and boisterous holiday parties about which other tenants repeatedly complained (eventually to the police) in his Santa Monica apartment on the 7th, 8th, 14th, and 15th. At these parties, a drunken guest threw a beer bottle through the front window of the apartment and another guest punched a few fist-sized holes in the walls. Santa Monica's rent-control ordinance requires that 1) before terminating a tenancy for causing excessive damage, the landlord must give the tenant a chance to pay the cost of repairs, and 2) in order to terminate for disturbing neighbors, the disturbances must continue following a written notice to cease.

Here's a letter addressing both issues. This should be followed by serving Paul with an unconditional three-day notice to quit if he doesn't pay for the damage and stop his raucous parties. It should be given to the tenant in the same way as a three-day notice is served (see Section C, above.)

December 17, 1986

Paul Partier
950 Parker St., Apt. 10
Santa Monica, CA

Dear Mr. Partier:

This letter is to advise you that the management of Monica Apartments intends to proceed to terminate your tenancy of the above-described premises if you continue to conduct yourself in a manner which seriously disturbs other tenants and results in the destruction of our property.

On December 7, 8, 14 and 15, you held loud and boisterous parties, which lasted until 3:00 A.M. and at which very loud music was played, guests spilled out into the streets, and the police were called on at least three of the four occasions. Please be advised that this conduct has destroyed the peace and quiet of other tenants, and, that if this conduct does not cease, your tenancy shall be terminated in accordance with both local and state law.

Please be further advised that on December 14 and/or 15, several of the party guests damaged our property, shattering the front window to your apartment and punching two holes in your bathroom wall. Pursuant to a properly-noticed inspection of the premises yesterday by myself and my maintenance person, I have concluded that the reasonable cost of repairing this damage is $350.00. Please be advised that if you fail to pay this sum to me within three days, your tenancy will be terminated in accordance with both local and state law.

Sincerely,

Marvin D. Manager
Marvin Manager

If Paul fails to pay the money for repairs and/or has another wild party, you would prepare and serve the following three-day notice to quit, and serve it on Paul.

THREE-DAY NOTICE TO QUIT

(Improper Subletting, Nuisance, Waste, or Illegal Use)

TO _____ Paul Partier _____ ,

TENANT(S) IN POSSESSION OF THE PREMISES AT

950 Parker Street, Apartment 10
(Street Address)

City of __Santa Monica__ , County of __Los Angeles__ , California

YOU ARE HEREBY NOTIFIED that you are required within THREE (3) DAYS from the date of service on you of this notice to vacate and surrender possession of the said premises by reason of your having committed the following nuisance, waste, unlawful use, or unlawful subletting:

(1) You have continued, following a written request to cease, dated December 17, 1986, to be so disorderly as to destroy the peace and quiet of other tenants, by having a loud party December 21, 1986, which lasted until 3:00 A.M. and at which very loud music was played until that time. Prior to this, you conducted four similar parties on December 7th, 8th, 14th, and 15th, and (2) you have failed following written request, to pay the reasonable cost of repairing a shattered window and holes in walls, caused by you or your guests at one or more of such parties.

As a result of your having committed the foregoing acts, the lease or rental agreement under which you occupy the said premises is terminated. In the event you fail to vacate and surrender possession of the said premises, legal proceedings will be instituted against you to recover possession, damages, and court costs.

DATE: December 22, 1986 ___*Keija Kiibermot*___
OWNER/MANAGER

---

d. **Illegal Use of the Premises:**
As we saw in Section C above, a tenant's illegal use of the premises constitutes a basis for eviction under state law, the landlord being allowed to use a three-day notice to quit in order to terminate the tenancy. Interestingly enough, some rent-control ordinances neglect to mention this as a ground for eviction. Does this mean

that you can't evict a tenant who, for example, runs a house of prostitution out of her apartment? The answer, of course, is "No." Since virtually all written leases and rental agreements (including our form lease/rental agreement in the back of the book) either specify that the property be used only as a residence and/or that illegal use of the property is forbidden, this would constitute a violation of the rental agreement for which a regular three-day notice to cure covenant or quit could be used.

2. Reasons Allowed for Termination with a 30-day Notice

All four reasons listed above, for which a tenant's tenancy can be terminated by state law with a three-day notice, and by local ordinance, apply whether the tenant's tenancy is one from month to month (or some other period) or for a fixed term. This is true because the reasons all involve misconduct for which a tenant can be considered to forfeit his tenancy.

The just-cause-for-eviction sections of most rent-control ordinances allow termination of the tenancy for other reasons in addition to those listed above. These reasons permit the termination of a month-to-month tenancy (but not a lease) by an unconditioned 30-day notice. These reasons include:

• The tenant refuses to allow the landlord access to the premises, but no lease or rental agreement clause requires this;

• The landlord, after having obtained all necessary permits, intends to extensively remodel the premises, convert the dwelling to a condominium unit, or demolish the structure; and

• The landlord is intending to move herself or a close relative into the dwelling.

Let's discuss these reasons in more detail.

a. **Tenant Refusal to Allow Access:** We said in Section 1 above that a three-day notice can be used to terminate tenancy where the tenant refuses to allow the landlord legal access to the property--provided such refusal is a violation of the rental agreement. If the rental agreement doesn't have an access clause, however, a 30-day notice must be used, but then only if the tenancy is from month to month. This sort of notice should be preceded with a warning letter of the type mentioned in Section 1, above. Also, the reason for termination should be stated in the 30-day notice in the same manner as in the three-day notice in the example.

b. **Remodeling, Conversion, or Demolition:** Most rent-control ordinances allow a month-to-month tenancy to be terminated with a 30-day notice on the basis that the landlord wishes to extensively remodel the premises, convert the property into a condominium unit, or demolish it. The landlord must first obtain all permits necessary, complying with other ordinances providing for notice to affected persons, the tenants included. Also, the 30-day notice should specify in detail the reason for termination, giving the date the permits were granted by the city or county.

A few landlords have abused ordinances which allow eviction for remodeling, either by claiming nonexistent needs for extensive remodeling, or failing to do the remodeling once the tenant left. In response, several cities have made these reasons more restricting and cumbersome to use. For example, Berkeley's ordinance requires a landlord seeking to evict a tenant for remodeling to give the tenant the right of first refusal to re-rent the property when the remodeling is done, and even to house the tenant in the interim if the landlord has any other vacant rental property in the city.

c. **Landlord or Close Relative to Move In:** Most rent-control ordinances allow a month-to-month tenancy to be terminated by 30-day notice when the landlord wants to live in the property himself or move in a close relative. Like the above reason, this basis for termination has also had its share of abuse, with some landlords falsely claiming to have relatives interested in moving into the property (which

would then be occupied by the relative for a very short time, if at all. Similarly, cities have made this reason more cumbersome to use. For example, Berkeley's ordinance limits permissible relatives to parents and children, and requires the termination notice to give the name and relationship of the person who will move in.

Also, the cities that require just cause for eviction now provide in their ordinances for heavy penalties against landlords who circumvent the just-cause-for-eviction requirement by using the "phony-relative" ploy (see also Chapter 4, Section F on penalties for attempted evasion of rent-control ordinance provisions.) The point is that assuming you seek to evict a tenant for one of the reasons allowed in the "just-cause-for-eviction" part of an applicable rent-control ordinance, make sure you are in compliance with local law. A sample 30-day notice listing reasons for termination in accordance with the requirements of a local rent-control ordinance is shown.

NOTICE OF TERMINATION OF TENANCY

TO _____·Helga Hellraiser_____ ,

TENANT(S) IN POSSESSION OF THE PREMISES AT:

_____1234 Grove Street, Apartment 5_____ ,
         (Street Address)

City of _Berkeley_ , County of _Alameda_ , California:

    YOU ARE HEREBY NOTIFIED that effective 30 DAYS from the date of service on you of this notice, the periodic tenancy by which you hold possession of the above-described premises is terminated, at which time you are required to vacate and surrender possession of the said premises. In the event you fail to do so, legal proceedings will be instituted against you to recover possession of the said premises, damages and costs of suit.

    1. You have continued, following a written request to cease, dated December 10, 1986 , to refuse me access to the premises as required by Civil Code Section 1954, on 12/11/86 , 12/12/86 , and 12/13/86 , despite

the fact that I gave you notice 24 hours in advance, in each case, of an intent to repair a defective heater. (Rent Stabilization Ordinance, Section 13(a)(6).

[OR]

2. I wish to have my son ORVILLE OWNERSON, reside in the premises, there being no other vacant comparable unit in the property. (Rent Stabilization Ordinance, Section 13(a)(9).)

DATED: December 15, 1986   *Tori Tenant*
                                          OWNER/MANAGER

---

3. Reasons Allowed for Termination When No Notice Is Required

Most just-cause provisions for rent-control ordinances also allow a landlord to evict a tenant who refuses to sign a new fixed-term lease after the old one expires. However, the new lease the landlord presents to the tenant must contain essentially the same terms as the old one, with no substantial change and must not contain any clauses forbidden by state law (see Chapter 2, Section E) or local ordinance. This basis for eviction applies only where:

1. A fixed-term lease expires on a certain date;

2. The landlord has not accepted any rent after that (so as to avoid converting the tenancy into a non-expiring tenancy); and

3. The tenant has refused to sign a new lease essentially identical to the earlier one. In this situation, the landlord does not have to give the tenant a written notice of any kind prior to filing an eviction lawsuit. This is because the tenancy ended of its own accord when the lease expired, and the tenant is refusing to extend it.

NOTE ON ADDITIONAL LOCAL REQUIREMENTS FOR TERMINATION: Whether a three-day or 30-day notice is used to terminate a tenancy, be sure to check any applicable ordinance for other requirements relating to the notice. The notice must always specify in detail the reason for termination, but there are often other requirements as well. For example, San Francisco's ordinance requires that the notice state, in addition to the reason for termination of the tenancy, that tenant assistance is available from the rent-control board, (the address and phone number of the rent board must be included) and Berkeley's ordinance requires that copies of all such notices be filed with the local rent board. Failure to comply with even the seemingly technical requirements may result in your losing a subsequent eviction lawsuit and being held liable for the tenant's court costs and attorney's fees.

E. Termination of Fixed-Term Lease by the Tenant

As we discussed in Chapter 2, a "lease" lasts for a fixed term, usually six months or a year. During the term of the lease, neither you nor the tenant may terminate the tenancy unless the other party "breaches" the lease by failing to fulfill his obligations. If everything goes well, the lease simply terminates of its own accord at the end of the lease term. Unfortunately, however, this description of how a lease works is often more theoretical than real. In fact, as we have discussed several times, because of the "mitigation of damages" rule, it's often easier for a tenant to legally end a lease than it is for a landlord to do the same.

One obvious problem for a landlord occurs when a tenant "breaks" a lease simply by leaving before the end of the term. This part of the chapter focuses on your rights and responsibilities in this situation as well as those of your tenant.

NOTE: If your tenant rents under a lease the terms of which have since expired, the tenancy is probably now on a month-to-month basis, assuming you have continued to accept monthly rent. If so, Section A of this chapter on month-to-month tenancy termination applies.

1. Tenant Leaves at End of Lease Term

a. No Notice Required

With a fixed-term lease, the lease simply expires of its own accord at the end of the term. No written notice is legally required. Any notice, written or oral, indicating the tenant's intent to leave before the natural expiration of the lease term is of no legal effect other than to tell you that the tenant is planning to "break the lease" by leaving early.

Even though a formal notice of "termination" is not legally required in a lease situation, you should as a practical matter routinely give tenants a 30-day notice if you don't wish to continue the tenancy when the lease expires. Although the tenant is theoretically required to leave at the end of the lease term, it has become so customary for a tenant to stay on a month-to-month basis, in the absence of anything said to the contrary, that it's an essential business practice to advise your tenant at least a month in advance if you won't be renewing or even extending the lease.

b. Application of Deposit to Last Month's Rent

Your tenant may not legally refuse to pay the rent for the last month of occupancy and insist that you "take it out of the security deposit," unless you have accepted a deposit specifically called "last month's rent. Any attempt by the tenant to refuse to pay the rent for his last month under the lease and to ask you to take it out of the security deposit can be met by your three-day notice, followed by an eviction lawsuit (see Section C of this chapter). However, if after a conversation with the tenant you are convinced that she will leave the place clean and undamaged, and will leave on time, you may want to voluntarily go along with this plan.

c. Acceptance of Rent Beyond the Last Month

Acceptance of rent for a period beyond the termination of a fixed-term lease extends the tenancy on a month-to-month basis, just as it does when you accept rent after the termination date of a month-to-month tenancy. If you refuse this rent, you may insist that the tenant(s) leave.

NOTE: If you've accepted "last month's rent," be sure not to accept any additional rent for the last month of the lease, unless you intend the tenancy to continue on a month-to-month basis.

2. Leaving Before the End of the Term

A tenant who leaves (whether or not she notifies you that she's leaving) before the expiration of a fixed-term lease is said to have "broken the lease." There are, of course, many other ways for a tenant to "breach" a lease, but the colloquial phrase "break the lease" usually means to move out early and refuse to pay the remainder of the rent due under the lease.

Let's review some information we discussed in more detail in Chapter 2. A tenant renting under a lease agrees at the outset to pay a fixed total rent (the monthly rent multiplied by the number of months the lease is to last). Payment is normally to be made in monthly installments over the term of the lease. This means the tenant is liable for the entire rent for the entire lease term (except where the landlord breaches an important lease provision first, thus excusing the tenant's breach). According to this rule, a landlord faced with a tenant leaving early could sue the tenant for the remaining rent she would have col-

lected had the tenant not left early.

Unfortunately, as we have noted, this general rule doesn't mean too much where a shortage of rental housing makes it easy to find a new tenant. This is because a tenant's liability for leaving too soon is limited by the landlord's duty to "mitigate damages" by finding a new rent-paying tenant. This is true whether the tenancy is under a fixed-term lease or a month-to-month arrangement, but applies most powerfully in the lease situation.

EXAMPLE: Steve Stability rented an apartment to Skip Sneak in January for a term of one year, the monthly rent being $1,000. Everything went well until September, when Skip skipped out on the lease. Under the general rule, Skip is theoretically liable to Steve for $3,000--the rent for October, November, and December. However, if Steve mitigated these damages by taking out an ad and re-renting on October 15, Skip would owe much less. If the new tenant paid $500 for the last half of October, and $1,000 in November and December, Steve must credit the total $2,500 he got from the new tenant against Skip's $3,000 liability. This leaves Skip liable for only $500 plus Steve's advertising costs of $20, for a total of $520.

Of course, the landlord's duty to mitigate damages only gets the tenant off the hook if it's possible to get a satisfactory new tenant to pay the same amount of rent or more. Most of the time it is, but occasionally a landlord might have problems, as could be the situation with student housing during the summer or vacation rentals off season.

One further note on mitigating damages. Often a tenant wishing to "break" the lease by leaving before it expires will approach the landlord and offer to find a suitable new tenant so that the flow of rent will remain uninterrupted. It is a good idea to cooperate with a tenant who suggests this, even if the lease has a clause against subletting, if you want the "lease breaking" tenant to owe you damages if a new tenant can't be found to pay the same rent. A landlord who refuses to cooperate by accepting an excellent new tenant is almost by definition refusing to mitigate damages, and may wind up with no recovery if he sues the outgoing tenant who broke the lease for damages. In this context, the "mitigation of damages" rule is, in effect, a hidden lease clause requiring the landlord to be reasonable about consenting to accept a new tenant to fill out the first tenant's lease term, even where the lease flatly prohibits a sublease. In fact, about the only criterion a landlord may legitimately use to reject a replacement tenant suggested by the outgoing one with an eye to still being able to collect damages from the departing tenant, is a bad credit or renting history. Of course, if the rental market is really tight in your area, and you can lease the unit easily at a higher rent, you may not care if a tenant breaks a lease, but will want to rent the property yourself and not bother with the tenant's help.

But assuming now that you and the outgoing lease-breaking tenant do agree on a replacement tenant, you can legally proceed in one of two ways. You can either agree to let the outgoing tenant sublet to the incoming one (in which case the outgoing tenant still remains liable for the remainder of the rent under the lease if the new tenant doesn't pay), or you may have the new tenant enter into a new lease with you

(in which case you might even want to raise the rent a little, if local rent control ordinances permit). As we discuss in some detail in Chapter 9, we believe the second alternative is the more desirable.

To summarize, where your fixed-term tenant leaves before the end of the lease, you're entitled to:

1. The remaining rent due under the lease, less

2. Any rent you could have collected from a new tenant between the time the tenant skipped out and the end of the lease term, plus

3. Any reasonable advertising expenses incurred in finding a new tenant.

F. Termination by Abandonment of Premises

This section describes legal means of possession of your rental property, without having to go to court, when you have reason to believe the tenant simply left without intending to come back, but didn't bother to tell you about it.

Often it's hard to tell whether a tenant has left for good. People do, after all, sometimes disappear for weeks at a time, going on vacations or elsewhere. And even when a tenant doesn't intend to come back, she may leave behind enough discarded clothing or furniture to make it appear that she may plan to return. We discuss what to do with abandoned property in Chapter 19.

Often the first hint you'll have that a tenant has abandoned the premises will be when you don't receive the rent. Or, you may get a call from a neighbor asking about a vacancy, or simply walk by a window and notice the lack of furniture. Unfortunately, the mere appearance that your rental property is no longer occupied doesn't give you the legal right to retake possession. It does, however, constitute legal justification to inspect the place to check for signs of abandonment (see Chapter 12 on privacy). And remember, you don't have to give 24 hours' advance notice of entering if it's "impractical" to do so, which is certainly the case if no one's been around for days.

Once you've determined that your tenant has probably skipped out with no intention of returning, you have several choices. Your first and most obvious is to assume the tenant won't return, and to proceed to clean up, dispose of any possessions left behind (see Chapter 19), and re-rent the property. This is perfectly okay if the tenant really doesn't come back, and may be your best bet if a tenant who has not paid rent has cleared out, leaving nothing behind. However, it does involve some legal risk. This occurs if the tenant does return to find the place rerented and her possessions gone. If you were too impatient to use the formal abandonment notice procedure discussed below, you could

face heavy liability in a lawsuit. This is especially true if you retake possession during a time for which the "departing" tenant has paid rent.

Your second choice is simply to hunt down the tenant in order to get a definite answer as to whether she intends to stay away or come back. Look at the tenant's rental application and phone each personal and business reference. If that doesn't work, try asking neighbors, and finally the police.

Why should you go to so much trouble? Because this approach beats the third alternative, which, although it protects you from liability, requires you to go without rent for a little over a month. In other words, from a business standpoint, it's far better to hunt the tenant down and get her to admit she isn't coming back, allowing you to retake possession immediately, than to have to follow the legally-correct procedure requiring you to leave the place vacant for a month.

The third procedure is the formal legal one. It requires that you try to notify the tenant in writing that you intend to terminate the tenancy as the result of the tenant's suspected abandonment of the premises. Unfortunately, you must wait until 14 days have passed without the tenant's having paid rent before you can initiate this procedure.* It involves mailing a notice to the tenant's address at the property (or any other known mailing address) on or after the 15th day of rent nonpayment. This notice should look like the sample below (a blank form is included in the Appendix of this book):

* During this period, you might as well prepare a three-day notice to pay rent or quit and serve it by posting and mailing (see Chapter 15). This way, if the tenant does show up later and indicates an intent not to leave after all, you can begin the unlawful detainer suit to get the tenant out if she won't pay the rent. However, in situations where the tenant doesn't show up, use of an unlawful detainer suit will be just as time-consuming as, and more costly than, the abandonment notice procedure discussed here.

NOTICE OF BELIEF OF ABANDONMENT

TO: _____Abraham Abandoner_____

TENANT(S) IN POSSESSION OF THE PREMISES AT:

<u>123 Skipout Street</u>
Street Address

City of <u>Fresno</u> , County of <u>Fresno</u> , California.

This notice is given pursuant to Section 1951.3 of the Civil Code concerning the real property leased by you at the above address. The rent on this property had been due and unpaid for 14 consecutive days and the lessor/landlord believes that you have abandoned the property.

The real property will be deemed abandoned within the meaning of Section 1951.2 of the Civil Code and your lease will terminate on _____ , 19__ , a date not less than 18 days after the mailing of this notice, unless before such date the undersigned receives at the address indicated below a written notice from you stating both of the following:

(1) Your intent not to abandon the real property;

(2) An address at which you may be served by certified mail in any action for unlawful detainer of the real property.

You are required to pay the rent due and unpaid on this real property as required by the lease, and your failure to do so can lead to a court proceeding against you.

DATE: April 15, 1986

Lenny Landlord (signature)
LESSOR (SIGNATURE)

Lenny Landlord
LESSOR NAME (PRINT)

456 State Sreet
ADDRESS

Fresno, California

Mail the notice to the tenant* by first class mail at the property with extra copies mailed to any other address for the tenant you know of.

In order to preserve her right to the property, the tenant must provide you with a written statement that indicates an intent not to abandon and

* The law also says the notice can be "served personally," in which case you need wait only 15, rather than 18, days before retaking possession, but if you can serve the notice personally, you should have long since asked the tenant if she intends to stay, and the whole notice procedure should be moot.

provide you with a mailing address at which she may be served by certified mail with an unlawful detainer suit. If you don't receive such a response by the 18th day after mailing the notice (not counting the day of mailing), you may retake possession of the premises. Just walk in--you don't have to go to the courthouse--and begin your usual preparation for rerenting. You should dispose of any of the tenant's abandoned possessions in the manner described in Chapter 19 of the next chapter.

G. What to Do When Some Tenants Leave and Others Stay

As we discussed in Chapter 9, a landlord should at all times know the names of all the adult occupants-- whether on the lease or rental agreement--of the property. This is because your ability to collect rent depends in part on your potential ability to sue by name and evict all of the occupants if the rent isn't paid.

Although it's very important to keep tabs on who's moving in, it's almost as important to know when one of several tenants moves out. Imagine a scenario where you rent to Tillie and Terence. Within a few months, Tillie moves out and some unnamed woman moves in. A few months later, another parting of the ways occurs, with Terry moving out and an unnamed man moving in. Whom do you sue for nonpayment of rent should Ms. Nameless and Mr. Anonymous stop paying rent?

When one of your tenants leaves and the other (whether a spouse, lover, or roommate) remains behind, good business practice, as well as sound legal reasons, require that you take the change into account rather than ignore it. However, your best course of action, from a legal point of view at least, depends on the extent to which the person leaving is still responsible for the rent in the event the person staying behind doesn't pay. We discuss the legal liability of co-tenants and sub-tenants in detail in Chapter 9. Here we review this material briefly.

1. Co-Tenant Liability

As you saw in Chapter 9, when two or more of your renters have both signed the same lease or rental agreement (or were both present when you orally agreed to rent to them), they are "co-tenants" with equal rights to occupy the premises and equal liability for the rent. This is why it's best to have all adult occupants sign the lease or rental agreement. A co-tenant who vacates and leaves a fellow co-tenant behind is still legally liable for the rent due under the lease or rental agreement until the lease period expires (unless you agree to an earlier termination) or until the month-to-month tenancy is terminated by 30-day notice.

For example, if you rent to Jack and Jill, who both sign a one-year lease, Jill is still jointly liable with Jack for the rent for the year even if Jill leaves and Jack stays. This means that if Jack doesn't pay the rent, you can sue Jill in small claims court for unpaid rent. It's important to remember, though, that this suit would have to be separate from any eviction suit-- in which only occupants can be named as defendants. See Volume II, on evictions.

If you had rented to Jack and Jill on a month-to-month basis, Jill would be liable for the monthly rent after leaving (or after Jack left), unless she properly terminated the tenancy, as to herself, by giving you a 30-day notice.* Still, as a practical matter, if Jack stopped paying rent after Jill left without giving a proper notice, you would sue only him in an unlawful detainer proceeding, since, as noted above, you can sue only occupants of the premises in that kind of suit. If you could find Jill, you could of course file a separate small claims suit against her for all unpaid rent.

2. Sub-Tenant Liability

As you saw in Chapter 9, a sub-tenant is a tenant of a tenant who occupies the premises by agreement with the original tenant. A sub-tenant can be a person who either took over the property after the original tenant left and with whom you didn't enter into a new lease or rental agreement, or one who simply lives with the person who has signed your rental agreement. Unfortunately, the fact that the lease or rental agreement prohibits subleasing does not necessarily mean that no valid sublease occurred or that there are no sub-tenants. All it means is that the tenant who signed your lease breached it by subletting, anyway. If this occurs, you can evict the tenant for violating the lease term, but if you don't, you normally have few legal rights vis-a-vis the sub-tenant who has entered into no tenant-landlord relationship with you. This means that you can't sue the sub-tenant--either in small claims court or in an eviction

suit for rent.* However, should you rent to a married couple and neglect to get both to sign the lease, the non-signing spouse, although a sub-tenant, is liable for the rent, because each spouse is legally responsible for the necessities of life of the other.

3. What to Do When a Co-Tenant Leaves

As is discussed in more detail in Chapter 9, when a co-tenant--one of two or more tenants named on the lease or rental agreement--leaves and someone else moves in, it's up to you to act decisively. True, if no new agreement is signed, the departing tenant will still be liable for the rent, but this will probably not be worth too much if she leaves for parts unknown. You are almost always better off to sign a lease or rental agreement with any new tenant if they are acceptable.** An added advantage of this is that it will be clear that the outgoing tenant is no longer entitled to possession of the property. This last point may be especially important where a couple (married or not) who shares the same bed, separate. If one of them leaves and then wants to come back--against the will of the other--you are powerless to keep that person out by changing the locks or by other means, if:

---

* However, if Jack and Jill were married, and did not intend to separate permanently, Jill might still be liable for the rent, even after giving such a 30-day notice, if Jack stayed on after that because she is legally responsible for her husband's necessities of life. Civil Code Section 5121.

* You can bring an eviction lawsuit against the sub-tenant based on nonpayment of rent, but you can get a judgment against the sub-tenant only for possession of the property and court costs, not for the rent itself.

** As we note in Chapter 9, San Francisco recognizes the concept of a "master tenant" by ordinance, in effect giving additional legal authority to the concept of one tenant renting to another. See Chapters 4 and 9 for more details.

a. She didn't terminate the month-to-month tenancy as to herself with a 30-day notice; or

b. In the case of a lease, no new lease was entered into; or

c. The couple is still married, even if a new agreement **has** been signed.*

If no new tenant plans to move in, you should determine whether the remaining one can afford the rent.** If so, you are still probably best off to definitively end your legal relationship with the departing tenant for the reasons stated above. If someone is moving in to replace the departing tenant, it's usually best to have the remaining tenant and the new tenant sign a new lease or rental agreement. The new roommate thus becomes jointly liable for the rent.

* Under Civil Code Section 5102, a spouse may not be excluded from the home of the other in the absence of a court order, even if a divorce is pending.

** If you live in a city with rent control, such as San Francisco, which recognizes the concept of vacancy decontrol, this may also be your chance to raise the rent if the remaining tenant was not part of the original group you rented to. Remember, in most cities that recognize the vacancy decontrol concept, you can only raise the rent in a shared housing when all the original tenants move out.

But what happens if the new tenant isn't acceptable to you? If she hasn't moved in, simply use your authority to deny permission to sublet. If she has moved in without your permission, promptly move to evict the tenant on the basis of his violation of the lease term prohibiting sublets. (You should also name the person moving in on the eviction action--see Volume II, on evictions.) If you rent under a month-to-month tenancy, a simple 30-day notice is probably your best bet.

H. Death of a Tenant

Occasionally, a landlord will be faced with the death of a tenant who lives alone. Because lawyers and public agencies are bound to be involved, you should be sure to comply with the law, even though your first urge may be to clear out the property and rent it as quickly as possible.

When you first suspect or learn of a death of a tenant, call the police or fire department. After the body is removed, you are required to take reasonable precautions to preserve the deceased tenant's property. Obviously, you don't want to be sued by the executor of the estate for giving away valuable property to relatives or to "friends," to the detriment of the true heirs. If the deceased was married and living with her spouse, you can safely let the spouse handle things. Otherwise, contact the next of kin, but allow them only to remove personal effects (such as the deceased's clothing) needed for the funeral. Keep everyone else out of the premises. If more than a negligible amount of property is in the dwelling, put a padlock on the door. Open it for the public administrator for the county, or to a court-appointed executor or administrator who can show you "Letters Testamentary" or

"Letters of Administration" (legal mumbo-jumbo for papers signed by a judge appointing a legal representative for the deceased's estate).

One of these procedures is almost sure to take place if the decedent had considerable valuable property. However, if her total estate was small ($60,000 or less) or she efficiently used probate avoidance techniques, there may well be no official probate procedure and hence no court-approved executor or administrator. In this situation, if a family member of the deceased's appears and wants to take the property, you can safely release it if you receive a copy of the decedent's will, establishing that the person in question is entitled to the property, along with a declaration under penalty of perjury signed by the person to whom the property has been left (Probate Code 630). If there is no will, however, and only a small amount of property remains on the premises, formal probate proceedings are unlikely and it's probably okay to release the property to close relatives--provided they sign a receipt for what they take. If you are in doubt, talk to a lawyer.

LIVING TOGETHER NOTE: If you rent to an unmarried couple, straight or gay, and one member of the couple dies without a will, you might be caught in a nasty crossfire between the blood relatives of the deceased and his domestic partner. In a living together situation, the blood relatives inherit unless the survivor and the deceased had a contract to share ownership of all property. This is pretty tricky stuff, and if a lot of property is involved, your best bet is to check with your lawyer.

After all the deceased tenant's property is removed, consider making a claim for any unpaid rent through the date the property remained on the premises. If a probate proceeding is initiated, you should submit a filled-out claim form (available from legal stationery stores or court clerks) to the probate clerk of the superior court. You have four months in which to file your claim, beginning when the court officially appoints the estate's executor. If the estate doesn't go through probate (many small estates do not), the best you can do is bill the next of kin, who it is hoped will feel some responsibility to pay.

18

When the Tenant Leaves

This chapter is devoted to the legal rules involved in taking care of a number of important issues when a tenant decides to move on. These include the entire process of itemizing and refunding security deposits and the occasional necessity of taking a tenant to small claims court to recover for unpaid rent, damages, or cleaning bills not covered by the deposit, or a previous judgment from an eviction lawsuit.*

A. Fixtures

What should you do when you encounter what in landlord-tenant law is re-

_____
* We talk about how to get a court judgment for eviction as part of an unlawful detainer lawsuit in Volume II: **The Landlord's Law Book: Evictions.**

ferred to as a "fixture," an item which has more or less been permanently attached to the wall, such as bookshelves bolted or nailed in? The general rule in the absence of a lease provision otherwise, is that a fixture attached to the premises by the tenant becomes a part of the premises, which rightfully belongs to the landlord. For example, a tenant who installs bookshelves to a wall, using bolts, nails or other fasteners which can't be removed without leaving unsightly marks or more serious damage, such as large holes, is legally required to leave the shelves in place. If she removed them anyway, she is essentially removing a part of what has become the premises. On the other hand, temporary fasteners, such as nails used to hang art which can be removed so as to leave only a small hole that at worst needs a dab of spackling paste and paint to render invisible, does not constitute a "fixture" which the tenant must leave in place when vacating the property.

What if the tenant has gone ahead anyway and added, for example, a row of bookshelves contrary to the provisions of the rental agreement. If the bookshelves are still there, you have the choice of simply leaving them in place, or of removing them, restoring the property to the same condition as before they were installed, and subtracting from the tenant's security deposit the amount necessary to effect the change. If you choose the latter course, you do not have to return the bookcases to the tenant since, after all, you've only removed something that has become part of the premises and hence your property.

Quite often, however, a landlord inspecting the property a tenant has just vacated will be confronted with large gaping holes that were used to attach bookshelves or another sort of fixture. In this event, your choice, whether or not you allowed the fixture to be installed, is to bill the tenant either for the cost of replacing the fixture that the tenant improperly removed or for the cost of restoring the wall (or floor, etc.) to its original condition.

B. Security Deposits

We discuss the legal rules affecting how much you can charge for a security deposit in Chapter 5. We review these in Section 1(a) below, but if you have problems in this area, your best bet is to read Chapter 5 before you continue. In Chapter 1, we suggest a number of practical things you can do at the beginning of a tenancy to increase the likelihood that you can ultimately recover for damages, cleaning costs, etc., if a tenant moves on leaving the premises in an unsatisfactory state. We do not repeat this material here, but limit ourselves to discussing deposit requirements in the context of what a landlord should do when the tenant moves out.

1. Avoiding Lawsuits Over Deposits

As any small claims court judge will tell you, disputes over whether or not a landlord properly withheld all or part of a tenant's security deposit account for a large percentage of the landlord-tenant disputes that wind up in court. Unfortunately, even though landlords commonly win the suits they initiate, they don't always gain very much, given the time that goes into bringing the suit and the often difficult and time-consuming job of collecting the judgment. Knowing this, our conclusion is that that your best protection against spending hours haggling over back rent, cleaning costs, and tenant's damage to your property as part of a formal court process is to know the law and plan ahead.

The law allows you to make certain legitimate deductions from a tenant's security deposit, provided you do it correctly. The basic rule is this: Within two weeks after a tenant who has paid a deposit leaves, you must mail a written, itemized accounting of deductions for back rent and costs for necessary cleaning and damage repair, together with a check for any balance, to the tenant's last known address, or forwarding address if you have one.* Failure to do this may subject you to liability for up to $200 punitive damages should the tenant sue you in small claims court. Please note the requirement that you itemize deductions. A few judges have been known to enforce this requirement strictly by denying landlords who have failed to itemize the right to claim any deductions, even in situations where they were, in fact, legitimate.

2. "Security Deposits" Defined

To review the material in Chapter 5 very briefly, California's security deposit law defines a "security deposit" as "any payment, fee deposit or charge, including, but not limited to, an advance payment of rent, used, or to be used, for any purpose, including, but not limited to," anything to compensate a landlord for back rent or cleaning or damage charges.

This means simply that a "security deposit" includes any money you collect from a tenant other than first month's rent. It specifically includes "last month's rent." In other words, whether you call your tenant's up-front money a "fee," "deposit," or "charge" for "rent," "cleaning," "damages," or even "keys," you have to account for it under the law applicable to refundable security deposits. Anything in a lease or rental agreement to the contrary is of no legal effect.** As noted in Chapter 5, it's better to call a security deposit just that, rather than allocating a portion of it to "last month's rent." This is because if you use the words "last month's rent," that portion of the deposit must be applied to the rent for the last month before the tenant leaves, so isn't available to pay

for any cleaning or damages after the tenant is gone. If instead, you simply refer to the deposit as a security deposit, you can allocate it to cleaning costs, damage costs, and/or last month's rent, as the requirements of the particular situation dictate.

3. When the Security Deposit Law Applies

California's security deposit law applies whenever a tenant, or all tenants (in roommate situations), who have jointly paid a deposit, leave. This means that when you rent to two or more co-tenants under the same agreement (i.e., where their names are all listed on the written lease or rental agreement), you don't have to return or otherwise account for any of the deposit until all tenants leave. In other words, you're entitled to the benefit of the entire deposit until the entire tenancy ends. Any question as to whether a departing co-tenant is entitled to any share of the deposit he originally paid should be worked out between the co-tenants. Obviously, there's nothing to legally prevent you from voluntarily working out an appropriate agreement with a departing tenant in this type of situation. But if you do, make sure you're adequately protected by the remainder of the deposit or require that the existing tenant (or maybe her new roommate) bring it up to an acceptable amount.

You must always follow the legal procedures having to do with the return of, or accounting for, security deposits outlined below, whether the tenant leaves voluntarily or involuntarily, with or without the threat or use of eviction proceedings. Quite a few landlords are under the mistaken belief that they don't have to account for the deposit to a tenant who's been evicted by court order following an unlawful detainer lawsuit, apparently thinking the tenant's misconduct allows a landlord to pocket the entire deposit without further formality. This is not true. Even if a judgment against a tenant for several month's unpaid rent exceeds the deposit, the landlord still must notify the tenant in writing within 14 days after he or she departs as to how the deposit is applied toward cleaning or damage charges and any court judgment for rent.

4. Inspecting the Premises

Although it's not legally required, we recommend that you or your manager arrange to check over the property with a disputing tenant the day she leaves. Done in a conciliatory, non-threatening way, this should alleviate some of the tenant's uncertainty concerning exactly what deductions (if any) will be made from her deposit. Although this puts you to some trouble, we believe it's worth it. After all, a tenant unpleasantly surprised by the amount of her deposit that you withhold is more likely to take the matter to court.

Whether or not the final inspection is made in the tenant's presence, we suggest you follow this procedure. Check each item on the landlord/tenant

checklist signed when the tenant moved in. Note its present condition on a new copy of the landlord/tenant checklist. If pictures were taken at the outset, these should similarly be used for comparison purposes when the tenant moves out if the premises are dirty or damaged. Obviously, the new pictures should be taken with a view toward graphically illustrating problem areas. Finally, if you have any reason to expect a particular tenant will take you to court over deductions you plan to make from a security deposit, have the unit examined by another person before it is cleaned up. This person should be available to testify in court if necessary.

5. How to Make Proper Deductions for Cleaning and Damages

You may deduct the following amounts from the tenant's deposit:*

a. Costs of Cleaning

The reasonable costs of cleaning include taking care of such things as flea infestations left behind by the tenant's animals, oven cleaning, removing decals from walls, removing mildew in the bathroom, and defrosting the refrigerator

As you can imagine, a large number of landlord-tenant disputes over deductions from security deposits deal with whether or not it was reasonable for the landlord to reclean the premises after the tenant moves. Unfortunately, legal standards in this area are vague. You may legally charge for any cleaning necessary to satisfy the "average" or

---

* Remember, if your property is located in a city such as Berkeley and Santa Monica, which requires you to pay interest on a tenant's entire deposit, you must also refund this amount. Check your local ordinance for detail of how to complete this.

"reasonable" incoming tenant. That isn't much help, is it? In practical terms, this means that you can't automatically charge a tenant for carpets, drapes, or wall cleaning as a standard policy. You must view the premises with an eye to how well the tenant cleaned and only charge extra if the property was left in a clearly substandard condition. Items for which cleaning is often necessary--and costly--include stained carpets, drapes (particularly smoker-contaminated ones), furniture (for furnished premises), and kitchen and bathroom equipment.

If you or your employees clean these items, you will need to impose a reasonable hourly charge. Several large management companies we know cost out cleaning time at $15 per hour, and this is accepted by small claims courts.* If you have cleaning done by an outside service, be sure to keep your cancelled checks, as well as their itemization of work done. By and large, these amounts are accepted by small claims courts unless they are clearly unreasonable. If you or a member of your family do the work, you are of course entitled to charge a reasonable hourly rate. However, if you have the work done by teenagers who you pay the minimum wage, you can expect trouble in court if you have charged the tenant a $15.00 hourly rate. Also, it's wise to try and patronize only those cleaning services whose employees are willing to testify for you, or at least send a letter describing what they did in detail if the tenant sues you in small claims court, contesting your deposit deductions.

Items for which cleaning is also necessary--though less expensive--in-

---

* This is justified as follows. Maintenance people get $6.50 - $8.00 per hour. With benefits, this adds up to over $10 per hour. Supervisors who must schedule maintenance and inspect the unit (this could be you) are paid a higher hourly rate but work on any one unit for a shorter period of time.

clude dirty walls, stove, refrigerator, and commodes, sinks and shower stalls. Again, it is always wise to take pictures of dirty premises and to arrange to have them viewed by several witnesses.

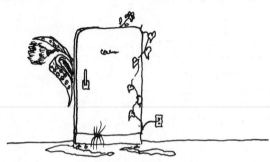

b. Repairing Damage To Property "Exclusive of Ordinary Wear and Tear"

This includes obvious sorts of damage, such as cigarette burns, childrens' crayon marks, holes in walls, broken tiles, etc., but also more subtle breakage, such as broken refrigerator parts, missing boiler pans, water damage from hanging plants, and urine stains from animals.

Almost as common as disputes over cleaning are those over whether or not damages were due to "ordinary wear and tear." A common argument is whether normal deterioration, or the tenant's carelessness, makes repainting necessary. Basically, this depends on the condition of the premises and how long the tenant has occupied them. One landlord we know uses the following approach when a tenant moves out and repainting is necessary, with excellent success. If the tenant has occupied the premises for six months or less, the full cost of repainting (labor and materials) is subtracted from their deposit. If the tenant lived in the unit between six months and a year, and the walls are dirty, two-thirds of the painting cost is subtracted from the deposit. Tenants who occupy a unit for between one and two years and leave dirty walls are charged one-third of the repainting cost. No one who stays for two years or more is ever charged a painting fee. No matter how dirty the walls become, the landlord would always repaint as a matter of course if this amount of time had passed since the previous painting.

Obviously, a rule of thumb of this type is only that, and must be modified occasionally to fit particular circumstances. And at times it's also important to distinguish between damage to walls and dirty paint. Generally, minor marks or nicks are your responsibility as ordinary wear and tear, while large marks or paint gouges are the responsibility of the tenant. Certainly, a large number of picture and/or tack holes in the wall and holes to hang plants in the ceiling that require filling with plaster, or otherwise patching and repainting, constitutes grounds for withholding the appropriate amount from the tenant's deposit, allowing for whether the unit needed repainting anyway, or had just been painted. Again, take pictures.

As to carpets, ordinary wear and tear obviously does not justify a charge against the tenant's deposit. Neither does moderate dirt or spotting, even if you can't get the stains out, if the tenant has occupied the unit for a number of years. On the other hand, large rips or indelible stains will justify your deducting for a replacement rug--pro-rated to subtract for the useful life expectancy of the rug already used up. The same applies with respect to drapes. The basic approach to take in all of these situations is to ask whether the tenant has damaged something that doesn't normally wear out, or has substantially shortened the life of something that does. If the answer is "Yes," you may charge the tenant the pro-rated cost of the item, taking into account how old it was, how long it might have lasted otherwise, and the cost of replacement. For example, if your tenant has ruined an

eight-year-old rug that had a life expectancy of 10 years, and for which a replacement would cost $1,000 at today's prices, you would charge the tenant $200 for the two years of life that would have remained in the rug had the tenant not ruined it.

Finally, if you use an estimate as a basis for charging a tenant for damage when you send the required notice within 14 days of the tenant leaving because you haven't had time to make the repairs, be sure to do so before the trial date, should the tenant sue you.

6. Making Deductions for Unpaid Rent

After deducting legitimate cleaning and damage charges from a tenant's security deposit, you can also deduct any unpaid rent.

a. Month-to-Month Tenancies

For month-to-month or other periodic tenancies, you can use the tenant's security deposit to cover any rent the departed tenant didn't pay. The dollar amount of your rent deduction should be pro-rated for the number of days the tenant failed to pay. In the case of a month-to-month tenancy where the tenant gave less than the required 30 days' notice before leaving, you are entitled to rent for the entire 30 days, unless you rerent or reasonably could have. Simply pro-rate the rent based on the number of days the tenant left early.

EXAMPLE 1: If your tenant pays you the rent of $600 for March--supposedly his last month--but stays until April 5 without paying anything more, you can deduct these last five days' rent from the security deposit by pro-rating the month's rent. In this case, you would be entitled to deduct one-sixth of the total month's rent, or $100.

EXAMPLE 2: After having paid her $600 monthly rent on October 1, Sheila Shortnotice informs you on the 15th that she's leaving on the 25th, thus giving you only 10 days' notice when you're entitled to 30. You're entitled to rent through the 30th day, counting from October 15, or November 14, unless you found a new tenant in the meantime, or reasonably could have.* Since the rent is paid through October 31, Sheila owes you the pro-rated rent for the 14 days in November. At $600 per month or $20 a day, this works out to $280, which can be deducted from Sheila's security deposit on account of the improperly short notice she gave you.

b. Leases

In the case of an unexpired fixed-term lease, you are entitled to the balance of the rent due under the lease, with credit for any rent you

---

* We discuss your responsibility to mitigate damages when a tenant moves in Chapter 17. Generally, with month-to-month tenants there is little real duty to mitigate damages unless the departing tenant produces a satisfactory new tenant who will begin paying rent immediately. Otherwise, it is generally (but not always) assumed that it is reasonable to take up to 30 days to find a new tenant and get them moved in.

receive from new tenants prior to the end of the term, or could receive if you make a diligent effort to rerent the property. (See Chapter 2, Section C and Chapter 17, Section C. In lease situations, if your tenant leaves more than one month early, your duty to mitigate damages is usually taken seriously by courts. In other words, if you withhold more than one month's rent from the tenant's deposit and you are challenged in court, a judge is likely to want to know why you couldn't rerent the property.)

Where you have to sue to evict and obtain a judgment for rent through the date of the judgment, you can subtract pro-rated rent for the period between the date of the judgment and the date the tenant actually leaves, as well as subtracting the amount of judgment itself from the deposit.

EXAMPLE 1: On January 1, Ludwig Von Lessor leased his 5-bedroom home to Skip Skipout and his family for $1,200 a month. On June 30, Skip skips out, even though six months remains on his lease. Under the lease, Skip was supposed to stay six more months at $1,200 a month, paying total rents of $7,200. Ludwig rerents the property on July 10, this time for $1,250 a month (prorated at $833 for the last 20 days in July), so that he'll receive a total rent of $7,083 through December 31, the date through which Skip agreed to stay under the terms of the original lease. Because this sum is $117 less than the $7,200 he would have received from Skip had he lived up to the lease, Ludwig may deduct $117 from Skip's deposit. In addition, if Ludwig expended a reasonable amount of money to find a new tenant (e.g., newspaper ads, rental agency commissions, etc.), he could also deduct this sum from the deposit.

EXAMPLE 2: You sue a tenant who fails to pay May's rent of $450, and get a judgment on June 10 for rent pro-rated through that date. The tenant doesn't leave until the 17th, when the sheriff comes and puts him out. You're entitled to the extra week's rent (seven days pro-rated at $15/day, or $105) that has accrued between judgment and eviction. You are, of course, also entitled to keep and credit any balance of the deposit against the judgment and deduct any necessary amount to take care of damage and cleaning costs.

7. Deduct for Cleaning and Damage Costs Before You Deduct for Unpaid Rent Covered by a Court Judgment

Always deduct for cleaning and damage costs and any rent amount not included in a court judgment before subtracting the amount of a court judgment for unpaid rent obtained as part of an eviction proceeding from a tenant's security deposit. The reason for this suggestion is simple. A judgment, once obtained, can be collected in all sorts of ways, such as garnisheeing the former tenant's wages or bank account if the security deposit is not large enough to cover it. However, you are much more limited when it comes to collecting money the tenant owes you for damages and dirty conditions which have not been reduced to a judgment. Indeed, the only way to collect these damages, short of filing suit and getting a judgment, is to subtract them directly from the security deposit.

What all this adds up to should be obvious. If you credit the court judg-

ment against the security deposit first, there may not be enough money left to compensate you for cleaning, damages to your property, or rent not reflected in the judgment. The unhappy result will then be that you will have to bring another lawsuit to collect this money. However, if, as we suggest, you approach the problem the other way around and credit the amount necessary to cover cleaning damage fees and any unpaid rent not covered in the judgment before you worry about the crediting the judgment amount, you will still have the judgment should the deposit prove not to be large enough to cover everything.

EXAMPLE: Amalia Amateur collected a $1,200 security deposit from Denny Deadbeat, whom she ultimately had to sue to evict for failure to pay rent. Amalia got a judgment for $160 court costs plus $1,000 unpaid rent through the date of the judgment. Denny didn't leave until the sheriff came, about six days later, thus running up an additional pro-rated rent of $180 not reflected in the judgment. Denny also left a mess that cost $500 to clean. In addition, he made fist-sized holes in the wall that cost $500 to repair. Amalia (not having read this book) first applied the $1,200 security deposit to the $1,160 judgment, leaving only $40 to apply toward the rent of $180 which was not reflected in the judgment, as well as the cleaning and repair charges, all of which totalled $1,180. Unfortunately, because Amalia subtracted the amount of the judgment from the security deposit, it is considered to be paid, leaving only $40 to apply to the other debts. Therefore, Amalia must now sue Denny again for the $1,160 he still owes her.

EXAMPLE: Now, let's change a few facts to assume that Priscilla Professional was Denny's landlady. In the same situation, Priscilla applied Denny's $1,200 deposit first to the cleaning and damage charges of $1,000 and then to the $180 rent not reflected in the judgment. This left $20 to apply to the $1,160 judgment, the balance of which she can collect by having the sheriff garnish Denny's wages or bank account.*

_____

* We discuss the importance of keeping track of where your tenant works and banks in Chapter 1. Obviously, you can't collect a judgment if you have no idea where a tenant is. The point is that Priscilla, unlike Amalia, doesn't have to sue Denny a second time to collect.

8. Notifying the Tenant of Security Deposit Deductions

After you've determined what, if anything, to withhold from the tenant's deposit (including "last month's rent," if not previously applied), you must notify the tenant of what you did in writing, justifying your actions. Returning to the previous example, here is the letter Priscilla Professional sent to Denny Deadbeat:

_____

November 30, 198_
123 Reality Road
San Jose, California

Denny Deadbeat
123 Lazy Lane, Apartment 4
Santa Clara, California

Dear Mr. Deadbeat,

The following is an itemization of my application of the $1,200 security deposit you paid me in January 198_ , when you moved into the premises at 123 Lazy Lane, Apartment 4, Santa Clara, California, to damages you made to that property. I am mailing this statement to the 123 Lazy Lane address because it is your last address known to me, in the hope that the Postal Service will forward it to you.

Carpet cleaning by Reddi Rug Refurbishers
(receipt copy enclosed) necessitated by
several large grease stains and imbedded
candle wax in living room rug: $160.00

Drapery Cleaning by Curtis Curtain Cleaners,
(receipt copy enclosed) necessitated by
heavy cigarette odor and multiple grease
stains in drapes throughout the apartment: $140.00

Sums paid to resident managers for 10 hours
cleaning at $10/hr. of debris-filled garage,
dirty stove and refrigerator, and stains and
marks on walls: $100.00

Plaster repair by Paula's Plastering
(receipt copy enclosed) of several fist-sized
holes in bedroom walls: $500.00

Painting of living room wall (newly painted
before you moved in by Pete's Painting
(receipt copy enclosed) of bedroom walls
to cover plaster repairs: $100.00

Rent pro-rated for 5 days at $15/day for
period between November 6 unlawful
detainer judgment and November 12 eviction
by Sheriff (representing rent not part of
judgment): $180.00

Total charges not included in judgment: $1,180.00

Deposit amount: $1,200.00

less above charges: $1,180.00

Balance: $ 20.00

     As you know, the municipal court awarded me a judgment against you
for unpaid rent and court costs in the total amount of $1160.00. There-
fore, I am applying the balance of your security deposit, after subtracting for damages to my property and unpaid rent not covered in the
judgment, to the amount of the judgment. Subtraction of the remaining
$20 of your balance from the $1160 judgment leaves $1140 owing on this
judgment. Please remit that amount to me at once or I shall be required
to garnish your wages at Laid-Back Mattress Testing Company.

                              Sincerely,

                              Priscilla Professional

Here's another example of a letter
to a tenant who left voluntarily:

                                        November 8, 198_
                                        123 Fourth St.
                                        La Jolla, CA

Tina Tenant
1234 Larchmont Lane
San Diego, CA

Dear Ms. Tenant:

     Here is the itemization, as required by Civil Code Section 1950.5,
of your $600.00 security deposit on the property at 5678 Lessee Lane in
San Diego, which you rented from me on a month-to-month basis on January
1, 198_ and vacated on October 31, 198_.

Repainting of living room walls, necessitated
by crayon and chalk marks--$350.00. (See
enclosed receipt from Precision Painters.)
Pro-rated $350.00 (4 years normal life--3
years' life at termination of tenancy).   = $262.50

```
5 days' pro-rated rent; 25 days' notice
to terminate month-to-month tenancy, given
October 5, unpaid portion of 30 days'
rent through November 5 @ $20.00/day
($600.00/month)                              =   $100.00


TOTAL CHARGES                                    $362.50

DEPOSIT AMOUNT                                   $600.00

LESS ABOVE CHARGES                               $362.50

    BALANCE REFUNDED TO YOU                      $237.50
    (Check enclosed)
```

Please note that your cashing of this check constitutes your acceptance that the same is payment in full of the balance of your security deposit. If you have any questions, please call me at 555-1359.

Sincerely,

Lena Landlady

IMPORTANT: Your deposit charge itemization letter should be mailed to the tenant at her last known address, or her forwarding address, along with a check for any balance you owe her, within two weeks of her departure. If the tenant hasn't left you a forwarding address (especially common for tenants who skip out on their rent or have to be evicted), you should mail the itemization and any balance to the address of the property itself. That, after all, is the tenant's last address known to you. If your former tenant has left a forwarding address with the post office, it will forward the mail. (If you put "Address Correction and Forwarding Requested" on the envelope, the Postal Service will notify you of the new address, for a nominal fee. This will help if the tenant's deposit doesn't cover all proper deductions and you want to sue in small claims court -- see Section C of this chapter.) If the tenant has left no forwarding address, the letter will come back to you. The postmarked envelope is your proof of your good-faith attempt to notify the tenant. It should protect you from the danger of being assessed up to $200 in punitive damages which a judge is empowered to assess you for bad-faith deposit withholding, if the tenant later takes you to small claims court and shows you made no effort to return his deposit within 14 days.

C. Small Claims Lawsuits Over Security Deposits

1. Trying to Settle a Potential Lawsuit

Regardless of how much you give your tenants the benefit of the doubt as to cleaning and/or damage deductions from deposits, and no matter how meticulous you are about properly accounting to your tenants for their deposits, many landlords sooner or later face the prospect of being sued by a tenant who disagrees with their assessment of the cost of damages or repairs. Because the amount of most residential security deposits is less than $1,500, most such suits are brought in small claims court ($1,500 is the maximum award available in small claims court). The purpose of this section, then, is to suggest several helpful strategies for dealing with ex-tenants' small claims suits over security deposits. We emphasize how a landlord should prepare and present a security deposit case in small claims court, rather than give you an overview on small claims court procedures generally. For more information on the latter, see Everybody's Guide to Small Claims Court, by Ralph Warner (Nolo Press).

A tenant may file suit two weeks after leaving the premises if no deposit refund (complete with an itemization of what the deposit was used for) or explanation of why one will not be forthcoming is received. If you return a part of a deposit sooner and the tenant does not agree with your arithmetic, she can bring suit immediately. However, a tenant may legally wait to sue you for at least two years.* It is very likely, however, if a tenant is going to sue, he'll do it fairly promptly. Just the same, don't throw out cleaning bills, receipts for repairs, and photographs showing dirt and damages, after only a few months, lest you be caught defenseless.

You will most likely first hear from a tenant dissatisfied with your deductions from her deposit by way of a letter or phone call demanding that you refund more than you did. This sort of demand is a requirement before anyone can begin a small claims suit.** In response to such a demand, your best bet is often to try and settle the suit immediately. This means working out a reasonable compromise with the tenant. We recommend that you be open to this idea of returning to the tenant some additional portions of the deposit even if you believe your original assessment of the cost of repairs and cleaning more than fair and you feel you will surely win in court if it goes that far. Why do we suggest a course of action which may seem wishy-washy to some readers? Because, as a businessperson, it usually doesn't make sense for you to spend a morning in court to argue over $50, $100, or even $200, especially when you consider that many small claims court judges are relatively inexperienced "pro tem" judges, who may not always see landlord-tenant lawsuits over damages in the same way you do.***

** C.C.P. Section 116.4(a) requires a person suing in small claims court to state under penalty of perjury that she "has demanded payment." If the tenant fails to do this, point it out to the judge. With luck, the judge might dismiss the suit on that basis.

***One landlord we know with thousands of units experiences about 250 move-outs each month. He receives about 10 complaints per month about the amount charged against deposits (charges vary widely with the circumstances, but average about $175). This landlord's general policy is to offer to settle for 50% of the disputed amount. He does this, not because he thinks his original assessment was wrong, but because he finds that coming to a settlement with a tenant costs him a lot less than fighting in court. However, if the settlement offer isn't accepted promptly by the tenant, our landlord fights to win and almost always does.

---

* The statute of limitations for a tenant's suit to recover a security deposit is two years if a failure to refund a deposit is viewed as a breach of an oral agreement (C.C.P. Section 339) and four years if a written lease or rental agreement is involved, and failure to return a deposit can be considered a breach of it (C.C.P. Section 337).

If you do arrive at a compromise settlement with your former tenant, you should insist that your payment be accepted as full satisfaction of your obligation to return the deposit. The best way to do this is to prepare and have the tenant sign a brief settlement agreement, such as the following:

SETTLEMENT AGREEMENT*

Larchmont Lessor, "Landlord," and Lisa Lessee, "Tenant," hereby agree as follows:

1. Landlord rented the premises at 1234 State Avenue, Apartment 5, Los Angeles, California, to Tenant on July 1, 198_, pursuant to a written rental agreement for a tenancy from month-to-month.

2. Pursuant to the said agreement, Tenant paid Landlord the sum of $1,000.00 as and for a security deposit.

3. On October 31, 198_, Tenant vacated the said premises.

4. Within two weeks after Tenant vacated the said premises, Landlord itemized various deductions from the said security deposit totalling $380.00 and refunded the balance of $620.00 to Tenant.

5. Tenant asserts that she is entitled to the additional sum of $300.00, only $80.00 of the said deductions being proper. Landlord asserts that all the deductions were proper and that he owes Tenant nothing.

6. In order to settle the parties' entire dispute, and to compromise Tenant's claim for return of her security deposit, Landlord pays to Tenant the sum of $150.00, receipt of which is hereby acknowledged by Tenant, as and for full satisfaction of her claim.

DATED: December 1, 198_

SIGNATURE: _____
　　　　　　　　Larchmont Lessor

DATED: December 1, 198_

SIGNATURE: _____
　　　　　　　　Lisa Lessee

---

* You could shorten this agreement by simply using the first two lines and the material in paragraph 6, along with the signature lines.

250

You can also accomplish this by writing the words "Accepted in full satisfaction of security deposit refund claim" on the back of the check you mail to the tenant, where the endorsement is made. If the check is cashed, it is evidence that the tenant accepted it as a full compromise settlement.

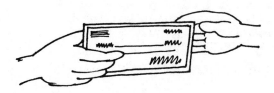

2. The Tenant Sues You

Obviously, there are times when you are dealing with a tenant who is so foolish and unreasonable that no compromise is possible and you have to meet the tenant in court. The first official notification of the court action you will receive will be a copy of the tenant's "Claim of Plaintiff" form. This will be served on you either by certified mail or by personal service. This form will notify you of the date, time, and place of the small claims hearing.

It's still not too late at this stage to try to work out a compromise settlement by paying part of what the tenant's suing for. However, if you compromise at this stage, you should do so only in exchange for a dismissal form signed by the tenant. This form is available from the small claims clerk.

Assuming you do end up in court (maybe you're just too damn mad, or too damn right, to give up a cent of what you are owed), you will want to actively gather your evidence. You don't

have to file any papers with the court clerk unless you want to counter sue for money you feel the tenant owes you.*

Although you might believe that since your former tenant is suing you (the tenant is the plaintiff and you are the defendant), the tenant should have the burden of proof. This is not true. By law, the landlord always has the burden of proving the premises needed cleaning or were damaged after the tenant left.** Thus, unless you affirmatively establish that the place was dirty or damaged, all your former tenant need prove to win her case is that a residential tenancy existed, that she paid you a deposit, and that you didn't return all of it. In other words, on the day of the hearing it is essential that you show up in court with as many of the following items of evidence as you can:

• Two copies of the landlord/tenant checklist which you should have filled out with the tenant when the tenant moved in and then again when she moved out (see Chapter 1, Section H, and Section B of this chapter). This is particularly important if the tenant admitted to damaged or dirty conditions on the checklist;

• Photos of the premises before the tenant moved in which show how clean and undamaged the place was;

• Photos after the tenant left which show a mess or damage;

---

* Normally, you would only want to do this if you kept the tenant's entire deposit and demanded that he pay you more. You'll obviously look silly if you refunded part of the deposit, thereby admitting the tenant only owes you the amount withheld, and then change your mind and sue for more. Incidentally, the general rule of law that says your failure to countersue a plaintiff precludes you from suing later on a claim arising out of the same subject matter, as the plaintiff's claim does not apply to small claims suits. [C.C.P. Section 426.60(b).] In other words, technically you can defend against the tenant's suit and still initiate your own later.

** Civil Code Section 1950.5(k).

• An itemization of hours spent by you or your repair or cleaning people on the unit, complete with the hourly costs for such work;

• Written statements from people doing cleaning work, as to the filthy conditions they found and what they had to do to remedy them;

• Damaged items small enough to bring into the courtroom (a curtain with a cigarette hole would be ever effective);

• Receipts for professional cleaning (particularly of carpets and drapes) and damage repair;

• One, or preferably two, witnesses who were familiar with the property and saw it just after the tenant left and who will testify that the place was a mess or that certain items were damaged. People who helped in the subsequent cleaning or repair are particularly effective witnesses. As noted above, written statements or declarations under penalty of perjury by people who can't come to court can be used, but they aren't as effective as live testimony, so use such statements only if the witness is unavailable. Here is a sample written statement:

DECLARATION OF CLEM CLEANER

I, Clem Cleaner, declare:

1. I am employed at A & B Maintenance Company, a contract cleaning and maintenance service located at 123 Abrego Street, Monterey, California. Lana Landlady, the owner of an apartment complex at 456 Seventh Street, Monterey, California, is one of our accounts.

2. On May 1, 198_, I was requested to go to the premises at 456 Seventh Street, Apartment 8, Monterey, California, to shampoo the carpets. When I entered the premises, I noticed a strong odor, part of what seemed like stale cigarette smoke. I also noticed an odor that seemed to come from the carpet.

3. When I began using a steam carpet cleaner on the living room carpet, I noticed a strong smell of urine. I stopped the steam cleaner, moved to a dry corner of the carpet, and pulled it from the floor. I then noticed a yellow color on the normally-white foam-rubber pad beneath the carpet, as well as a strong smell of urine, apparently caused by a pet (probably a cat) having urinated on the carpet. On further examination of the parts of the carpet, I noticed similar stains and odors throughout the carpet and pad.

4. In my opinion, the living room carpet and foam-rubber pad underneath need to be removed and replaced and the floor should be sanded and sealed.

I declare under penalty of perjury under the laws of the State of California that the foregoing is true and correct.

DATED: June 15, 198_

SIGNATURE: _____
                    Clem Cleaner

The small claims hearing should go something like this:*

---

* In small claims court people don't sit in a witness box. They normally stand behind a table facing the judge and explain their version of the dispute. In some courts, however, judges use other procedures, such as requesting that all parties and witnesses approach the judge's bench and explain what went on in conversational tones.

Clerk: "Calling the case of **Linda Lessor v. Lana Lessee.**"

Judge: "Well, Ms. Lessee, since you're the plaintiff, please tell me your version of the facts first."

Lana Lessee: "I moved into apartment "A" at 1700 Walnut St. in Costa Mesa in the spring of 198_. I paid my landlady here my first month's rent of $900 plus a $900 security deposit. When I moved out, she withheld $540 of this, returning only $360. As I believe this constitutes a willful denial of my rights under Civil Code Section 1950.5, I am asking for not only the $540 she owes me, but $200 in punitive damages, for a total of $740. Here is a copy of the rental agreement [HANDS IT TO THE CLERK], which specifically states, my deposit is to be returned to me if the apartment is left clean and undamaged. When I moved into apartment A, it was a mess. It's a nice little apartment, but the people who lived there before me were sloppy. The stove was filthy, as was the bathroom, the refrigerator, the floors, and just about everything else. But I needed a place to live and this was the best available, so I moved in despite the mess. I painted the whole place--everything. My landlady gave me the paint, but I did all of the work. And I cleaned the place thoroughly too. It took me three days. I like to live in a clean house."

Judge: [LOOKING AT ONE OF THE TENANT'S WITNESSES] "Do you have any personal knowledge of what this apartment looked like?"

Frank Friend: "Yes, I helped Lana move in and move out. I simply don't understand what the landlady is fussing about. The place was a mess when she moved in, and it was clean when Lana moved out."

Judge: "Ms. Lessor, you may now tell your side of the story. I should remind you that even though you are the defendant, you have the burden of proving that the amounts you withheld were reasonable."

Linda Lessor: "Your Honor, it is true, as Ms. Lessee testified, that the people who lived in the apartment before her were sloppy. They left things a mess alright, but my manager and I cleaned it up the day before Ms. Lessee actually moved in. Here are several photographs we took after the previous tenant, "Dirty Dan" Dimwit moved out [HANDS PHOTOS TO CLERK]. My manager, Mannie, and I spent a long day cleaning the place before Ms. Lessee moved in. We took this second set of photos to show the contrast after we cleaned it, in case Mr. Dimwit ever sued us for his deposit, which, as it turned out, he never dared do. Anyway, the point is that these photos [HANDS TO THE CLERK] also show the apartment just before Ms. Lessee moved in. Also, when Ms. Lessee moved in, she signed this inventory sheet [HANDS TO CLERK] indicating that all parts of the premises were clean and undamaged, right after she and Mannie Manager--who is here to testify--inspected the premises together. It's true that Ms. Lessee did some painting, but this was in exchange for a reduction of her first month's rent of $150 and our supplying the paint. Mr. Manager will also testify to his inspection of the premises after Ms. Lessee left and present the pictures he took on the day she left. But before he does, I should add that Ms. Lessee gave me only ten days' verbal notice, on October 15, before she left the apartment on October 25. Her rent was paid through the 31st, but I was unable to rerent the property until November 10, despite the ads I put in the paper as soon as she gave me her notice. Because she didn't give me the full 30 days' notice, I charged her 10 days pro-rated rent of $150 for the rent I didn't receive within the 30-day period, as well as $120 for cleaning the apartment. I believe this was reasonable under the circumstances."

Judge: [LOOKING AT MANNIE MANAGER] "What do you have to add, Mr. Manager?"

Mannie Manager: "Well, Your Honor, I did inspect the premises with Ms. Lessee when she first moved in. She stated everything looked fine and signed the landlord/tenant checklist I gave her. When she moved out on October 25, I went into the apartment and took these pictures. [HANDS THEM TO THE CLERK TO GIVE TO THE JUDGE]. Although the place wasn't a real mess, it still wasn't clean enough to re-rent right away either. The pictures I took clearly show mildew in the refrigerator, and a dirty oven. They also show a large dirt-stained area in the hall carpet, as well as a foot-square area where candlewax was imbedded in the bedroom carpet. I hired a professional cleaning service to clean the refrigerator, stove, and carpet, for which I have a receipt [HANDS TO CLERK]. The total was $120.

After you and your witnesses have presented your evidence as in the above example, the judge may ask a few questions and may render a decision right there. More likely, the judge will take the matter "under submission," and you will be notified of the result by mail. If you lose the small claims case, you must pay the judgment within 20 days (unless you appeal), or the tenant will be able to attach your bank account or other property, or even to put a lien on the property.

As a defendant, you have the right to appeal an adverse small claims decision to the superior court for a new trial, where you may be represented by an attorney (not allowed in small claims court). Before you do so, however, you should consider that the superior court judge will more than likely lean toward affirming the decision of the small claims judge. Also, if you hire an attorney, you may have to pay your own attorney's fees, even

if you win.* Finally, if the judge feels that you appealed the case just to harass the plaintiff, and that you had no valid defense, she can assess you an extra $250.**

Finally, you should know that nothing that happens in small claims court affects the validity of any judgment you may have (e.g., one arising out of an earlier eviction suit) against the tenant. In other words, if you got a judgment against a tenant for $1,200 for unpaid rent as part of an eviction action, this judgment is still good, even though a tenant gets a judgment against you for $200 in small claims court based on your failure to return her deposit.

---

* Even if the lease or rental agreement has an attorney's fees clause providing that the prevailing party in any suit be awarded attorney's fees, many judges hearing small claims appeals feel that the small claims statute (C.C.P. Section 117.12) limiting attorney's fees to $15.00 (and then only if the plaintiff wins) overrides any other provision for attorney's fees.
** C.C.P. Section 117.12.

254

3. You Sue the Tenant

Occasionally, you may wish to use the courts to file a lawsuit against a departed former tenant. This will happen when your tenant skips out owing back rent before you can file an unlawful detainer suit and the tenant's security deposit won't cover the amount owed. It is also likely to occur if the tenant trashes your property so severely as to more than use up the deposit. These situations can often be avoided through good property management practices, such as carefully screening prospective tenants at the outset, making sure to insist on a large security deposit and not waiting more than a week after the rent is due to bring an unlawful detainer action. Occasionally, however, you end up with a real stinker of a tenant who, despite your best efforts to avoid it, leaves owing you a considerable amount. In such situations, you will want to consider the possibility of taking your ex-tenant to small claims court.

Although small claims court is best avoided for bringing eviction suits, mostly because it's a lot slower than the regular court system and easier for the tenant to defend (we discuss the whys and wherefores of this in Volume II: **The Landlord's Law Book: Evictions**), the reverse is true for lawsuits designed to collect damages. In this situation, small claims court is both faster and easier to use than municipal court as long as your claim doesn't exceed $1,500, the limit for which you can sue in small claims court.

Again, rather than explaining in its entirety how small claims court works and setting forth all the procedures and possibilities, we refer you to Nolo Press's book on the subject, **Everybody's Guide to Small Claims Court**, by Ralph Warner. Here we discuss only the basics of suing a tenant for back rent and/or damages not covered by the tenant's deposit.

a. Deciding Whether or Not to Sue

Before you rush off to your local small claims court to file a claim against your former tenant, you should first ask yourself three questions:

• Do I have a valid case?*

• Can I locate the departed tenant? and

• Can I collect a judgment if I win?

If the answer to any of these questions is "No," think twice about initiating a suit. Pay particular attention to question 3, which involves your determination of how you will collect a judgment.

Quite simply, the best way to collect any judgment against your ex-tenant is to garnish her wages. If she's working, there is an excellent chance of collecting if payment is not made voluntarily. You can't garnish a welfare, social security, unemployment, pension or disability check, or a federal paycheck. So, if the person sued gets her income from one of these sour-

---

* If you are a landlord with many rental units and use a local small claims court regularly, make particularly sure the cases you bring are good ones. That is, the charges you make for cleaning and damages repairs, etc. are valid. You do not want to lose your credibility with the court in future cases by even appearing to be unfair.

ces, you may be wasting your time unless you can identify some other asset that you can efficiently get your hands on.

But what about these other assets? Can't a judgment be collected from lots of sources other than wages? Yes, bank accounts, motor vehicles and real estate are other common collection sources. But people who run out on their debts don't always have much in a bank account (or they may have moved the account to make it difficult for you to locate it), and much of their personal property may be exempt under California debt protection laws. These are discussed in detail in **Billpayer's Rights** by Honigsberg and Warner, Nolo Press, but to take a few examples--equity in motor vehicles owned by the debtor is exempt up to $1,200, and the tools of a person's trade are exempt up to $2,500, ordinarily and reasonably necessary household furnishings, appliances, clothing, are all exempt, as is money in bank accounts which can be traced to exempt assets such disability and unemployment benefits, etc.

Assuming you decide that it is worthwhile to go after your tenant for money owed, your first step is to write a letter asking her to pay the amount of your claim. Although this may seem like an exercise in futility, the law requires that you make a demand for the amount sued for before filing in small claims court. This demand can be combined with your written itemization as to how you applied the tenant's security deposit to the charges [see Section C(1), above]. A good tactic is to describe the charges for cleaning and/or damages in detail, mostly for the benefit of the small claims judge who will read it if you end up in court.* A letter that both explains how the tenant's deposit was credited against your claim for back rent, cleaning and damage charges and demands payment of the balance would look something like this:

---

* At the small claims hearing, you should offer a copy of the letter to the judge, noting that you're doing so for the purpose of showing that you made the required demand before suing. Although the judge will pay more attention to what you say in court rather than what you said in the demand letter, a coherent set of facts in writing certainly doesn't hurt.

December 20, 198_
123 Pine Street
Monterey, California

Mauve Doubt
8910 Pine Avenue
Pacific Grove, California

Dear Ms. Doubt:

As your know, you rented the premises at 456 Pine Avenue, Apartment 7, Pacific Grove, California from me on a month-to-month basis, beginning January 1 of this year at the rate of $650 per month, payable in advance on the first of each month, paying me the first month's rent plus a $600 security deposit. This letter is to advise you how I credited that deposit, as required by Civil Code Section 1950.5.

You vacated the premises on December 5. However, you failed to notify me until December 4 that you were moving. As a result, I was unable to re-rent the property until today (December 20), even after placing daily newspaper ads in the **Monterey Muckraker**. (It's very difficult to rent an apartment during the holiday season.) Because of your failure to give me the required 30 days' notice, I have lost 20 days' rent which amounts to $400 and have spent $50 for the want-ads.

In addition, I was required to spend $80 to have the living room rug professionally cleaned because of a two-foot diameter red stain. Finally, it was necessary to have the entire apartment repainted because of the odd bright colors you used to paint several rooms, including pink, light blue and purple rainbows in the bedroom, and the fact that all other painting was poorly done (e.g., paint dripped on floor, light switches painted with wrong type paint, streaks in the bedroom etc.). All this required several coats of paint to cover; my total cost was $350 (receipt enclosed), which I paid to Pam's Professional Painting.

To summarize, you are liable for $400 rent and $50 advertising costs as the result of your failure to give me 30 days' notice, $80 charge for carpet cleaning, and a $350 charge for repainting, for a total of $880. Application of your $600 security deposit to this amount leaves $280 owing. Please mail your payment to the address above. If I do not hear from you within two weeks, I will be required to take appropriate legal action.

Sincerely,

Lorraine Landperson

A letter like the one above serves several purposes. First, it satisfies the requirements of the security deposit law by telling the tenant how her security deposit was applied. Second, it makes a formal demand for the balance the tenant owes. Finally, in the likely event the tenant doesn't pay and you have to go to small claims court, it states a clear and coherent set of facts the judge has the opportunity to read.

b. How to Sue

If you don't receive a response to your demand letter within a reasonable time (or if the tenant does respond-- with a razzberry), file your suit. You can file suit in the judicial district in which your premises are located or in which the tenant now resides, whichever is most convenient for you.

To start your case, go to the small claims clerk's office, pay a small filing fee (which you can recover if you win), and fill out a form called "Plaintiff's Statement to Clerk." When you have completed it, give it to the court clerk, who will then use it to

type out a "Claim of Plaintiff" form and assign your case a number. You will be asked to sign this form under penalty of perjury. A copy of the "Claim of Plaintiff" will go to the judge, and another must be served on the defendant.

If the person you're suing lives in the same county in which the suit is brought, your hearing date should be between 10 and 40 days from the time the papers are filed. If the defendant lives outside of the county where you bring suit, the case will be heard between 30 and 70 days from that date.

When you file your papers, you should also arrange with the clerk for a court date. Get a date that is convenient for you. You need not take the first date the clerk suggests. Be sure to leave yourself enough time to get a copy of the "Claim of Plaintiff" form served on the defendant(s). If you fail to serve your papers properly on the defendant in time, there is no big hassle--just notify the clerk, get a new court date, and try again.

Small claims court sessions are usually between 9:00 a.m. and 3:00 p.m. on working days. Larger counties are required to hold at least one evening or Saturday session per month. Ask the clerk for a schedule.

As in a regular lawsuit, all the persons you name in a small claims case must be served with the papers. You can often serve your "Claim of Plaintiff" by certified mail. The clerk of the court does the mailing for you. The fee in California is modest and is recoverable if you win. This method of service is both cheap and easy, but it depends for its success on the defendant signing for the letter. Many individuals routinely sign to accept mail. However, some people never do, knowing instinctively, or perhaps from past experience, that nothing good ever comes by certified mail. The consensus among court clerks as to the percentage of certified mail services that

are accepted is about 40%. The "Claim of Plaintiff" can also be served on each defendant personally, using the sheriff, marshal, private process server or any adult, except you, or you can use substituted service. Substituted service involves giving a copy of the papers to a person at the defendant's home or workplace with a second copy mailed to her there. (See C.C.P. Section 415.20.)

The defendant is entitled to receive service of the "Claim of Plaintiff" form at least five days before the date of the court hearing, if he is served within the county in which the courthouse is located. If the defendant is served in a county other than the one where the trial is to take place, he must be served at least 15 days before the trial date.

Once you've obtained your court date and had your former tenant served with the "Claim of Plaintiff," you are ready to prepare for trial. A suit against a tenant for back rent and cleaning and/or damage costs is handled in much the same way as is your defense against a tenant's suit for recovery of the security deposit, except that you, being the plaintiff, present your case first. We refer you to Section B(1) of this chapter on small claims suits over deposits, as well as to Nolo's small claims manual, **Everybody's Guide to Small Claims Court.**

19

How to Deal With Property Abandoned by a Tenant

A. Personal Property

This chapter outlines the proper steps to take to deal with property left behind by tenants who have moved out, so that the vacated premises can be readied for the next tenant. Obviously, you want to do this in a way that protects you from claims by the tenant who has moved out that you have destroyed or stolen her property. (In legal jargon, this is known as "unlawful conversion.")

Whether a tenant vacates voluntarily, or with the aid of the sheriff or marshal, landlords all too often must not only clean up, and repair damage, but also dispose of a pile of junk.

Removing obvious trash is normally no problem, but even here you must exercise care. If you toss a moth-eaten book in the dumpster that turns out to have been a valuable first edition, you could have problems. Indeed, it's wise to realize that, as a general rule, the more valuable the property left behind by a tenant, the more formalities you must comply with when disposing of it. In rare instances, a tenant against whom you have a judgment for unpaid rent or damages to your premises may leave valuable property behind which she never claims. If so, you can safely have the property sold and the money applied to pay your judgment if you follow the legal procedures outlined in this chapter.

1. Inventorying the Property and Preparing a "Notice of Right to Claim Abandoned Property"

The process of dealing with a tenant's property can begin only after you have legally gained possession of the premises. This occurs when a tenant finally leaves voluntarily (whether or not she gives you the keys),* or, if there is an eviction procedure and the tenant hangs on to the bitter end when the sheriff, marshal, or constable escorts her off the premises. Incidentally, contrary to the Dickensian depictions of tenant advocates, the belongings of evicted tenants are not put into the street. The law enforcement officer performing an eviction will allow the tenant to carry out a few armloads of personal possessions, leaving the remainder to be locked in the premises and stored by you until the tenant can arrange to take them away.

If the tenant's property that is left behind is worth less than $300, you basically have no problem once you send the tenant a proper notice. This is because Civil Code Section 1988 allows you to deal with property worth less than this amount in any way you wish. We discuss what to do with property worth more than $300 below.

Okay, now let's assume that you have entered your rental premises legally after a tenant has left and discover property in addition to obvious trash or garbage. What should you do? Simply follow these steps:

Step 1: Contact the tenant informally, if possible, and arrange to have the property picked up. Look through the tenant's rental application and phone personal or business references listed there if you are unable to contact the tenant otherwise.

Step 2: If this leads nowhere, your next step is to take an inventory of the abandoned property. An objective witness (tenant/neighbor) is valuable here if you want to protect yourself from any charge that you have not done this honestly. Items locked in trunks, suitcases, etc., or tied in boxes, may be described by reference to the trunk or box without listing the contents. (You may, however, open boxes, etc. to check items for value, since your method of disposing of the property depends on its total value.)

Step 3: Decide whether the value of all the property--what you could get for it at a well-attended flea market or garage sale--is worth more than $300. If it's worth less than that, you can keep it, sell it, or throw it away if the tenant fails to respond to your notice, as described in Step 4 below. Otherwise, you must auction it off in the manner indicated in Subsection 2, below. Several larger landlords we know routinely put all the material left behind by the tenant in large plastic bags, which they tag and keep in their own storage room for six months or so. A few times a year, they give everything that hasn't been claimed to the Goodwill.

Step 4: Prepare a Notice of Right to Reclaim Abandoned Property (a blank form is included in the Appendix of this book), listing the name of the tenant (and any other person you believe has an interest in the property), the address of the premises, a description of the property, and a place where the property may be claimed. If there are too many items of property to list on the form, you can list them on a separate sheet of paper attached as "Attachment A." You should also check

---

* If you gained possession of the property after having heard nothing from the tenant for 18 days since mailing a Notice of Belief of Abandonment (see Chapter 17), you should understand that your mailing of the abandonment notice relating to the premises has nothing to do with any property abandoned. In other words, it only allows you to enter legally after the premises were abandoned, not dispose of property.

the appropriate box on the form as to whether the property, in your opinion, is worth more or less than $300. A sample notice follows:

NOTICE OF RIGHT TO RECLAIM ABANDONED PROPERTY

To: _____
(Name of former tenant(s) and possible owners of property)

When the premises at _____
(Address of premises)

City of _____ , County of _____ , California, were

vacated, the following personal property remained:

_____

_____

[ ] Continued on Attachment "A" hereto.

You may claim this property at:

_____
(Address at which property may be claimed)

City of _____ , County of _____ , California.

Unless you pay the reasonable cost of storage for all the above-described property, and take possession of the property which you claim not later than eighteen (18) days after the date of mailing of this notice indicated below, this property may be disposed of pursuant to Civil Code Section 1988.

[ ] Because this property is believed to be worth less than $300, it may be kept, sold, or destroyed without further notice if you fail to reclaim it within the time limit indicated.

[ ] Because this property is believed to be worth more than $300, it will be sold at a public sale after notice has been given by publication, if you fail to reclaim it within the time limit indicated. You have the right to bid on the property at this sale. After the property is sold and the cost of storage, advertising, and sale is deducted, the remaining money will be paid over to the county. You may claim the remaining money at any time within one year after the county receives the money.

DATE OF MAILING: _____

_____
OWNER/MANAGER (SIGNATURE)

_____
(ADDRESS OF OWNER/MANAGER)

Step 5: Mail the notice to the tenant's last known address, which will usually be the address of your property. The postal service will forward the notice if the tenant has left a forwarding address.

Step 6: Surrender the property if the tenant contacts you within 18 days after you mailed the notice and arranges to pay you the reasonable storage charge. You can insist on being paid the pro-rated daily rental value for keeping the property on your premises and/or any out-of-pocket costs you incur after that for renting storage space. You can also subtract the value of your time for packing it up in the first place. However, in most situations where there is not a lot of property, we recommend that you give the tenant his belongings and forget about any charges, particularly if you didn't incur any out-of-pocket expenses. It's just not worth it to get in fights over $75 worth of used books, records, and tennis sneakers. If you insist on too high a storage charge, and the tenant refuses to pay it, you will end up having to keep or sell the property. This may result in a tenant suing you and raises the possibility a judge may hold you liable for the entire value of the property because your storage charge wasn't reasonable in the first place.

WARNING: Even if the tenant owes you a substantial sum for back rent, damages, etc., you may not insist on payment of that amount as a condition of returning the tenant's property, even if you've obtained a court judgment. (In order to properly keep the property to have it sold and applied against such a judgment, you must have the sheriff seize it and auction it off. The costs of doing this may exceed the value of the property, however.)

Step 7: If your former tenant or other owner of the property doesn't contact you within 18 days of mailing the letter, you may keep, sell, give away, use or do anything else you wish with the property if it is all worth less than $300. In other words, it's yours. To recover from you for wrongfully disposing of the property, the tenant would have to convince a probably-skeptical judge that the property was worth over $300 and that your belief that it was worth less was unreasonable.

2. Property Worth Over $300

Very seldom will a departing tenant leave behind personal effects worth more than $300. Indeed, one management company that handles several thousand units, and has done so for 30 years, tells us that they have only had this occur once. However, in the rare event this does occur, Civil Code Section 1988 requires that you publish a notice in the newspaper and then arrange for the property to be sold at a public auction. The ad must be published after the 18-day period for the tenant to claim her belongings has expired (Step 4, above), and at least five days before the date of the auction. A "flea market" or "garage sale" does not comply with the law, which requires a "public sale by competitive bidding," i.e., an auction. You must hire a licensed and bonded public auctioneer. (See the "Auctioneer" listing in the yellow pages of your telephone directory.)

Place your ad in the legal section of a local newspaper.* See Civil Code Sections 1988(b) and (c) for more details on how this works. Basically, the ad must describe the property in the same way you described it in the "Notice of Right to Claim Abandoned Property," discussed in Step 4, above. Send your ad to the newspaper in care of the legal ads person in the want-ad department.

Proceeds from the sale go first to pay your reasonable costs of the storage, advertising, and sale. According to Section 1988, the balance is supposed to be paid within 30 days of the sale, to the county, which will hold it for one year, unless you have a judgment for unpaid rent, in which instance you can keep the amount necessary to pay the judgment. (In order to do this, however, you will have to take the judgment and a "Writ of Execution," available from the court clerk, to the sheriff or marshal and give them the appropriate fee and written instructions to "levy" on the tenant's funds in the county's control. Ask the sheriff's or marshal's office for details.) In the unlikely event that money is left over, ask the county clerk for details, including a form to account for the sale proceeds. The county gets to keep the money if the tenant or other owner of the property doesn't claim it within a year.

Why should you go to all this trouble? After all, no law-enforcement agency will prosecute you for failing to comply with this law. The answer is that following this procedure will protect you from any liability in the event the tenant, or other owner of the property, shows up later and sues you for unlawful "conversion" of her property [see Civil Code Section 1989(c)]. Also, if the property is worth a lot more than $300, there may be enough money left over from the proceeds of the sale, after subtracting your costs for storage, advertising and conducting the action, to apply to any judgment you have against the tenant.

EXAMPLE: After Laura Landperson went to court and obtained a judgment for eviction and $1,000 back rent against her tenant, Abbie Abandoner, Abbie simply took off for parts unknown. Strangely enough, Abbie left behind a good quality color TV, a piano, and a starving Persian cat. Following a notice (to which Abbie didn't respond) and a public auction which brought in $750, Laura applied the money as follows: $100 storage charges, including care and feeding of the cat and pro-rated rental value for the days the property was on the premises, $90 for the cost of running the legal ad, and the auctioneer's $200 fee. This left $350 for Laura to have the sheriff apply against her $1,000 judgment.

---

* The newspaper must be one of "general circulation" that has paid subscribers in the county. Most daily newspapers qualify; weekly "throwaway" newspapers delivered free of charge and which depend on advertising for all their revenue do not. See Government Code Section 6066.

WARNING: If the tenant owes you money even for back rent, you can't use the proceeds of the sale to pay that debt unless you have a court judgment. This is because the proceeds, after subtracting costs of storage, advertising, and sale, are still the tenant's property, and you are not allowed to take someone else's property except to pay off a judgment.

In the above example, Laura, in order to enforce her "judgment lien" against Abbie's property, should instruct the auctioneer to hold the funds in Abbie's name. She should then have the clerk of the court that issued the judgment issue a "Writ of Execution," which she would, in turn, take to the local sheriff or marshal, with appropriate instructions to "levy on" (attach) the funds held by the auctioneer. Why shouldn't Laura have the auctioneer give her the money and credit it against the judgment herself? Because, following the formal procedures, as described above, will give her the best protection against future liability should a tenant show up later and threaten to sue you for "conversion" of her property. However, as a practical matter, if Laura did informally credit the excess auction proceeds toward the judgment and account for it properly to the tenant if and when she shows up later, it's unlikely a judge would penalize her, assuming her accounting was honest. And even if she did, Laura would have the right to offset her judgment against the tenant's claims for any wrongful disposition of the property.

B. Motor Vehicles

Occasionally, a departing tenant will leave an inoperable "junker" automobile in the parking lot or garage. Unfortunately, motor vehicles are a special category of personal property to which the procedures listed in Section A above do not apply. Whether the tenant has used the street in front of your property, or the property itself, as a junkyard, you should call the local police, giving the vehicle's license number, make, and model, and indicate where it's parked. If the car is parked on the street, the police will arrange to have it towed away 72 hours later, placing a notice to that effect on the windshield. See Vehicle Code Section 22651(k).

If it's parked on your property, the police will normally arrange for its removal after sending out an officer to see if it appears to be abandoned and tagging it. See Vehicle Code Sections 22523(b) and 22669. Cities have slightly different ordinances to cover this situation. In some, there is a small charge, but in many others, they recover towing and storage costs from the sale of the car. Several landlords have reported that the police are slow to pick up motor vehicles abandoned on private property and try to tell landlords that it's their responsibility to do a lien sale through the Department of Motor Vehicles. If a car is worth a fair amount, this is a viable alternative, as you can use the money you get from the sale to satisfy any judgment you have against the tenant.

But, as this involves a fair amount of paperwork, a lien sale is often more trouble than it's worth.

Your best approach is usually to insist that the police help you. Get a copy of the local abandoned property ordinance and refer to it if they resist. Finally, several landlords have reported that when all else failed, they said a few magic words and one dark night the abandoned vehicle disappeared from their property and reappeared on the street. We, of course, can't recommend this last course of action.

Appendix

Time Estimate for Repair

FROM: _____

_____

_____

DATE: _____

TO: _____

_____

_____

Dear Resident:

Thank you for promptly notifying us of the following problem with your unit:

_____

We expect to have the problem corrected on _____ , 19 __ , due to the following: _____

_____ .

We regret any inconvenience this delay may cause. Please do not hesitate to point out any other problems that may arise.

Sincerely,

_____

Notice of Intent to Enter Premises

FROM: _____

_____

_____   _____ , 19____

TO: _____

_____

_____

Dear Mr. /Ms. _____ :

Please be advised that the management of_____ would like to

enter your apartment on _____ , 19__ at _____ a.m. /p.m. for the following

reason(s):

( ) To make or arrange for the following repairs(s) and/or improvement(s):

_____

_____

_____

( ) To exhibit the premises to: ( ) a prospective tenant, ( ) workers and/or

contractors regarding the above repair or improvement,

( ) Other: _____

_____

If you wish to be present, or have a friend or associate be present, at that

time, you may, of course, make the appropriate arrangements. If you have any

questions, please call me at_____.

This notice is given in accordance with the provisions of Section 1954 of the

California Civil Code.

Sincerely,

_____

Notice of Change of Terms of Tenancy

TO _____ ,
          (Name)

TENANT(S) IN POSSESSION OF THE PREMISES AT:

_____
          (Street Address)

City of _____ , County of _____ , California.

YOU ARE HEREBY NOTIFIED that the terms of tenancy under which you occupy the above-described premises are changed as follows:

( ) The monthly rent will be increased to_____ , payable in advance.

( ) Other: _____

     _____

     _____ .

YOU ARE FURTHER NOTIFIED that the said change in terms of tenancy shall be effective,

( ) On _____ .
          (Date)

( ) On the 30th day following service on you of this notice. If the above-described change of terms of tenancy is an increase in rent, the amount due on the next following due date, pro-rated at the current rental rate prior to the said 30th day, and pro-rated at the increased rate thereafter, is $ _____ .

DATED: _____

_____
OWNER/MANAGER

3-DAY NOTICE
to Pay Rent or Quit

TO _____

TENANT(S) IN POSSESSION OF THE PREMISES AT

_____
(Street Address)

City of _____ , County of _____ , California

YOU ARE HEREBY NOTIFIED that the rent on the above-described premises occupied by you, in the amount of $ _____ , for the period from _____ to _____ , is now due and payable.

YOU ARE HEREBY REQUIRED to pay the said rent within THREE (3) days from the date of service on you of this notice or to vacate and surrender possession of the premises. In the event you fail to do so, legal proceedings will be instituted against you to recover possession of the premises, declare the forfeiture of the rental agreement or lease under which you occupy the premises, and recover rents, damages and costs of suit.

DATE: _____   _____
                                                    OWNER/MANAGER

3-Day Notice to
Perform Covenant or Quit

TO _____

TENANT(S) IN POSSESSION OF THE PREMISES AT

_____,
(Street Address)

City of _____, County of _____, California

YOU ARE HEREBY NOTIFIED that you are in violation of the lease or rental agreement under which you occupy the above-described premises in that you have violated the covenant to:

_____

_____

in the following manner:

_____

_____

YOU ARE HEREBY REQUIRED to remedy the said violation and perform the said covenant within THREE (3) DAYS from the date of service on you of this notice or to vacate and surrender possession of the said premises. In the event you fail to do so, legal proceedings will be instituted against you to recover possession of the said premises, declare the forfeiture of the said rental agreement or lease under which you occupy the said premises, and recover damages and court costs.

DATED: _____   _____
                                              OWNER/MANAGER

3-Day Notice to Quit

(Improper Subletting, Nuisance, Waste, or Illegal Use)

TO _____,

TENANT(S) IN POSSESSION OF THE PREMISES AT

_____
(Street Address)

City of _____, County of _____, California

    YOU ARE HEREBY NOTIFIED that you are required within THREE (3) DAYS from the date of service on you of this notice to vacate and surrender possession of the said premises by reason of your having committed the following nuisance, waste, unlawful use, or unlawful subletting:

_____

_____

_____

    As a result of your having committed the foregoing acts, the lease or rental agreement under which you occupy the said premises is terminated. In the event you fail to vacate and surrender possession of the said premises, legal proceedings will be instituted against you to recover possession, damages, and court costs.

DATE:_____   _____
                                            OWNER/MANAGER

Notice of Belief of Abandonment

TO: _____

TENANT(S) IN POSSESSION OF THE PREMISES AT:

_____
                   Street Address

City of _____ , County of _____ , California.

    This notice is given pursuant to Section 1951.3 of the Civil Code concerning the real property leased by you at the above address. The rent on this property had been due and unpaid for 14 consecutive days and the lessor/landlord believes that you have abandoned the property.

    The real property will be deemed abandoned within the meaning of Section 1951.2 of the Civil Code and your lease will terminate on _____ , 19__ , a date not less than 18 days after the mailing of this notice, unless before such date the undersigned receives at the address indicated below a written notice from you stating both of the following:

    (1) Your intent not to abandon the real property;

    (2) An address at which you may be served by certified mail in any action for unlawful detainer of the real property.

    You are required to pay the rent due and unpaid on this real property as required by the lease, and your failure to do so can lead to a court proceeding against you.

DATE: _____

_____
LESSOR (SIGNATURE)

_____
LESSOR NAME (PRINT)

_____
  ADDRESS

_____

Notice of Right to Reclaim Abandoned Property

To:

_____
(Name of former tenant(s) and possible owners of property)

When the premises at _____
(Address of premises)

City of _____ , County of _____ , California, were

vacated, the following personal property remained:

_____

_____

[ ] Continued on Attachment "A" hereto.

You may claim this property at:

_____
(Address at which property may be claimed)

City of _____ , County of _____ , California.

    Unless you pay the reasonable cost of storage for all the above-described pro-
perty, and take possession of the property which you claim not later than eighteen
(18) days after the date of mailing of this notice indicated below, this property
may be disposed of pursuant to Civil Code Section 1988.

[ ] Because this property is believed to be worth less than $300, it may be
kept, sold, or destroyed without further notice if you fail to reclaim it
within the time limit indicated.

[ ] Because this property is believed to be worth more than $300, it will be
sold at a public sale after notice has been given by publication, if you
fail to reclaim it within the time limit indicated. You have the right to
bid on the property at this sale. After the property is sold and the cost
of storage, advertising, and sale is deducted, the remaining money will be
paid over to the county. You may claim the remaining money at any time
within one year after the county receives the money.

DATE OF MAILING: _____

_____
OWNER/MANAGER (Signature)

_____   _____
(PHONE)   (ADDRESS OF OWNER/MANAGER)

Index

About the Authors

DAVID W. BROWN practices law in the Monterey, California area, where he has represented both landlords and tenants in hundreds of court cases--most of which he felt could have been avoided if both sides were more fully informed about landlord/tenant law. Brown, a graduate of Stanford University (chemistry) and the University of Santa Clara School of Law, also teaches law at the Monterey College of Law and is the author of **Fight Your Ticket** and a co-author of **How to Change Your Name**. He is currently a landlord and was a tenant for many years.

RALPH WARNER is a founder and publisher of Nolo Press, and an expert on landlord/tenant law. He is the co-author of **The California Tenants' Handbook**. Ralph has been a landlord, tenant, and for several years, a property manager. Having become fed up with all these roles, he bought a single-family house.

About the Illustrator

LINDA ALLISON was born before the invention of the computer and has been one step ahead of the game ever since. There is no truth to the rumor that she just sits around the house all day and makes little drawings.

Legal Books for Landlords

THE LANDLORD'S LAW BOOK: EVICTIONS.

Volume II. This is the companion book to
Rights and Responsibilities. When all else
fails and you must evict a tenant, this
book shows you how to do it legally and
efficiently. Complete with tear-out forms
and instructions and hints about what to
watch for and avoid. Available in
Available Spring 1986
California Edition $24.95

CALIFORNIA CIVIL CODE

(West Publishing) Statutes covering a
wide variety of topics, rights and duties
in the landlord/tenant relationship, marriage and divorce, contracts, transfers
of real estate, consumer credit, power of
attorney, and trusts.
California only $18.00

CALIFORNIA CODE OF CIVIL PROCEDURE

(West Publishing) Statutes governing most
judicial and administrative procedures:
unlawful detainer (eviction) proceedings,
small claims actions, homestead procedures, wage garnishments, recording of
liens, statutes of limitation, court
procedures, arbitration, and appeals.
California only $18.00

To order any of these books, use the
Order Form at the end of the book.

SOFTWARE

ESTATE PLANNING & PROBATE

willmaker

Nolo Press/Legisoft
Recent statistics say chances are better than 2 to 1 that you haven't written a will, even though you know you should. WillMaker makes the job easy, leading you step by step in a fill-in-the-blank format. Once you've gone through the program, you print out the will and sign it in front of witnesses. Because writing a will is only one step in the estate planning process, WillMaker comes with a 200-page manual providing an overview of probate avoidance and tax planning techniques.
National 3rd Ed.

Apple, IBM, Macintosh	$59.95
Commodore	$39.95

california incorporator

Attorney Mancuso and Legisoft, Inc.
About half of the small California corporations formed today are done without the services of a lawyer. This easy-to-use software program lets you do the paperwork with minimum effort. Just answer the questions on the screen, and California Incorporator will print out the 35-40 pages of documents you need to make your California corporation legal.

California Edition (IBM)	$129.00

for the record

By attorney Warner & Pladsen. A book/software package that helps to keep track of personal and financial records; create documents to give to family members in case of emergency; leave an accurate record for heirs, and allows easy access to all important records with the ability to print out any section
National Edition

Macintosh	$49.95

nolo's simple will book & nolo's simple willbook with tape

Attorney Denis Clifford
We feel it's important to remind people that if they don't make arrangements before they die, the state will give their property to certain close family members. If there are nieces, nephews, godchildren, friends or stepchildren you want to leave something to, you need a will. If you want a particular person to receive a particular object ,you should have a will. It's easy to write a legally valid will using this book, and once you've done it yourself you'll know how to update it whenever necessary.
National 1st Ed.

National 1st Ed.	$14.95
wi/30-min audio cassette	$19.95

plan your estate: wills, probate avoidance, trusts & taxes

Attorney Denis Clifford
A will is only one part of an estate plan. The first concern is avoiding probate so that your heirs won't receive a greatly diminished inheritance years later. This book shows you how to create a "living trust" and gives you the information you need to make sure whatever you have saved goes to your heirs, not to lawyers and the government.

California 6th Ed.	$15.95

the power of attorney book

Attorney Denis Clifford
The Power of Attorney Book concerns something you've heard about but probably would rather ignore: Who will take care of your affairs, make your financial and medical decisions, if you can't? With this book you can appoint someone you trust to carry out your wishes.

National 2ndEd.	$17.95

how to probate an estate

Julia Nissley
When a close relative dies, amidst the grieving there are financial and legal details to be dealt with. The natural response is to rely on an attorney, but that response can be costly. With How to Probate an Estate, you can have the satisfaction of doing the work yourself and saving those fees.

California 3rd Ed.	$24.95

the california non-profit corporation handbook

Attorney Anthony Mancuso

Used by arts groups, educators, social service agencies, medical programs, environmentalists and many others, this book explains all the legal formalities involved in forming and operating a non-profit corporation. Included are all the forms for the Articles, Bylaws and Minutes you will need. Also included are complete instructions for obtaining federal 501(c)(3) exemptions and benefits. The tax information in this section applies wherever your corporation is formed.

California 4th Ed. $24.95

how to form your own corporation

Attorney Anthony Mancuso

More and more business people are incorporating to qualify for tax benefits, limited liability status, the benefit of employee status and the financial flexibility. These books contain the forms, instructions and tax information you need to incorporate a small business.

California 7th Ed. $29.95
Texas 4th Ed. $24.95
New York 2nd. Ed. $24.95
Florida 1st Ed. $19.95

1988 calcorp update package

Attorney Anthony Mancuso

This update package contains all the forms and instructions you need to modify your corporation's Articles of Incorporation so you can take advantage of new California laws. $25.00

the california professional corporation handbook

Attorney Anthony Mancuso

Health care professionals, marriage, family and child counsellors, lawyers, accountants and members of certain other professions must fulfill special requirements when forming a corporation in California. This edition contains up-to-date tax information plus all the forms and instructions necessary to form a California professional corporation. An appendix explains the special rules that apply to each profession.

California 3rd Ed. $29.95

marketing without advertising

Michael Phillips & Salli Rasberry

There are good ideas on every page. You'll find here the nitty gritty steps you need to–and can–take to generate sales for your business, no matter what business it is.—Milton Moskowitz, syndicated columnist and author of The 100 Best Companies to Work For in America

Every small business person knows that the best marketing plan encourages customer loyalty and personal recommendation. Phillips and Rasberry outline practical steps for building and expanding a small business without spending a lot of money.

National 1st Ed. $14.00

the partnership book

Attorneys Clifford & Warner

Lots of people dream of going into business with a friend. The best way to keep that dream from turning into a nightmare is to have a solid partnership agreement. This book shows how to write an agreement that covers evaluation of partner assets, disputes, buy-outs and the death of a partner.

National 3rd Ed. $18.95

nolo's small business start-up

Mike McKeever

...outlines the kinds of credit available, describing the requirements and pros and cons of each source, and finally shows how to prepare cashflow forecasts, capital spending plans, and other vital ideas. An attractive guide for would-be entrepreneurs.—ALA Booklist

Should you start a business? Should you raise money to expand your already running business? If the answers are yes, this book will show you how to write an effective business plan and loan package.

National 3rd Ed. $17.95

the independent paralegal's handbook: how to provide legal services without going to jail

Attorney Ralph Warner

Warner's practical guide highlights the historical background of self-help law, and then gives a great deal of nuts-and-bolts advice on establishing and maintaining a paralegal office ...Highly recommended...—Library Journal

A large percentage of routine legal work in this country is performed by typists, secretaries, researchers and various other law office helpers generally labeled paralegals. For those who would like to take these services out of the law office and offer them at a reasonable fee in an independent business, attorney Ralph Warner provides both legal and business guidelines.

National 1st Ed. $12.95

getting started as an independent paralegal (two audio tapes)

Attorney Ralph Warner

This set of tapes, approximately three hours in all, is a carefully edited version of Nolo Press founder Ralph Warner's Saturday Morning Law School class. It is designed for people who wish to go into business helping consumers prepare their own paperwork in uncontested actions such as bankruptcy, divorce, small business incorporations, landlord-tenant actions, probate, etc. Also covered are how to set up, run, and market your business, as well as a detailed discussion of Unauthorized Practice of Law. The tapes are designed to be used in conjunction with The Independent Paralegal's Handbook.

National 1st Ed. $24.95

bankruptcy: do-it-yourself

Attorney Janice Kosel

Personal bankruptcy grew 35% in 1986 to over 400,000 nationwide. This book covers Chapter 7, the total discharge of personal debt through bankruptcy. In fact, most people using this book are guided to constructive alternatives to bankruptcy.

National 6th Ed. $17.95

collect your court judgment

Scott, Elias & Goldoftas

After you win a judgment in small claims, municipal or superior court, you still have to collect your money. Here are step-by-step instructions on hwo to collect your judgment from the debtor's bank accounts, wages, business receipts, real estate or other assets.

California 1st Ed. $24.95

chapter 13: the federal plan to repay your debts

Attorney Janice Kosel

For those who want to repay their debts and think they can, but are hounded by creditors, Chapter 13 may be the answer. Under the protection of the court you may work out a personal budget and take up to three years to repay a percentage of your debt and have the rest wiped clean.

National 3rd Ed. $17.95

make your own contract

Attorney Stephen Elias

If you've ever sold a car, lent money to a relative or friend, or put money down on a prospective purchase, you should have used a contract. Perhaps everything went without a hitch. If it didn't, though, you probably experienced a lot of grief and frustration.

Here are clearly written legal form contracts to: buy and sell property, borrow and lend money, store and lend personal property, make deposits on goods for later purchase, release others from personal liability, or pay a contractor to do home repairs.

National 1st Ed. $12.95

social security, medicare & pensions: a sourcebook for older americans

Attorney Joseph L. Matthews & Dorothy Matthews Berman

Social security, medicare and medicaid programs follow a host of complicated rules. Those over 55, or those caring for someone over 55, will find this comprehensive guidebook invaluable for understanding and utilizing their rightful benefits. A special chapter deals with age discrimination in employment and what to do about it.

National 4th Ed. $14.95

everybody's guide to small claims court

Attorney Ralph Warner

So, the dry cleaner ruined your good flannel suit. Your roof leaks every time it rains, and the contractor who supposedly fixed it won't call you back. The bicycle shop hasn't paid for the tire pumps you sold it six months ago. This book will help you decide if you have a case, show you how to file and serve papers, tell you what to bring to court, and how to collect a judgment.

California 7th Ed. $14.95
National 3rd Ed. $14.95

billpayers' rights

Attorneys Warner & Elias

Lots of people find themselves overwhelmed by debt. The law, however, offers a number of legal protections for consumers and Billpayers' Rights shows people how to use them.

Areas covered include: how to handle bill collectors, deal with student loans, check your credit rating and decide if you should file for bankruptcy.

California 8th Ed. $14.95

29 reasons not to go to law school

Ralph Warner & Toni Ihara

Lawyers, law students, their spouses and consorts will love this little book with its zingy comments and Thurberesque cartoons, humorously zapping the life of the law.— Peninsula Times Tribune

Filled with humor and piercing observations, this book can save you three years, $70,000 and your sanity.

3rd Ed. $9.95

murder on the air

Ralph Warner & Toni Ihara

Here is a sure winner for any friend who's spent more than a week in the city of Berkeley...a catchy little mystery situated in the environs and the cultural mores of the People's Republic.—The Bay Guardian

Flat out fun...—San Francisco Chronicle $5.95

poetic justice

Ed. by Jonathan & Andrew Roth

A unique compilation of humorous quotes about lawyers and the legal system, from Socrates to Woody Allen.

    $8.95

the criminal records book

Attorney Warren Siegel

We've all done something illegal. If you were one of those who got caught, your juvenile or criminal court record can complicate your life years later. The good news is that in many cases your record can either be completely expunged or lessened in severity.

The Criminal Records Book takes you step by step through the procedures to: seal criminal records, dismiss convictions, destroy marijuana records, reduce felony convictions.

California 2nd Ed. $14.95

draft, registration and the law

Attorney R. Charles Johnson

This clearly written guidebook explains the present draft law and how registration (required of all male citizens within thirty days of their eighteenth birthday) works. Every available option is presented along with a description of how a draft would work if there were a call tomorrow.

National 2nd Ed. $9.95

fight your ticket

Attorney David Brown

At a trade show in San Francisco recently, a traffic court judge (who must remain nameless) told our associate publisher that he keeps this book by his bench for easy reference.

If you think that ticket was unfair, here's the book showing you what to do to fight it.

California 3rd Ed. $16.95

how to become a united states citizen

Sally A. Abel

This bilingual (English/Spanish) book presents the forms, applications and instructions for naturalization. This step-by-step guide will provide information and answers for legally admitted aliens who wish to become citizens.

National 3rd Ed. $12.95

how to change your name

Attorneys Loeb & Brown

Wish that you had gone back to your maiden name after the divorce? Tired of spelling over the phone V-e-n-k-a-t-a-r-a-m-a-n S-u-b-r-a-m-a-n-i-a-m?

This book explains how to change your name legally and provides all the necessary court forms with detailed instructions on how to fill them out.

California 4th Ed. $14.95

legal research: how to find and understand the law

Attorney Stephen Elias

Legal Research could also be called Volume-Two-for-all-Nolo-Press-Self-Help-Law-Books. A valuable tool for paralegals, law students and legal secretaries, this book provides access to legal information. Using this book, the legal self-helper can find and research a case, read statutes, and make Freedom of Information Act requests.

National 2nd Ed. $14.95

family law dictionary

Attorneys Leonard and Elias

Written in plain English (as opposed to legalese), the Family Law Dictionary has been compiled to help the lay person doing research in the area of family law (i.e., marriage, divorce, adoption, etc.). Using cross referencs and examples as well as definitions, this book is unique as a reference tool.

National 1st Edition $13.95

intellectual property law dictionary

Attorney Stephen Elias

This book uses simple language free of legal jargon to define and explain the intricacies of items associated with trade secrets, copyrights, trademarks and unfair competition, patents and patent procedures, and contracts and warranties.—IEEE Spectrum

If you're dealing with any multi-media product, a new business product or trade secret, you need this book.

National 1st Ed. $17.95

the people's law review:
an access catalog to law without lawyers

Edited by Attorney Ralph Warner

Articles, interviews and a resource list introduce the entire range of do-it-yourself law from estate planning to tenants' rights. The People's Law Review also provides a wealth of background information on the history of law, some considerations on its future, and alternative ways of solving legal problems.

National 1st Ed. $8.95

how to do your own divorce

Attorney Charles E. Sherman

This is the book that launched Nolo Press and advanced the self-help law movement. During the past 17 years, over 400,000 copies have been sold, saving consumers at least $50 million in legal fees (assuming 100,000 have each saved $500—certainly a conservative estimate).

California 14th Ed.	$14.95
Texas 2nd Ed.	$12.95

(Texas Ed. by Sherman & Simons)

california marriage & divorce law

Attorneys Warner, Ihara & Elias

Most people marry only with the idea they are in love— that's not enough. This book should be a text in every California high school and college.—Phyllis Eliasberg, Consumer Reporter, CBS News

For a generation, this practical handbook has been the best resource for the Californian who wants to understand marriage and divorce laws. Even if you hire a lawyer to help you with a divorce, it's essential that you learn your basic legal rights and responsibilities.

California 9th Ed. $15.95

practical divorce solutions

Attorney Charles Ed Sherman

Written by the author of *How to Do Your Own Divorce* (with over 500,000 copies in print), this book provides a valuable guide both to the emotional process involved in divorce as well as the legal and financial decisions that have to be made.

Getting the "legal divorce," says Sherman, is "a ceremony you have to go through." The real divorce involves the many emotional and practical aspects of your life that are inevitably altered. To ensure the best possible outcome you must educate yourself. The worst thing you can do, he counsels, is to run directly to a lawyer and get involved in an uncontrolled battle.

California 1st Ed. $12.95

how to adopt your stepchild in california

Frank Zagone & Mary Randolph

For many families that include stepchildren, adoption is a satisfying way to guarantee the family a solid legal footing. This book provides sample forms and complete step-by-step instructions for completing a simple uncontested adoption by a stepparent.

California 3rd Ed. $19.95

how to modify and collect child support in california

Attorneys Matthews, Siegel & Willis

California has established landmark new standards in setting and collecting child support. Payments must now be based on both objective need standards and the parents' combined income.

Using this book, custodial parents can determine if they are entitled to higher child support payments and can implement the procedures to obtain that support.

California 2nd Ed. $17.95

a legal guide for lesbian and gay couples

Attorneys Curry & Clifford

The edge of the law… will be much less fearful for those who have this book. Full of clear language and concern for realistic legal expectations, this guide well serves and supports the spirit of the law.—Los Angeles Times

In addition to its clear presentation of "living together" contracts, A Legal Guide contains crucial information on the special problems facing lesbians and gay men with children, civil rights legislation, and medical/legal issues.

National 4th Ed. $17.95

the living together kit

Attorneys Ihara & Warner

Few unmarried couples understand the laws that may affect them. Here are useful tips on living together agreements, paternity agreements, estate planning, and buying real estate.

National 5th Ed. $17.95

your family records

Carol Pladsen & Attorney Denis Clifford

…a cleverly designed and convenient workbook that provides a repository for legal, financial and tax data as well as family history. —Los Angeles Times

Most American families keep terrible records. Typically, the checkbook is on a shelf in the kitchen, insurance policies are nowhere to be found, and jewelry and cash are hidden in a coffee can in the garage. Your Family Records is a sensible, straightforward guide that will help you organize your records before you face a crisis.

National 2nd Ed. $14.95

for sale by owner
George Devine
In 1986 about 600,000 homes were sold in California at a median price of $130,000. Most sellers worked with a broker and paid the 6% commission. For the median home that meant $7,800. Obviously, that's money that could be saved if you sell your own house. This book provides the background information and legal technicalities you will need to do the job yourself and with confidence.
California 1st Ed. $24.95

homestead your house
Attorneys Warner, Sherman & Ihara
Under California homestead laws, up to $60,000 of the equity in your home may be safe from creditors. But to get the maximum legal protection you should file a Declaration of Homestead before a judgment lien is recorded against you. This book includes complete instructions and tear-out forms.
California 6th Ed. $8.95

the landlord's law book:
vol. 1, rights & responsibilities
Attorneys Brown & Warner
Every landlord should know the basics of landlord-tenant law. Everything from the amount you can charge for a security deposit to terminating a tenancy, to your legal responsibility for the illegal acts of your manager is closely regulated by the law. In short, the era when a landlord could substitute common sense for a detailed knowledge of the law is gone forever. This volume covers: deposits, leases and rental agreements, inspections (tenants' privacy rights), habitability (rent withholding), ending a tenancy, liability, and rent control.
California 2nd Ed. $24.95

the landlord's law book: vol. 2, evictions
Attorney David Brown
Even the most scrupulous landlord may sometimes need to evict a tenant. In the past it has been necessary to hire a lawyer and pay a high fee. Using this book you can handle most evictions yourself safely and economically.
California 1st Ed. $24.95

tenants' rights
Attorneys Moskowitz & Warner
Your "security building" doesn't have a working lock on the front door. Is your landlord liable? How can you get him to fix it? Under what circumstances can you withhold rent? When is an apartment not "habitable?" This book explains the best way to handle your relationship with your landlord and your legal rights when you find yourself in disagreement.
California 9th Ed. $14.95

the deeds book:
how to transfer title to california real estate
Attorney Mary Randolph
If you own real estate, you'll almost surely need to sign a new deed at one time or another. The Deeds Book shows you how to choose the right kind of deed, how to complete the tear-out forms, and how to record them in the county recorder's public records. It also alerts you to real property disclosure requirements and California community property rules, as well as tax and estate planning aspects of your transfer.
California 1st Ed. $15.95

how to copyright software
Attorney M.J. Salone
Copyrighting is the best protection for any software. This book explains how to get a copyright and what a copyright can protect.
National 2nd Ed. $24.95

the inventor's notebook
Fred Grissom & Attorney David Pressman
The best protection for your patent is adequate records. The Inventor's Notebook provides forms, instructions, references to relevant areas of patent law, a bibliography of legal and non-legal aids, and more. It helps you document the activities that are normally part of successful independent inventing.
National 1st Ed. $19.95

legal care for your software
Attorneys Daniel Remer & Stephen Elias
If you write programs you intend to sell, or work for a software house that pays you for programming, you should buy this book. If you are a freelance programmer doing software development, you should buy this book.— Interface
This step-by-step guide for computer software writers covers copyright laws, trade secret protection, contracts, license agreements, trademarks, patents and more.
National 3rd Ed. $29.95

patent it yourself
Attorney David Pressman
You've invented something, or you're working on it, or you're planning to start...Patent It Yourself offers help in evaluating patentability, marketability and the protective documentation you should have. If you file your own patent application using this book, you can save from $1500 to $3500.
National 1st Ed. $24.95

SELF-HELP LAW BOOKS & SOFTWARE

ORDER FORM

Quantity	Title	Unit Price	Total

Prices subject to change

Subtotal _____

Tax (CA only): San Mateo, San Diego, LA, & Bart Counties 6 1/2%
Santa Clara & Alameda 7%
All others 6%

Tax_____

Postage & Handling

No. of Books	Charge
1	$2.50
2-3	$3.50
4-5	$4.00

Over 5 add 6% of total before tax

Postage & Handling_____

Total_____

Please allow 1-2 weeks for delivery.
Delivery is by UPS; no P.O. boxes, please.

Name_____

Address _____

_____

☐ VISA   ☐ Mastercard

_____Exp._____

Signature _____

Phone (   )_____

ORDERS: Credit card information or a check may be sent to:

Nolo Press
950 Parker St.
Berkeley CA 94710

Use your credit card and our **800 lines** for faster service:

ORDERS ONLY
(M-F 9-5 Pacific Time)**:**

US:	**800-992-NOLO**
Outside (415) area **CA:**	**800-445-NOLO**
Inside (415) area **CA:**	**(415) 549-1976**

For general information call: **(415) 549-1976**

☐ Please send me a catalogue

Notice of Termination of Tenancy

TO _____ ,

TENANT(S) IN POSSESSION OF THE PREMISES AT:

_____ ,
(Street Address

City of _____ , County of _____ , California:

    YOU ARE HEREBY NOTIFIED that effective 30 DAYS from the date of service on you of this notice, the periodic tenancy by which you hold possession of the above-described premises is terminated, at which time you are required to vacate and surrender possession of the said premises. In the event you fail to do so, legal proceedings will be instituted against you to recover possession of the said premises, damages and costs of suit.

    [If you are in a rent-control city which requires that you state a reason for terminating a tenancy, insert it here.]

DATED: _____   _____
OWNER/MANAGER